OXFORD PAPERBACK REFERENCE

A Dictionary of

Accounting

P9-DJA-481

Compiled by Market House Books Ltd.

Editor

R. Hussey, PhD, MSc, FCCA
   NWIS Professor of Financial Services,
   University of the West of England

Market House Books Ltd. – Editorial Staff

Alan Isaacs
Elizabeth Martin
Anne Stibbs
Fran Alexander

Contributors

M. Bendrey, MSc, FCMA, FCCA, ACIS
M. Bishop, BA, DMS, ACCA
C. Eastaugh, BSc, ACA, ATII, MCT
A. Hansford, BA, ATII
R. Hussey, PhD, MSc, FCCA

Oxford Paperback Reference

The most authoritative and up-to-date reference books for both students and the general reader

Abbreviations
Accounting
Art and Artists
Ballet
Biology
Botany
Business
Card Games
Chemistry
Christian Church
Classical Literature
Computing
Dates
Earth Sciences
Ecology
English Christian Names
English Etymology
English Language
English Literature
English Place-Names
Finance
Food and Nutrition
Fowler's Modern English Usage
Geography
Irish Mythology
King's English
Law
Literary Terms
Mathematics

Medical Dictionary
Modern Quotations
Modern Slang
Music
Nursing
Opera
Philosophy*
Physics
Politics*
Popes
Popular Music
Proverbs
Quotations
Sailing Terms
Saints
Science
Ships and the Sea
Sociology
Superstitions
Theatre
Twentieth-Century History
Twentieth-Century Poetry*
Weather Facts
Women Writers
Word Games
World Mythology
Zoology

forthcoming

A Dictionary of
Accounting

Edited by
R. HUSSEY

Oxford   New York

OXFORD UNIVERSITY PRESS

1995

Oxford University Press, Walton Street, Oxford OX2 6DP

Oxford New York
Athens Auckland Bangkok Bombay
Calcutta Cape Town Dar es Salaam Delhi
Florence Hong Kong Istanbul Karachi
Kuala Lumpur Madras Madrid Melbourne
Mexico City Nairobi Paris Singapore
Taipei Tokyo Toronto

and associated companies in
Berlin Ibadan

Oxford is a trade mark of Oxford University Press

British Library Cataloguing in Publication Data
Data available

Library of Congress Cataloging in Publication Data available
Data available
ISBN 0-19-280029-9

10 9 8 7 6 5 4 3 2 1

Printed in Great Britain by
Biddles Ltd
Guildford and King's Lynn

Preface

In recent years there have been dramatic changes in accounting and finance on both a national scale and an international scale. Legislation has increased, powerful regulatory institutions have been established, and new accounting techniques and financial products have found global recognition. These changes have had a major impact on all our lives. Not only are matters of personal interest, such as pensions and mortgages, becoming more complex, but even sophisticated financial products, such as derivatives, make headline news.

A Dictionary of Accounting is intended for all those interested in the financial world. It will be of immense value to students of all kinds, especially students of accounting and of business courses, from the secondary school level to postgraduate courses at university. It will also be a major source of reference for businessmen and their professional advisers, who require an authoritative and up-to-date guide to assist them in their work.

The dictionary provides extensive coverage of the terms commonly used in financial accounting and reporting, management accounting, taxation, treasury management, and financial management. These disciplines themselves use terms derived from, or associated with, commerce, law, and computing; where it has been thought helpful, definitions have been included here from companion volumes in the Oxford Paperback Reference series – *A Dictionary of Finance* and *A Concise Dictionary of Business*. We have also given a broad coverage of accounting terms and concepts used in the USA, where they differ from those current in the UK. Another major feature of the dictionary is its explanation of the jargon used in the financial world, both in the USA and the UK.

R.H.

AAA Abbreviation for *American Accounting Association.

AAPA 1. Abbreviation for *Association of Authorized Public Accountants. **2.** Abbreviation for Associate of the Association of Authorized Public Accountants.

AAT Abbreviation for *Association of Accounting Technicians.

abacus An ancient device for performing arithmetic calculations by sliding beads along rods or in grooves. Despite the spread of electronic calculators and computers, the abacus is still widely used in the Far East.

ABB Abbreviation for *activity-based budgeting.

abbreviated accounts A company qualifying as a small or medium-sized company under the UK Companies Act (1989) may file abbreviated accounts with the *Registrar of Companies instead of the full report and accounts (*see* annual accounts). These accounts, previously known as modified accounts, are an additional set of *financial statements drawn from the full financial statements, specifically for the purpose of delivery to the Registrar; they thus become a public document and must be accompanied by a special report of the *auditors.

ABC method *See* activity-based costing.

ability-to-pay taxation A form of taxation in which taxes are levied on the basis of the taxpayers' ability to pay. This form of taxation leads to the view that as income or wealth increases, its marginal utility (its value to its owner) decreases so that progressive rates of tax can be levied on the higher slices. Typical taxes of this sort in the UK are *income tax and *inheritance tax. *Compare* benefit taxation.

abnormal loss The loss arising from a manufacturing or chemical process through abnormal waste, shrinkage, seepage, or spoilage in excess of the *normal loss. It may be expressed as a weight or volume or in other units appropriate to the process; it is usually valued on the same basis as the *good output. An **abnormal gain** is an unexpected surplus of output that may occur if the actual loss is less than anticipated.

abnormal shrinkage *See* abnormal loss.

abnormal spoilage *See* abnormal loss.

abnormal waste *See* abnormal loss.

above par *See* par value.

above-the-line Denoting entries above the horizontal line on a company's *profit and loss account that separates the entries that establish the profit (or loss) from the entries showing how the profit is distributed. Prior to the introduction of *Financial Reporting Standard 3, 'Reporting Financial Performance', in October 1992, it was understood that any exceptional items that were within the ordinary activities of the business were shown above the line, while any extraordinary items that were outside the ordinary activities of the business were shown below it. There was, however, criticism that the definitions of extraordinary and exceptional items could be manipulated to improve the *earnings per share figure. For example, if a building was sold for a large profit it could be interpreted as being exceptional and included in the earnings per share, whereas if it was sold at a loss it could be interpreted as being extraordinary and not included in the earnings per share. Since the introduction of FRS 3, both exceptional and extraordinary items are shown above the line and are included in the earnings per share. *Compare* below-the-line.

abridged accounts Financial statements other than the full report and accounts of a company (*see* annual accounts); they are defined in the legislation as *non-statutory accounts. Under the UK Companies Act (1989) a company has to make a statement on any non-statutory accounts it issues to the effect that they are not the full statutory accounts.

absorbed overhead (recovered overhead; applied overhead) The amount of the *overhead of an organization charged to, or borne by, the *production of that organization for the accounting period under consideration when the technique of *absorption costing is used. Absorbed overhead is obtained by multiplying the actual production for the period by the *absorption rate.

absorption (cost absorption; overhead absorption) An accounting process used in *absorption costing in which the *overhead of an organization is borne by the production of that organization by the use of *absorption rates.

absorption account An account opened when a system of *double-entry cost accounting is in operation to show the amount of *overhead that has been absorbed by the production.

absorption costing The cost accounting system in which the *overheads of an organization are charged to the production by means of the process of *absorption. Costs are first apportioned to *cost centres, where they are absorbed using *absorption rates. *Compare* marginal costing.

Production measure	Absorption rate
units, weight, or volume	rate per unit, weight, or volume
direct labour hours	rate per direct labour hour
machine hours	rate per machine hour
direct labour cost	% on direct labour cost
direct material cost	% on direct material cost
prime cost	% on prime cost
standard hours	rate per standard hour

absorption rate (overhead absorption rate; recovery rate) The rate or rates calculated in an *absorption costing system in advance of an accounting period for the purpose of charging the *overheads to the *production of that period. Absorption rates are calculated for the accounting period in question using the following formula:

budgeted overhead/budgeted production.

In absorption costing production may be expressed in a number of different ways; the way chosen to express production will determine the absorption rate to be used. The seven major methods of measuring production, together with their associated absorption rate, are given in the table above. The rate is used during the accounting period to obtain the *absorbed overhead by multiplying the actual production achieved by the absorption rate.

abusive tax shelter In the USA, a limited partnership that the *Internal Revenue Service considers is claiming illegal tax deductions, often by increasing the value of purchased property as a basis for inflated *depreciation write-offs.

ACA Abbreviation for Associate of the *Institute of Chartered Accountants in England and Wales.

ACCA Abbreviation for Associate of the *Chartered Association of Certified Accountants.

accelerated cost recovery system In the USA, a system of *depreciation designed to encourage capital investment by businesses. It permits a quicker recovery of an asset's cost to provide higher tax benefits in the earlier years of its use. A higher depreciation charge is made to the *profit and loss account in the early years, thus reducing the amount of profit assessable for tax.

accelerated depreciation A rate of *depreciation of assets that is faster than the useful-life basis normally used to calculate depreciation. For example, a computer may be expected to have a useful life of four years when it is purchased; however, as a result of new product innovation, it is replaced after two years. If the useful-life basis had been used, the full cost would not have been charged to the accounts until the end of the fourth year; by accelerating the depreciation the full charge would be made earlier, reflecting the short life cycle of high-technology products. In the USA, the accelerated depreciation may be used to gain tax advantages (*see* accelerated cost recovery system).

acceleration The action of a lender in demanding early repayment when a borrower defaults.

acceptance commission *See* acceptance credit.

acceptance credit A means of financing the sale of goods, particularly in international trade. It involves a commercial bank or merchant bank extending credit to a foreign importer whom it deems creditworthy. An acceptance credit is opened against which the exporter can draw a *bill of exchange. Once accepted by the bank, the bill can be discounted on the *money market or allowed to run to maturity. In return for this service the exporter pays the bank a fee known as the **acceptance commission.**

acceptance supra protest (acceptance for honour) The acceptance or payment of a *bill of exchange, after it has been dishonoured, by a person wishing to save the honour of the drawer or an endorser of the bill.

accommodation bill A *bill of exchange signed by a person (the accommodation party) who acts as a guarantor. The accommodation party is liable for the bill should the acceptor fail to pay at maturity. Accommodation bills are sometimes known as **windbills** or **windmills**. *See also* kite.

accommodation party The person who signs an *accommodation bill as drawer, acceptor, or endorser and acts as the guarantor.

accord and satisfaction A device enabling one party to a contract to avoid an obligation that arises under the contract, provided that the other party agrees. The accord is the agreement by which the contractual obligation is discharged and the satisfaction is the *consideration making the agreement legally operative. Such an agreement only discharges the contractual obligation if it is accompanied by consideration. For example, under a contract of sale the seller of goods may discharge the contractual obligation by delivering goods of different quality to that specified in the contract, provided there is agreement with the buyer (the accord) and a reduction in the contract price (the satisfaction) is offered. The seller has therefore 'purchased' release from the obligation. Accord and satisfaction refer to the discharge of an obligation arising under the law of tort.

accountability An obligation to give an account. For limited companies, it is assumed that the directors of the company are accountable to the shareholders and that this responsibility is discharged, in part, by the directors providing an annual report and accounts (*see* annual accounts). In an accountability relationship there will be at least one principal and at least one agent. This forms the basis of an *agency relationship.

accountancy **1.** The profession in which *accountancy bodies regulate the activities of accountants. **2.** The process of *accounting.

accountancy bodies Organizations, established in most countries in the world, to regulate the activities of accountants; their members are normally entitled to use the title *chartered accountant, *certified accountant, or *certified public accountant. Membership is normally controlled by examination and the members are expected to comply with the regulations of their body. In the UK and the USA the accountancy profession is powerful and active. It takes a significant role in the regulation of financial accounting and reporting by issuing *accounting standards. In the UK, the profession is somewhat fragmented due to the number of separate accountancy bodies. Although there have been attempts to integrate these into one body, this has not yet been achieved. The professional bodies in the UK making up the *Consultative Committee of Accountancy Bodies are the *Chartered Association of Certified Accountants, the *Chartered Institute of Management Accountants, the *Chartered Institute of Public Finance and Accountancy, the *Institute of Chartered Accountants in England and Wales, the *Institute of Chartered Accountants in Ireland, and the *Institute of Chartered Accountants of Scotland.

accountant A person who has passed the accountancy examinations of one of the recognized *accountancy bodies and completed the required work experience. Each of the bodies varies in the way they train their students and the type of work expected to be undertaken. For example, accountants who are members of the *Chartered Institute of Public Finance and Accountancy generally work in local authorities, the National Health Service, or other similar public bodies, while members of the *Chartered Institute of Management Accountants work in industry. Wherever accountants work, their responsibilities centre on the collating, recording, and communicating of financial information and the preparation of analyses for decision-making purposes.

accountant's lien The right to retain possession of goods or property that belongs to another until that person pays debts due to the possessor of the goods or property.

account code A number given to an account from a *chart of accounts. Each number in the code will represent some feature; for example, asset type, location, department with responsibility for maintaining it, etc.

accounting The process of identifying, measuring, recording, and communicating economic transactions. Measurement is normally made in monetary terms and the accountant will prepare records in the form of *financial statements, such as a *profit and loss account and *balance sheet. Accounting can be subdivided into *financial accounting, which is mainly concerned with the legal aspects of the subject and reporting to parties external to an organization, and *management accounting, which is mainly concerned with providing information helpful to managers running a business. Accounting includes various activities, such as conducting *audits, *book-keeping, and *taxation. *See also* acquisition accounting; merger accounting.

accounting bases The methods used for applying fundamental *accounting concepts to financial transactions and items when preparing *financial statements. The particular bases adopted by an organization will form its *accounting policies.

accounting code (cost code; expenditure code; income code) In modern accounting systems, a numerical reference given to each account to facilitate the recording of voluminous accounting transactions by computer.

accounting concepts (accounting conventions; accounting principles; fundamental accounting concepts) The fundamental principles applied to financial statements. The main ones are: *going concern, *consistency, *prudence, and *matching (or accruals).

accounting conventions *See* accounting concepts.

accounting cushion In the USA, the practice of making larger provisions for expenses in one year, in order to minimize them in future years. Effectively, earnings will be understated in the present year but will be overstated in a subsequent year.

accounting cycle The sequence of steps in accounting for a financial transaction entered into by an organization. First, it is recorded in the *books of account and finally it will be aggregated with other transactions in the *financial statements for a financial period.

accounting entity A unit for which accounting records are maintained and for which *financial statements are prepared. As an accounting concept, it is assumed that the financial records are prepared for a particular unit or entity. By law, limited companies constitute the accounting entity. For sole traders and partnerships accounts are also prepared to reflect the transactions of the business as an accounting entity, not those of the owner(s) of the business. Changing the boundaries of the accounting entity can have a significant impact on the accounts themselves, as these will reflect the purpose of the accounts and for whom they are prepared.

accounting equation (balance-sheet equation) The formula underlying a *balance sheet; it can be expressed as:

$$\text{assets} = \text{liabilities} + \text{capital}.$$

An increase or decrease in the total assets of a concern must be accompanied by an equal increase or decrease in the liabilities and capital in order to ensure that a balance sheet will always balance. This formula expresses an *accounting entity view of the business, whereas the *proprietary view would deduct liabilities from assets to calculate the owners' stake in the business.

accounting event A transaction or change (internal or external) recognized by the accounting recording system. Events are recorded as debit and credit entries. For example, when a sale is made for cash the double entry for the sales transaction would be debit bank, credit sales (*see* double-entry book-keeping).

accounting exposure *See* translation exposure.

accounting manual A document that gives details of a business's accounting policies and procedures; it often includes a list of account codes or a *chart of accounts. An example of an accounting policy would be the way in which the company treats depreciation, including the method selected and the useful economic life used for each asset type. The procedure would explain how to apply the policy; for example, how to work out the depreciation charge for the year, which is then debited to the *profit and loss account and credited to the *provision for depreciation. Other procedures relating to depreciation would show how to deal with both the revaluation of assets and the sale of assets.

accounting period 1. The period for which a business prepares its accounts. Internally, *management accounts may be produced monthly or quarterly. Externally, *financial accounts are produced for a period of 12 months, although this may vary when a business is set up or ceases or if it changes its accounting year end. **2. (chargeable account period)** A period in respect of which a *corporation tax assessment is raised. It cannot be more than 12 months in length. An accounting period starts when a company begins to trade or immediately after a previous accounting period ends. An accounting period ends at the earliest of:

• 12 months after the start date,
• at the end of the company's period of account,
• the start of a winding-up,
• on ceasing to be UK resident.

accounting plan A detailed accounting guide provided by a number of European countries, such as France and Spain. The guide gives definitions of accounting terms, rules for valuation and measurement, model financial statements, and a *chart of accounts. This legalistic approach to the preparation of *financial statements contrasts with the approach in the UK, where greater emphasis is placed on ensuring that the financial statements present a true and fair view of the financial status of a particular organization.

accounting policies The specific *accounting bases adopted and consistently followed by an organization in the preparation of its *financial statements. These bases will have been determined by the organization to be the most appropriate for presenting fairly its financial results and operations; they will concentrate on such specific topics as *pension schemes, *goodwill, *research and development costs, and *foreign exchange. Under Statement of Standard Accounting Practice 2, companies are required to disclose their accounting policies in their *annual accounts.

accounting principles *See* accounting concepts.

Accounting Principles Board (APB) In the USA, the forerunner of the *Financial Accounting Standards Board. It was established by the *Institute of Certified Public Accountants in 1959 and issued Opinions until 1973. Several of the 31 Opinions issued significantly improved the theory and practice of accounting and still form part of *generally accepted accounting principles (GAAP).

accounting profit The amount of profit calculated by using generally accepted principles of accounting instead of tax rules. At its simplest the profit is the revenue for an accounting period less the expenses incurred, using the concept of accrual accounting. There are a number of theoretical and practical problems in arriving at the amount, for both revenue and expenses; the result is that the accounting profit has less precision than many believe. One of the consequences of this imprecision is that a number of organizations are tempted to present profits in their best light. *Accounting standards attempt to prevent any abuses.

accounting rate of return An accounting ratio that expresses the profit of an organization before interest and taxation, usually for a year, as a percentage of the capital employed at the end of the period. Variants of the measure include using profit after interest and taxation, equity capital employed, and the average of opening and closing capital employed for the period.

accounting records The records kept by a company to comply with the Companies Act (1984), which requires companies to keep accounting records sufficient to show and explain their transactions and to prepare accounts that give a true and fair view of their activities. Accounting records take the form of a manual or computerized ledgers, journals, and the supporting documentation.

accounting reference date The date at the end of an *accounting reference period.

accounting reference period The financial year for a company, as notified to the *Registrar of Companies. For companies incorporated after 1 April 1990, it is normally taken as the last day of the month in which the anniversary of incorporation falls.

accounting series releases In the USA, official pronouncements relating to accounting issued by the *Securities and Exchange Commission. They are now codified as *Financial Reporting Releases.

accounting standard A definitive standard for financial accounting and reporting established in the form of a *Statement of Standard Accounting Practice (SSAP) issued by the *Accounting Standards Committee or, since 1990, a *Financial Reporting Standard (FRS) issued by the *Accounting Standards Board in the UK. In the USA the issue of accounting standards is the responsibility of the *Financial Accounting Standards Board. Standards set out rules and procedures relating to the measurement, valuation, and disclosure of accounting transactions. In recent years there have been attempts in a number of countries to improve accounting standards by developing a *conceptual framework.

Accounting Standards Board (ASB) The recognized body for setting accounting standards in the UK. It was established in 1990 to replace the *Accounting Standards Committee (ASC) following the recommendations contained in the *Dearing Report. Under the Companies Act (1985), companies (except *small companies and *medium-sized companies) must state whether their accounts have been prepared in accordance with the relevant *accounting standards and give details and reasons for any material departures from those standards. The ASB issues *Financial Reporting Exposure Drafts (FREDs), *Financial Reporting Standards (FRS), and through its offshoot, the *Urgent Issues Task Force, reports known as Abstracts. The ASB is a subsidiary of the *Financial Reporting Council.

Accounting Standards Committee (ASC) A joint committee of the *Consultative Committee of Accountancy Bodies set up in 1976 as a successor to the *Accounting Standards Steering Committee. Membership of the ASC was part-time and unpaid; because serious doubts concerning its effectiveness were raised, in 1990 it was replaced by the *Accounting Standards Board. In its life the ASC issued 25 *Statements of Standard Accounting Practice (SSAPs), many of which were adopted by the ASB. The ASC was also responsible for issuing *Statements of Recommended Practice (SORPs). Despite its failings, the ASC did much to improve the general level of financial reporting and accounting in the UK.

Accounting Standards Steering Committee (ASSC) A committee set up in 1970 by the *Institute of Chartered Accountants in England and Wales following serious criticism of the accountancy profession in the 1960s; it later became the *Accounting Standards Committee.

accounting system The system designed to record the accounting transactions and events of a business and account for them in a way that complies with its policies and procedures. The basic elements of the accounting system are concerned with collecting, recording, evaluating, and reporting transactions and events.

account payee only Words printed between two vertical lines in the centre of a UK cheque that, in accordance with the Cheque Act (1992), make the cheque non-transferable. This is to avoid cheques being endorsed and paid into an account other than that of the payee, although it should be noted that banks may argue in some circumstances that they acted in good faith and without negligence if an endorsed cheque is honoured by the bank. In spite of this most cheques are now overprinted 'account payee only', and the words 'not negotiable' are sometimes added.

accounts 1. The *profit and loss accounts and the *balance sheet of a company. 2. *See* books of account.

accounts payable (trade creditors) The amounts owed by a business to suppliers (e.g. for raw materials). Accounts payable are classed as current liabilities on the balance sheet (*see* circulating assets), but distinguished from *accruals and other non-trade creditors (such as the Inland Revenue).

accounts receivable (trade debtors) The amounts owing to a business from customers for invoiced amounts. Accounts receivable are classed as current assets on the balance sheet (*see* circulating assets), but distinguished from prepayments and other non-trade debtors. A provision for bad debts is often shown against the accounts receivable balance in line with the *prudence concept. This provision is based on the company's past history of bad debts and its current expectations. A general provision is often based on a percentage of the total credit sales, for example 2% of credit sales made during the period.

accounts receivable collection period The time given to customers in which to pay their accounts. It is common to require customers to pay within 30 days, although in practice the collection period is often not respected. As late-paying customers can often cause major cash-flow problems, a chronological analysis of outstanding debtor amounts should be produced monthly to ensure that all outstanding amounts are followed up by reminders.

accretion An increase in the value of an asset as a result of a physical change (e.g. a growing crop), as opposed to an increase in value as a result of a change in its market price.

accrual (accrued charge; accrued expense; accrued liability)
An estimate in the accounts of a business of a liability that is not supported by an invoice or a request for payment at the time the accounts are prepared. An accrual is a *current liability on the *balance sheet and will be charged under expenses in the *profit and loss account. Expenses are accrued as set out in the *accruals concept outlined in Statement of Standard Accounting Practice 2. An example of an accrual would be telephone expenses, which are billed in arrears. At the end of the accounting period, if no bill has been received, an estimate (based on past bills) would be made and credited to an accruals account; the corresponding debit would be made to the telephone expense account. The telephone expense account is then cleared to the profit and loss account.

accrual accounting A system of accounting in which *revenue is recognized when it is earned and expenses are recognized as they are incurred. Accrual accounting is a basic *accounting concept used in the preparation of the *profit and loss account and *balance sheet of a business. It differs from *cash-flow accounting, which recognizes transactions when cash has been received or paid. In preparing *financial statements for an *accounting period using accrual accounting, there will inevitably be some estimation and uncertainty in respect of transactions. The reader of the financial statements therefore cannot have the same high level of confidence in these statements as in those using cash-flow accounting.

accruals concept One of the four fundamental concepts contained in Statement of Standard Accounting Practice 2, 'Disclosure of Accounting Policies', and one of the principles in the Companies Act (1985). It requires that revenue and costs are recognized as they are earned or incurred, not as money is received or paid. Income and expenses should be matched with one another, as far as their relationship can be established or justifiably assumed, and dealt with in the *profit and loss account of the period to which they relate.

However, if there is a conflict between the accruals concept and the *prudence concept, the latter prevails. *Accruals and prepayments are examples of the application of the accruals concept in practice. For example, if a rates bill for both a current and future period is paid, that part relating to the future period is carried forward as a current asset (a prepayment) until it can be matched to the future periods.

accrued benefits Benefits due under a pension scheme in respect of service up to a given time, irrespective of whether the rights to the benefits are vested or not. Accrued benefits may be calculated in relation to current earnings of protected final earnings. *Statement of Standard Accounting Practice 24, 'Accounting for Pension Costs', contains mandatory regulations on accounting for pension costs in financial accounts.

accrued benefits method An actuarial valuation method in which the actuarial value of liabilities relates at a given date to:
• the benefits, including future increases promised by the rules, for the current and deferred pensioners and their dependants;
• the benefits that the members assumed to be in service on the given date will receive for service up to that date only.
Allowance may be made for expected increases in earnings after the given date, and for additional pension increases not promised by the rules. The given date may be a current or future date. The further into the future the adopted date lies, the closer the results will be to those obtained by a prospective benefits valuation method.

accrued charge *See* accrual.

accrued expense *See* accrual.

accrued income (accrued revenue) Income that has been earned during an accounting period but not received by the end of it. Accrued income is dealt with as set out in the *accruals concept outlined in Statement of Standard Accounting Practice 2. For example, interest may have been earned but not received; it should be included in the profit figure (subject to the overriding *prudence concept) and classified as a current asset on the balance sheet (*see* circulating assets).

accrued liability *See* accrual.

accrued revenue *See* accrued income.

accumulated depreciation (aggregate depreciation) The total amount of the *depreciation written off the cost price or valuation of a *fixed asset since it was brought into the balance sheet of an organization.

accumulated dividend A dividend that has not been paid to a holder of *cumulative preference shares and is carried forward (i.e. accumulated) to the next accounting period. It represents a liability to the company. The Companies Act requires that where any fixed cumulative dividends on a company's shares are in arrears, both the amount of the arrears and the period(s) in arrears must be disclosed for each class of shares.

accumulated earnings *See* accumulated profits.

accumulated fund (capital fund) A fund held by a non-profitmaking organization (such as a club or society) to which a surplus of income over expenditure is credited and to which any deficit is debited. The value of the accumulated funds can be calculated at any time by valuing the net assets (i.e. assets less liabilities) of the organization. The accumulated fund is the equivalent of the capital of a profit-making organization.

accumulated profits (accumulated earnings) The amount showing in the *appropriation of profits account that can be carried forward to the next year's accounts, i.e. after paying dividends, taxes, and putting some to reserve.

accumulating shares Ordinary shares issued to holders of ordinary shares in a company, instead of a dividend. Accumulating shares are a way of replacing annual income with capital growth; they avoid income tax but not capital gains tax. Usually tax is deducted by the company from the declared dividend, in the usual way, and the net dividend is then used to buy additional ordinary shares for the shareholder.

acid-test ratio *See* liquid ratio.

ACIS Abbreviation for Associate of the *Institute of Chartered Secretaries and Administrators.

ACMA Abbreviation for Associate of the *Chartered Institute of Management Accountants.

acquisition accounting The accounting procedures followed when one company is taken over by another. The fair value of the purchase consideration should, for the purpose of consolidated financial statements, be allocated between the underlying net tangible and intangible assets, other than goodwill, on the basis of the fair value to the acquiring company. Any difference between the fair value of the consideration and the aggregate of the fair values of the separable net assets (including identifiable intangibles, such as patents, licences, and trademarks) will represent goodwill. The results of the acquired company should be brought into the consolidated *profit and loss account from the date of acquisition only.

In certain circumstances *merger accounting may be used when accounting for a business combination. Acquisition accounting differs from merger accounting in that shares issued as purchase consideration are valued at their market price, not par value (*see* share premium account), a goodwill figure may arise on consolidation, and pre-acquisition profits are not distributable. Merger accounting treats both parties as if they had always been combined, and values the purchase consideration at par.

Acquisition accounting and merger accounting were covered by Statement of Standard Accounting Practice 23, 'Accounting for Acquisitions and Mergers', until September 1994, when the Accounting Standards Board issued *Financial Reporting Standards 6, 'Acquisitions and Mergers', and Financial Reporting Standard 7, 'Fair Values in Acquisition Accounting', which replaced SSAP 23.

ACT 1. Abbreviation for *advance corporation tax. **2.** Abbreviation for *Association of Corporate Treasurers.

active stocks Securities that are frequently traded on a particular stock exchange or in a particular period.

activity An operation that takes place within an organization and causes costs to be incurred. Examples are receipt of raw materials, production planning, and machine set-up. *See also* cost driver.

activity-based budgeting (ABB) Establishing the *activities that incur costs in each function of an organization, defining the relationships between activities, and using the information to decide how much resource should be allowed for each activity in the *budget. ABB also attempts to determine how well a particular section of the budget is being managed and to explain any variances from budgeted expenditure.

activity-based costing (ABC method; activity costing) A system of costing proposed by Professors Johnson and Kaplan in their book *Relevance Lost: The Rise and Fall of Management Accounting* (1987), in which they questioned accounting techniques based on *absorption costing. Their method recognizes that costs are incurred by each *activity that takes place within an organization and that products (or customers) should bear costs according to the activities they use. *Cost drivers are identified, together with the appropriate cost pools, which are used to charge costs to products.

activity-based management The use made by the management of an organization of *activity-based costing. The identification of *activities and *cost drivers encourages the management to review how projected cost levels compare with the activity levels achieved.

activity costing *See* activity-based costing.

activity ratio A ratio used in *management accounting consisting of the *production achieved for an accounting period divided by the production level regarded as achievable for that period.

actual cost The actual expenditure incurred in carrying out the *activities of an organization.

actuals (physicals) Commodities that can be purchased and used, rather than goods traded on a *futures contract, which are represented by documents (although the documents give a right to physical possession of the goods, futures contracts are often cancelled out by offsetting a purchase against a sale).

actuarial method A method used in *lease accounting to apportion rentals on the basis of compound *interest; it is also used in accounting for pensions to determine the charge to the *profit and loss account.

actuary A person trained in the mathematics of statistics and probability theory. Some are employed by insurance companies to calculate probable lengths of life and advise insurers on the amounts that should be put aside to pay claims and the amount of premium to be charged for each type of risk. Actuaries also advise on the administration of pension funds. The work of the actuary is separate from that of the accountant, although there are certain areas in which they are required to collaborate, particularly in accounting for pension costs under *Statement of Standard Accounting Practice 24.

added-value statement *See* value-added statement.

additional paid-in capital In the USA, the excess received from stockholders over the *par value of the stock issued.

additional voluntary contribution (AVC) Additional pension-scheme contributions that employees can make, at their discretion, in order to increase the benefits available from their pension fund on retirement. Additional voluntary contributions can be paid into an employers' scheme or to a scheme of the employee's choice (a free-standing AVC). The employee's total pension contributions must not exceed the limit of 15% of current salary. AVCs are restricted to the difference between 15% of salary and the standard pension contributions. AVCs will be used to increase the pension payable and only in exceptional circumstances will they increase the tax-free lump sum payable on retirement.

adjudication 1. The judgment or decision of a court, especially in bankruptcy proceedings. **2.** An assessment by the Commissioners of Inland Revenue of the amount of stamp duty due on a document. A document sent for adjudication will either be stamped as having no duty to pay or the taxpayer will be advised how much is due. An appeal may be made to the High Court if the taxpayer disagrees with the adjudication.

adjusted gross income In the USA, the difference between the gross income of a taxpayer and the adjustments to income.

adjusted trial balance A *trial balance to which adjustments have been made; for example, there may be *prepayments and *accruals that need to be taken into account. Separate columns are used for these adjustments, one for debits and one for credits. Once the trial balance has been adjusted in this way, it forms the basis for the *profit and loss account and *balance sheet.

adjusting entries Entries made at a *balance-sheet date under an *accrual accounting system to ensure that the income and expenditure of the business concerned are included in the correct period. Examples of adjustments include those made for *depreciation, *prepayments, *accruals, and closing stock (items that will not be sold until future periods).

adjusting events (post-balance-sheet events) Events that occur between a balance-sheet date and the date on which *financial statements are approved, providing additional evidence of conditions existing at the balance-sheet date. For example, a valuation of a property held at the balance-sheet date that provides evidence of a permanent diminution in value would need to be adjusted in the financial statements. Such events include those that, because of statutory or conventional requirements, are reflected in financial statements. Statement of Standard Accounting Practice 17, 'Accounting for Post Balance Sheet Events', requires that such material events should be reflected in the actual account balances in the financial accounts, where they purport to give a true and fair view.

A **non-adjusting event** concerns conditions that did not exist at the balance-sheet date; such events may need to be disclosed in the notes to the accounts. An issue of shares after the post-balance-sheet period would be an example of a non-adjusting event. If an event would be classed as non-adjusting, but the application of the *going-concern concept to the whole, or a material part, of the company is not appropriate, it should be treated as an adjusting event. For example, if serious industrial action has occurred, which if it continues could threaten the continued existence of the business, an appropriate provision should be made in the accounts.

adjusting journal entry (AJE) An entry made in a *journal, or journal format records, to record a movement, such as a prepayment at year end, which has to be posted to a ledger account.

administration cost variance The difference between the *administration overheads budgeted for in an accounting period and those actually incurred.

administration expenses *See* administration overheads.

administration order 1. An order made in a county court for the administration of the estate of a judgment debtor. The order normally requires the debtor to pay the debts by instalments; so long as this is done, the creditors referred to in the order cannot enforce their individual claims by other methods without the leave of the court. Administration orders are issued when the debtor has multiple debts but it is thought that *bankruptcy can be avoided. 2. An order of the court under the Insolvency Act (1986) made in relation to a company in financial difficulties with a view to securing its survival as a going concern or, failing that, to achieving a more favourable realization of its assets than would be possible on a *liquidation. While the order is in force, the affairs of the company are managed by an **administrator**.

administration overheads (administration expenses) The part of the general *overheads of an organization that are incurred in carrying out its administrative activities. They include general office salaries, stationery, telephones, etc.

administrative receiver A *receiver appointed by the holder of a *floating charge covering the whole, or substantially all, of a company's assets in order to recover money due to a secured creditor. The administrative receiver has the power to sell the assets that are secured by the charge or to carry on the company's business.

administrator 1. Any person appointed by the courts, or by private arrangement, to manage the property of another. 2. Any person appointed by the courts to take charge of the affairs of a deceased person, who died without making a will. This includes collection of assets, payment of debts, and distribution of the surplus to those persons entitled to inherit, according to the laws of intestacy (*see* intestate). The administrator must be in possession of letters of administration as proof of the authority vested by the courts.

administratrix A female *administrator.

ADR Abbreviation for *American depositary receipt.

ADST Abbreviation for *approved deferred share trust.

ad valorem duty A form of stamp duty applied to certain legal instruments. The duty is based on a percentage of the consideration for the transaction effected by the instrument. Conveyance or transfer of property is subject to 1% ad valorem duty, over a certain value (currently £30,000), and the transfer of shares, by way of instrument, is subject to an ad valorem duty of 1/2%.

advance A payment on account or a loan. In a *partnership it refers to any amount paid into the partnership in excess of the agreed capital contributions. Under the Partnership Act (1890) interest is payable on advances, unless the partners agree to the contrary. On dissolution the advance would be repaid after any external creditors were paid but before the distribution of capital to the partners.

advance corporation tax (ACT) An advance payment of *corporation tax. It is paid when a company makes a *qualifying distribution. For the financial year 1 April 1995 to 31 March 1996 ACT is calculated at a rate of 20/80 dividend paid. The ACT is due for payment 14 days after the *return period in which the dividend is paid. ACT paid in an *accounting period can be set against the *gross corporation tax due for the period, up to the maximum set-off of 20% of *total profits.

advancement Payment by a parent (during his or her lifetime) to a child of an amount that the child would receive as beneficiary, or as heir, on the death of that parent.

adverse opinion An opinion expressed by an *auditor in an *audit report to the effect that the financial statements do not give a true and fair view of the organization's activities. This situation usually arises if there is a disagreement between the auditor and the directors, and the auditor considers the effect of the disagreement is so material or pervasive that the financial statements are seriously misleading. Audit reports are covered by the *Auditing Practices Board's Statement of Auditing Standard 600, 'Auditors' Reports on Financial Statements'.

adverse variance (unfavourable variance) In *standard costing and *budgetary control, the differences between actual and budgeted performance of an organization if the differences create a deduction from the budgeted profit. For example, this may occur if the actual sales revenue is less than that budgeted or the actual costs exceed budgeted costs. *Compare* favourable variance.

advice note A document issued by a supplier of goods advising the customer that the goods have been sent. The advice note is generally received before the goods themselves.

affiliate A company linked in some sense to another company. The concept has no legal status in the UK.

affinity card A *credit card issued to an affinity group (such as the members of a club, college, etc.) in the USA. In the UK, an affinity card is linked to a particular charity; the credit-card company pledges to make a donation to a specified charity for each card issued and may also donate a small proportion of the money spent by card users. In the UK, affinity cards are sometimes called **charity cards**.

after date The words used in a *bill of exchange to indicate that the period of the bill should commence from the date inserted on the bill, e.g. '... 30 days after date, we promise to pay ...'. *Compare* after sight; at sight.

after sight The words used in a *bill of exchange to indicate that the period of the bill should commence from the date on which the drawee is presented with it for acceptance, i.e. has sight of it. *Compare* after date; at sight.

age allowance The *personal allowance available to taxpayers aged 65 and over. The age allowance for taxpayers aged 65–74 is £4630 and for those 75 and over is £4800, for 1995–96. There is an income limit of £14,600 for age allowance. The allowance is reduced at a rate of £1 off the allowance for every £2 by which the income exceeds the income limit, until the basic personal allowance is reached, which is £3525 for 1995–96.

age analysis A listing of debtors' accounts (i.e. the amounts owing to a business), usually produced monthly, which analyses the age of the debts by splitting them into such categories as those up to one month old, two months old, and more than two months old. As a basic part of the credit control system, the analysis should be regularly examined so that any appropriate follow-up action may be taken.

agency agreement An agreement between a customer and a bank allowing the customer to bank cheques at a branch of that bank, usually for logistical reasons. The cheques thus enter the clearing system, although the customer does not have an account with that bank. A charge is made by the bank for this service.

agency fee (facility fee) An annual fee paid to an agent for the work and responsibility involved in managing a loan after it has been signed.

agency relationship A relationship in which a principal engages an agent to perform some service on his or her behalf; this involves delegating authority by the principal. As it has to be assumed that the agent will not always act in the best interests of the principal, the principal incurs costs in monitoring and controlling the behaviour of the agent. In turn, the agent will incur bonding costs in convincing the principal that the interests of the principal will not be harmed. The agent may also take decisions that do not always maximize the welfare of the principal; these decisions can result in what is called a residual loss. The sum of the monitoring and bonding costs together with the residual loss form the **agency costs**. Even in an unregulated economy managers may choose to provide financial statements, examined by independent auditors, to shareholders and creditors in order to reduce agency costs. By supplying informative financial statements to external parties on the basis of information held by them, managers may avoid costly disputes and more expensive mechanisms for controlling their actions. These aspects of an agency relationship are sometimes referred to as **agency theory**.

agent A person appointed by another person, known as the principal, to act on his or her behalf. The directors of a company are agents of the shareholders (the principal). *See* agency relationship.

aggregate depreciation *See* accumulated depreciation.

AGM Abbreviation for *annual general meeting.

agreed bid A *takeover bid that is supported by a majority of the shareholders of the target company, whereas a **hostile bid** is not welcomed by the majority of the shareholders of the target company.

agricultural property relief An *inheritance tax relief available on the transfer of agricultural property when certain conditions are met. For 1995–96 the relief is at a rate of 100%. At the time of the transfer the agricultural property must have been occupied by the donor for agriculture throughout the previous two years, or if it was tenanted it must have been owned for seven years and occupied for agriculture by the donor or someone else throughout the period.

AIAB Abbreviation for Associate of the *International Association of Bookkeepers.

AIBD Abbreviation for Association of International Bond Dealers.

AICPA Abbreviation for *American Institute of Certified Public Accountants.

AJE Abbreviation for *adjusting journal entry.

alienation of assets The sale by a borrower of some or all of the assets that form the actual or implied security for a loan. It is therefore common practice to include a clause in the document setting up a loan, which restricts the disposal of the borrower's assets to specific circumstances.

alimony payment In the USA, payments in a divorce settlement. They are treated as deductions from *adjusted gross income by the payer, but the recipient treats them as income for tax purposes.

all-financial resources concept In the USA, the basis for preparing a statement of changes in financial position. The statement presents transactions affecting *working capital and transactions not affecting working capital if they are of a material noncurrent nature, such as the acquisition of a fixed asset in exchange for a long-term liability.

all-inclusive income concept A concept used in drawing up a *profit and loss account, in which all items of profit and loss are included in the statement to arrive at a figure of *earnings; this is the approach adopted in the UK and the USA. Although it is claimed that this basis gives the fullest picture of the operation of an enterprise, it does lead to a volatility in earnings figures as one-off costs, such as redundancies and sale of assets, will be included. To assist prediction of future profits, users are often more interested in the sustainable profits, which are shown using *reserve accounting, which is the alternative basis for drawing up a profit and loss account.

allocation 1. (cost allocation) Charging the whole element of a cost directly to a *cost centre or *cost unit because the cost centres or cost units are directly incurring those costs. If a cost cannot be allocated in this way the techniques of *apportionment or *absorption are used. 2. The number of shares in a new issue allotted (*see* allotment) to an investor or syndicate of investors.

allotment A method of distributing previously unissued shares in a limited company in exchange for a contribution of capital. An application for such shares will often be made after the issue of a prospectus on the *flotation of a public company or on the privatization of a state-owned industry. The company accepts the application by dispatching a **letter of allotment** to the applicant stating how many shares have been allotted; the applicant then has an unconditional right to be entered in the *register of members in respect of those shares. If the number of shares applied for exceeds the number available (oversubscription), allotment is made by a random draw or by a proportional allocation. Applicants that have been allotted fewer shares than they applied for receive a cheque for the unallotted balance (an application must be accompanied by a cheque for the full value of the shares applied for).

allotted shares Shares distributed by *allotment to new shareholders (allottees). The shares form part of the allotted share capital. *See also* issued share capital.

allowable capital loss *See* capital loss.

allowance 1. An amount deducted from an invoice; for example, to compensate for damaged goods. 2. An amount given to an employee for expenses, such as the cost of travel. 3. *See* tax allowance.

allowance for doubtful accounts *See* provision for bad debts.

all-purpose financial statements In the USA, financial statements intended to be seen by a diverse range of interest groups. In the UK, they are known as *general purpose financial statements. The major drawback of an all-purpose approach to financial reporting is that none of the groups of users receive financial statements that include the information they specifically require; to attempt to produce one document to satisfy the needs of all groups is impractical. The result is a compromise document that attempts to satisfy the needs of most users reasonably well, but in the end may satisfy no one.

alpha risk and beta risk Risks that occur in the sampling procedure undertaken by an *auditor. An auditor may reject a population that should have been accepted (alpha risk) or accept it when it should have been rejected (beta risk).

alternative accounting rules Alternative rules for valuing certain assets under the Companies Act (1985). These rules modify the *historical-cost convention. According to the modified rules intangible assets may be valued at current cost (with the exception of goodwill). Tangible fixed assets may be included at market value, determined as at their last valuation date, or at current cost. Fixed-asset investments may be valued at market value, determined as at their last valuation date, or at a value determined on any basis considered by the directors to be appropriate to the circumstances. Current-asset investments and stock may be included at current cost, unless the *net realizable value is lower, in which case this must be used. Any permanent diminution in value must be provided for. Accounts prepared under the alternative accounting rules are described as being prepared under the **modified historical-cost convention.**

alternative budgets Financial or quantitative budgets produced for consideration by the management of an organization in addition to the budgets adopted. The alternative budgets are based upon alternative policies, which may or may not be pursued by the organization at a later date.

amalgamation The combination of two or more companies. The combination may be effected by one company acquiring others, by the merging of two or more companies, or by existing companies being dissolved and a new company formed to take over the combined business. *Financial Reporting Standard 6, 'Acquisitions and Mergers', regulates the accounting of business combinations. *See also* acquisition accounting; merger accounting.

American Accounting Association (AAA) An influential organization with a membership consisting primarily of academic accountants. Originally founded in 1916 as the American Association of University Instructors in

Accounting, the Association adopted its present name in 1936. The Association has contributed to the development of accounting theory through the publication of reports, papers, and journals.

American depositary receipt (ADR) A receipt issued by a US bank to a member of the US public who has bought shares in a foreign country. The certificates are denominated in US dollars and can be traded as a security in US markets. The advantages of ADRs are the reduction in administration costs and the avoidance of stamp duty on each transaction.

American Institute of Certified Public Accountants (AICPA) The professional organization of practising certified public accountants. The Institute, which was founded in 1887, provides technical advice and guidance to its members and such government bodies as the *Securities and Exchange Commission. It issues many influential publications in the areas of accounting, auditing, and taxation.

American option An *option that can be exercised on any business day prior to its expiry date. *Compare* European option.

American Society of Women Accountants An organization whose membership consists of practising women accountants; its aim is to promote women's interests in the accounting profession.

amortization 1. The process of treating as an expense the annual amount deemed to waste away from a fixed asset. The concept is particularly applied to leases, which are acquired for a given sum for a specified term at the end of which the lease will have no value. It is customary to divide the cost of the lease by the number of years of its term and treat the result as an annual charge against profit. While this method does not necessarily reflect the value of the lease at any given time, it is an equitable way of allocating the original cost between periods. *Compare* depreciation.

Goodwill may also be amortized. *Statement of Standard Accounting Practice 22 recommends as its preferred method the writing-off in the year of purchase of all purchased goodwill. The charge should be to the reserves and not to the *profit and loss account. However the standard also permits the writing-off of goodwill to the profit and loss account in regular instalments over the period of its economic life. Home-grown goodwill, if it is in the balance sheet at all, should be similarly dealt with by one of the two methods above.
2. The repayment of debt by a borrower in a series of instalments over a period. Each payment includes interest and part repayment of the capital.
3. The spreading of the *front-end fee charged on taking out a loan over the life of a loan for accounting purposes.
4. In the USA, another word for *depreciation.

amortization schedule A schedule that summarizes the dates on which specified amounts must be paid in the repayment of a loan.

amortized cost That part of the value of an asset that has been written off; it represents the *accumulated depreciation to date.

amortizing loan A loan in which the repayment is made in more than one instalment. *Compare* bullet loan.

AMPS Abbreviation for *auction market preferred stock.

analysis of variance (ANOVA) An analysis of the variance in the total profit of an organization into sub-variances to indicate the major reasons for the difference between budgeted profit and actual profit. Typically, the total profit variance may be analysed into the following sub-variances:
    *sales margin volume variance,
    *sales margin price variance,
    *direct materials total cost variances,
    *direct labour variances,
    *variable overhead cost variance,
    *overhead efficiency or productivity variance,
    *fixed overhead expenditure variance,
    *overhead volume variance.

analytical auditing An analytical approach to an *audit that compares figures and other financial and non-financial data, either internally or with external data, to decide whether the picture presented appears to be reasonable. Analytical auditing is used in the initial planning stage of an audit, during the audit, or in its final stages when the tests of details have been completed. *See also* analytical review.

analytical review An audit test designed to provide evidence of the completeness, accuracy, and validity of *financial accounts and statements. Analytical review is a type of *substantive test that may be used in planning and undertaking an audit. It works by comparing figures and other financial and non-financial data, either internally or with external data, to decide whether they are reasonable. Procedures range from simple comparisons (e.g. comparing current amounts with those of earlier years) to more sophisticated methods using computer audit software and advanced statistical techniques (e.g. multiple regression analysis).

ancillary credit business A business involved in credit brokerage, debt adjusting, debt counselling, debt collecting, or the operation of a credit-reference agency. **Credit brokerage** includes the effecting of introductions of individuals wishing to obtain credit to persons carrying on a consumer-credit business. **Debt adjusting** is the process by which a third party negotiates terms for the discharge of a debt due under consumer-credit agreements or consumer-hire agreements with the creditor or owner on behalf of the debtor or hirer. The latter may also pay a third party to take over an obligation to discharge a debt or to undertake any similar acitivity concerned with its liquidation. **Debt counselling** is the giving of advice (other than by the original creditor and certain others) to debtors or hirers about the liquidation of debts due under consumer-credit agreements or consumer-hire agreements. A **credit-reference agency** collects information concerning the financial standing of individuals and supplies this information to those seeking it. The Consumer Credit Act (1974) provides for the licensing of ancillary credit businesses and regulates their activities.

Annual Abstract of Statistics An annual publication of the Central Statistical Office giving UK industrial, vital, legal, and social statistics.

annual accounts (annual report; report and accounts) The *financial statements of an organization, generally published annually. In the UK, incorporated bodies have a legal obligation to publish annual accounts and file them at Companies House. Annual accounts consist of a *profit and loss account, *balance sheet, *cash-flow statement (if required), and *statement of total recognized gains and losses, together with supporting notes and the directors' report and *auditors' report. Companies falling into the legally defined *small companies and *medium-sized companies categories may file *abbreviated accounts that may not have been audited (*see* small-company audit exemptions). Some bodies are regulated by other statutes; for example, many financial institutions and their accounts will have to comply with their own regulations. Non-incorporated bodies, such as partnerships, are not legally obliged to produce accounts but may do so for their own information, for their banks if funding is being sought, and for the Inland Revenue for taxation purposes.

annual exemption An *exempt transfer under *inheritance tax legislation allowing £3000 to be given each year as a gift without liability to inheritance tax. This has remained unchanged since 6 April 1981. Husband and wife each have their own exemption. If the exemption is not used or not fully used during a *fiscal year, the amount not used can be carried forward to the next tax year only, to cover gifts made in that following year.

annual general meeting (AGM) An annual meeting of the shareholders of a company, which must be held every year; the meetings may not be more than 15 months apart. Shareholders must be given 21 days' notice of the meeting. The usual business transacted at an AGM is the presentation of the audited accounts, the appointment of directors and auditors, the fixing of their remuneration, and recommendations for the payment of dividends. Other business may be transacted if notice of it has been given to the shareholders.

annualization In the USA, a procedure specified by the Internal Revenue Code in which taxable income for part of a year is multiplied by 12 and divided by the number of months involved to give a monthly amount.

annual percentage rate (APR) The annual equivalent *rate of return on a loan or investment in which the rate of interest specified is chargeable or payable more frequently than annually. Most investment institutions are now required by law to specify the APR when the interest intervals are more frequent than annual. Similarly those charge cards that advertise monthly rates of interest (say, 2%) must state the equivalent APR. In this case it would be $[(1.02)^{12} - 1] = 26.8\%$.

annual report *See* annual accounts.

annual return A document that must be filed with the Registrar of Companies within 14 days of the *annual general meeting of a company. Information required on the annual return includes the address of the registered office of the company and the names, addresses, nationality, and occupations of its directors. The *financial statements, *directors' report, and *auditors' report must be annexed to the return. Legally defined *small companies and *medium-sized companies may file *abbreviated accounts. Unlimited companies are exempt from filing the financial statements and dormant companies may not have to be audited. There are penalties for late filing of accounts.

annuitant A person receiving an *annuity.

annuity **1.** A contract in which a person pays a premium to an insurance company, usually in one lump sum, and in return receives periodic payments for an agreed period or for the rest of his or her life. An annuity has been described as the opposite of a life assurance as the policyholder pays the lump sum and the insurer makes the regular payments. Annuities are often purchased at a time of prosperity to convert capital into an income during old age. *See also* annuity certain; deferred annuity. **2.** A payment made on such a contract.

annuity certain An *annuity in which payments continue for a specified period irrespective of the life or death of the person covered. In general, annuities cease on the death of the policyholder unless they are annuities certain.

annuity method A method of calculating the *depreciation on a fixed asset. The objective of the method is to produce an approximately constant annual charge for the total depreciation and cost of capital of an asset. It is calculated in such a way that a low depreciation charge is made in the earlier years when interest costs are high, and a higher charge is made in the later years when interest costs are lower. It is less popular than the *straight-line method or the *diminishing-balance method.

ANOVA Abbreviation for *analysis of variance.

ante-date To date a document before the date on which it is drawn up. This is not necessarily illegal or improper. For instance, an ante-dated cheque is not in law invalid. *Compare* post-date.

anti-trust laws Laws passed in the USA, from 1890 onwards, making it illegal to do anything in restraint of trade, set up monopolies, or otherwise interfere with free trade and competition.

Anton Piller order A court injunction ordering the defendant to allow the plaintiff to enter named premises to search for and take copies of specified articles and documents. These orders are obtained by the plaintiff 'ex parte' (without the other party being present in court) to enable the preservation of evidence in cases in which the plaintiff has grounds to think it will be destroyed. It is especially useful in 'pirating' cases. The order is not a search warrant, so entry cannot be forced, but the defendant will be in contempt of court if entry is refused. A solicitor must serve the order. It is named after an order made in the High Court in 1976 against Anton Piller KG.

APACS Abbreviation for *Association for Payment Clearing Services.

APB **1.** Abbreviation for *Accounting Principles Board. **2.** Abbreviation for *Auditing Practices Board.

APC Abbreviation for *Auditing Practices Committee.

application and allotment account A ledger account used in the process of applications for and *allotment of a company's share capital. When the shares are offered, potential shareholders (applicants) apply to buy them on an *application form with a cheque to cover the cost of the shares. This is known as the **application process**. On receipt of the applicants' money, the company debits the bank account with the cash received and credits an application and allotment account. When the shares are allocated to the applicants they become the **allottees**, i.e. the new shareholders; this is known as the **process of allotment** The book-keeping entries on allotment involve debiting the application and allotment account and crediting the share capital or share premium, as appropriate. If the applications exceed the number of shares available, each applicant receives a scaled down number of shares and the excess application money is returned. The application and allotment account may also be split into two separate accounts: the application account and the allotment account.

application controls Controls relating to the transactions and standing data for each computer-based accounting system; they are, therefore, specific to each such application. Application controls, which may be manual or programmed, are designed to ensure the completeness and accuracy of the accounting records and the validity of the entries made. An example of an application control designed to check completeness would be a manual or programmed agreement of control totals, i.e. the total of the source documents and the total of the amounts input would be compared. Other examples of application controls include checks to ensure that the correct master files and standing data files are used, that data has been updated, and that output reports are both complete and accurate. *See also* computer-assisted audit techniques.

application for listing The process by which a company applies to a stock exchange for its securities to be traded on that exchange. In obtaining the listing a company will be required to abide by the rules of the exchange. The advantage for a company in obtaining a listing is that it will be able to raise funds by issuing shares on the stock exchange and the marketability of the shares it issues will attract investors. *See also* flotation; listing requirements.

application form A form, issued by a newly floated company with its prospectus, on which members of the public apply for shares in the company. *See also* allotment.

application for quotation An application by a *public limited company for a quotation on the *London Stock Exchange. The company is scrutinized by the Quotations Committee to see if it complies with the regulations and if its directors have a high reputation. If the application is accepted the company is given a quotation on one of the Stock Exchange's markets.

applications software Computer programs that are designed for a particular purpose or application. For example, accounts programs, games programs, and educational programs are all applications software.

applied overhead *See* absorbed overhead.

applied research Original or critical investigations undertaken to gain new scientific or technical knowledge with respect to a specific practical objective. For example, any testing in the search for a product alternative would generally be classified as applied research. It is the 'specific practical objective' that distinguishes applied research from pure research, which is primarily undertaken to acquire new scientific or technical knowledge for its own sake. Any pure or applied research expenditure should be written off to the *profit and loss account as incurred; *development costs may be carried forward in certain specified circumstances. *Statement of Standard Accounting Practice 13,

'Accounting for Research and Development', defines research and development and lays down their accounting treatment.

apportionment (cost apportionment) Charging a proportion of a cost to a *cost centre or *cost unit because the cost centres or cost units are not directly incurring those costs although they share in incurring them. A *basis of apportionment is always required. For example, local authority business rates for premises are seldom incurred by individual cost centres, therefore floor area is often used as a basis of apportionment to share these costs between appropriate cost centres.

appraisal The assessment of alternative courses of action with a view to establishing which action should be taken. Appraisals may be financial, economic, or technical in emphasis.

appreciation 1. An increase in the value of an asset, usually as a result of inflation. This usually occurs with land and buildings. *See* asset stripping. **2.** An increase in the value of a currency with a *floating exchange rate relative to another currency. *Compare* depreciation; devaluation.

apprentice A young employee who signs a contract (an **indenture** or **articles of apprenticeship**) agreeing to be trained in a particular skill for a set amount of time by a specific employer. During this time the wages will be relatively low but on completion of the apprenticeship they increase to reflect the increased status of the employee and to recognize the skills acquired.

appropriation The allocation of the *net profits of an organization in its accounts. For example, in a company appropriations are usually in the form of cash *dividends or *scrip dividends to shareholders, transfers to reserves, and amounts for taxation. In a partnership appropriations tend to be in the form of salaries, interest on capital, and profit.

appropriation account 1. An account used in partnership accounts to attribute the various appropriations, such as interest on capital, salaries, and profit shares, to the partners. **2.** A financial statement prepared by a government department to show its expenditure and receipts for a financial year.

approved deferred share trust (ADST) A trust fund set up by a British company, and approved by the Inland Revenue, that purchases shares in that company for the benefit of its employees. Tax on dividends is deferred until the shares are sold and is then paid at a reduced rate.

APR Abbreviation for *annual percentage rate.

a priori theories of accounting Theories developed from assumptions, rather than experience, that apply deductive reasoning in measurement and valuation systems of accounting. The assumptions may be based on a mixture of empirical observations of accounting practice and the postulates of economic theory. The 1960s was a particularly fruitful period for a priori research in financial accounting.

arbitrage 1. The non-speculative transfer of funds from one market to another to take advantage of differences in interest rates, exchange rates, or commodity prices between the two markets. It is non-speculative because an arbitrageur will only switch from one market to another if the rates or prices in both markets are known and if the profit to be gained outweighs the costs of the operation. Thus, a large stock of a commodity in a user country may force its price below that in a producing country; if the difference is greater than the cost of shipping the goods back to the producing country, this could provide a profitable opportunity for arbitrage. Similar opportunities arise with *bills of exchange, bonds, shares, and foreign currencies. **2.** Any form of speculation involving an open position in bond, share, commodity, or currency markets.

arbitrage pricing theory An explanation of movements in security prices that takes into account more than one variable. *See* capital asset pricing model.

arbitration The determination of a dispute by an arbitrator or arbitrators rather than by a court of law. Any civil (i.e. noncriminal) matter may be settled in this way; commercial contracts often contain **arbitration clauses** providing for this to be done in a specified way. If each side appoints its own arbitrator, as is usual, and the arbitrators fail to agree, the arbitrators are often empowered to appoint an **umpire**, whose decision is final. Arbitration is made binding on the parties by the Arbitration Acts (1950 and 1975). Various industries and chambers of commerce set up tribunals for dealing with disputes in their particular trade or business.

archive A store for documents and magnetic disks or tapes containing records that are seldom used. Most computer users maintain an archive holding copies of disks or tapes containing vital information. If the original disk or tape becomes damaged, the archive copy is used to reinstate the information lost from the damaged master disk or tape.

arithmetic average (arithmetic mean) An average in which individual numbers or quantities are added together and divided by their total number. For example, the average of 6, 7, and 11 is $(6 + 7 + 11)/3 = 8$. *Compare* geometric mean; weighted average.

arm's length transaction A transaction entered into by unrelated parties, each acting in their own best interests in paying or charging prices based on fair market values. In the preparation of financial statements it is normally assumed that all transactions are conducted at arm's length, although it is appreciated that this may not be the case with companies belonging to the same group, who make special arrangements between themselves for taxation or other reasons. Because of the possibility of transactions being carried out at other than arm's length and the reader of financial statements being unaware of this fact, there has been some pressure to issue an *accounting standard on *related-party transactions.

arrears A liability that has not been settled by the due date. For example, *cumulative preference shares entitle the shareholders to receive an annual fixed dividend. If this is not paid, the dividend is said to be in arrears and this fact must be disclosed in the notes to the financial statements.

article of incorporation In the USA, an official document that details a company's existence. It is similar to the UK *memorandum of association.

articles of association The document that governs the running of a company. It sets out voting rights of shareholders, conduct of shareholders' and directors' meetings, powers of the management, etc. Either the articles are submitted with the *memorandum of association when application is made for incorporation or the relevant model articles contained in the Companies Regulations (Tables A to F) are adopted. Table A contains the model articles for companies limited by shares. The articles constitute a contract between the company and its members but this applies only to the rights of shareholders in their capacity as members. Therefore directors or company solicitors (for example) cannot use the articles to enforce their rights. The articles may be altered by a special resolution of the members in a general meeting.

articles of partnership *See* partnership agreement.

articulated accounts Accounts prepared under the *double-entry book-keeping system, in which the retained profit figure on the *profit and loss account equals the increase in net worth of the business on the *balance sheet, subject to any other increases, such as an injection of new capital.

artificial intelligence The ability of a computer to perform tasks normally associated with human intelligence, such as reasoning and learning from experience. There has been considerable progress in the field recently, particularly in those applications that make use of the computer's calculating power. Chess-playing computers that can beat most human players seem to be intelligent, yet their skill relies only on their ability to calculate better than their human opponents. A more important development, the expert system, makes use of the computer's ability to store, organize, and retrieve large volumes of information. Also called intelligent knowledge-based systems, these store the knowledge and experience of an expert in a particular field. The system can be questioned by a non-expert and will give the answer that the expert would give. These systems are used for a wide range of tasks, such as analysis of company results, review of loan applications, buying stocks and shares, medical diagnosis, identifying poisons, and prospecting for oil.

artificial person A person whose identity is recognized by the law but who is not an individual. For example, a company is a person in the sense that it can sue and be sued, hold property, etc., in its own name. It is not, however, an individual or real person.

ASB Abbreviation for *Accounting Standards Board.

ASC Abbreviation for *Accounting Standards Committee.

ASCII Acronym for American Standard Code for Information Interchange. This is a standard code adopted by many computer manufacturers to simplify the transfer of information between computers. The code represents the numbers, letters, and symbols used in computing by a standard set of numbers. For example, the capital letter A is represented by the number 65, B is represented by the number 66, and so on. Many computers can convert their output to ASCII code, in which form it can be transferred to, and recognized by, other computers.

A shares Ordinary shares in a company that usually do not carry voting rights. **Non-voting ordinary shares** are issued by a company when it wishes to raise additional capital without committing itself to a fixed dividend and without diluting control of the company. They are, however, unpopular with institutional investors (who like to have a measure of control with their investments) and are therefore now rarely issued.

ASOBAT Acronym for *A Statement of Basic Accounting Theory*, an influential publication by the American Accounting Association. It argued for a user-friendly approach to financial statements and considered the qualitative characteristics of such statements.

as per advice Words written on a *bill of exchange to indicate that the drawee has been informed that the bill is being drawn on him or her.

ASSC Abbreviation for *Accounting Standards Steering Committee.

assembler A computer program that takes instructions prepared by the computer user in a kind of shorthand (called *assembly language) and converts them into a form that the computer can understand.

assembly language A type of *low-level language used to program computers. Each instruction is a short mnemonic, or 'memory-jogger', that describes one operation to be performed by the machine. For instance, for a particular machine the assembly-language instruction ADD B adds a number to the total already in the computer memory. A special program, called an **assembler**, is needed to convert the mnemonics into a form, called machine code, that the computer can understand. In practice, most programming is done using high-level languages, such as BASIC or PASCAL, that use abstract constructs, which have no one-for-one correspondence with machine-code instructions. In this case the translation into machine code is done by a program called an interpreter, or a compiler.

assented stock A security, usually an ordinary share, the owner of which has agreed to the terms of a *takeover bid. During the takeover negotiations, different prices may be quoted for assented and **non-assented stock**.

assessable capital stocks In the USA: **1.** Capital stock of banks, subjecting stockholders to liabilities in excess of the sum originally subscribed **2.** Capital stock not fully paid and therefore subject to calls.

asset Any object, tangible or intangible, that is of value to its possessor. In most cases it either is cash or can be turned into cash; exceptions include prepayments, which may represent payments made for rent, rates, or motor licences, in cases in which the time paid for has not yet expired. Tangible assets include land and buildings, plant and machinery, fixtures and fittings, trading stock, investments, debtors, and cash; intangible assets include goodwill, patents, copyrights, and trademarks. *See also* deferred debit.

   For *capital gains tax purposes, an asset consists of all forms of property, whether situated in the UK or abroad, including options, debts, incorporeal property, currency (other than sterling), and any form of property either created by the person disposing of it or owned without being acquired. It must, however, consist of some form of property for which a value can be ascertained. Some assets are exempt from *capital gains tax.

asset-backed fund A fund in which the money is invested in tangible or corporate assets, such as property or shares, rather than being treated as savings loaned to a bank or other institution. Asset-backed funds can be expected to grow with inflation in a way that bank savings cannot.

asset classification The classification of assets as required by law on a
*balance sheet. Assets must be classified as fixed (i.e. held for use on a
continuing basis) or current (i.e. not intended for continuing use but held on a
short-term basis). Fixed assets are further classified as intangible (e.g. goodwill)
or tangible (e.g. land and buildings). Fixed assets must be depreciated (*see*
depreciation) over their useful economic life to comply with the Companies Act
and *Statement of Standard Accounting Practice 12, 'Accounting for
Depreciation'. Current assets include stock, debtors, prepayments, cash at bank,
and cash in hand. Fixed assets may be shown at *historical cost less
accumulated depreciation, or under the *alternative accounting rules. Current
assets must be shown at the lower of historical cost (or *current cost under the
alternative accounting rules) and *net realizable value.

asset cover A ratio that provides a measure of the solvency of a company; it
consists of its *net assets divided by its *debt. Those companies with high asset
cover are considered the more solvent.

asset deficiency The condition of a company when its *liabilities exceed its
*assets. Although each particular circumstance must be interpreted in its own
context, the financial viability of an organization with an asset deficiency must
be in question.

asset revaluation reserve *See* revaluation reserve account.

assets register *See* fixed-assets register.

asset stripping The acquisition or takeover of a company whose shares are
valued below their *asset value, and the subsequent sale of the company's most
valuable assets. Asset stripping was a practice that occurred primarily in the
decade after World War II, during which property values were rising sharply.
Having identified a suitable company, an entrepreneur would acquire a
controlling interest in it by buying its shares on the stock exchange; after
revaluing the properties held, some or all of them could be sold for cash, which
would be distributed to shareholders (which now included the entrepreneur).
Subsequently, the entrepreneur could either revitalize the management of the
company and later sell off the acquired shareholding at a profit or, in some
cases, close the business down. Because the asset stripper is totally heedless of
the welfare of the other shareholders, the employees, the suppliers, or creditors
of the stripped company, the practice is now highly deprecated.

asset valuation An assessment of the value at which the *assets of an
organization, usually the *fixed assets, should be entered into its balance sheet.
The valuation may be arrived at in a number of ways; for example, a
revaluation of land and buildings would often involve taking professional
advice.

asset value (per share) The total value of the assets of a company less its
liabilities, divided by the number of ordinary shares in issue. This represents in
theory, although probably not in practice, the amount attributable to each
share if the company was wound up. The asset value may not necessarily be the
total of the values shown by a company's balance sheet, since it is not the
function of balance sheets to value assets. It may, therefore, be necessary to
substitute the best estimate that can be made of the market values of the assets
(including goodwill) for the values shown in the balance sheet. If there is more

than one class of share, it may be necessary to deduct amounts due to shareholders with a priority on winding up before arriving at the amounts attributable to shareholders with a lower priority.

assignment 1. The act of transferring, or a document (a **deed of assignment**) transferring, property to some other person. Examples of assignment include the transfer of rights under a contract or benefits under a trust to another person. *See also* assignment of lease. **2.** The transfer of a bank loan from the lending bank to another bank in order to reduce the credit risk of the lending bank. This practice is contrary to the principles of *relationship banking.

assignment of lease The transfer of a lease by the tenant (assignor) to some other person (assignee). Leases are freely transferable at common law although it is common practice to restrict assignment by conditions (covenants) in the lease. An assignment that takes place in breach of such a covenant is valid but it may entitle the landlord to put an end to the lease and re-enter the premises. An assignment of a legal lease must be by deed. An assignment puts the assignee into the shoes of the assignor, so that there is 'privity of estate' between the landlord and the new tenant. This is important with regard to the enforceability of covenants in the lease (*see* covenant). An assignment transfers the assignor's whole estate to the assignee, unlike a sub-lease (*see* head lease).

assignment of life policies Transfer of the legal right under a life-assurance policy to collect the proceeds. Assignment is only valid if the life insurer is advised and agrees; life assurance is the only form of insurance in which the assignee need not possess an insurable interest. In recent years policy auctions have become a popular alternative to surrendering endowment assurances. In these auctions, a policy is sold to the highest bidder and then assigned to him or her by the original policyholder.

associated company A company associated with another company that it controls. Associated companies are also defined as companies under the control of the same person or persons.

associated undertaking An *undertaking that is not defined as a *subsidiary undertaking but is one in which the group has a *participating interest and exercises a *significant influence over its operations and financial policies.

Association for Payment Clearing Services (APACS) An association set up by the UK banks in 1985 to manage payment clearing and overseas money transmission in the UK. The three operating companies under its aegis are: BACS Ltd, which provides an automated service for interbank clearing in the UK; Cheque and Credit Clearing Co. Ltd, which operates a bulk clearing system for interbank cheques and paper credits; and CHAPS, which provides electronic funds transfer. In addition EftPos UK Ltd is a company set up to develop electronic funds transfer at the point of sale. APACS also oversees London Dollar Clearing, the London Currency Settlement Scheme, and the cheque card and eurocheque schemes in the UK.

Association of Accounting Technicians An association set up in 1980 by the *Consultative Committee of Accountancy Bodies (CCAB) to provide a second-tier accounting qualification. This qualification can enable an individual to obtain subsequently a full CCAB qualification.

Association of Authorized Public Accountants (AAPA) An association in the UK of qualified accountants who have been authorized by the Board of Trade to carry out *audits of companies. Fellows of the Association are designated FAPA and Associates are designated AAPA.

Association of Corporate Treasurers (ACT) An organization set up to encourage and promote the study and practice of treasury management in companies. A small organization in relation to the professional accounting bodies, it has become influential in the field of corporate treasurership. Fellows of the Association are designated FCT and members as MCT.

assurance Insurance against an eventuality (especially death) that must occur. *See* life assurance.

assured The person named in a life-assurance policy to receive the proceeds in the event of maturity or the death of the life assured. As a result of the policy, the person's financial future is 'assured'.

at and from Denoting a marine hull insurance cover that begins when the vessel is in dock before a voyage, continues during the voyage, and ends 24 hours after it has reached its port of destination.

ATII Abbreviation for Associate of the *Chartered Institute of Taxation (formerly Associate of the Taxation Institute Incorporated), a professional qualification achieved by passing the Institute's examination. Most members with the qualification are partners or senior employees of accountancy or solicitors' firms, working mainly in the tax field. Some members work in banks, the Inland Revenue, insurance, industry, or commerce.

at sight The words used on a *bill of exchange to indicate that payment is due on presentation. *Compare* after date; after sight.

ATT Abbreviation for Associate of the Association of Tax Technicians, a qualification undertaken by employees working in taxation at a level below that of members of the *Chartered Institute of Taxation. The Association was set up in 1989 under the sponsorship of the Institute of Taxation (now the Chartered Institute of Taxation).

attachment The procedure enabling a creditor, who has obtained judgment in the courts (the judgment creditor), to secure payment of the amount due from the debtor. The judgment creditor obtains a further court order (the garnishee order) to the effect that money or property due from a third party (the garnishee) to the debtor must be frozen and paid instead to the judgment creditor to satisfy the amount due. For instance, a judgment creditor may, through a garnishee order, attach the salary due to the debtor from the debtor's employer (the garnishee).

attainable standard In *standard costing, a cost or income standard set at a level that is attainable by the operators under the conditions applicable during the relevant cost period.

attest To bear witness to an act or event. The law requires that some documents are only valid and binding if the signatures on them have been attested to by a third party. This also requires the third party's signature on the document. For instance, the signature of the purchaser of land under a contract must be attested to by a witness.

attest function The provision of an *audit opinion as to the truth and fairness of the *financial statements of an organization.

at-the-money option A call or put *option in which the exercise price is approximately the same as the current market price of the underlying security.

attributable profit The part of the total estimated profit earned on a long-term contract, after allowing for estimated remedial and maintenance costs and any other non-recoverable costs, that fairly reflects the profit attributable to that part of the work completed at a specified accounting date.

attribute A characteristic that each member of a population either has or does not have. For example, if an auditor is examining the invoices of a company to establish whether each document has been signed and approved, the population will be the invoices, the attribute is the signature.

attributes sampling An examination of less than 100% of a population to determine the proportion of the population that has a specified *attribute. Attributes sampling is mostly used in *compliance tests, in which the characteristic being sought is a deviation from required control procedures.

auction market preferred stock (AMPS) A type of funding instrument issued in the US domestic market. The cost is extremely competitive when economic factors are favourable because the price is determined by auction. Unfortunately problems arise with regard to price and liquidity when the borrower is in difficulties.

audit An independent examination of, and the subsequent expression of opinion on, the financial statements of an organization. This involves the auditor in collecting evidence by means of *compliance tests (tests of control) and *substantive tests (tests of detail). External audits (i.e. audits performed by an auditor external to the organization) are required under statute for limited companies by the Companies Act and for various other undertakings, such as housing associations and building societies, by other acts of parliament. Internal audits are performed by auditors within an organization, usually an independent department, such as an internal-audit department. Internal auditors examine various areas, including financial and non-financial concerns, with emphasis on ensuring that internal controls are working effectively. Internal auditors may assist the external auditor of an organization. Non-statutory audits can be performed at the request of the owners, members, or trustees of an undertaking, for example. Forms of *financial statements, other than the annual accounts, may also be audited; for example, summaries of sales made by an organization. *See also* statutory audit; auditors' report; small-company audit exemption; internal audit; analytical auditing; independence of auditors.

Audit Agenda A discussion paper published by the *Auditing Practices Board (APB) at the end of 1994. It details current thinking on the form an *audit should take. It builds upon the report 'The Future Development of Auditing', published by the APB in 1992, and focuses on the need to recognize that the audit requirements of large listed companies differ from those of owner-managed companies. It advocates an extended audit for large listed and major public entities. The discussion paper also places an emphasis on the detection of fraud and recommends the commissioning of periodic *forensic accounting by listed companies.

Audit Commission The shortened name of the Audit Commission for Local Authorities in England and Wales, which was established by the Local Government Finance Act (1982). Since the passing of this act and the National Health and Community Care Act (1990), the Audit Commission has been responsible for all local authority and health authority external audit work.

audit committee A committee of non-executive directors the establishment of which was recommended for listed companies by the code of practice set out in the *Cadbury Report. The function of audit committees is to check the powers of executive directors, with particular reference to the financial reporting and auditing functions. Such committees would enhance the independence of auditors by allowing them to report to a body that is independent of the executive directors; this development could be further advanced in the future by giving the audit committee responsibility for the appointment, remuneration, and removal of the auditors. The establishment of audit committees remains a recommendation, not a requirement, in the UK.

audit completion checklist A list of items to be checked by audit staff to ensure that the *financial statements being audited give a true and fair view. The list will include all statutory disclosures and accounting standard requirements; for example, 'Have all the accounting policies been disclosed as required by *Statement of Standard Accounting Practice 2, 'Disclosure of Accounting Policies'?' The checklist may be used throughout the audit but is more specifically designed to be used as a final check before handing the files to the reporting partner of the audit firm for signature.

audit evidence The evidence required by an auditor on which to base an *audit opinion on the *financial statements of the company whose accounts are being audited. Sources of information include the accounting systems and the underlying documentation of the enterprise, its tangible assets, management and employees, its customers, suppliers, and any other third parties who have dealings with, or knowledge of, the enterprise or its business. The evidence will be obtained by means of *compliance tests (tests of controls) and *substantive tests (tests of details and analytical review). Techniques involved in gathering the evidence include inspection, observation, enquiry, computation, and analytical work.

audit exemption The exemption from a statutory annual *audit performed by a registered auditor that can be claimed by companies with a turnover of not more than £90,000 (and a balance-sheet total of not more than £1.4 million). Companies with a turnover in the range £90,000 to £350,000 (and a balance-sheet total of not more than £1.4 million) may claim exemption from the audit requirement but still need a reporting accountant's report. The report must state that the accounts are, in the opinion of the accountant, in agreement with the accounting records kept by the company and that the accounts have been drawn up in a manner consistent with the provisions of the Companies Act (1985). Also, the accountant must report that, on the basis of the information contained in the accounting records, the company is entitled to the exemption on the basis of size. The audit exemption report was initially known as a **compilation report** but this term is now obsolete. *See also* small-company audit exemption.

audit expectations gap The gap between the role of an *auditor, as perceived by the auditor, and the expectations of the users of *financial statements. It may be subdivided into a gap in communications and a gap in performance. The communications gap is caused by public expectations being unreasonable; for example, users of accounts may expect all fraud to have been discovered by a statutory audit, whereas the auditor is only expected to plan the audit to prevent and detect fraud to comply with *Statement of Auditing Standard 110, 'Fraud and Error'. The communications gap could be closed by ensuring that the users of accounts understand what an audit is and what its limitations are. The performance gap occurs when public expectations are reasonable but the auditor's performance does not fulfil them, i.e. there is a shortfall in the auditor's performance. This can only be overcome by improving the quality of the auditor's work.

audit fee (auditors' remuneration) The amount payable to an *auditor for an *audit; this has to be approved at the *annual general meeting of a company. In the *financial statements, audit fees must be distinguished from fees payable to the auditor for non-audit work.

auditing guidelines Documents originally issued by the former *Auditing Practices Committee (APC). APC guidelines have been adopted by the *Auditing Practices Board (APB), which now has the responsibility for issuing all auditing pronouncements. Guidelines are not prescriptive, but they give guidance as to the methods of applying auditing standards. Auditors could be asked to explain any departures from the guidelines if their failure to follow auditing standards is being investigated. Guidelines are generally grouped into three areas: industry-specific, detailed operational, and reporting guidelines.

Auditing Practices Board (APB) A body constituted in 1991 to replace the *Auditing Practices Committee (APC). Intended to be more independent of the auditing profession than the APC, the APB has half of its members drawn from outside practice, for example from universities and from the legal profession. Its objectives are to guide the development of auditing practice in the UK and the Republic of Ireland in order to establish the highest standards of auditing. To do this it seeks to meet the developing needs of users of financial information and thus to ensure public confidence in the auditing process. It is empowered to issue Statements of Auditing Standards (SASs) in its own right, and also supplements these with the issue of Practice Notes (PN) and Bulletins (*see* auditing standards).

Auditing Practices Committee (APC) A committee of the *Consultative Committee of Accountancy Bodies set up in 1976 and replaced by the *Auditing Practices Board in 1991. During the period 1980 to 1991 it was responsible for issuing two *auditing standards: 'The Auditor's Operational Standard' (April 1980) and 'The Audit Report' (March 1989; now superseded), and 38 auditing guidelines.

auditing standards Standards issued by the *Auditing Practices Committee between 1980 and 1991. The *Auditing Practices Board (APB) standards are known as *Statements of Auditing Standards (SAS). An SAS contains basic principles and essential procedures with which auditors are required to comply (except where otherwise stated in the SAS concerned) in the conduct of any audit of financial statements. Auditing standards do not need to be applied to matters whose effect is, in the auditor's judgment, not material. The APB also issues *Practice Notes (to assist the auditor in applying auditing standards of general application to particular circumstances and industries) and **Bulletins** (designed for issue when guidance is required on new or emerging issues). Practice Notes and Bulletins are not prescriptive; they are an indication of current good practice.

Auditing Standards Board In the USA, the organization responsible for the issue of *Statements of Auditing Standards.

audit manual A written document that explains the auditing policies and procedures of a firm.

audit opinion An opinion contained in an *auditors' report. It expresses a view as to whether or not the *financial statements audited have been prepared consistently using appropriate accounting policies, in accordance with relevant legislation, regulations, or applicable accounting standards. The opinion also has to state that there is adequate disclosure of information relevant to the proper understanding of the financial statements. If the auditors are satisfied on these points, and if any departure from legislation, regulations, or applicable accounting standards has been justified and adequately explained in the financial statements, an unqualified opinion will be given. If the scope of the auditors' examination has been limited, or the auditors disagree materially with the treatment or disclosure of a matter in the financial statements, or they do not comply with relevant accounting or other requirements, a qualified opinion will be issued. *See* adverse opinion; disclaimer of opinion; proper accounting records.

auditor A person or firm appointed to carry out an *audit of an organization. In the UK, since the Companies Act (1989) an external auditor must be a registered auditor or a member of a recognized supervisory body and be eligible for appointment under the rules of that body. The four recognized bodies, given approval in 1991, were the *Chartered Association of Certified Accountants, the *Institute of Chartered Accountants in England and Wales (ICAEW), the *Institute of Chartered Accountants of Scotland (ICAS), and the *Institute of Chartered Accountants in Ireland (ICAI). Since 1991, the *Association of Authorized Public Accountants (AAPA) has also been recognized in principle. The recognized supervisory bodies are required to have rules designed to ensure that persons eligible for appointment as company auditors are either individuals who hold the appropriate qualification or firms controlled by properly qualified persons. These bodies must also ensure that eligible persons continue to maintain the appropriate level of competence and must monitor and enforce compliance with their rules. These rules do not apply to internal auditors. *See also* independence of auditors.

auditors' remuneration *See* audit fee.

auditors' report (audit report) A report by the auditors appointed to *audit the accounts of a company or other organization. Auditors' reports may take many forms depending on who has appointed the auditors and for what purposes. Some auditors are engaged in an internal audit while others are appointed for various statutory purposes. The auditors of a limited company are required to form an opinion as to whether the annual accounts of the company give a true and fair view of its profit or loss for the period under review and of its state of affairs at the end of the period; they are also required to certify that the accounts are prepared in accordance with the requirements of the Companies Act (1985). The auditors' report is technically a report to the members of the company and it must be filed together with the accounts with the Registrar of Companies under the Companies Act (1985). Under this Act, the auditors' report must also include an audit of the directors' report with respect to consistency. *See also* qualified audit report.

audit panel A panel that the *Auditing Practices Board, in its report *Future Development of Auditing (1992), suggested should be appointed to enhance the independence of auditors. The panel would represent the shareholders of all listed companies, and could be modelled on the Takeover Panel (*see* City Code on Takeovers and Mergers). The panel's duties could include overseeing the appointment of auditors, thus giving the auditor a body, independent of the client, to report to.

audit plan (audit planning memorandum) A document outlining the *audit strategy to be applied to each manageable area of the accounting system and *financial statements of an audit client. The plan would take into account the assessed levels of inherent risk (i.e. the susceptibility of account balances or classes of transactions to material misstatement) and control risk (the risk that material misstatements are not prevented or detected by the internal control system); it would also outline the nature, timing, and extent of audit procedures.

audit programme A document listing the individual audit tests to be performed to achieve an *audit strategy. The tests will check that the accounting system operates in the manner recorded. For example, a credit sales transaction will be traced through to payment. *Compliance tests will be made to check that the internal control system is working. *Substantive tests of details (e.g. account balances and transactions) and an analytical review (an overall analysis of the *financial statements) will also be outlined. The audit programme gives guidance to the audit staff involved and provides a record of work done and the conclusions drawn; it therefore provides a basis for effective quality control and meeting *audit evidence requirements.

audit report *See* auditors' report.

audit risk The risk that an *auditor fails to qualify the *audit report when the *financial statements are materially misleading, i.e. do not give a true and fair view. The audit risk consists of three components: the **inherent risk** (the likelihood of misstatements occurring in the absence of controls), the **control risk** (the risk that misstatements may not be prevented or detected on a timely basis by the internal control system), and the **detection risk** (the risk that the auditor's *substantive tests will not detect a misstatement that exists on an account balance or class of transactions). A quantification of each of these elements, when multiplied together, gives a measure of the audit risk.

audit rotation The practice of appointing an *audit firm for a set period, such as five years, after which it must give up the position. The aim is to reduce the effective control of the auditor by directors, who may threaten to remove the auditors if they do not comply with their requirements. The *Auditing Practices Board, in its report 'The Future Development of Auditing' (1992), suggested audit rotation as one possible way of enhancing the auditors' independence. However, the practice is generally criticized on the grounds of cost, disruption, and the consequent reduced quality of the audit work.

audit software Computer programs used by an auditor to examine an enterprise's computer files. Utility programs may be used, for example, for sorting and printing data files. Package or tailor-made programs may be used to interrogate the computer-based accounting system of a client. The auditor may also use more sophisticated audit software for *compliance tests and *substantive tests. *Computer-assisted audit techniques (CAATs) include the use of *embedded audit facilities, enabling program codes and additional data to be incorporated into the client's computerized accounting system to facilitate a continuous review of the system. There are two main examples of embedded audit facilities: *Integrated Test Facilities (ITF), which involve the creation of a fictitious entity to which transactions are posted for checking purposes; and *Systems Control and Review Files (SCARF), which collect certain predefined transactions for further examination.

audit strategy The overall plan for an *audit, which gives the framework for detailed decisions regarding the nature, timing, and extent of the *substantive tests to be employed.

audit trail The trail of documents and records examined during an *audit, showing how a transaction has been dealt with by an organization from start to finish. Documents will require cross-referencing so the trail is not broken. For example, a sales transaction can be traced from the item of stock sold, to the invoice, through the sales day book, to the sales account, and finally to the bank account.

audit working papers Files built up during an *audit that contain detailed evidence and information gathered during the audit. Typical contents include information of continuing importance (e.g. the organizational plan of a company), planning information, assessment of the client's accounting and internal control systems, details of work carried out and by whom, financial information and summaries, evidence of work having been appropriately reviewed, and the conclusions reached. These files provide the reporting partner of the audit firm with the evidence necessary to form an opinion; they are also useful for future reference.

authorized auditor An individual granted authorization by the Board of Trade or the Secretary of State to be the auditor of a company, under the Companies Act (1967). Authorizations were granted on the basis of the experience of the individual involved; however, the power to grant authorizations ended in April 1978. Under the Companies Act (1989) an authorized auditor is eligible for appointment as an auditor of an unquoted company but is not qualified to be the auditor of any other company. *See also* auditor.

authorized investments Legally authorized investments suitable for trust funds.

authorized minimum share capital In the UK, the statutory minimum of £50,000 for the share capital of a public company. There is no minimum share capital for private companies.

authorized share capital (nominal share capital; nominal capital; registered capital) The maximum amount of share capital that may be issued by a company, as detailed in the company's memorandum of association. The authorized share capital must be disclosed on the face of the *balance sheet or alternatively in the notes to the accounts. See also authorized minimum share capital; issued share capital.

available hours 1. The number of hours available to complete a job, task, or process. 2. The number of working hours available during an accounting period expressed as either machine hours, direct labour hours, or production hours.

aval A guarantee of payment by a third party, often a bank, on a *bill of exchange or promissory note.

AVC Abbreviation for *additional voluntary contribution.

AVCO Abbreviation for *average cost.

average collection period See debtor collection period.

average cost 1. The average cost per unit of output calculated by dividing the *total costs, both *fixed costs and *variable costs, by the total units of output. 2. (AVCO; weighted-average cost) A method of valuing units of *raw material or *finished goods issued from stock; it involves recalculating the unit value to be used for pricing the issues after each new consignment of raw materials or finished goods has been added to the stock. The average cost is obtained by dividing the total stock value by the number of units in stock. Because the issues are at an average cost, it follows that the valuation of the closing stock should be made on the same average cost basis. The method may also be used in *process costing to value the work in process at the end of an accounting period.

average costing A method of obtaining unit costs in which the items produced have a high degree of homogeneity. The unit cost is obtained by dividing the total production cost by the number of items produced. See also continuous-operation costing; process costing.

average life A somewhat artificial measure sometimes used to compare bonds of different duration and different repayment schedules. It is calculated as the average of the periods for which funds are available, weighted by the amounts available in each of these periods.

avoidable costs Costs that are not incurred if a particular course of action is taken or an alternative decision is made. For example, if a specific product is not produced, material and labour costs may not be incurred. In this instance material and labour costs are avoidable costs. *Variable costs are often avoidable costs, whereas *fixed costs, such as business rates, are not avoidable in the short term.

B

BAA Abbreviation for *British Accounting Association.

backdate **1.** To put an earlier date on a document than that on which it was compiled, in order to make it effective from that earlier date. **2.** To agree that salary increases, especially those settled in a pay award, should apply from a specified date in the recent past.

back duty An amount of tax that should have been paid in previous years but was not assessed because the taxpayer failed to disclose full income details to the Inland Revenue. A back duty case may arise when a source of income has been omitted totally from a tax return or when the level of business profits has been understated. If an Inspector of Taxes believes that back duty is payable, an enquiry will be instigated. If back duty is found to be payable it is likely that there will be interest and *penalties added to the tax charge.

backflush accounting A method of costing a product based on a management philosophy that includes having the minimum levels of stock available; in these circumstances, the valuation of stocks becomes less important, making the complex use of *absorption costing techniques unnecessary. Backflush accounting works backwards; after the actual costs have been determined they are allocated between *stocks and *cost of sales to establish profitability. There is no separate accounting for *work in progress.

backlog depreciation A *depreciation charge that occurs when an asset is revalued. The additional depreciation that arises as a consequence of the increase in the value of the asset also increases the accumulated depreciation; this increase is known as backlog depreciation.

back-to-back credit (countervailing credit) A method used to conceal the identity of the seller from the buyer in a credit arrangement. When the credit is arranged by a British finance house, the foreign seller provides the relevant documentation. The finance house, acting as an intermediary, issues its own documents to the buyer, omitting the seller's name and so concealing the seller's identity.

back-up copy A copy of information held in a computer taken in case the original is lost or destroyed. If the original information is on disk, the back-up copy should be on a completely different disk, or tape, and stored in a separate location from the original. Any sensible business will have back-up copies of all information held on its computer. How frequently the copies are made will depend upon how rapidly the information changes, its difficulty of replacement, and its importance.

BACS Abbreviation for *Bankers Automated Clearing System. *See also* Association for Payment Clearing Services.

bad debt An amount owed by a debtor that is unlikely to be paid; for example, due to a company going into liquidation. The full amount should be written off to the *profit and loss account of the period or to a provision for bad and *doubtful debts as soon as it is foreseen, on the grounds of prudence.

bad debts recovered Debts originally classed as *bad debts and written off to the *profit and loss account (or to a provision for bad and *doubtful debts) but subsequently recovered either in part of in full. Bad debts recovered should be written back to the profit and loss account of the period (or to a provision for bad and doubtful debts).

bailment A delivery of goods from the **bailor** (the owner of the goods) to the **bailee** (the recipient of the goods), on the condition that the goods will ultimately be returned to the bailor. The goods may thus be hired, lent, pledged, or deposited for safe custody. A delivery of this nature is usually also the subject of a contract; for example, a contract with a bank for the deposit of valuables for safekeeping. Nonetheless, in English law a bailment retains its distinguishing characteristic of a business relationship that arises outside the law of contract and is therefore not governed by it.

balance The amount representing the difference between the debit and credit sides of an account. It is included on the side of the lesser total, to ensure it equals the greater total. A balance is brought down on to the opposite side of the account. For example, if the total credits on an account exceed the total debits, a balance is inserted on the debit side and then brought down on to the credit side.

balance off The practice of totalling the debit and credit sides of an account and inserting a *balance to make them equal at the end of a financial accounting period. For example, on the *debtors control account amounts owed will be debited, amounts settled will be credited. When balancing off the account the balance inserted will be on the credit side, representing amounts owed that have still not been settled. On the first day of the next accounting period, the balance will be brought forward from the credit side to the debit side, representing the opening amount of debtors.

balance sheet A statement of the total assets and liabilities of an organization at a particular date, usually the last day of the *accounting period. The first part of the statement lists the fixed and current assets and the liabilities, the second part shows how they have been financed; the totals for each part must be equal. Under the Companies Act the balance sheet is one of the primary statements to be included in the financial accounts of a company. The Companies Act requires that the balance sheet of a company must give a true and fair view of its state of affairs at the end of its financial year, and must comply with statute as to its form and content. There are two possible *balance-sheet formats. In both formats, corresponding amounts for the preceding financial year should be shown. A balance sheet does not necessarily value a company, as some assets may be omitted, or given an unrealistic value.

balance-sheet asset value The book value of an asset as shown on the *balance sheet. For tangible fixed assets this is the cost less accumulated depreciation (although freehold land is generally not subject to depreciation). Intangible assets are shown at cost less *amortization. Current assets are valued at the lower of cost and *net realizable value. Under the *alternative accounting rules, the historical cost of certain assets (for example, buildings and stocks) may be replaced by current cost.

balance-sheet audit An *audit limited to verification of the existence, ownership, valuation, and presentation of the assets and liabilities in a balance sheet. For example, the existence of a building would be satisfied by an inspection, an examination of the deeds would provide evidence of ownership. The valuation of the building could be based on historical cost, in which case the original purchase contract would be examined, alternatively it may have been revalued, in which case the documentation for the revaluation would need to be examined; this may need to be supported by further enquiry. The balance-sheet presentation and disclosures for the building would be checked against the Companies Act and requirements of *accounting standards.

balance-sheet equation *See* accounting equation.

balance-sheet formats Methods of presenting a *balance sheet, as contained in the Companies Act. There are two formats: one vertical (format 1) and one horizontal (format 2). Both formats give the same basic disclosures, but format 1 also requires the calculation and disclosure of the net current assets and liabilities. The items are classified under letters, Roman numerals, and Arabic numbers. Items preceded by letters and Roman numerals must be shown on the face of the balance sheet, while those preceded by Arabic numbers may be shown in the notes to the accounts. Unless the directors believe there are valid arguments for a change, a company must adhere to the format it has chosen. Details of any changes and the reasons for making them must be disclosed in the notes to the accounts.

balance-sheet total The total net worth of an organization as shown at the bottom of the *balance sheet, i.e. the fixed assets plus net current assets less long-term liabilities. In the qualification conditions for *small company and *medium-sized company exemptions, the balance-sheet total is the total of fixed and current assets before deduction of current and long-term liabilities.

balancing allowance The allowance available on disposal of an asset when the proceeds are less than the *written-down value for tax purposes. For example, if the written-down value of an asset is £23,000 and on disposal the proceeds totalled £15,000, there would be a balancing allowance of the difference of £8000. *Compare* balancing charge.

balancing charge The charge that may be assessable to *corporation tax on the disposal of an asset when the proceeds realized on the sale of the asset exceed the *written-down value, for tax purposes. The balancing charge amounts to the difference between the proceeds and the written-down value. For example, if the written-down value is £23,000 and the proceeds on disposal were £30,000, there would be a balancing charge of the difference of £7000. The balancing charge is deducted from the other allowances for the period. If the charge exceeds the allowances available, the net amount is added to the profit for the period and assessed to tax.

balancing figure A figure that is inserted to make one total equal another. *See* balance; balance off.

balloon **1.** A large sum repaid as an irregular instalment of a loan repayment.

2. In the USA, the final loan repayment, when this amount is significantly more than the prior repayments.

bank A commercial institution licensed as a taker of deposits. Banks are concerned mainly with making and receiving payments on behalf of their customers, accepting deposits, and making short-term loans to private individuals, companies, and other organizations. In the UK, the banking system comprises the Bank of England (the central bank), the *commercial banks, *merchant banks, branches of foreign and Commonwealth banks, the TSB Group, the *National Savings Bank, and the National Girobank (*see* giro). The first (1990) *building society to become a bank in the UK was the Abbey National, after its public *flotation. In other countries banks are also usually supervised by a government-controlled central bank.

bank certificate A certificate, signed by a bank manager, stating the balance held to a company's credit on a specified date. It may be asked for during the course of an audit.

bank charge The amount charged to a customer by a bank, usually for a specific transaction, such as paying in a sum of money by means of a cheque or withdrawing a sum by means of an automated teller machine. However, modern practice is to provide periods of commission-free banking by waiving most charges on personal current accounts. The commercial banks have largely been forced to take this step as a result of the free banking services offered by *building societies. However, business customers invariably pay tariffs in one form or another.

bank confirmation A request made by an *auditor to a bank to confirm details of an audit client's bank accounts, together with any other assets held by the bank, and any other financial information.

bank deposit A sum of money placed by a customer with a bank. The deposit may or may not attract interest and may be instantly accessible or accessible at a time agreed by the two parties. Banks may use a percentage of their customers' deposits to lend on to other customers; thus most deposits may only exist on paper in the bank's books. Money on deposit at a bank is usually held in either a *deposit account or a *current account, although some banks now offer special high-interest accounts.

bank draft (banker's cheque; banker's draft) A cheque drawn by a bank on itself or its agent. A person who owes money to another buys the draft from a bank for cash and hands it to the creditor who need have no fear that it might be dishonoured. A bank draft is used if the creditor is unwilling to accept an ordinary cheque.

Bankers Automated Clearing System (BACS) A company owned by the UK banks that operates a computerized payments clearing service. It is commonly used by companies for paying employees. *See also* Association for Payment Clearing Services.

banker's cheque *See* bank draft.

banker's discount The discount calculated by a bank when purchasing a *bill of exchange.

banker's draft *See* bank draft.

banker's order An order to a bank by a customer to pay a specified amount at specified times (e.g. monthly or quarterly), until the order is cancelled, from a specific bank account of the customer to another named bank account.

banker's payment A *bank draft drawn in favour of another bank, as settlement of business between the two banks.

banker's reference (status enquiry) A report on the creditworthiness of an individual supplied by a bank to a third party, such as another financial institution or a bank customer. References and status enquiries are often supplied by specialist credit-reference agencies, who keep lists of defaulters, bad payers, and people who have infringed credit agreements. References must be very general and recent legislation has given new rights to the subjects of such reports, which restrict their value even further.

bank float The time spent by a remittance in the banking system, during which the sum of money is available to neither the payer nor the payee.

Bank for International Settlements (BIS) An international bank originally established in 1930 as a financial institution to coordinate the payment of war reparations between European central banks. It was hoped that the BIS, with headquarters in Basle, would develop into a European central bank but many of its functions were taken over by the *International Monetary Fund (IMF) after World War II. Since then the BIS has fulfilled several roles including acting as a trustee and agent for various international groups, such as the OECD, European Monetary Agreement, etc. The frequent meetings of the BIS directors have been a useful means of cooperation between central banks, especially in combating short-term speculative monetary movements. Since 1986 the BIS has acted as a clearing house for interbank transactions in the form of *European Currency Units. The BIS also sets *capital adequacy ratios for banks in European countries.

The original members were France, Belgium, West Germany, Italy, and the UK but now most European central banks are represented as well as the USA, Canada, and Japan. The London agent is the Bank of England, whose governor is a member of the board of directors of the BIS.

bank giro credit *See* bank transfer; giro.

bank interest The interest charge made by a bank to a person or company, based on the daily cleared overdraft balance or a committed loan. The *interest rate will usually be the *base rate plus between 1% and 5%.

bank loan (bank advance) A specified sum of money lent by a bank to a customer, usually for a specified time, at a specified rate of interest. In most cases banks require some form of security for loans, especially if the loan is to a commercial enterprise, although if a bank regards a company as a good credit risk, loans may not be secured. *See also* overdraft.

bank mandate A document given by a customer of a bank to the bank, requesting that the bank should open an account in the customer's name and honour cheques and other orders for payment drawn on the account. The mandate specifies the signatures that the bank should accept for transactions on the account and also contains specimens of the signatures.

bank overdraft *See* overdraft.

bank reconciliation statement A statement that reconciles the bank balance in the books of an organization with the *bank statement. Differences may be due to cheques drawn by the organization but not yet presented to the bank, bank charges deducted from the account not yet notified to the organization, and payments made to the bank but not yet recorded by the organization. Bank reconciliations are usually performed weekly or monthly and are a form of internal control check.

bank report A report made by a bank at the request of an *auditor of a business, giving details of the business's dealings with the bank during a specified period.

bankruptcy The state of an individual who is unable to pay his or her debts and against whom a **bankruptcy order** has been made by a court. Such orders deprive bankrupts of their property, which is then used to pay their debts. Bankruptcy proceedings are started by a petition, which may be presented to the court by (1) a creditor or creditors; (2) a person affected by a voluntary arrangement to pay debts set up by the debtor under the Insolvency Act (1986); (3) the Director of Public Prosecutions; or (4) the debtor. The grounds for a creditors' petition are that the debtor appears to be unable to pay his or her debts or to have reasonable prospects of doing so, i.e. that the debtor has failed to make arrangements to pay a debt for which a statutory demand has been made or that a judgment debt has not been satisifed. The debts must amount to at least £750. The grounds for a petition by a person bound by a voluntary arrangement are that the debtor has not complied with the terms of the arrangement or has withheld material information. The Director of Public Prosecutions may present a petition in the public interest under the Powers of Criminal Courts Act (1973). The debtor may also present a petition on the grounds of being unable to pay his or her debts.

Once a petition has been presented, the debtor may not dispose of any property. The court may halt any other legal proceedings against the debtor. An interim receiver may be appointed. This will usually be the *official receiver, who will take any necessary action to protect the debtor's estate. A special manager may be appointed if the nature of the debtor's business requires it.

The court may make a bankruptcy order at its discretion. Once this has happened, the debtor is an undischarged bankrupt, who is deprived of the ownership of all property and must assist the official receiver in listing it, recovering it, protecting it, etc. The official receiver becomes manager and receiver of the estate until the appointment of a **trustee in bankruptcy**. The bankrupt must prepare a statement of affairs for the official receiver within 21 days of the bankruptcy order. A **public examination** of the bankrupt may be ordered on the application of the official receiver or the creditors, in which the bankrupt will be required to answer questions about his or her affairs in court.

Within 12 weeks the official receiver must decide whether to call a **meeting of creditors** to appoint a trustee in bankruptcy. The trustee's duties are to collect, realize, and distribute the bankrupt's estate. The trustee may be appointed by the creditors, the court, or the Secretary of State and must be a qualified insolvency practitioner or the official receiver. All the property of the bankrupt is available to pay the creditors, except for the following: equipment necessary for him or her to continue in employment or business, necessary domestic equipment; and income required for the reasonable domestic needs of the bankrupt and his or her family. The court has discretion whether to order sale of a house in which a spouse or children are living. All creditors must prove their claims to the trustees. Only unsecured claims can be proved in bankruptcy. When all expenses have been paid, the trustee will divide the estate. The Insolvency Act (1986) sets out the order in which creditors will be paid (*see* preferential creditor). The bankruptcy may end automatically after two or three years, but in some cases a court order is required. The bankrupt is discharged and receives a certificate of discharge from the court.

bankruptcy order *See* bankruptcy.

bankruptcy petition A petition presented by: creditor(s), the Director of Public Prosecutions, a person affected by a voluntary arrangement set up by a debtor, or the debtor, to the court to initiate *bankruptcy proceedings against a specified person.

bank statement A record of an account produced by a bank, usually at regular intervals, and sent to the customer. It gives a summary of the account transactions that have occurred during the period, for example cheques drawn and received, cash withdrawn and paid in, standing orders paid, bank charges deducted, etc.

bank transfer (bank giro credit) A method of making payments in which the payer may make a payment at any branch of any bank for the account of a payee with an account at any branch of the same or another bank.

bar chart (bar diagram) A chart that presents statistical data by means of rectangles (i.e. bars) of differing heights. For example, the sales figures for a range of products for an accounting period may be presented in this way, the different sizes of the bars enabling the users to see at a glance how each product has performed during the period.

bargain purchase option *See* capital lease.

bargain renewal option *See* capital lease.

barter A method of trading in which goods or services are exchanged without the use of money. It is a cumbersome system, which severely limits the scope for trade. Means of exchange, such as money, enable individuals to trade with each other at much greater distance and through whole chains of intermediaries, which are inconceivable in a barter system.

base currency The currency used as the basis for an exchange rate, i.e. a foreign currency rate of exchange is quoted per single unit of the base currency, usually sterling or US dollars.

base metals The metals copper, lead, zinc, and tin.

base rate 1. The rate of interest used as a basis by banks for the rates they charge their customers. In practice most customers will pay a premium over base rate to take account of the bank's risk involved in lending, competitive market pressures, and to regulate the supply of credit. **2.** An informal name for the rate at which the Bank of England lends to the *discount houses, which effectively controls the lending rate throughout the banking system. The

abolition of the minimum lending rate in 1981 heralded a loosening of
government control over the banking system, but the need to increase interest
rates in the late 1980s (to control inflation and the *balance of payments deficit)
led to the use of this term in this sense.

base stock A certain volume of stock, assumed to be constant in that stock
levels are not allowed to fall below this level. When the stock is valued, this
proportion of the stock is valued at its original cost. This method is not
normally acceptable under Statement of Standard Accounting Practice 9 for
financial accounting purposes.

basic costing method The major costing method adopted by an
organization. The basic costing method may be *absorption costing, *marginal
costing, *process costing, or *average costing. *See also* standard costing.

basic earnings per share The *earnings per share calculated by dividing
the earnings for a financial period by the number of shares in issue without
taking into account any obligations that the company has outstanding that
would lead to dilution.

basic rate of income tax A rate of income tax between the lower and
higher rates. In the UK it is 25%, which is applied to *taxable income, for
1995–96, in the band £3201 to £24,300. *See also* higher-rate tax; lower rate of
income tax.

basic standard A cost or income standard set in *standard costing to form
the basis upon which other standards are set. For example, the number of
labour minutes allowed per unit of product produced would be a basic standard
to which the current wage rates can be applied in order to produce a *current
standard.

basic wage rate The wage rate paid to an operator for a specified time
period worked; it excludes any payments for incentive bonus, shift premium,
overtime, working conditions, and other premium payments that, when added
to the basic wage rate, make up the final gross pay.

basis of apportionment The basis used for the *apportionment of costs
between a number of *cost centres when the costs are to be shared between
them equitably. This occurs when the *allocation of an overhead cannot be
directly attributed to one particular cost centre. For example, rent and business
rates are seldom incurred by individual cost centres, therefore floor area is
often used as a basis of apportionment to share the costs between appropriate
cost centres.

basis of assessment The *schedules under which personal income or
business profits are assessed in the UK for each tax year. The individual rules
for each schedule identify the profits or income to be assessed in that year. In
many cases this is not the profits or income arising in the actual year. In the
case of a partnership that has been trading for many years, the profits for the
year to 30 April 1994, i.e. those arising during the period 1 May 1993 to 30 April
1994, will form the basis of the assessment for the tax year 1995–96. This is
known as the **prior-year basis of assessment**. Other income received during the
year, e.g. building society interest received, is assessed on an actual basis and so

for 1995–96 the basis of assessment will be the tax year, i.e. the interest received during the year 6 April 1995 to 5 April 1996. *See* current-year basis.

basis period The period, usually a year, during which profits earned or income generated form the *basis of assessment for the tax year. Profits of an ongoing partnership for the year to 30 April 1998 are used as the basis for assessment of tax, under the *current-year basis of assessment, in the tax year 1998–99.

basis point One hundredth of one per cent; this unit is often used in finance when prices involve fine margins.

batch A measure of production often used if the individual units of production are small or homogeneous. In this case the costs of production are best expressed per batch, by combining a specified number of units together to form a batch. This method of production is known as **batch processing**.

batch costing A form of costing in which the unit costs are expressed on the basis of a *batch produced. This is particularly appropriate where the cost per unit of production would result in an infinitesimal unit cost and where homogeneous units of production can conveniently be collected together to form discrete batches.

b/d Abbreviation for *brought down.

BDV Abbreviation for *budget day value.

bear A dealer on a stock exchange, currency market, or commodity market who expects prices to fall. A **bear market** is one in which a dealer is more likely to sell securities, currency, or goods than to buy them. A bear may even sell securities, currency, or goods without having them. This is known as selling short or establishing a **bear position**. The bear hopes to close (or cover) a short position by buying in at a lower price the securities, currency, or goods previously sold. The difference between the purchase price and the original sale price represents the successful bear's profit. A concerted attempt to force prices down by one or more bears by sustained selling is called a **bear raid**. In a **bear squeeze**, sellers force prices up against someone known to have a bear position to cover. *Compare* bull.

bearer A person who presents for payment a cheque or *bill of exchange marked 'pay bearer'. As a bearer cheque or bill does not require endorsement it is considered a high-risk form of transfer.

bearer security (bearer bond) A security for which proof of ownership is possession of the security certificate; this enables such bonds to be transferred from one person to another without registration. No register of ownership is kept by the company in whose name it is issued. This is unusual as most securities are registered, so that proof of ownership is the presence of the owner's name on the security register. *Eurobonds are bearer securities, enabling their owners to preserve their anonymity, which can have taxation advantages. Bearer bonds are usually kept under lock and key, often deposited in a bank. Dividends are usually claimed by submitting coupons attached to the certificate.

bed and breakfast An operation on the London Stock Exchange in which a shareholder sells a holding one evening and makes an agreement with the broker to buy the same holding back again when the market opens the next morning. The object is to establish a loss, which can be set against other profits for calculating capital gains tax. In the event of an unexpected change in the market, the deal is scrapped.

bed and PEP A similar operation to *bed and breakfast, except that in this case a shareholding is sold one evening and repurchased at the beginning of the next day's trading for the shareholder's own *personal equity plan (PEP), in order to comply with the regulations for self-select PEPs.

bellweather security In the USA, a security considered to be a good guide to the direction in which the market is moving.

below-the-line Denoting entries below the line on a company's *profit and loss account that separates the entries that establish the profit (or loss) from the entries that show how the profit is distributed or where the funds to finance the loss have come from. *Compare* above-the-line.

beneficiary 1. A person for whose benefit a trust exists. 2. A person who benefits under a will. 3. A person who receives money from the proceeds of a *letter of credit. 4. A person who receives payment at the conclusion of a transaction, e.g. a retailer who has been paid by a customer by means of a credit card.

benefit–cost ratio The evaluation of a proposed activity by determining the value of the anticipated benefits likely to accrue compared to the costs that will be incurred. If the benefits exceed the costs the activity is financially attractive, although there may be many non-financial factors to take into account before making a final decision. The benefits, some of which may be of a qualitative nature, may be enjoyed by some groups and the costs borne by others, which may make the analysis more complex.

benefits in kind Benefits other than cash arising from employment. The UK tax legislation seeks to assess all earnings to tax, whether they be in the form of cash or in kind. The treatment of benefits depends on the level of total earnings, including the value of any benefits, and whether the employee is a director of a company. For employees earning less than £8500, the benefits are only assessable if they are capable of being turned into cash, such as credit tokens or vouchers, living accommodation, and payment by the employer of an employee's personal liability. For all directors and higher-paid employees, with total earnings (including benefits) in excess of £8500, the benefits must be reported on form P11D by the employer at the end of the *fiscal year. This form will include details of company cars and associated fuel provided by the employer, beneficial loans, mobile telephones, medical insurance provided by the employer, subscriptions paid, and any costs paid on the employee's behalf. These benefits will be assessed to tax. This often takes the form of a restriction to the *income tax code.

benefit taxation A form of taxation in which taxpayers pay tax according to the amounts of benefit that they receive from the system. Such a system of taxation is, in practice, very difficult to apply unless specific charges are made for specific services, such as metered electricity charges. *Compare* ability-to-pay taxation.

bequest A gift made by a *will.

BES Abbreviation for *business expansion scheme.

beta coefficient A measure of the volatility of a share. A share with a high beta coefficient is likely to respond to stock market movements by rising or falling in value by more than the market average. *See also* capital asset pricing model.

betterment In the USA, the replacement of a major item of plant or machinery by one that will provide better performance; betterment thus involves capital expenditure.

b/f Abbreviation for *brought forward.

BGC Abbreviation for bank giro credit. *See* bank transfer.

bid 1. The price (often called the **bid price**) at which a *market maker will buy shares: the lower of the two figures quoted on the *TOPIC screens of the *SEAQ system, the higher being the *offer price; the difference between the two prices is known as the **bid–offer spread**. Some dealers prefer to rely on the figure quoted, others prefer to haggle over the price. *Compare* offer price. **2.** An approach by one company to buy the share capital of another; an attempted takeover. **3.** The price at which a buyer is willing to close a deal. If the seller has made an *offer that the buyer considers too high, the buyer may make a bid at a lower price (or on more advantageous terms). Having received a bid, the seller may accept it, withdraw, or make a counteroffer. Once the buyer has made a bid the original offer no longer stands.

bid price *See* bid.

Big Bang The upheaval on the *London Stock Exchange (LSE) when major changes in operation were introduced on 27 October 1986. The major changes enacted on that date were: (a) the abolition of LSE rules enforcing a single-capacity system; (b) the abolition of fixed commission rates charged by *stockbrokers to their clients. The measures were introduced by the LSE in return for an undertaking by the government (given in 1983) that they would not prosecute the LSE under the Restrictive Practices Act. Since 1986 the Big Bang has also been associated with the globalization and modernization of the London securities market.

big GAAP The *generally accepted accounting principles applied to large entities. *Compare* little GAAP.

bilateral bank facility A *facility provided by a bank to a corporate customer. The agreement is restricted to the two parties, which enables a relationship to develop between the bank and the customer (*see* relationship banking). *Compare* syndicated bank facility.

bilateral netting A method of reducing bank charges in which two related companies offset their receipts and payments with each other, usually monthly. In this way a single payment and receipt is made for the period instead of a number, which saves on both transaction costs and paperwork. *See also* multilateral netting.

bill *See* bill of exchange; bill of sale; bill of quantities.

bill broker (discount broker) A broker who buys *bills of exchange from traders and sells them to banks and *discount houses or holds them to maturity. Many now deal exclusively in Treasury bills.

billion Formerly, one thousand million (10^9) in the USA and one million million (10^{12}) in the UK; now it is almost universally taken to be one thousand million.

bill of entry A detailed statement of the nature and value of a consignment of goods prepared by the shipper of the consignment for customs entry.

bill of exchange An unconditional order in writing, addressed by one person (the drawer) to another (the drawee) and signed by the person giving it, requiring the drawee to pay on demand or at a fixed or determinable future time a specified sum of money to or to the order of a specified person (the payee) or to the bearer. If the bill is payable at a future time the drawee signifies acceptance, which makes the drawee the party primarily liable upon the bill; the drawer and endorsers may also be liable upon a bill. The use of bills of exchange enables one person to transfer to another an enforceable right to a sum of money. A bill of exchange is not only transferable but also negotiable, since if a person without an enforceable right to the money transfers a bill to a holder in due course, the latter obtains a good title to it. Much of the law on bills of exchange is codified by the Bills of Exchange Act (1882). *See* accommodation bill; bills in a set; dishonour.

bill of quantities (bill of materials) A document drawn up by a quantity surveyor showing in detail the materials and parts required to build a structure (e.g. factory, house, office block), together with the price of each component and the labour costs. The bill of quantities is one of the tender documents that goes out to contractors who wish to quote for carrying out the work.

bill of sale **1.** A document by which a person transfers the ownership of goods to another. Commonly the goods are transferred conditionally, as security for a debt, and a **conditional bill of sale** is thus a mortgage of goods. The mortgagor has a right to redeem the goods on repayment of the debt and usually remains in possession of them; the mortgagor may thus obtain false credit by appearing to own them. An **absolute bill of sale** transfers ownership of the goods absolutely. The Bills of Sale Acts (1878 and 1882) regulate the registration and form of bills of sale. **2.** A document recording the change of ownership when a ship is sold; it is regarded internationally as legal proof of ownership.

bill rate (discount rate) The rate on the *discount market at which *bills of exchange are discounted (i.e. purchased for less than they are worth when they mature). The rate will depend on the quality of the bill and the risk the purchaser takes. First-class bills, i.e. those backed by banks or well-respected finance houses, will be discounted at a lower rate than bills involving greater risk.

bills payable The amounts owed by a business to *creditors, such as suppliers.

bills receivable The amounts owed to a business by its *debtors (i.e. its customers).

BIMBO Abbreviation for buy-in management buyout: a form of *management buyout in which management invests in the venture together with outsider venture capitalists, who have more managerial control than is usual with a management buyout.

bin card (store card) A card attached to each site or bin in which individual items of *stock are stored to record the receipts, issues, and balances of each item of stock in units. The bin card balance should indicate the physical stock available at any time; regular reconciliations with the physical quantities should be made to ensure accuracy.

BIS Abbreviation for *Bank for International Settlements.

black knight A person or firm that makes an unwelcome *takeover bid for a company. *Compare* grey knight; white knight.

blackleg 1. An employee who refuses to join a trade union. 2. An employee who refuses to stop work when the rest of his co-unionists have declared a strike.

black market An illegal market for a particular good or service. It can occur when regulations control a particular trade (as in arms dealing) or a particular period (as in wartime). *Compare* grey market.

Black Wednesday Wednesday, 16 September 1992, when sterling left the Exchange Rate Mechanism, which led to a 15% fall in its value against the Deutschmark (*see* European Monetary System). Because of the improved economic performance of the UK following the event, it is also known as **White Wednesday**.

blank bill A *bill of exchange in which the name of the payee is left blank.

blank cheque A cheque in which the amount payable is not stated. The person writing the cheque (the drawer) may impose a maximum amount to be drawn by the cheque by writing on it, for example, 'Not more than £100'.

blank endorsed *See* endorsement.

blanket rate A production overhead *absorption rate used for a factory as a whole; it replaces the practice of calculating a rate for each individual *cost centre.

blank transfer A share transfer form in which the name of the transferee and the transfer date are left blank. The form is signed by the registered holder of the shares so that the holder of the blank transfer has only to fill in the missing details to become the registered owner of the shares. Blank transfers can be deposited with a bank, when shares are being used as a security for a loan. A blank transfer can also be used when shares are held by *nominees, the beneficial owner holding the blank transfer.

block A group of numbers, characters, or words that is transferred as a unit between the parts of a computer system, for example between the computer terminal and a disk drive. Also, when information is stored on disks or tape, it is divided into blocks, stored on separate physical areas of the disk or tape. The blocks are separated from each other by inter-block gaps.

blocked funds Money that cannot be transferred to another country because of *exchange controls.

block grant A grant made to an organization in the public sector, in which the organization is allowed to decide by its own procedures how to spend the grant.

blue chip Colloquial name for any of the ordinary shares in the most highly regarded companies traded on a stock market. Originating in the USA, the name comes from the colour of the highest value chip used in poker. Blue-chip companies have a well-known name, a good growth record, and large assets. The main part of an institution's equity portfolio will consist of blue chips.

blue-collar worker A manual worker, normally one working on the shop floor, as opposed to an office worker, who is known as a white-collar worker. The blue collar refers to the blue overalls often worn in factories and the white collar to the normal office attire of a white shirt and a tie.

blue-sky law In the USA, a law providing for state regulation and supervision for issuing investment securities in that state. It includes broker licensing and the registration of new issues.

Board of Customs and Excise The government department responsible for collecting and administering customs and excise duties and *value added tax. The Commissioners of Customs were first appointed in 1671 by Charles II; the Excise department, formerly part of the Inland Revenue Department, was merged with the Customs in 1909. The Customs and Excise have an investigation division responsible for preventing and detecting evasions of revenue laws and for enforcing restrictions on the importation of certain goods (e.g. arms, drugs, etc.). Their statistical office compiles overseas trade statistics from customs import and export documents.

Board of Inland Revenue A small number of higher civil servants, known individually as Commissioners of Inland Revenue, responsible to the Treasury for the administration and collection of the principal direct taxes in the UK, but not the indirect VAT and excise duties. They are responsible for income tax, capital gains tax, corporation tax, inheritance tax, petroleum revenue tax, and stamp duties. Under the Taxes Management Act (1970), they are under a duty to appoint inspectors and collectors of taxes who, in turn, act under the direction of the board. They also advise on new legislation and prepare statistical information.

body corporate A *corporation consisting of a body of persons legally authorized to act as one person, while being distinct from that person. For example, the shareholders of a company are separate from the company. References to a body corporate in the Companies Act (1985) do not include a corporation sole, in which only one individual forms the corporation, for example a bishop or the sovereign.

boilerplate A copy intended for use in making other copies. It is sometimes used to describe a group of instructions that is incorporated in different places in a computer program or the detailed standard form of words used in a contract, guarantee, etc.

bona fide In good faith, honestly, without collusion or fraud. A bona fide purchaser for value without notice is a person who has bought property in good faith, without being aware of prior claims to it (for example, that it is subject to a trust). The purchaser will not be bound by those claims, unless (if the property is land) they were registered.

bona vacantia Goods without an apparent owner. An example could be the possessions of a person with no living relatives who has died intestate. The Crown is entitled to any personal property without an apparent owner. The prerogative may also be extended to real estate by the doctrine of **escheat**, the return of ownerless land to the superior landowner.

bond An IOU issued by a borrower to a lender. Bonds usually take the form of fixed-interest securities issued by governments, local authorities, or companies. However, bonds come in many forms: with fixed or variable rates of interest, redeemable or irredeemable, short- or long-term, secured or unsecured, and marketable or unmarketable. Fixed-interest payments are usually made twice a year but may alternatively be credited at the end of the agreement (typically 5 to 10 years). The borrower repays a specific sum of money plus the face value (PAR) of the bond. Most bonds are unsecured and do not grant shares in an organization (*see* debenture). Bonds are usually sold against loans, mortgages, credit-card income, etc., as marketable securities. A discount bond is one sold below its face value; a premium bond is one sold above par.

bonds with warrants Fixed-rate *bonds with warrants attached giving long-term options linked usually to ordinary shares. They differ from *convertibles in that the fixed-rate bonds and the warrants are frequently separated and marketed to separate groups of investors.

bonus dividend A *dividend issued to a shareholder in addition to those expected. Typically, two dividends are issued each year. If an additional dividend is paid to shareholders, perhaps because of a takeover, this is known as a bonus dividend.

bonus issue *See* scrip issue.

bonus shares Shares issued to the existing shareholders of a company following a *scrip issue. The number of shares received depends on the level of the shareholding prior to the bonus issue. The number of bonus shares is usually one share for a specified number of shares held before the issue. For example, if the specified number is four this would be denoted as a 1:4 bonus issue. It is also possible to have a 2:1 bonus, when two shares are issued for every one held.

book-keeper A person employed to keep the *books of account for a business. Such a person may be a member of the *Association of Accounting Technicians.

book-keeping The keeping of the *books of account of a business. The records kept enable a *profit and loss account and the *balance sheet to be compiled. Most firms now use *business software packages of programs to enable the books to be kept by computer.

book of prime entry A book or record in which certain types of transaction are recorded before becoming part of the *double-entry book-keeping system. The most common books of prime entry are the *day book, the *cash book, and the *journal.

books of account The books in which a business records its transactions using *ledgers, *journals, and other accounting records. If the business is a limited company the accounting records must show in sufficient detail the position of the company at any time.

bootstrap **1.** A cash offer for a controlling interest in a company. This is followed by an offer to acquire the rest of the company's shares at a lower price. The purpose is twofold: to establish control of the company and to reduce the cost of the purchase. **2.** A technique enabling a computer to load a program of instructions. Before computer hardware can function, a program must be loaded into it. However, as a program is needed in the computer to enable it to load a program, preliminary instructions are stored permanently in the computer making it possible for longer programs to be accepted.

borrowed capital *See* loan capital.

bottom line The profit figure used as the earnings figure in the earnings-per-share calculation of a company to comply with *Statement of Standard Accounting Practice 3, 'Earnings per Share'. The introduction of *Financial Reporting Standard 3, 'Reporting Financial Performance', in October 1992 amended SSAP 3 to include extraordinary items in the bottom-line earnings figure in the earnings-per-share calculation. This has reduced the significance of the concept. *See also* above-the-line.

bought day book In the USA, the purchases journal that gives details of all the items a business has bought. The totals from the bought day book are regularly transferred to the *nominal ledger account.

bought deal A method of raising capital for a new issue of *bonds, acquisitions, etc., as an alternative to a *rights issue or *placing. The borrower invites banks or groups of banks to bid for new issues of bonds or shares, selling them to the highest bidder, who then sells them to the rest of the market in the expectation of making a profit. The borrower is guaranteed that the new issue is successful. Bought deals originated in the USA and are becoming increasingly popular in the UK, although they remain controversial as they violate the principle of *pre-emption rights. *Compare* competitive bought deal; placed deal. *See also* vendor placing.

bought ledger In the USA, the *creditors' ledger recording amounts owed by a business.

branch accounting An accounting system in which each department or branch of a business is established as a separate *cost centre or *accounting centre. The net profit per branch may be added together to arrive at the profit for the whole business. **Branch accounts** may be prepared to show the performance of both a main trading centre (i.e. the head office) and subsidiary trading centres (i.e. branches) but with all the accounting records being maintained by head office. Alternatively, **separate entity** branch accounts are prepared in which branches maintain their own records, which are later combined with head-office records to prepare accounts for the whole business.

branch accounts *See* branch accounting.

brands Intangible assets, such as a product or company name, sign, symbol, design, or reputation, which if operated in combination will lead to greater benefits from the sales or service through brand differentiation. The accounting treatment for brands is closely linked to the controversy surrounding accounting for *goodwill. Some companies, neither wishing to write off an amount representing goodwill immediately to their reserves nor to amortize it, have shown an amount for brands on their balance sheets. These amounts may remain on the balance sheet without amortization. Some companies have also chosen to place on their balance sheets internally created brands, as well as those acquired. Although there is general agreement that the existence of brands can have a beneficial impact on the earnings of a company, there is less agreement on the reliability for valuing brands in the balance sheet. In the USA it is standard practice to capitalize and amortize goodwill and all intangibles are treated in the same fashion; thus in the USA brands are not an important accounting issue.

breach of contract A failure by a party to a contract to perform obligations under that contract or an indication of an intention not to do so. An indication that a contract will be breached in the future is called **repudiation** or an **anticipatory breach**; it may be either expressed in words or implied from conduct. Such an implication arises when the only reasonable inference from a person's acts is an intention not to fulfil his or her part of the bargain. For example, an anticipatory breach occurs if a person contracts to sell a car to A but sells and delivers it to B before the delivery date agreed with A. The repudiation of a contract entitles the injured party to treat the contract as discharged and to sue immediately for *damages for the loss sustained. The same procedure only applies to an actual breach if it constitutes a **fundamental breach**, i.e. a breach of a major term of the contract. In either an anticipatory or an actual breach, the injured party may, however, decide to affirm the contract instead. When an actual breach relates only to a minor term of the contract (a warranty) the injured party may sue for damages but has no right to treat the contract as discharged. The process of treating a contract as discharged by reason of repudiation or actual breach is sometimes referred to as rescission. Other remedies available under certain circumstances for breach of contract are an injunction and specific performance.

breach of trust The contravention by a *trustee of the duties imposed by a *trust. If one of several trustees agrees to a breach of trust by a co-trustee, this also constitutes a breach of trust.

breakeven analysis (cost-volume-profit analysis; CVP analysis)
The technique used in *management accounting in which costs are analysed according to *cost behaviour characteristics into *fixed costs and *variable costs and compared to sales revenue in order to determine the level of sales volume, sales value, or production at which the business makes neither a profit nor a loss (*see* breakeven point). The technique is also used in decision-making to assist management to determine such questions as the profit or loss likely to arise from any given level of production or sales, the impact on profitability of

changes in the fixed or variable costs, and the levels of activity required to generate a desired profit. Breakeven analysis may either be carried out by drawing a *breakeven chart or by calculation. For example, the formula for determining the level of activity required to generate a desired profit is:

(total fixed costs + desired level of profit)/contribution per unit of production. *See also* contribution.

breakeven chart (breakeven graph) A graph on which an organization's total costs, analysed into *fixed costs and *variable costs, are drawn over a given range of activity, together with the sales revenue for the same range of activity. The point at which the sales-revenue curve crosses the total-cost curve is known as the *breakeven point (expressed either as sales revenue or production/sales volume). The breakeven chart, like *breakeven analysis, may also be used to determine the profit or loss likely to arise from any given level of production or sales, the impact on profitability of changes in the fixed or variable costs, and the levels of activity required to generate a required profit.

breakeven point The level of production, sales volume, percentage of capacity, or sales revenue at which an organization makes neither a profit nor a loss. The breakeven point may either be determined by the construction of a *breakeven chart or by calculation. The formulae are:

breakeven point (units) = total fixed costs/contribution per unit;

breakeven point (sales) = (total fixed cost × selling price per unit)/contribution per unit.

See also contribution.

break-up value 1. The value of an asset on the assumption that an organization will not continue in business. On this assumption the assets are likely to be sold piecemeal and probably in haste. **2.** The *asset value per share of a company.

bribery and corruption Offences relating to the improper influencing of people in positions of trust. The offences commonly grouped under this expression are now statutory. Under the Public Bodies Corrupt Practices Act (1889), amended by the Prevention of Corruption Act (1916), it is an offence corruptly to offer to a member, officer, or servant of a public body any reward or advantage to do anything in relation to any matter with which that body is concerned; it is also an offence for a public servant or officer to corruptly receive or solicit such a reward. The Prevention of Corruption Act (1906) amended by the 1916 Act is wider in scope. Under this Act it is an offence corruptly to give or offer any valuable consideration to an agent to do any act or show any favour in relation to the principal's affairs.

bridging loan A loan taken on a short-term basis to bridge the gap between the purchase of one asset and the sale of another. It is particularly common in the property and housing market.

British Accounting Association (BAA) The major body of accounting academics in the UK, originally founded as the Association of University Teachers in Accounting. It has approximately 1000 members, a number from overseas, and issues a quarterly journal, the *British Accounting Review*.

broker An agent who brings two parties together, enabling them to enter into a contract to which the broker is not a principal. The broker's remuneration consists of a **brokerage**, which is usually calculated as a percentage of the sum involved in the contract but may be fixed according to a tariff. Brokers are used because they have specialized knowledge of certain markets or to conceal the identity of a principal, in addition to introducing buyers to sellers. *See* bill broker; stockbroker.

brought down (b/d) In book-keeping, describing an opening balance that has been transferred from the previous period.

brought forward (b/f) In book-keeping, describing an amount that is the total of the corresponding column on the previous page.

bucket shop A derogatory colloquial name for a firm of brokers, dealers, agents, etc., of questionable standing and frail resources, that is unlikely to be a member of an established trade organization.

budget **1.** A financial or quantitative statement, prepared prior to a specified accounting period, containing the plans and policies to be pursued during that period. It is used as the basis for *budgetary control. Generally a *functional budget is drawn up for each functional area within an organization, but in addition it is also usual to produce a *capital budget, a *cash-flow budget, *stock budgets, and a *master budget, which includes a budgeted profit and loss account and balance sheet. **2. (the Budget)** In the UK, the government's annual budget, which is presented to parliament by the Chancellor of the Exchequer towards the end of the calendar year (usually in November or December). It contains estimates for the government's income and expenditure, together with the tax rates and the fiscal policies designed to meet the government's financial goals for the succeeding fiscal year.

budgetary control The process by which *financial control is exercised within an organization using *budgets for income and expenditure for each *function of the organization in advance of an accounting period. These budgets are compared with actual performance to establish any *variances. Individual function managers are made responsible for the controllable activities within their budgets, and are expected to take remedial action if the *adverse variances are regarded as excessive.

budget centre A section or area of an organization under the responsibility of a manager for which *budgets are prepared; these budgets are compared with actual performance as part of the *budgetary control process. A budget centre may be a *function, department, section, individual, *cost centre, or any combination of these that the management wishes to treat as a budget centre. It is usual to produce regular financial statements on the basis of each budget centre so that each budget-centre manager is aware of its budgeted and actual performance and any *variances that arise.

budget committee The committee responsible for the operation of the *budgetary control process within an organization. The membership and responsibilities of the committee vary between organizations, but a typical committee might comprise a chief executive as chairman, the functional managers as members, and a financial manager as committee secretary or *budget director. The committee is responsible for ensuring the formulation of the budgets according to the directives and policies communicated by the board of *directors, scrutinizing the various budgets for coordination and acceptability, and ultimately submitting the budgets (or budget revisions) to the board of directors for approval.

budget cost allowance The amount of budgeted expenditure that a *cost centre or *budget centre is allowed to spend according to its budget, having regard to the level of *activity (or other basis of cost incurrence) actually achieved during the *budget period. The budget cost allowance is usually based on the level of activity achieved and whether the *cost item is classified as a *fixed cost or a *variable cost.

budget day value (BDV) The value of an asset on 6 April 1965. This value is used primarily in *capital gains tax computations as this was the date on which the tax was introduced. Gains of long-held assets are assessed from budget day value, with the gains arising prior to this date being excluded.

budget director The member of a *budget committee who is responsible for the administration of the *budgetary control process. The precise responsibilities vary between organizations, but the budget director acts as secretary to the budget committee and in this capacity coordinates the flow of information from the managers of the *budget centres to the budget committee and from the budget committee to the board of directors.

budgeted capacity The productive *capacity available in an organization for a budget period as expressed in the *budget for that period. It may be expressed in terms of *direct labour hours, *machine hours, or *standard hours.

budgeted cost A cost included in a *budget representing the cost expected to be incurred by a *budget centre, *cost centre, *cost unit, product, process, or job.

budgeted revenue The income level included in a *budget representing the income that is expected to be achieved during that budget period.

budget expenditure head A way of analysing a budget and presenting financial statements under major headings, each budget heading being the responsibility of a particular manager. Under some circumstances a manager may be responsible for more than one budget expenditure head.

budget manual A manual setting out the administrative procedures and operations that should be applied in the operation of the *budgetary control system. It covers guidelines for the operation of the *budget committee and the *budget centres and includes such information as levels of responsibility, budget timetable, budget preparation, and budget-revision procedures.

budget period A period for which a *budget is prepared and during which it is intended to apply. It is usual for the budget period to be a year, but it is often broken down into shorter control periods, such as a month or a quarter. The budget periods should coincide with the *accounting periods adopted by the organization.

building society A financial institution that accepts deposits, upon which it pays interest, and makes loans for house purchase or house improvement secured by *mortgages. They developed from the *Friendly Society movement in the late 17th century and are non-profitmaking. They are regulated by the

Building Societies Act (1986). The societies accept deposits into a variety of accounts, which offer different interest rates and different withdrawal terms, or into 'shares', which often require longer notice of withdrawal. Interest on all building-society accounts is paid net of income tax, the society paying the tax direct to the Inland Revenue. The societies attract both large and small savers, with average holdings being about £5000.

Loans made to persons wishing to purchase property are usually repaid by regular monthly instalments of capital and interest over a number of years. Another method, which has grown in popularity, is an endowment mortgage in which the capital remains unpaid until the maturity of an assurance policy taken out on the borrower's life; in these arrangements only the interest and the premiums on the assurance policy are paid during the period of the loan.

Since the 1986 Act, building societies have been able to widen the range of services they offer; this has enabled them to compete with the *commercial banks in many areas. They offer cheque accounts, which pay interest on all credit balances, cash cards, credit cards, loans, money transmission, foreign exchange, personal financial planning services (shares, insurance, pensions, etc.), estate agency, and valuation and conveyancing services. The distinction between banks and building societies is fast disappearing, indeed some building societies have obtained the sanction of their members to become *public limited companies. These changes have led to the merger of many building societies to provide a national network that can compete with the major commercial banks. Competition is well illustrated in the close relationship of interest rates between banks and building societies as they both compete for the market's funds. Moreover, the competition provided by the building societies has forced the banks into offering free banking services, paying interest on current accounts, and Saturday opening.

bull A dealer on a stock exchange, currency market, or commodity market who expects prices to rise. A **bull market** is one in which a dealer is more likely to be a buyer than a seller, even to the extent of buying without having made a corresponding sale, thus establishing a **bull position**. A bull with a long position hopes to sell these purchases at a higher price after the market has risen. *Compare* bear.

bulldog bond An unsecured or secured *bond issued in the UK domestic market by a non-UK borrower.

bullet The final repayment of a loan, which consists of the whole of sum borrowed. *See* bullet loan.

Bulletins *See* auditing standards.

bullet loan A loan in which the principal is repaid in a final *bullet, although interest may be paid in interim payments. *Compare* amortizing loan.

burden In the USA, another word for *overheads.

burn-out turnaround The process of restructuring a company that is in trouble by producing new finance to save it from liquidation, at the cost of diluting the shareholding of existing investors.

business combination The combining of two or more companies by means of acquisition or merger. *See* acquisition accounting; merger accounting.

business entity concept The concept that *financial accounting and reporting relates to the activities of a specific business entity and not to the activities of the owners of that entity.

business expansion scheme (BES) A former UK investment scheme giving full tax relief for *higher-rate taxpayers making investments in qualifying companies. The scheme ended on 31 December 1993, when it was replaced by the *enterprise investment scheme.

business name The name under which a business trades. According to the Business Names Act (1985), if a business is conducted under a name other than that of the proprietor, it must display at its place of business the business name, its activity, and the name of the proprietor. All business stationery must carry both the business name and the names of the owners. The name of the business must be registered with the *Registrar of Companies.

business plan A detailed plan setting out the objectives of a business over a stated period, often three, five, or ten years. A business plan is drawn up by many businesses, especially if the business has passed through a bad period or if it has had a major change of policy. For new businesses it is an essential document for raising capital or loans. The plan should quantify as many of the objectives as possible, providing monthly *cash flows and production figures for at least the first two years, with diminishing detail in subsequent years; it must also outline its strategy and the tactics it intends to use in achieving its objectives. Anticipated *profit and loss accounts should form part of the business plan on a quarterly basis for at least two years, and an annual basis thereafter. For a group of companies the business plan is often called a **corporate plan**.

business property relief An *inheritance tax relief available on certain types of business property. For a business or interest in a business, including a partnership share, the relief is 100%. Land or buildings owned and used in a company under the control of the donor, or a partnership in which the donor was a partner, attract 50% relief.

business rates The local tax paid in the UK by businesses. It is calculated annually by the local authority in which the business is situated and is based on the rateable value of the property occupied by the organization.

business reply service A service offered by the Post Office enabling a company to supply its customers with a prepaid business reply card, envelope, or label (either first- or second-class postage) so that they can reply to direct-mail shots, ask for follow-up literature, pay bills promptly, etc., free of postal charges.

business segments The material and separately identifiable parts of the business operations of a company or group whose activities, assets, and results can be clearly identified. Companies are obliged to disclose in their annual report and accounts certain financial information relating to business segments (*see* annual accounts). Although Statement of Standard Accounting Practice 25 provides guidance as to what comprises a business segment, because the final decision has to be taken by their managements some inconsistencies appear in the information provided by companies.

business software package One of a wide range of software programs sold in packages to enable computers to be used for a variety of business uses. They range in complexity and expense from those needed to operate a PC to the suite of programs required by a mainframe. A typical package would include one or more of: book-keeping programs, which provide facilities for keeping sales, purchase, and nominal ledgers; accounting packages, enabling balance sheets, budgetary control, and sale and purchase analysis to be undertaken automatically; payroll packages, dealing with wages, salaries, PAYE, National Insurance, pensions, etc.; *database management systems to maintain company records; communications software to allow two or more computers to work together; and wordprocessors. The programs comprising the package are designed to work together and use each other's data; sometimes a single program provides one or more of these functions.

Business Statistics Office Until August, 1989, a department of the Department of Trade and Industry, since then a department of the Central Statistical Office. It collects statistics of British businesses and publishes *Business Monitors*.

buy-in The purchase of a holding of more than 50% in a company by (or on behalf of) a group of executives from outside the company, who wish to run the company.

buyout The purchase of a substantial holding in a company by its existing managers. *See* management buyout.

by-product A product from a process that has secondary economic significance compared to the *main product of the process. For example, while the primary reason for cracking oil is to produce petroleum, other products produced as a result of the process, such as lubricating oil, paraffin, and other distillates, are by-products. *See also* joint products; process costing.

CAATs Abbreviation for *computer-assisted audit techniques.

Cadbury Report The report of the committee set up in May 1991 by the Financial Reporting Council, the London Stock Exchange, and the accountancy profession, under the chairmanship of Sir Adrian Cadbury, to consider the financial aspects of corporate governance. The Cadbury Report was published in May 1992 for comment; the final report was published on 1 December 1992. The main recommendation of the committee was that the boards of all listed companies registered in the UK should comply with a code of practice and state in their financial accounts whether or not they have complied with it, identifying any areas of non-compliance. This code includes the provisions that non-executive directors should be appointed for specified terms and re-appointment should not be automatic, that such directors should be selected through a formal process, and that both their selection and their appointment should be a matter for the board as a whole.

cafeteria plan In the USA, an agreement that permits employees to select a fringe benefit from a variety of such benefits (including cash); under the tax code, the benefit is not included in the gross income of the participants solely because the participants are required to choose from a variety of benefits.

CAFR Abbreviation for *comprehensive annual financial report.

callable bonds Fixed-rate bonds, usually *convertibles, in which the issuer has the right, but not the obligation, to redeem (call) the bond at par during the life of the bond. The call exercise price may be at par, although it is usually set at a premium. A **grace period** (i.e. a period during which the borrower is unable to call the bond) will usually be included in the terms of the agreement; conversion after the grace period will only be possible if certain conditions are met, usually related to the price of the underlying share.

called-up share capital The amount of the *issued share capital of a company for which payment has been requested (called up). Some shares are paid for in part, for example on allotment, with subsequent calls for payment. When all calls have been paid, the called-up share capital will equal the **paid-up share capital**.

call option *See* option.

Canadian Institute of Chartered Accountants (CICA) The professional body of practising accountants in Canada; it was originally founded in 1902 as the Dominion Association of Chartered Accountants.

cap A ceiling on a charge; for example, an interest-rate cap would set a maximum interest rate to be charged on a loan, regardless of prevailing general interest-rate levels. A lender would charge a fee for including a cap at the outset to offset this risk. Caps may also limit annual increases to a certain level. *See also* collar.

capacity The level of productive capacity that an organization can attain under particular circumstances. It may be expressed in terms of *direct labour hours, *machine hours, or *standard hours. *See also* budgeted capacity.

capacity usage variance *See* idle capacity variance.

capacity variances In *standard costing, the *favourable variance or *adverse variance that arises as a result of the use of the actual *capacity compared to the *budgeted capacity available. The *variance is calculated by the formula:

(actual hours worked − budgeted hours available) × *absorption rate per standard hour.

Caparo case The case of Caparo Industries plc *v.* Dickman and others. In 1990 the House of Lords decided that auditors owe a duty of care to existing shareholders as a body rather than to individual shareholders.

capital **1.** The total value of the assets of a person less liabilities. **2.** The amount of the proprietors' interests in the assets of an organization, less its liabilities. **3.** The money contributed by the proprietors to an organization to enable it to function; thus **share capital** is the amount provided by way of shares and the **loan capital** is the amount provided by way of loans. However, the capital of the proprietors of companies not only consists of the share and loan capital, it also includes retained profit, which accrues to the holders of the ordinary shares. *See also* reserve. **4.** In economic theory, a factor of production, usually either machinery and plant (**physical capital**) or money (**financial capital**). However, the concept can be applied to a variety of other assets. Capital is generally used to enhance the productivity of other factors of production (e.g. combine harvesters enhance the productivity of land; tools enhance the value of labour) and its return is the reward following from this enhancement. In general, the rate of return on capital is called *profit.

capital account **1.** An account in the financial records of a company limited by shares showing the total amounts for each class of share capital, for example the *preference share capital and the *ordinary share capital. The list of individual shareholders is kept in the *register of members. **2.** An account showing the capital of each partner in a partnership. This account also records the partners' capital contributions, goodwill valuation, and revaluations. In sole tradership accounts, the capital account records the interest the sole trader holds in the business.

capital allowances Allowances against UK income tax or corporation tax available to a business, sole trader, partnership, or limited company that has spent capital on *plant and machinery used in the business. Capital allowances are also given on commercial buildings in enterprise zones, agricultural buildings, industrial buildings, and hotels. The level of allowances varies according to the different categories of asset. From 1 November 1993 the allowance for plant and machinery was restricted to a 25% *writing-down allowance with no *first-year allowance. From the same date an allowance of 4% calculated by the *straight-line method is available on industrial buildings, with no initial allowance. Under the prior-year basis, capital allowances are treated as a separate deduction from the adjusted profits for tax purposes. Under the *current-year basis, this will change and the allowances will be treated as a further expense. The capital allowance period reflects the period during which the accounts are prepared.

capital asset *See* fixed asset.

capital asset pricing model (CAPM) A model designed to assist a firm in choosing its investment and financing policy in order to maximize the price or value of its equity shares by determining the equilibrium relationship between return and risk. The model may also be used to determine the *discount rate or *cost of capital to be used in the organization's investment decisions. It is used in *portfolio theory, in which the expected rate of return (E) on an investment is expressed in terms of the expected rate of return (r_m) on the market portfolio and the *beta coefficient (β), i.e.
$$E = R + \beta(r_m - R),$$
where R is the risk-free rate of return.

capital budget (capital expenditure budget; capital investment budget) The section of the *master budget that covers the amount of *capital expenditure an organization expects to undertake within a given *budget period.

capital budgeting (capital investment appraisal; investment appraisal) The process by which an organization appraises a range of different investment projects with a view to determining which is likely to give the highest financial return. The approaches adopted include *net present value, *internal rate of return, *profitability index, the *accounting rate of return, and the *payback period method. *See also* cost-benefit analysis; economic appraisal.

capital costs *See* capital expenditure.

capital cover The capital value of a *portfolio, often a portfolio of property, divided by the capital sum to be financed. The lower the capital cover, the higher the risk.

capital duty A duty imposed by the European Community in 1973 to replace certain elements of the UK's stamp duty. Capital duty was abolished with effect from 16 March 1988.

capital employed Either the sum of the shareholders' equity in a company and its long-term debts or the *fixed assets of a company plus its *net current assets. However, this term is neither legally defined nor required to be disclosed in a *balance sheet, although it is an important element of *ratio analysis.

capital expenditure (capital costs; capital investment; investment costs; investment expenditure) The *expenditure by an organization of an appreciable sum for the purchase or improvement of a *fixed asset; the amount expended would warrant the item being depreciated over an estimated useful life of a reasonably extended period. Capital expenditure is not charged against the profits of the organization when it takes place, but is regarded as an investment to be capitalized in the *balance sheet as a fixed asset and subsequently charged against profits by depreciating the asset over its estimated useful life.

capital expenditure budget *See* capital budget.

capital fund *See* accumulated fund.

capital gain The gain on the disposal of an asset calculated by deducting the cost of the asset from the proceeds received on its disposal. Under *capital gains tax legislation the *chargeable gain for individuals is adjusted to take account of *indexation. For assets acquired on or after 31 March 1982, the cost of the asset is subject to indexation and the indexed cost is deducted from the proceeds of sale to establish the chargeable gain. For assets acquired before 31 March 1982 the cost can be replaced by the 31 March 1982 valuation of the asset. This would be used if the 31 March 1982 valuation is higher than the cost. The 31 March 1982 value is then subject to indexation and the chargeable gain is calculated by deducting the indexed 31 March 1982 value from the proceeds of sale.

capital gains tax (CGT) A UK tax on *capital gains, introduced on 6 April 1965. It is charged on the total amount of the *chargeable gains accruing to a *chargeable person in a *fiscal year after deducting any allowable *capital losses for the year or capital losses brought forward from a previous year. The rate of capital gains tax depends on the other income for the year; it can be charged at a rate of 20%, 25%, or 40%, or a mixture of these. Gains arising on disposal of assets on or after 29 November 1994 may be deferred if the gain is reinvested in shares acquired under the *enterprise investment scheme within specified time limits.

capital gearing *See* gearing.

capital instruments The means used by companies to raise finance, including *shares, *debentures, and loans; it also includes *options and *warrants that give the holder the right to subscribe for or to obtain capital instruments.

capital investment *See* capital expenditure.

capital investment appraisal *See* capital budgeting.

capital investment budget *See* capital budget.

capitalization 1. The act of providing *capital for a company or other organization. **2.** The structure of the capital of a company or other organization, i.e. the extent to which its capital is divided into share or loan capital and the extent to which share capital is divided into ordinary and preference shares. *See also* thin capitalization. **3.** The conversion of the reserves of a company into capital by means of a *scrip issue.

capitalization issue *See* scrip issue.

capitalization of borrowing costs The cost of borrowing specifically to fund the purchase of a fixed asset or the development of investment property. It may be included in the capitalized cost of the fixed asset.

capital lease In the USA, a lease that does not legally constitute a purchase although the leased asset should be recorded as an asset on the lessee's books if any one of the following four criteria is met:
- the lease transfers ownership of the property to the lessee at the end of the lease term;
- a **bargain purchase option** exists; i.e. an option exists enabling the lessee to

buy the leased property at the end of the lease for a minimal amount or to renew the lease for a nominal rental (a **bargain renewal option**);
• the lease term is 75% or more of the life of the property;
• the *present value of minimum lease payments equals or exceeds 90% of the fair value of the property.
See also finance lease.

capital loss (allowable capital loss) The excess of the cost of an asset over the proceeds received on its disposal. *Indexation of the cost of the asset, or indexation of the 31 March 1982 value, for those assets acquired before 31 March 1982, could be deducted from the proceeds to establish the indexed capital loss on disposals prior to 30 November 1993. The Finance Act (1994) introduced a restriction on the use of indexation to create or increase a capital loss, with a degree of transitional relief for disposals made in 1993–94 and 1994–95.

capital maintenance concept 1. The **financial capital maintenance concept** is that the capital of a company is only maintained if the financial or monetary amount of its *net assets at the end of a financial period is equal to or exceeds the financial or monetary amount of its net assets at the beginning of the period, excluding any distributions to, or contributions from, the owners.
2. The **physical capital maintenance concept** is that the physical capital is only maintained if the physical productive or operating capacity, or the funds or resources required to achieve this capacity, is equal to or exceeds the physical productive capacity at the beginning of the period, after excluding any distributions to, or contributions from, owners during the financial period.

capital market A market in which long-term *capital is raised by industry and commerce, the government, and local authorities. The money comes from private investors, insurance companies, pension funds, and banks and is usually arranged by issuing houses and *merchant banks. *Stock exchanges are also part of the capital market in that they provide a market for the shares and loan stocks that represent the capital once it has been raised. It is the presence and sophistication of their capital markets that distinguishes the industrial countries from the developing countries, in that this facility for raising industrial and commercial capital is either absent or rudimentary in the latter.

capital redemption reserve A reserve created if a company purchases its own shares in circumstances that result in a reduction of share capital. It is a reserve that cannot be distributed to the shareholders and thus ensures the maintenance of the capital base of the company and protects the *creditors' buffer. *See also* permissible capital payment.

capital reduction *See* reduction of capital.

capital reserve A reserve that cannot be distributed, for example a *capital redemption reserve. The concept of a capital reserve is referred to in the Companies Act (1948).

capital risk The risk, in a lending operation, that the capital amount of the investment may be less than its *par value, even at maturity.

capital stock In the USA, the equity shares in a corporation. The two basic types of capital stock are *common stock and *preferred stock.

capital structure (financial structure) The balance between the assets and liabilities of a company, the nature of its assets, and the composition of its borrowings. The assets may be fixed (tangible or intangible) or current (stock, debtors, or creditors); the borrowings may be long- or short-term, fixed or floating, secured or unsecured. Ideally the assets and liabilities should be matched. *See also* gearing.

capital surplus In the USA, the difference between the *par value of a share and its *issue price. It is the equivalent of a *share premium in the UK.

capital transactions Transactions relating to share capital and reserves, long-term debt capital, or fixed assets of a company, as opposed to *revenue transactions. For example, the purchase of a building is a capital transaction, while the maintenance of a building is a revenue transaction.

capital transfer tax (CTT) A tax introduced into the UK in 1974 to replace estate duty and to deal with some of the anomalies arising from it. The capital transfer tax legislation introduced tax on lifetime transfers of money and assets as well as on the estate on death. The rate of CTT on death was affected by all the lifetime gifts made with, initially, no restriction for those within a certain period before death. CTT applied to lifetime gifts made after 26 March 1974 and to estates from 13 March 1975. In March 1986 sweeping changes to capital transfer tax were made and the name was changed to *inheritance tax.

capital turnover The ratio of sales of a company or other organization to its capital employed (i.e. its assets less current liabilities). It is presumed that the higher this ratio, the better the use that is being made of the assets in generating sales.

CAPM Abbreviation for *capital asset pricing model.

capped floating-rate note (capped FRN) *See* floating-rate note.

captive finance company A finance company controlled by an industrial or commercial company.

captive insurance company An insurance company set up by one or more commercial or industrial companies with the object of insuring their risks.

carriage inwards Delivery costs of goods purchased. If the costs relate to *fixed assets, they may be capitalized with the cost of the fixed asset on the *balance sheet.

carriage outwards Delivery costs of goods sold. This is a business expense, which is written off to the *profit and loss account for the period.

carried down (c/d) In book-keeping, describing an amount that is to be transferred as the opening balance in the next period.

carried forward (c/f) In book-keeping, describing the total of a column of figures that is to be the first item in the corresponding column on the next page.

carrying amount The balance-sheet value of an asset or liability. For example, a *fixed asset, such as a building, will be shown at the historical cost less the accumulated *depreciation to date, using the *historical-cost convention. Under *alternative accounting rules it can be shown at the revalued amount less the accumulated depreciation to date.

carrying cost The cost of holding stock from the date of receipt to the date of disposal, or for any other specified period. These costs include warehousing, insurance, and security.

cash *Legal tender in the form of banknotes and coins that are readily acceptable for the settlement of debts.

cash accounting **1.** An accounting scheme for *value added tax enabling a *taxable person to account for VAT on the basis of amounts paid and received during the period of the VAT return. Relief for bad debts is automatically available under this scheme. In order to qualify for the scheme *taxable supplies must not be expected to exceed £350,000 in the coming 12-month period. A business already in the scheme is allowed a 25% tolerance limit and so is permitted to stay in the scheme if turnover does not exceed £437,500. **2.** *See* cash-flow accounting.

cash at bank The total amount of money held at the bank by a person or company, either in current or deposit accounts. It is included in the *balance sheet under *circulating assets.

cash basis of accounting Accounting based on the cash concept rather than the *accruals concept. Transactions are recorded on the date that cash is received or paid out and are included in the *profit and loss account in which these payments occur. Under this system there is no accounting for debtors, prepayments, creditors, accruals, stocks, and fixed assets.

cash book A book in which bank cash transactions are recorded. These include receipts (from customers) and payments (to suppliers) as well as bank charges, interest received, etc. A cash book is a type of *journal, recording transactions in date order; the balance will be included in the *trial balance. The cash book is regularly reconciled with the *bank statement as an internal control check. Cash transactions not made through the bank are generally recorded in a petty-cash book.

cash budget *See* cash-flow budget.

cash cow A business, or part of a company, that regularly generates useful sales and profits without the need for large capital expenditure. Growth prospects, however, are usually expected to be unexciting.

cash discount A *discount receivable or allowable for settling an invoice for cash, or within a specified period. In the *profit and loss account, discounts receivable are classed as revenue; discounts allowable as expenditure.

cash dividend A *dividend paid in cash rather than shares. Cash dividends are paid net of income tax, credit being given to the shareholder for the tax deducted. *See also* advance corporation tax.

cash equivalents Highly liquid investments that are capable of being converted into known amounts of cash without notice and that were within three months of maturity when acquired; from this total must be deducted bank advances that are repayable within three months from the date of the advance. Cash equivalents are an important element of a *cash-flow statement as required by *Financial Reporting Standard 1. There has been some controversy regarding the requirement for three months maturity, which is an issue to be reconsidered when the standard is reviewed.

cash float Notes and coins held for the purpose of being able to give change to customers.

cash flow The movement of cash into and out of a business.

cash-flow accounting (CFA; cash accounting) A system of accounting that records only the cash payments and receipts relating to transactions made by a business, rather than when the money is earned or when expenses are incurred, as in *accrual accounting. It is claimed to be easier to understand and less arbitrary in its allocation processes than accrual accounting. It may be used in place of or in addition to accrual accounting and is reflected in a *cash-flow statement.

cash-flow budget (cash budget; cash-flow forecast; cash-flow projection; financial budget) A *budget that summarizes the expected cash inflows and the expected cash outflows of an organization over a *budget period, usually prepared on a monthly basis. It is the result of the analysis in cash-flow terms of the *functional budgets and the *capital budget, adjusted by other cash-flow items, such as interest, tax, and dividend payments. It is used as a planning aid to determine when cash surpluses are likely to be available for investment or when cash deficits are likely to arise requiring additional finance.

cash-flow statement A statement showing the inflows and outflows of cash and *cash equivalents for a business over a financial period. The inflows and outflows are classified under the headings of operating activities, returns on investments and servicing of finance, taxation, investing activities, and financing. *Financial Reporting Standard 1 issued by the *Accounting Standards Board requires certain companies to publish a cash-flow statement in their annual report and accounts (*see* annual accounts).

cash-flow to total-debt ratio A ratio for assessing the solvency of a company, calculated by dividing the *cash flow from operations by the total *liabilities. It indicates a company's ability to satisfy its debts.

cash-payments journal A journal recording payments of cash from an organization's bank account. This journal may be combined with a *cash-receipts journal to form a *cash book.

cash ratio (liquidity ratio) The ratio of the cash reserve that a bank keeps in coin, banknotes, etc., to its total liabilities to its customers, i.e. the amount deposited with it in current accounts and deposit accounts. Because cash reserves earn no interest, bankers try to keep them to a minimum, consistent with being able to meet customers' demands. The usual figure for the cash ratio is 8%. The Bank of England may from time to time set specific levels of cash, which the banks must deposit with it. In the USA there have always been strict cash ratios set by the Federal Reserve Bank.

cash-receipts journal A journal recording receipts of cash into an organization's bank account. This journal may be combined with a *cash-payments journal to form a *cash book.

cash sale A sale made for cash, rather than on credit terms. Cash sales should be entered in the *cash book rather than the *sales day book.

cash to current liabilities ratio A ratio for assessing the solvency of a company, calculated by dividing the cash, near cash, and marketable securities by the *current liabilities. It indicates a company's ability to satisfy short-term financial obligations.

CCA Abbreviation for *current cost accounting.

CCAB Abbreviation for *Consultative Committee of Accountancy Bodies.

c.c.c. Abbreviation for *cwmni cyfyngedig cyhoeddus: the Welsh equivalent of plc.

CCE Abbreviation for *current cash equivalent.

CD Abbreviation for *certificate of deposit.

c/d Abbreviation for *carried down.

CEDEL Abbreviation for *Centrale de Livraison de Valeurs Mobilières.

ceiling In the USA, an amount equal to the *net realizable value of an asset. The market cannot exceed the ceiling (upper limit) when employing the lower of cost or market method of *inventory valuation. If market is greater than the ceiling, the latter is chosen.

central bank A bank that provides financial and banking services for the government of a country and its commercial banking system as well as implementing the government's monetary policy. The main functions of a central bank are: to manage the government's accounts; to accept deposits and grant loans to the commercial banks; to control the issue of banknotes; to manage the public debt; to help manage the exchange rate when necessary; to influence the interest rate structure and control the money supply; to hold the country's reserves of gold and foreign currency; to manage dealings with other central banks; and to act as lender of last resort to the banking system. Examples of major central banks include the Bank of England in the UK, the Federal Reserve Bank of the USA, the Bundesbank in Germany, the Banque de France, and the Bank of Japan.

Centrale de Livraison de Valeurs Mobilières (CEDEL) A settlement service for *eurobonds in Luxembourg. It is owned by a consortium of international banks. *See also* Euroclear.

certificate of deposit (CD) A negotiable certificate issued by a bank in return for a term deposit of up to five years. They originated in the USA in the 1960s. From 1968, a sterling CD was issued by UK banks. They were intended to enable the *merchant banks to attract funds away from the clearing banks with the offer of competitive interest rates. However, in 1971 the clearing banks also began to issue CDs as their negotiability and higher average yield had made them increasingly popular with the larger investors.

A secondary market in CDs has developed, made up of the *discount houses and the banks in the interbank market. They are issued in various amounts between £10,000 and £50,000, although they may be subdivided into units of the lower figure to facilitate negotiation of part holdings.

certificate of incorporation The certificate that brings a company into existence; it is issued to the shareholders of a company by the Registrar of Companies. It is issued when the *memorandum of association and *articles of association have been submitted to the Registrar of Companies, together with other documents that disclose the proposed registered address of the company, details of the proposed directors and company secretary, the nominal and issued share capital, and the capital duty. The statutory registration fee must also be submitted. Until the certificate is issued, the company has no legal existence.

certificate of insurance A certificate giving abbreviated details of the cover provided by an insurance policy. In a motor-insurance policy or an employers'-liability policy, the information that must be shown on the certificate of insurance is laid down by law and in both cases the policy cover does not come into force until the certificate has been delivered to the policyholder.

certificate of origin A document that states the country from which a particular parcel of goods originated. In international trade it is one of the shipping documents and will often determine whether or not an import duty has to be paid on the goods and, if it has, on what tariff. Such certificates are usually issued by a chamber of commerce in the country of origin.

certificate of value A statement made in a document certifying that the transaction concerned is not part of a transaction (or series of transactions) for which the amount involved exceeds a certain value. The statement is made in relation to stamp duty, denoting that either it is not payable or it is payable at a reduced rate.

certificate to commence business A document issued by the *Registrar of Companies to a public company on incorporation; it certifies that the nominal value of the company's *allotted share capital is at least equal to the authorized minimum of £50,000. Until the certificate has been issued, the company cannot do business or exercise its borrowing powers.

certified accountant A fellow or associate of the *Chartered Association of Certified Accountants.

certified check In the USA, a depositor's cheque (check), which a bank guarantees to pay.

certified public accountant (CPA) A member of the *American Institute of Certified Public Accountants. The title is conferred by state authorities; a certified public accountant is licensed to give an *audit opinion on a company's financial statements.

cessation In the context of a business, the ceasing of trading.

c/f Abbreviation for *carried forward.

CFA Abbreviation for *cash-flow accounting.

CGT Abbreviation for *capital gains tax.

chairman The most senior officer in a company, who presides at the *annual general meeting of the company and usually also at meetings of the board of directors. This officer may combine the roles of chairman and managing director, especially in a small company of which he is the majority shareholder, or he may be a figurehead, without executive participation in the day-to-day running of the company. He is often a retired managing director. In the USA the person who performs this function is often called the president. If this office is filled by a woman, she is known as a **chairwoman** or **chairperson**. To avoid this complication the officer is now often referred to as the **chair**.

chairman's report (chairman's statement) A report by the chairman of a company in the annual report and accounts (*see* annual accounts), addressed to the *members of the company, giving an overview of the company's activities during the financial period. These statements are not prescribed by regulation and often present a favourable view of the activities and prospects of an organization. The report often also gives a survey of what can be expected in the coming year. It is signed by the chairman, who usually reads it at the *annual general meeting.

CHAPS Abbreviation for Clearing House Automated Payment System. *See* Association for Payment Clearing Services.

chapter 7 In the USA, the statute of the Bankruptcy Reform Act (1978) that refers to liquidation proceedings. It provides for a trustee appointed by the court to make a management charge, secure additional financing, and operate the business in order to prevent further loss. The intention of the statute, which is based on fairness and public policy, is to accept that honest debtors may not always be able to discharge their debts fully and to give them an opportunity to make a fresh start both in their business and personal lives. *Compare* chapter 11.

chapter 11 In the USA, the statute of the Bankruptcy Reform Act (1978) that refers to the reorganization of partnerships, corporations, and municipalities, as well as sole traders, who are in financial difficulties. Unless the court rules otherwise, the debtor remains in control of the business and its operations. By allowing activities to continue, debtors and creditors can enter into arrangements, such as the restructuring of debt, rescheduling of payments, and the granting of loans. *Compare* chapter 7.

charge **1.** A legal or equitable interest in land, securing the payment of money. It gives the creditor in whose favour the charge is created (the **chargee**) the right to payment from the income or proceeds of sale of the land charged, in priority to claims against the debtor by unsecured creditors. **2.** An interest in company property created in favour of a creditor (e.g. as a *debenture holder) to secure the amount owing. Most charges must be registered by the *Registrar of Companies (*see also* register of charges). A *fixed charge (or specific charge) is attached to a specific item of property (e.g. land); a *floating charge is created in respect of circulating assets (e.g. cash, stock in trade), to which it will not attach until **crystallization**, i.e. until some event (e.g. winding-up) causes it to become fixed. Before crystallization, unsecured debts can be paid out of the assets charged. After, the charge is treated as a fixed charge and therefore unsecured debts (except those given preference under the Companies Acts) rank after those secured by the charge. A charge can also be created upon shares. For example, the articles of association usually give the company a lien in respect of unpaid calls, and company members may, in order to secure a debt owed to a third party, charge their shares, either by a full transfer of shares coupled with an agreement to retransfer upon repayment of the debt or by a deposit of the share certificate.

chargeable account period *See* accounting period.

chargeable assets All forms of property, wherever situated, unless they are specifically designated as non-chargeable. Exempt assets, for *capital gains tax, include motor cars, National Savings Certificates, foreign currency for private use, betting winnings, damages for personal or professional injury, life-insurance policies for those who are the original beneficial owners, works of art of national importance given for national purposes, principal private residences, *gilt-edged securities, certain chattels (*see* chattel exemption), and investments under *personal equity plans.

chargeable event **1.** Any transaction or event that gives rise to a liability to income tax or to *capital gains tax. **2.** The withdrawal or partial surrender of certain non-qualifying life-assurance policies, such as single premium bonds in which a single lump sum is payable. The proceeds of such policies are free of income tax at the *basic rate and capital gains tax. A chargeable event occurs when during the lifetime of the policy a withdrawal is made of more than 5% of the premiums paid. The amount withdrawn over the 5% is the chargeable event, which is subject to *higher-rate tax.

chargeable gain In the UK, a *capital gain arising as a result of the disposal of an asset, unless the legislation provides otherwise. The exceptions are:
• gains resulting from proceeds that are taxable under *income tax or *corporation tax;
• gains covered by various exemptions (e.g. personal exemption from capital gains tax of £6000 for 1995–96 for a tax year);
• gains not charged in full, as part of the gain occurred before 6 April 1965.
See also indexation allowance.

chargeable person Any person resident, or ordinarily resident, in the UK during the year in which a *chargeable gain assessable to *capital gains tax was made as the result of that person disposing of an asset.

chargeable transfer Certain lifetime gifts that are transfers of value not covered by any of the exemptions and are therefore liable to *inheritance tax. If such a lifetime gift is not a *potentially exempt transfer, it is a chargeable transfer. If the gift is a potentially exempt transfer, but death occurs within seven years, then that potentially exempt transfer becomes a chargeable transfer.

charge account (credit account) An account held by a customer at a retail shop that allows payment of any goods purchased at the end of a stated period (usually one month). While the large stores usually offered this facility without charging interest, it is now usual for interest to be charged on any amounts unpaid after the stated period. The customer is identified by means of a plastic **charge card**. If this is lost or stolen it is the customer's responsibility to notify the store immediately.

charge and discharge accounting A form of accounting used in the manorial system of the Middle Ages, in which individuals charge themselves with sums or estate they should receive and credit themselves with sums paid out.

charge card *See* charge account.

charges forward An instruction to the effect that all carriage charges on a consignment of goods will be paid by the consignee after he receives them.

charges register *See* register of charges.

charitable contribution A donation made by a business to an organization being run for charitable purposes.

charity accounts The accounts of a charitable organization showing receipts (such as donations, grants, and fund-raising amounts received) and payments made (such as expenses, grants, and donations given). The specific regulations the charity will be required to conform to depend upon its legal form and its size. The Charities Act (1993) introduced a new accounting regime for charities.

Charity Commissioners The board that acts as both an adviser to, and an investigator of, charities. It is responsible to parliament and is governed by the Charities Act (1993).

charter A document of incorporation issued by a government.

chartered accountant In the UK, a person who is a member of the *Institute of Chartered Accountants in England and Wales, the *Institute of Chartered Accountants of Scotland, or the *Institute of Chartered Accountants in Ireland.

Chartered Association of Certified Accountants The association that was formed in 1938 as the Association of Certified and Corporate Accountants, as a result of the amalgamation of the Corporation of Accountants (Glasgow; 1891) and the London Association of Accountants (1904). In 1941 the Institute of Certified Public Accountants joined the association.

chartered company A company incorporated by Royal Charter rather than by the Companies Act or by a private act of parliament.

Chartered Institute of Management Accountants (CIMA) The association that was founded in 1919 as the Institute of Cost and Works Accountants. Its members work mainly in industry and commerce. *See also* management accounting.

Chartered Institute of Public Finance and Accountancy (CIPFA) The association that was founded in 1885 as the Corporate Treasurers and Accountants Institute. Its members work principally in public-sector accounting.

Chartered Institute of Taxation (until 1994 the Institute of Taxation) A professional institute for those engaged in working within the taxation field, in accountancy practices, legal firms, banks, and in commerce. An Associate of the Institute is designated *ATII and a Fellow *FTII. *See also* ATT.

chartist An *investment analyst who uses charts and graphs to record past movements of the share prices, P/E ratios, turnover, etc., of individual companies to anticipate the future share movements of these companies. Claiming that history repeats itself and that the movements of share prices conform to a small number of repetitive patterns, chartists have been popular, especially in the USA, in the past. It is now more usual for analysts to use broader techniques in addition to those used by chartists.

chart of accounts A detailed listing of all the accounts used by an organization, showing classifications and subclassifications. For example, each letter or number in an *account code will indicate a feature, such as transaction type and the department responsible.

chattel exemption A gain on the disposal of a chattel that is exempt from *capital gains tax if the proceeds of the disposal are less than £6000. It does not apply to *wasting assets.

check *See* cheque.

cheque A preprinted form on which instructions are given to an account holder (a bank or building society) to pay a stated sum to a named recipient. It is the most common form of payment of debts of all kinds (*see also* current account).

In a **crossed cheque** two parallel lines across the face of the cheque indicate that it must be paid into a bank account and not cashed over the counter (a **general crossing**). A **special crossing** may be used in order to further restrict the negotiability of the cheque, for example by adding the name of the payee's bank. Under the Cheques Act (1992) legal force is given to the words 'account payee' on cheques, making them non-transferable and thus preventing fraudulent conversion of cheques intercepted by a third party. An **open cheque** is an uncrossed cheque that can be cashed at the bank of origin. An **order cheque** is one made payable to a named recipient 'or order', enabling the payee to either deposit it in an account or endorse it to a third party, i.e. transfer the rights to the cheque by signing it on the reverse. In a **blank cheque** the amount is not stated; it is often used if the exact debt is not known and the payee is left to complete it. However, the drawer may impose a maximum by writing 'under £...' on the cheque. A **rubber cheque** is one that is 'bounced' back to the drawer because of insufficient funds in the writer's account; a **stale cheque** is one in which more than three months have elapsed between the cheque's date and its presentation. In the USA the word is spelled **check**. *See also* bank draft.

cheque-in facility A machine that will print on a cheque the amount of the cheque in machine-readable form. These machines are used mainly by banks to assist them in processing cheques, although companies are being encouraged to use them in order to reduce their bank charges.

Chinese wall A notional information barrier between the separate divisions, departments, or teams of a business to ensure that no improper or price-sensitive unpublished information passes between them.

CHIPS Abbreviation for *Clearing House Interbank Payments System.

CICA Abbreviation for *Canadian Institute of Chartered Accountants.

CIMA Abbreviation for *Chartered Institute of Management Accountants.

CIPFA Abbreviation for *Chartered Institute of Public Finance and Accountancy.

circularization of debtors A technique used by an *auditor in which all *debtors to a company are asked to confirm the amounts outstanding (**positive circularization**) or to reply if the amount stated is incorrect or in dispute (**negative circularization**). The object is to ensure that the debts do exist and are correctly valued in the financial statements of a company.

circulating assets (circulating capital; current assets; floating assets) The assets of an organization that are constantly changing their form and are circulating from cash to goods and back to cash again. Cash is used to purchase raw materials, which become work in progress when issued to a production department. The work in progress becomes finished goods, which once they are sold, become debtors or cash from an accounting point of view. Debtors are ultimately changed into cash when they pay, thus completing the cycle. *Compare* fixed asset.

City The financial district of London in which are situated the head offices of the banks, the money markets, the foreign exchange markets, the commodity and metal exchanges, the insurance market (including Lloyd's), the *London Stock Exchange, and the offices of the representatives of foreign financial institutions. Occupying the square mile on the north side of the River Thames between Waterloo Bridge and Tower Bridge, it has been an international merchanting centre since medieval times.

City Code on Takeovers and Mergers A code first laid down in 1968, and subsequently modified, giving the practices to be observed in company takeovers (*see* takeover bid) and *mergers. Encouraged by the Bank of England, the code was compiled by a panel (the **Takeover Panel**) including representatives from the London Stock Exchange Association, the Issuing Houses Association, the London Clearing Bankers, and others. The code does not have the force of law but the panel can admonish offenders and refer them to their own professional bodies for disciplinary action.

The code attempts to ensure that all shareholders, including minority shareholders, are treated equally, are kept advised of the terms of all bids and counterbids, and are advised fairly by the directors of the company receiving the bid on the likely outcome if the bid succeeds. Its many other recommendations are aimed at preventing directors from acting in their own interests rather than those of their shareholders, ensuring that the negotiations are conducted openly and honestly, and preventing a spurious market arising in the shares of either side.

class action A legal action in which a person sues as a representative of a class of persons who share a common claim.

clawback The right to recall new shares issued by means of a *vendor placing to outsiders. Existing shareholders have a right to recall these shares if the vendor placing represents 10% or more of the issued share capital.

cleared balance A balance on a bank account, excluding any receipts that do not yet represent *cleared value.

cleared for fate Denoting the date on which the payer's bank has confirmed that funds are available to provide value for a transfer in accordance with the instructions given in a cheque, etc. *See* clearing cycle.

cleared value Denoting the time at which a credit to a customer's bank account becomes available to him. The *cleared balance is used for calculating interest and for establishing the undrawn balance of an agreed overdraft facility. *See also* clearing cycle.

clearing cycle The process by which a payment made by cheque, etc., through the banking system is transferred from the payer's to the payee's account. Historically, in the UK the average time for the clearing cycle to be completed was three days, although by 1994 this had been reduced to two days in many cases. However, with this reduction in the cycle, the payee's bank may not have received confirmation from the payer's bank that funds are available to provide value, *cleared for fate.

clearing house A centralized and computerized system for settling indebtedness between members. The best known in the UK is the *Association for Payment Clearing Services (APACS), which enables the member banks to offset claims against one another for cheques and orders paid into banks other than those upon which they were drawn. Similar arrangements exist in some commodity exchanges, in which sales and purchases are registered with the clearing house for settlement at the end of the accounting period. *See also* Centrale de Livraison de Valeurs Mobilières.

Clearing House Interbank Payments System (CHIPS) A US bankers' *clearing house for paying and accepting funds. It is an electronic system operated through terminals in bank branches. Participating banks must be members of the New York Clearing House Association or affiliates of it, for example foreign banks operating in the USA can only take part through selected correspondents among the 12 New York Clearing Houses. Outside New York, similar transactions are undertaken through Fedwire, a clearing system for members of the Federal Reserve System.

Clearing Houses Automated Payment System (CHAPS) *See* Association for Payment Clearing Services.

clock card *See* time card.

close company A company resident in the UK that is under the control of five or fewer participators or any number of participators who are also directors. There is also an alternative asset-based test, which applies if five or fewer participators, or any number who are directors, would be entitled to more than 50% of the company's assets on a winding-up. The principal consequences of being a close company are that certain payments made to shareholders can be treated by the Inland Revenue as a *distribution, as can loans or quasi-loans. Close investment companies do not qualify for the reduced rate of *corporation tax. There are a number of other consequences. In the USA close companies are known as **closed companies**.

closed-end funds Funds in which the capital is fixed, such as those held by investment companies, rather than open-ended, such as unit trusts.

close investment holding company A *close company that does not exist wholly or mainly as a trading company, a property company letting to third parties, or a holding company of a trading company.

closely held corporation In the USA, a public corporation that has only a limited number of *stockholders and consequently few of its shares are traded.

closing balance The debit or credit balance on a ledger at the end of an *accounting period, which will be carried forward to the next accounting period. A debit closing balance (such as an *accrual) will be carried forward to the credit side of a ledger and a credit closing balance (such as a prepayment) will be carried forward to the debit side of a ledger.

closing entries Final entries made at the end of an *accounting period to close off the income and expense ledgers to the *profit and loss account.

closing-rate method A method of restating the figures in a balance sheet in another currency using the closing rate of exchange for all assets and *liabilities, i.e. the rate of exchange quoted at the close of business on the balance-sheet date.

closing stock The *stock remaining within an organization at the end of an *accounting period as *raw materials, *work in progress, or *finished goods. It is necessary to establish the level of closing stocks so that the cost of their creation is not charged against the profits of the period (*see* opening stock). Closing stocks are therefore valued and deducted from the costs of the period and appear as *circulating assets in the *balance sheet.

club deal *See* syndicated bank facility.

cluster sampling A method of selecting a sample in which the population is divided into clusters (groups) from each of which a random sample is taken. This technique is used in an *audit. For example, groups of, say, invoices are chosen at random by the auditor and then each item in each group is examined in detail.

CoCoA *See* continuously contemporary accounting.

COGS Abbreviation for *cost of goods sold.

cold calling A method of selling a product or service in which a sales representative makes calls, door-to-door, by post, or by telephone, to people who have not previously shown any interest in the product or service. In the UK, the selling of investments by cold calling is regulated by the *Financial Services Act (1986).

collar An *option that, in return for a premium, fixes the maximum (**cap**) and minimum (**floor**) rate of interest payable on a loan.

collateral A form of *security, especially an impersonal form of security, such as life-assurance policies or shares, used to secure a bank loan. In some senses such impersonal securities are referred to as a secondary collateral, rather than a primary security, such as a guarantee.

collateralize In the USA, to pledge assets to secure a debt. If the borrower defaults on the terms and conditions of the agreement the assets will be forfeited.

collecting bank (remitting bank) The bank to which a person who requires payment of a cheque (or similar financial document) has presented it for payment.

collection account A bank account opened for the specific purpose of reducing *bank float for remittances from specific customers or groups of customers, usually those that are abroad or who pay in a foreign currency.

collection period The time, expressed in days, weeks, or months, that it takes to obtain payment of a debt by a customer.

collective bargaining Bargaining between employers and employees over wages, terms of employment, etc., when the employees are represented by a trade union or some other collective body.

collectivism An economic system in which much of the planning is carried out by a central government and the means of production owned by the community. This system was formerly common in several eastern-bloc countries.

Collector of Taxes A civil servant responsible for the collection of taxes for which assessments have been raised by *Inspectors of Taxes and for the collection of tax under *PAYE.

collusion 1. An agreement between two or more parties in order to prejudice a third party, or for any improper purpose. Collusion to carry out an illegal, not merely improper, purpose is punishable as a conspiracy. 2. In legal proceedings, a secret agreement between two parties as a result of which one of them agrees to bring an action against the other in order to obtain a judicial decision for an improper purpose. 3. A secret agreement between the parties to a legal action to do or to refrain from doing something in order to influence the judicial decision. For instance, an agreement between the plaintiff and the defendant to supress certain evidence would amount to collusion. Any judgment obtained by collusion is a nullity and may be set aside.

columnar accounts Accounts set out in several columns; it is common to present a trial balance in this way. By adding across the columns adjustments are automatically fed into the financial statements.

co-managers Banks that rank after *lead managers in marketing a new issue, usually a *eurobond. They are usually chosen for their ability to place a large portion of the issue with their customers.

combined financial statement In the USA, the aggregation of the *financial statements of a related group of entities in order to present the financial information as if the group was a single entity. Intercompany transactions are eliminated from combined financial statements.

comfort letter *See* letter of comfort.

commercial bank A privately owned UK bank, licensed under the Banking Act (1987) to provide a wide range of financial services, both to the general public and to firms. The principal activities are operating cheque current accounts, receiving deposits, taking in and paying out notes and coin, and making loans. Additional services include trustee and executor facilities, the supply of foreign currency, the purchase and sale of securities, insurance, a credit-card system, and personal pensions. They also compete with the *finance houses and *merchant banks by providing venture capital and with *building societies by providing mortgages.

The number of commercial banks has gradually reduced following a series of mergers. The main banks with national networks of branches are the 'Big Four' (National Westminster, Barclays, Lloyds, and the Midland), the Abbey National, the Royal Bank of Scotland, the Bank of Scotland, the Ulster Bank, and the TSB Group plc. They are also known as **High-Street banks** or **joint-stock banks**.

commercial credit risk *See* credit risk.

commercial paper A relatively low-risk short-term (maturing at 60 days or less in the US but longer in the UK) unsecured form of borrowing. Commercial paper is often regarded as a reasonable substitute for Treasury bills, certificates of deposit, etc. The main issuers are large creditworthy institutions, such as insurance companies, bank trust departments, and pension funds. In the UK, sterling commercial paper was first issued in 1986. Commercial paper is now available in Australia, France, Hong Kong, the Netherlands, Singapore, Spain, and Sweden.

commission A payment made to an intermediary, such as an agent, salesman, broker, etc., usually calculated as a percentage of the value of the goods sold. Sometimes the whole of the commission is paid by the seller (e.g. an estate agent's commission in the UK) but in other cases (e.g. some commodity markets) it is shared equally between buyer and seller. In advertising, the commission is the discount (usually between 10% and 15%) allowed to an advertising agency by owners of the advertising medium for the space or time purchased on behalf of their clients. A **commission agent** is an agent specializing in buying or selling goods for a principal in another country for a commission.

commissions paid account An account used to record commissions paid by an organization to agents and others. In a double-entry system, the commissions paid account is debited and the bank account (or the creditors' account until it is paid) is credited. This account may be combined with the *commissions received account.

commissions received account An account used to record commissions received by an organization. In a double-entry system, the commissions received account will be credited and the bank account (or the debtors' account until it is received) is debited. This account may be combined with the *commissions paid account.

commitment fee A fee charged by a bank to keep open a line of credit or to continue to make available unused loan facilities. Usually the annual charge is made by the lender on the daily undrawn balance of the facility and is often expressed in *basis points.

commitments for capital expenditure Expenditure on fixed assets to which a company is committed for the future. The aggregate amounts of contracts for capital expenditure not provided for in the accounts for the year and the aggregate amount of capital expenditure authorized by the directors but not yet accounted for should be disclosed in the notes to the accounts (according to the Companies Act, Schedule 4). These disclosures will usually be made in the directors' report.

committed costs Costs, usually *fixed costs, that the management of an organization have a long-term responsibility to pay. Examples include rent on a long-term lease and depreciation on an asset with an extended life.

committed facility An agreement between a bank and a customer to provide funds up to a specified maximum at a specified *interest rate (usually based upon an agreed margin over the *London Inter Bank Offered Rate) for a certain period. The total cost will be the interest rate plus the *mandatory liquid asset cost. The agreement will include the conditions that must be adhered to by the borrower for the facility to remain in place. *Compare* uncommitted facility. *See also* revolving bank facility.

commodity 1. A raw material traded on a *commodity market, such as grain, coffee, cocoa, wool, cotton, jute, rubber, pork bellies, or orange juice (sometimes known as **soft commodities** or **softs**) or metals and other solid raw materials (known as **hard commodities**). In some contexts soft commodities are referred to as **produce**. 2. A good regarded in economics as the basis of production and exchange.

commodity code Codes applied to each classification of direct material and other products used or produced by an organization. The codes facilitate recording in the material and finished goods control systems.

common costs 1. In *process costing, those costs incurred by a process before the point at which the *joint products or *by-products are subjected to separate treatment. The common costs, therefore, must be borne by all the output, i.e. by the *main product, the joint products, and the by-products. *See also* joint costs. 2. Costs regarded as unchanged as a result of a managerial decision. For example, if an increase in production is being considered, the total rent payable would be described as a cost common to both the situations before and after the production increase as the rent did not change as a result of the decision to increase production. 3. Costs that are common to a number of processes or products and are therefore shared by them. Common costs are usually *fixed costs and require *apportionment to the appropriate processes or products.

common-size financial statements A method of analysing and comparing financial statements by expressing the individual elements as percentages of the total. For example, with *profit and loss accounts all the costs would be expressed as a percentage of the sales figure. It is then possible to compare these percentages with those for another company or the industry average; these comparisons enable conclusions to be drawn on the performance of the company.

common stock In the USA, the equivalent of the ordinary shares in a public company or privately held firm that give the holders voting and dividend rights. Common stock holders are paid after bondholders and the holders of *preferred stock in the event of corporate bankruptcy.

commorientes Persons who die at the same time. If two people die simultaneously, or if it is uncertain who died first, it is assumed that the older person died first in so far as the devolution of their property is concerned. Thus, if two people are killed in a car crash, a bequest from the younger to the elder is treated as having lapsed.

Companies Acts The UK acts of parliament that are concerned with companies. The first act bearing this name was passed in 1862. Many subsequent measures have been enacted, but since 1980 they have been strongly influenced by the European Union and the company law harmonization programme. The Companies Act (1985) served to consolidate a number of earlier measures.

Companies House (Companies Registration Office) The office of the *Registrar of Companies, formerly in London but now in Cardiff. It contains a register of all UK private and public companies, their directors, shareholders, and balance sheets. All this information has to be provided by companies by law and is available to any member of the public for a small charge.

company A corporate enterprise that has a legal identity separate from that of its members; it operates as one single unit, in the success of which all the members participate. An **incorporated company** is a legal person in its own right, able to own property and to sue and be sued in its own name. A company may have limited liability (a *limited company), so that the liability of the members for the company's debts is limited. An **unlimited company** is one in which the liability of the members is not limited in any way. There are various different types of company: a **chartered company** is one formed under Royal Charter; a **joint-stock company** is a company in which the members pool their stock, trading on the basis of their joint stock.

A **registered company**, one registered under the Companies Acts, is the most common type of company. A company may be registered either as a public limited company or a private company. A **public limited company** must have a name ending with the initials 'plc' and have an authorized share capital of at least £50,000, of which at least £12,500 must be paid up. A **private company** is any registered company that is not a public company. The shares of a private company may not be offered to the public for sale. A **statutory company** is a company formed by special act of parliament.

There are legal requirements placed on companies to make certain financial information regarding their activities public. Such information normally comprises a *profit and loss account and *balance sheet and is included with other financial and non-financial information in an annual report and accounts (*see* annual accounts). The term is often used more widely to refer to any association of persons, such as a *partnership, joined together for the purpose of conducting a business, although legally there are significant differences.

company auditor A person appointed as an *auditor of a company under the Companies Act, which requires that a company's annual *financial statements must be audited. Since 1989 only registered auditors are eligible for appointment.

company doctor **1.** A businessman or -woman or an accountant with wide commercial experience, who specializes in analysing and rectifying the problems of ailing companies. The company doctor may either act as a consultant or may recommend policies and be given executive powers to implement them. **2.** A medical doctor employed by a company, either full-time or part-time, to look after its staff, especially its senior executives, and to advise on medical and public-health matters.

company formation The procedure to be adopted for forming a company in the UK. The subscribers to the company must send to the *Registrar of Companies a statement giving details of the registered address of the new company together with the names and addresses of the first directors and secretary, with their written consent to act in these capacities. They must also give a declaration (**declaration of compliance**) that the provisions of the Companies Acts have been complied with and provide the memorandum of association and the articles of association. Provided all these documents are in order the Registrar will issue a certificate of incorporation and a certificate enabling it to start business. In the case of a *public limited company additional information is required.

company limited by guarantee An incorporated organization in which the liability of members is limited by the *memorandum of association to amounts that they have agreed to undertake to contribute in the event of winding up. This is a less popular form of company than the *company limited by shares.

company limited by shares An incorporated organization in which the liability of members is limited by the *memorandum of association to the amounts paid, or due to be paid, for shares. In the UK this is the most popular form of company.

company officers *See* officers of a company.

company seal The common seal with the company's name engraved on it in legible characters. It is used to authenticate share certificates and other important documents issued by the company. The articles of association set out how and when the seal is to be affixed to contracts. Unless it is affixed to any contract required by English law to be made under seal, the company will not be bound by that contract.

company secretary An *officer of a company. The appointment is usually made by the directors. The secretary's duties are mainly administrative, including preparation of the agenda for directors' meetings. However, the modern company secretary has an increasingly important role; he or she may manage the office and enter into contracts on behalf of the company. Duties imposed by law include the submission of the annual return and the keeping of minutes. The secretary of a public company is required to have certain qualifications, set out in the Companies Act (1985). *See* Institute of Chartered Secretaries and Administrators.

comparative advantage The relative efficiency in a particular economic activity of an individual or group of individuals over another economic activity, compared to another individual or group. One of the fundamental propositions of economics is that if individuals or groups specialize in activities in which their comparative advantage lies, then there are gains from trade. This proposition, first outlined by David Ricardo (1772–1823), is one of the main arguments for free trade and against such restrictions as tariffs and quotas.

comparative amount *See* corresponding amount.

comparative figures Figures given for previous years in the *financial statements of an organization for the purpose of comparison. Corresponding figures for the previous financial year are required by law. If accounting policies have changed or a prior-year adjustment has been made, comparative figures may need to be adjusted to make them meaningful.

compatibility The ability of two or more different types of computer to use the same programs and data. Two computers are said to be compatible if the same machine code can run on both without alteration. Computers from different manufacturers are rarely compatible, unless this is a deliberate feature of the design. For example, many microcomputers are designed to be compatible with the IBM PC. Manufacturers are increasingly making their small machines compatible with their larger ones. This is called **upward compatibility**: programs written for the smaller computer will run on the larger, but not vice versa. This ensures that customers can easily upgrade their machines when necessary. The term is also used of parts of a computer system, either hardware (e.g. terminals) or software (e.g. spreadsheets), meaning that two or more specified brands or versions can be substituted for each other.

The term **plug compatible** describes peripheral devices that can be joined to a computer by a standard interface, or plug.

compensating balance A sum of money deposited at a bank by a customer as a condition for the bank to lend money to the customer.

compensating error An error that is not revealed in a trial balance because one error is cancelled out by another error or errors.

compensation for loss of office A lump-sum ex gratia payment made to an employee or director as compensation for the termination of a *service contract. The payment can be wholly or partly tax free provided that the employee is not entitled to the compensation under the service contract. *See* golden handshake.

competitive bought deal A form of underwriting agreement, generally similar to a straightforward *bought deal, in which the borrower seeks simultaneous competitive quotations from a number of banks for the purchase of an entire new issue of bonds, or similar securities, at a fixed price.

compilation report *See* audit exemption.

completion risk The inherent risk in *limited recourse financing of a construction project that construction will not be completed. *Compare* technological risk; supply risk.

compliance audit An *audit of *internal control procedures to evaluate how well they operate in practice. For example, a sample of invoices could be checked to ensure that they have been properly authorized (indicated by a signature or stamp). *See also* compliance tests.

compliance tests Tests used during an *audit to determine the effectiveness of a company's control procedures. The extent of compliance testing will depend upon the extent to which specific controls are relied upon. Results of compliance testing will indicate the necessary level of substantive testing (tests of transactions, balances, etc.). If controls are found to be working well, substantive testing may be reduced to some extent. *See also* compliance audit.

composite rate A special rate of tax that applied to banks and building societies from 1951 to 1991. This rate of tax was used to deduct tax from interest payments. The main disadvantage of the tax was that non-taxpayers were unable to reclaim the tax deducted from the interest paid to them. The change in 1991 resulted in tax being paid at basic rate, which could be reclaimed. A provision was also introduced enabling non-taxpayers to elect to have the interest paid gross.

composition *See* scheme of arrangement.

compound discount The difference between the value of an amount in the future and its present discounted value. For example, if £100 in five years' time is worth £65 now, the compound discount will be £35. The compound discount will depend upon the rate of discount applied.

compound interest *See* interest.

comprehensive annual financial report (CAFR) In the USA, the official annual report of the government.

comprehensive auditing *See* value for money audit.

comprehensive income The total of the operating profits and the holding gains of a company for an accounting period. The operating profit is the difference between the operating income and expenditure. The holding gains result from any increases in the value of assets between their dates of purchase and their dates of sale. Using *historical cost accounting no distinction is made between operating profits and holding gains. One criticism of this form of accounting is that, by not recognizing holding gains, profits can be overstated and distributed; this could affect the running of the company. *Current cost accounting is based on the maintenance of physical operating capacity and isolates holding gains.

comptroller The title of the financial director in some companies or chief financial officer of a group of companies. The title is more widely used in the USA than in the UK. *See also* controller.

compulsory liquidation (compulsory winding-up) The winding-up of a company by a court. A petition must be presented both at the court and at the registered office of the company. Those by whom it may be presented include: the company, the directors, a creditor, an official receiver, and the Secretary of State for Trade and Industry. The grounds on which a company may be wound up by the court include: a special resolution of the company that it be wound up by the court; that the company is unable to pay its debts; that the number of members is reduced below two; or that the court is of the opinion that it would be just and equitable for the company to be wound up. The court may appoint a provisional liquidator after the winding-up petition has been presented; it may also appoint a special manager to manage the company's property. On the grant of the order for winding-up, the official receiver becomes the *liquidator and continues in office until some other person is appointed, either by the creditors or the members. *Compare* members' voluntary liquidation.

computer-assisted audit techniques (CAATs) Techniques developed by auditors for performing *compliance tests and *substantive tests on computer systems for firms in which the data being audited is processed by computers and held on computer files. There are two main categories of technique. (1) The auditor creates a set of input data to be processed by the computer programs; the results are then checked against the expected results. (2) Computer audit software is used by the auditor to select data from a number of files. Various operations are then performed on the data and the results are transferred to a special audit file to be printed out in a required format. *See also* embedded audit facility; integrated test facility.

conceptual framework A statement of theoretical principles that provides guidance for financial accounting and reporting. In the UK the conceptual framework is called the *Statement of Principles and has been issued by the *Accounting Standards Board. In the USA the *Financial Accounting Standards Board issues Statements of Financial Accounting Concepts under its conceptual framework project.

confidence level (confidence coefficient) The probability that a range of numbers calculated from a sample of a population includes the value of the population parameter being estimated.

confirmation A technique used by an *auditor to obtain third-party evidence in support of information supplied by a client. For example, confirmation may be sought from a bank of balances held by a client. *See also* circularization of debtors.

confirmation note A document confirming the main facts and figures of a deal between two parties, usually a deal that has been agreed verbally or by telephone. The *London code of conduct recommends that the dealer records the telephone calls and that both parties send confirmation notes.

confirmed irrevocable letter of credit *See* letter of credit.

confirming house An organization that purchases goods from local exporters on behalf of overseas buyers. It may act as a principal or an agent, invariably pays for the goods in the exporters' own currency, and purchases on a contract that is enforceable in the exporters' own country. The overseas buyer, who usually pays the confirming house a commission or its equivalent, regards the confirming house as a local buying agent, who will negotiate the best prices on its behalf, arrange for the shipment and insurance of the goods, and provide information regarding the goods being sold and the status of the various exporters.

confiscation risk The risk that assets in a foreign country may be confiscated, expropriated, or nationalized; a non-resident owner's control over the assets may also be interfered with.

conglomerate A group of companies merged into one entity, although they are active in totally different fields. A conglomerate is usually formed by a company wishing to diversify so that it is not totally dependent on one industry. Many tobacco firms and brewers have diversified in this way.

connected person In the context of Companies Act (disclosure requirements for directors and connected persons), a director's spouse, child, or stepchild (under 18 years of age), a body corporate with which a director is associated, a trustee for a trust that benefits a director or connected person, or a partner of a director.

consent letter A letter contained in a prospectus in which an expert (e.g. a firm of accountants) consents to the issue of the prospectus, together with the inclusion of any report written by that expert or any references made to that expert.

consideration 1. A promise by one party to a *contract that constitutes the price for buying a promise from the other party to the contract. A consideration is essential if a contract, other than a deed, is to be valid. It usually consists of a promise to do or not to do something or to pay a sum of money. 2. The money value of a contract for the purchase or sale of securities on the London Stock Exchange, before commissions, charges, stamp duty, and any other expenses have been deducted.

consignee 1. Any person or organization to whom goods are sent. 2. An agent who sells goods, usually in a foreign country, on *consignment on behalf of a principal (consignor).

consignment 1. A shipment or delivery of goods sent at one time. 2. Goods sent **on consignment** by a principal (consignor) to an agent (consignee), usually in a foreign country, for sale either at an agreed price or at the best market price. The agent, who usually works for a commission, does not normally pay for the goods until they are sold and does not own them, although usually having possession of them. The final settlement, often called a **consignment account**, details the cost of the goods, the expenses incurred, the agent's commission, and the proceeds of the sale.

consignment note A document accompanying a consignment of goods in transit. It is signed by the *consignee on delivery and acts as evidence that the goods have received. It gives the names and addresses of both consignor and consignee, details the goods, usually gives their gross weight, and states who has responsibility for insuring them while in transit. It is not a negotiable document and in some circumstances is called a **way bill**.

consignment stock Stock held by one party (the dealer) but legally owned by another; the dealer has the right to sell the stock or to return it unsold to its legal owner. It is sometimes difficult to distinguish between the commercial realities of the transaction and the legal agreement. In accounting it is important that the concept of *substance over form is applied and that the *financial statements reflect the commercial reality. The *Accounting Standards Board has issued Financial Reporting Standard 5, 'Reporting the Substance of Transactions', to resolve these issues.

consignor 1. Any person or organization that sends goods to a *consignee. 2. A principal who sells goods on *consignment through an agent (consignee), usually in a foreign country.

consistency concept A concept used in accounting that ensures consistency of treatment of like items within each accounting period and from one period to the next. It also ensures that *accounting policies are consistently applied. It is a principle contained in the Companies Act and in the Statement of Standard Accounting Practice 2, 'Disclosure of Accounting Policies'.

consolidated accounts *See* consolidated financial statements.

consolidated balance sheet The balance sheet of a group providing the financial information contained in the individual financial statements of the parent company of the group and its subsidiary undertakings, combined subject to any necessary *consolidation adjustments. It must give a true and fair view of the state of affairs of a group as at the end of the financial year, and its form and content should comply with Schedule 4 of the Companies Act. If the balance sheet formats require the disclosure of the balances attributable to group undertakings (creditors, debtors, investments), the information should be analysed to show the amounts attributable to parent and fellow subsidiary undertakings of the parent company, and amounts attributable to unconsolidated subsidiaries.

consolidated cash-flow statement The information contained in the individual cash-flow statements of a group of undertakings combined by *consolidation, subject to any *consolidation adjustments. Cash-flow statements are regulated by *Financial Reporting Standard 1, 'Cash Flow Statements'.

consolidated financial statements (consolidated accounts; group accounts; group financial statements) The financial statements of a group of companies obtained by *consolidation. These are required by the Companies Act and *Financial Reporting Standard 2, 'Accounting for Subsidiary Undertakings'. The information contained in the individual financial statements of a group of undertakings is combined into consolidated financial statements, subject to any *consolidation adjustments. The consolidated accounts must give a true and fair view of the profit or loss for the period and the state of affairs as at the last day of the period of the undertakings included in the consolidation. Subsidiary undertakings within the group may be excluded from consolidation (*see* exclusion of subsidiaries from consolidation), and the parent company itself may be exempt from preparing consolidated accounts (*see* exemptions from preparing consolidated financial statements).

consolidated goodwill The difference between the fair value of the consideration given by an acquiring company when buying a business and the aggregate of the fair values of the separable net assets acquired. Goodwill is generally a positive amount. Goodwill should be eliminated by writing it off immediately to the reserves or alternatively by amortization to the profit and loss account over its useful life, to comply with *Statement of Standard Accounting Practice 22, 'Accounting for Goodwill'. *See also* negative goodwill on consolidation.

consolidated income and expenditure account The information contained in the individual income and expenditure accounts of a *group of organizations combined by *consolidation into a single document for the group. This is subject to any necessary *consolidation adjustments.

consolidated profit The combined profit of a *group of organizations presented in the *consolidated profit and loss account. Any intra-group items should be eliminated by *consolidation.

consolidated profit and loss account A combination of the individual *profit and loss accounts of the members of a *group of organizations, subject to any *consolidation adjustments. The consolidated profit and loss account must give a true and fair view of the profit and loss of the undertakings included in the consolidation. A parent company may be exempted, under section 230 of the Companies Act, from publishing its own profit and loss account if it prepares group accounts. The individual profit and loss account must be approved by the directors, but may be omitted from the company's annual accounts. In such a case, the company must disclose its profit or loss for the financial year and also state in its notes that it has taken advantage of this exemption.

consolidation The process of adjusting and combining financial information from the individual financial statements of a parent undertaking and its subsidiaries to prepare *consolidated financial statements. These statements should present financial information for the group as a single economic entity. For example, if one subsidiary has sold a fixed asset to another subsidiary in the group for a profit, this transaction should be eliminated in both the consolidated profit and loss account and the consolidated balance sheet.

consolidation adjustments Adjustments that need to be made in the process of the *consolidation of the accounts of a group of organizations. If there have been intra-group transactions, such as sales from one subsidiary company to another, any profits or losses resulting from these transactions should be eliminated from the *consolidated financial statements. For example, if one group undertaking has sold a fixed asset to another at a profit, the profit should be eliminated from the profit and loss account and also from the book value of the asset.

consortium relief A modified form of *group relief applying to consortia. A consortium exists if 20 or fewer UK resident companies each own at least 5% of the ordinary share capital of the consortium company and together the consortium members hold at least 75% of the ordinary shares of the consortium company. Losses can be surrendered between the consortium members and the consortium company. The loss that can be surrendered is restricted to the proportion of the claimant's profits that corresponds with the surrendering company's interest in the consortium.

constant dollar *See* current cost.

constant purchasing power accounting *See* current purchasing power accounting.

constraint A factor of production, a shortage of which prevents an organization achieving higher levels of performance. A constraint results from the impact of a *limiting factor (or principal budget factor), which must be eliminated or reduced before the constraint is removed. For example, at various times a shortage of skilled labour, materials, production capacity, or sales volume may constitute a limiting factor. Constraints are also brought into the statement of problems in *linear programming.

Consultative Committee of Accountancy Bodies (CCAB) A committee set up in 1970 by the six *accountancy bodies to foster closer cooperation. At the time of the *Accounting Standards Committee it was a valuable part of the process of setting standards but has lost that role with the establishment of the *Accounting Standards Board. It still plays an active part in many financial accounting and reporting issues.

consumable materials Materials that are used in a production process although, unlike *direct materials, they do not form part of the *prime cost. Examples are cooling fluid for production machinery, lubricating oil, and sanding discs. In circumstances in which direct materials of small value are used, such as cotton or nylon thread or nails and screws, they are sometimes treated in the same way as consumable materials.

Consumer Price Index In the USA, the measure of price level calculated monthly by the Bureau of Labor Statistics. It is commonly known as the cost-of-living index and gives the cost of specific consumer items compared to the base year of 1967. *Compare* Retail Price Index.

contingencies Potential gains and losses known to exist at the balance-sheet date although the actual outcomes will only be known after one or more events have occurred (or not occurred). Depending on the nature of a particular contingency, it may be appropriate to include it in the *financial statements or to show it as a *note to the accounts; *Statement of Standard Accounting Practice 18 provides guidance on this issue. Generally, accountants apply the concept of *prudence and will disclose information on contingent losses more readily than on contingent gains.

contingency theory of management accounting The theory that there is no single management accounting system acceptable to all organizations or any system that is satisfactory in all circumstances in a single organization. Consequently, accounting systems are contingent upon the circumstances that prevail at any time; they must be capable of development in order to take into consideration such factors as changes in the environment, competition, organizational structures, and technology.

contingent agreement *See* earn-out agreement.

contingent consideration A payment that is contingent on a particular factor or factors occurring. The concept often used in relation to *earn-out agreements.

contingent contract *See* earn-out agreement.

contingent gain A gain that depends upon the outcome of some contingency. For example, if a company is making a substantial legal claim against another organization, the company has a contingent gain (depending upon the successful outcome of the claim). Contingent gains should not be accrued in *financial statements but a material contingent gain should be disclosed in the financial statements if it is considered probable that the gain will be realized. Accounting for a contingent gain is therefore subjective; this can be reduced to some extent by seeking independent expert advice. *Compare* contingent loss.

contingent liability A liability that, at a balance-sheet date, can be anticipated to arise if a particular event occurs. Typical examples include a court case pending against the company, the outcome of which is uncertain, or loss of earnings as a result of a customer invoking a penalty clause in a contract that may not be completed on time. Under the Companies Act (1985), such liabilities must be explained by a note on the company balance sheet.

contingent loss A loss that depends upon the outcome of some contingency. For example, if there is a substantial legal claim for damages against a company, there is a contingent loss, if the claim has to be settled. A material contingent loss should be accrued in the financial statements if it is considered probable that a future event will confirm the loss and if it can be estimated with reasonable accuracy at the date on which the financial statements are approved by the board of directors. If the loss is not accrued, it should be disclosed, unless the possibility of making the loss is remote. Accounting for a contingent loss is therefore subjective; this can be reduced to some extent by seeking independent expert advice. *Compare* contingent gain.

continuous budget A budget for a future month or a quarter, which is added to an organization's budget as the latest month or quarter is dropped. The budget for the entire period is revised and updated as necessary, which encourages management to consider continuously short-range plans of the organization.

continuously contemporary accounting (CoCoA) A method of accounting that defines a company's financial position as the ability of that enterprise to adapt to a changing environment; it permits the recognition of general price level changes. Although favoured by some academics, practitioners have shown little interest.

continuous-operation costing A system of costing applied to industries in which the method of production is in continuous operation; examples include electricity generation and bottling. Because the product is homogeneous, this costing system is essentially a form of *average costing in which the unit cost is obtained by dividing the total production cost by the number of items produced. *Compare* process costing.

continuous stocktaking (continuous inventory; continuous stock-checking; perpetual audit) A system of stocktaking designed to ensure that all the items of stock are physically counted and reconciled with the *accounting records shown on the *bin cards and the *stock ledger within a specified period. For example, a stocktaking team may be working continuously so that all items of stock are checked four times a year, when adjustments are made to the accounting records to adjust them to the physical stock. Continuous stocktaking is useful for determining the availability of each item of stock and establishing when stock levels reach *reorder levels.

contra A book-keeping entry on the opposite side of an account to an earlier entry, with the object of cancelling the effect of the earlier entry.

contra accounts Accounts that can be offset, one against the other. For example, if Company A owes money to Company B and Company B also owes money to Company A, the accounts can be offset against each other, enabling both debts to be settled by one payment.

contract A legally binding agreement. Agreement arises as a result of an *offer and acceptance, but a number of other requirements must be satisfied for an agreement to be legally binding. There must be *consideration (unless the contract is by deed); the parties must have an intention to create legal relations; the parties must have capacity to contract (i.e. they must be competent to enter a legal obligation, by not being a minor, mentally disordered, or drunk); the agreement must comply with any formal legal requirements; the agreement must be legal; and the agreement must not be rendered void either by some common-law or statutory rule or by some inherent defect.

In general, no particular formality is required for the creation of a valid contract. It may be oral, written, partly oral and partly written, or even implied from conduct. However, certain contracts are valid only if made by deed (e.g. transfers of shares in statutory *companies, transfers of shares in British ships, legal *mortgages, certain types of *lease) or in writing (e.g. *hire-purchase agreements, *bills of exchange, promissory notes, contracts for the sale of land made after 21 September 1989), and certain others, though valid, can only be enforced if evidenced in writing (e.g. guarantees, contracts for the sale of land made before 21 September 1989). *See also* service contract. Certain contracts, though valid, may be liable to be set aside by one of the parties on such grounds as misrepresentation or the exercise of undue influence. *See also* breach of contract.

contract cost The total cost of a *long-term contract, obtained by using *contract costing techniques.

contract costing A costing technique applied to *long-term contracts, such as civil-engineering projects, in which the costs are collected by contract. A particular problem of long-term projects is the determination of annual profits to be taken to the profit and loss account when the contract is incomplete. This requires the valuation of work in progress at the end of the financial year.

contract for service A contract undertaken by a self-employed individual. The distinction between a contract for service (self-employed) and a *service contract (employee) is fundamental in establishing the tax position. With a contract for service the person may hire and pay others to carry out the work, will be responsible for correcting unsatisfactory work at their own expense, and may make losses as well as profits.

contract of employment *See* service contract.

contract of service *See* service contract.

contribution (contribution margin) The additional profit that will be earned by an organization after the *breakeven-point production is exceeded. The **unit contribution** is the difference between the unit selling price of a product and its *marginal cost of production. The **total contribution** is the product of the unit contribution and the number of units produced. This is based on the assumptions that the marginal cost and the sales value will be constant.

contribution income statement The presentation of an *income statement or *profit and loss account using the *marginal costing or variable costing layout in which the *fixed costs are not charged to the individual products produced as in *absorption costing but are treated as a deduction from the total *contribution of all the products. A simplified contribution income statement would appear as follows:

	Product A	Product B	Total
Sales revenue	2000	5000	7000
Variable costs	1400	2900	4300
Contribution	600	2100	2700
Total fixed costs			1200
Total profit			1500

contribution margin ratio (contribution-to-sales ratio; production–volume ratio; profit–volume ratio) The ratio of the contribution per product to the sales value, often expressed as a percentage. It is a way of ranking a range of products in terms of their relative profitability, the highest percentage indicating the highest contribution per pound of sales. *See also* limiting factor.

contributory pension A pension in which the employee, as well as the employer, contributes to the pension fund. *Compare* non-contributory pension scheme.

control The ability to direct the financial and operating policies of another undertaking with a view to gaining economic benefits from its activities. One company is said to control another company if it holds more than 50% of that company's share capital, voting power, distributable income, or net assets in a winding-up. If one company has control in this sense over another, the two companies should produce *consolidated financial statements.

control accounts Accounts in which the balances are designed to equal the aggregate of the balances on a substantial number of subsidiary accounts. Examples are the sales ledger control account (or total debtors account), in which the balance equals the aggregate of all the individual debtors' accounts, the purchase ledger control account (or total creditors account), which performs the same function for creditors, and the stock control account, whose balance should equal the aggregate of the balances on the stock accounts for each item of stock. This is achieved by entering in the control accounts the totals of all the individual entries made in the subsidiary accounts. The purpose is twofold: to obtain total figures of debtors, creditors, stock, etc., at any given time, without adding up all the balances on the individual records, and to have a crosscheck on the accuracy of the subsidiary records.

controllable costs Costs identified as being controllable and therefore able to be influenced by a particular level of management. Information about those costs is therefore directed to the correct management personnel in the appropriate *operating statements. In any system of *responsibility accounting, managers can only be regarded as responsible for those costs over which they have some control.

controllable variance A variance arising in *standard costing or *budgetary control that is regarded as controllable by the manager responsible for that area of an organization. The variance occurs as a result of the difference between the *budget cost allowance and the actual cost incurred for the period. *See also* controllable costs.

controlled foreign company A foreign company in which a UK company has a 10% stake or more. The UK resident company can be charged to UK tax in respect of profits from the controlled foreign company if the rate of tax paid by the foreign company is less than 75% of the rate that would be payable by the UK company.

controller In the USA, the chief accounting executive of an organization. The controller will normally be concerned with financial reporting, taxation, and auditing but will leave the planning and control of finances to the *treasurer. *See also* comptroller.

controlling interest An interest in a company that gives a person control of it. For a shareholder to have a controlling interest in a company, he would normally need to own or control more than half the voting shares. However, in practice, a shareholder might control the company with considerably less than half the shares, if the shares that he does not own or control are held by a large number of people. For legal purposes, a director is said to have a controlling interest in a company if he alone, or together with his wife, minor children, and the trustees of any settlement in which he has an interest, owns more than 20% of the voting shares in a company or in a company that controls that company.

control period The span of time for which budgeted figures are compared with actual results. Splitting up the financial year into control periods makes control of the figures more manageable.

control risk The risk that misstatements in the *financial statements of a company will not be prevented or detected on a timely basis by the internal control system of a business. It is a part of the *audit risk; an assessment of the control risk must be made for each audit objective. In assessing the control risk, an auditor will need to be familiar with the accounting and internal control system and test its effectiveness in operation by means of *compliance tests.

convention A general agreement or customary practice.

conversion The tort (civil wrong) equivalent to the crime of theft. It is possible to bring an action in respect of conversion to recover damages, but this is uncommon.

conversion cost The costs incurred in a production process as a result of which raw material is converted into finished goods. The conversion costs usually include *direct labour and *production overheads but exclude the costs of direct material itself.

conversion premium *See* convertible.

convertible 1. A fixed-rate *bond issued by a company that can be converted into shares in that company during the life of the convertible. The holder has the right, but not the obligation, to exchange it for shares; the alternative is to hold the convertible until maturity. The exchange ratio of shares to bonds (called the **conversion premium**) is fixed in advance. The dates on which the option to convert (called the **conversion intervals**) are also set in advance. 2. A government security in which the holder has the right to convert a holding into new stock instead of obtaining repayment. *See also* convertible unsecured loan stock.

convertible unsecured loan stock (CULS) Unsecured *loan stock that entitles the holder to exchange the loan stock for another security, usually ordinary shares in the company, at some future date.

conveyancing The transfer of ownership of land from the person currently holding title to a new owner.

corporate governance The manner in which organizations, particularly limited companies, are managed and the nature of *accountability of the managers to the owners. This topic has been of increased importance since the publication of the *Cadbury Report (1992), which sets out guidance in a Code of Practice. There is a stock-exchange requirement for listed companies to state their compliance with this Code; a number of companies now provide information on corporate governance in their annual report and accounts (*see* annual accounts).

corporate modelling The use of simulation models to assist the management of an organization in carrying out planning and decision making. A budget is an example of a corporate model.

corporate report 1. A comprehensive package of information that describes the economic activities of an organization; for *limited companies it is in the form of the annual report and accounts (*see* annual accounts). 2. A discussion document issued by the *Accounting Standards Steering Committee in 1975, which proposed various improvements for financial reporting. The document has attracted considerable academic attention, although it is hard to claim that it has made any significant impact on company practice.

corporate social reporting Issues, such as *employee reports, ethical reporting, *green reporting, and other matters that may be considered of interest to readers of the *annual and report accounts of a company in addition to information that caters for the financial interests of the shareholders. From time to time companies do disclose such information in their annual report, although it remains largely a voluntary activity.

corporation A succession of persons or body of persons authorized by law to act as one person and having rights and liabilities distinct from the individuals forming the corporation. The artificial personality may be created by royal charter, statute, or common law. The most important type is the registered *company formed under the Companies Act. **Corporations sole** are those having only one individual forming them; for example, a bishop, the sovereign, the Treasury Solicitor. **Corporations aggregate** are composed of more than one individual, e.g. a limited company. They may be formed for special purposes by statute; the BBC is an example. Corporations can hold property, carry on business, bring legal actions, etc., in their own name. Their actions may, however, be limited by the doctrine of *ultra vires.

corporation aggregate *See* corporation

corporation sole *See* corporation; body corporate.

corporation tax (CT) Tax charged on the total profits of a company *resident in the UK arising in each *accounting period. The rate of corporation tax depends on the level of profits of the company. The small companies rate of 25% applies to companies with total profits plus *franked investment income of £300,000 or less. Full-rate corporation tax of 33% applies to companies with total profits and franked investment income of over £1.5 million, both limits being those for the *financial year 1994. There is a *marginal relief for those companies with total profits plus franked investment income between those two limits.

correcting entry An entry made in an accounting system to correct an error.

correspondent bank A bank in a foreign country that offers banking facilities to the customers of a bank in another country. These arrangements are usually the result of agreements, often reciprocal, between the two banks. The most frequent correspondent banking facilities used are those of money transmission.

corresponding amount (comparative amount) An amount in the published financial accounts of a limited company that relates to the previous financial year. For example, the accounts will show the total sales for the current year and a corresponding amount for the previous year. Corresponding amounts are required by the Companies Act to provide a comparison. However, if the corresponding amounts are not comparable (e.g. as a result of a change of accounting policy), they should be restated; particulars of the adjustment and reasons for it should be disclosed in the notes to the accounts.

COSA Abbreviation for *cost of sales adjustment.

cost The expenditure on goods and services required to carry out the operations of an organization. There are a number of different ways of defining cost, the major ones being *average cost, *first-in-first-out cost, *historical cost, *last-in-first-out cost, and *replacement cost. *See also* fixed cost; marginal cost; opportunity cost.

cost absorption *See* absorption.

cost accounting The techniques used in collecting, processing, and presenting financial and quantitative data within an organization to ascertain the cost of the *cost centres, the *cost units, and the various operations. Cost accounting is now regarded as a division of *management accounting, which also incorporates the techniques of planning, decision making, and control. In large organizations, the management team usually includes a **cost accountant**.

Cost Accounting Standards Board A board established in the USA in 1970 by Congress to promote consistency in cost-accounting practices and to assist in the reporting of actual costs of government contracts. The board's responsibilities were taken over in 1980 by the Government Accounting Office.

cost accumulation The process of collecting costs as a product progresses through the production system, enabling the total cost of manufacture to be built up in a sequential fashion.

cost allocation *See* allocation.

cost apportionment *See* apportionment.

cost ascertainment The process of determining the costs of the operations, *processes, *cost centres, and *cost units within an organization.

cost attribution The procedures by which costs are charged to or made the responsibility of particular *cost centres, and ultimately charged to the products manufactured or services provided by the organization. Procedures used to achieve cost attribution include *absorption costing, *marginal costing, and *process costing.

cost behaviour The changes that occur to total costs as a result of changes in activity levels within an organization. The total of the *fixed costs tends to remain unaltered by changes in activity levels in the short term, whereas the total of the *variable costs tends to increase or decrease in proportion to activity. There are also some costs that demonstrate *semi-variable cost behaviour, i.e. they have both fixed and variable elements. The study of cost behaviour is important for *breakeven analysis and also when considering decision-making techniques.

cost-benefit analysis A technique used in *capital budgeting that takes into account the estimated costs to be incurred by a proposed investment and the estimated benefits likely to arise from it. In a *financial appraisal the benefits may arise from an increase in the revenue from a product or service, from saved costs, or from other cash inflows, but in an *economic appraisal the economic benefits, such as the value of time saved or of fewer accidents resulting from a road improvement, often require to be valued.

cost centre The area of an organization for which costs are collected for the purposes of *cost ascertainment, planning, decision making, and control. Cost centres are determined by individual organizations; they may be based on a function, department, section, individual, or any group of these. Cost centres are of two main types: **production cost centres** in an organization are those concerned with making a product, while **service cost centres** provide a service (such as stores, boilerhouse, or canteen) to other parts of the organization.

cost classification The process of grouping expenditure according to common characteristics. Costs are initially divided into *capital expenditure and *revenue expenditure. In a production organization the revenue expenditure is classified sequentially to enable a product cost to build up in the order in which these costs tend to be incurred. Revenue costs would normally include:
   direct material,
   direct labour,
   production overheads,
   administration overheads,
   selling overheads,
   distribution overheads,
   research overheads.

cost code *See* accounting code.

cost control The techniques used by various levels of management within an organization to ensure that the costs incurred fall within acceptable levels. Cost control is assisted by the provision of financial information to management by the accountant and by the use of such techniques as *budgetary control and *standard costing, which highlight and analyse any variances.

cost control account *See* cost ledger control account.

cost convention The custom used as a basis for recording the costs to be charged against the profit for an accounting period. The cost convention used may be based on *historical cost, *current cost, or *replacement cost.

cost driver Any *activity or series of activities that takes place within an organization and causes costs to be incurred. Cost drivers are used in a system of *activity-based costing to charge costs to products or services. Cost drivers are applied to **cost pools**, which relate to common activities. Cost drivers are not restricted to departments or sections, as more than one activity may be identified within a department. Examples of cost pools and the relevant cost drivers are given in the table below.

Cost pool	Cost driver
power	number of machine operations, machine hours
material handling	quantity/weight of material handled
material receipt	number of batches of material received
production planning	number of jobs planned
sales administration	number of customer orders received
machine set-up costs	number of jobs run
buying	number of orders placed

cost estimation The procedure that uses estimated unit costs for both *direct costs and *overheads in order to build up the estimated costs of products, services, and processes for the purposes of planning, control, and pricing.

cost function A formula or equation that represents the way in which particular costs behave when plotted on a graph. For example, the most common cost function represents the total cost as the sum of the *fixed costs and the *variable costs in the equation $y = a + bx$, where y = total cost, a = total fixed cost, b = variable cost per unit of production or sales, and x = number of units produced or sold.

costing methods The techniques and procedures used in *cost accounting and *management accounting to obtain the costs of services, products, processes, and *cost centres to provide the information required to undertake *performance measures, decision making, planning, and control. These techniques include *absorption costing, *marginal costing, and *process costing.

costing principles The rules that provide an acceptable treatment of the costs incurred by an organization, in *cost accounting and *management accounting. Examples include the principles used in valuing stocks and the principle that in establishing product costs an allowance for any *normal loss must be included.

cost item A category of costs incurred by an organization that are of a similar nature; they are collected together both for the purposes of reporting and because they can be subjected to similar treatment by the costing system. Examples of cost items are rent, consumable materials, and sundry selling expenses.

cost ledger The *books of account in which the *cost accounting records are contained. These records may be kept manually or be computer-based and may be either separate or integrated with the financial records.

cost ledger control account (cost control account) The *control account that appears in the financial accounting ledger in an accounting system in which separate books are maintained for the financial and costing records.

The balance on the cost ledger control account agrees with the net total of the entries made in the *cost ledger. Including the cost ledger control account in the financial accounting ledger makes the latter a self-balancing record from which a *trial balance can be extracted.

cost of capital The return, expressed in terms of an interest rate, that an organization is required to pay for the capital used in financing its activities. As the capital of an organization can be a mix of *equity share capital, *loan capital, and *debt, there is considerable debate as to whether or not the cost of capital increases as the *gearing increases. Another approach to establishing the cost of capital is to compute a unique *weighted average cost of capital for each organization, based on its particular mix of capital sources. The cost of capital is often used as a *hurdle rate in *discounted cash flow calculations.

cost of carry The difference between a financial instrument's *gross redemption yield and the cost of financing it.

cost of goods manufactured The total production cost of the finished goods transferred from the production facility of an organization during an accounting period. It is made up of the total expenditure for the period on *direct materials, *direct labour, and *production overheads adjusted by the opening and closing stocks of raw materials and the *work in progress at the beginning and end of the period. The cost of goods manufactured is often computed in the *manufacturing account or in a **cost of goods manufactured statement** for a period.

cost of goods sold (COGS) In a sales organization, the *opening stock at the beginning of an accounting period plus the purchases for the period, less the closing stock at the end of the period. In a manufacturing organization the purchases for the period would be replaced by the production of finished goods for the period. The cost of goods sold figure is deducted from the *sales revenue to obtain the gross profit for the period.

cost of sales adjustment (COSA) An adjustment to the trading profit of an organization as a result of a *holding gain on the cost of the stock sold. This occurs in *current cost accounting.

cost-plus contract A contract entered into by a supplier in which the goods or services provided to the customer are charged at cost plus an agreed percentage markup. This method of pricing is very common if the cost of production of the commodity is unknown or in a contract for research work. However, because simple cost-plus contracts do not encourage suppliers to minimize their costs, there has been a move away from this type of contract in UK government orders with private industry.

cost-plus pricing 1. The basic cost price charged in a *cost-plus contract. 2. An approach to establishing the selling price of a product or service in a commercial organization, in which the total cost of the product or service is estimated and a percentage markup is added in order to obtain a profitable selling price. A variation to this approach is to estimate the costs to a particular stage, say the costs of production only, and then to add a percentage markup to cover both the other overheads (including administration, selling, and distribution costs) and the profit margin.

cost pool A collection of costs charged to products by the use of a common *cost driver. Examples are material handling costs, based on the quantity or weight of material handled, and production planning, based on the number of jobs planned.

cost prediction The estimation of future cost levels based on historical *cost behaviour characteristics, using such statistical techniques as *linear regression.

cost sheet A form used in costing to collect together all the costs of a service, product, process, or *cost centre, for presentation to the management or for use in the costing system.

cost standard A predetermined level of cost expected to be incurred by a *cost item used in the supply, production, or operation of a service, product, process, or *cost centre. A cost standard is often applied to a *performance standard in order to calculate *standard overhead costs.

cost unit A unit of production for which the management of an organization wishes to collect the costs incurred. In some cases the cost unit may be the final item produced, for example a chair or a light bulb, but in other more complex products the cost unit may be a sub-assembly, for example an aircraft wing or a gear box. Cost units may also be expressed as batches of items, particularly when the unit cost of the individual product would be very small; for example, the cost unit for a manufacturer of pens might be the cost per thousand pens.

cost-volume-profit analysis *See* breakeven analysis.

council tax A UK local-government tax raised according to property valuation. Replacing the community charge from 1993–94, the tax is charged on the value of a property as defined by a series of bands. Different bands apply to different regions of the UK. Council tax will assume that two people live at the address, with rebates for single occupancy, and provides for a scale of earnings exemptions.

countervailing credit *See* back-to-back credit.

country cheques *See* town clearing.

country risk The possibility that a foreign government will either prevent the fulfilment of a contract entered into by a UK company or take over control of the management of overseas subsidiaries.

coupon 1. One of several dated slips attached to a *bearer bond, which must be presented to the agents of the issuer or the company to obtain an interest payment or dividend. *Eurobonds are issued in this form. **2.** The rate of interest on a bond's *par value, which the issuer promises to pay the holder of the bond.

coupon stripping A financial process in which the *coupons are stripped off a *bearer bond and then sold separately as a source of cash, with no capital repayment; the bond, bereft of its coupons, becomes a *zero coupon bond and is also sold separately. The process represents a type of *synergy, in which the sum of the values of the parts is worth more than the whole.

covenant 1. A promise made in a deed which may or may not be under seal. A covenant is frequently used as a means of providing funds to a body of persons or *trust established for charitable purposes. In such a **deed of covenant**, the payer covenants to pay an agreed sum to the charity, from which income tax at the *basic rate has been deducted. The charity can reclaim the tax so deducted and if the payer is a higher-rate taxpayer, a further claim for tax relief (currently 15% of the grossed up payment) can be made by the payer. For example, if the payment to a charity is £75, the gross payment would be £100, and the taxpayer could claim a further £15 in tax relief. Covenants may be entered into concerning the use of land, frequently to restrict the activities of a new owner or tenant (e.g. a covenant not to sell alcohol or run a fish-and-chip shop). Such covenants may be enforceable by persons deriving title from the original parties. This is an exception to the general rule that a contract cannot bind persons who are not parties to it. **2.** A loan agreement in the form of a covenant will include a series of undertakings, the breaching of which will make the loan repayable immediately. The undertakings can be split between *ratio covenants and *non-ratio covenants. The breaching of an undertaking will also be an *event of default.

covering An action taken to reduce or eliminate the risk involved in having an *open position in a financial, commodity, or currency market.

CPA **1.** Abbreviation for *certified public accountant. **2.** Abbreviation for *critical-path analysis.

CPM Abbreviation for critical-path method. *See* critical-path analysis.

CPP accounting *See* current purchasing power accounting.

creative accounting Misleadingly optimistic, though not illegal, forms of accounting. This can occur because there are a number of accounting transactions that are not subject to regulations or the regulations are ambiguous. Companies sometimes make use of these ambiguities in order to present their financial results in the best light possible. In particular, companies often wish to demonstrate increasing *accounting profits and a strong balance sheet. Examples of transactions in which creative accounting has taken place concern *consignment stocks and *sale and repurchase agreements. In these contexts, creative accounting will involve the separation of legal title from the risks and rewards of the activities, the linking of several transactions to make it difficult to determine the commercial effect of each transaction, or the inclusion in an agreement of options, which are likely to be exercised. Creative accounting is now less prevalent than it was in the 1980s. This is due both to the recession, which has led to a less tolerant view of *financial statements, and to the activities of the *Accounting Standards Board and the *Urgent Issues Task Force, which have addressed some of the worst abuses.

credit **1.** The reputation and financial standing of a person or organization. **2.** The sum of money that a trader allows a customer before requiring payment. **3.** The ability of members of the public to purchase goods with money borrowed from finance companies, banks, and other money lenders. **4.** An entry on the right-hand side of an account in *double-entry book-keeping, showing a positive asset.

credit account *See* charge account.

credit balance A balancing amount of an account in which the total of credit entries exceeds the total of debit entries. Credit balances represent revenue, liabilities, or capital.

credit control Any system used by an organization to ensure that its outstanding debts are paid within a reasonable period. It involves establishing a **credit policy**, *credit rating of clients, and chasing accounts that become overdue. *See also* factoring.

credit entry An entry made on the right hand side of an account, representing an increase in a liability, revenue, or equity item or a decrease in an asset or expense. For example, when a supplier is paid there will be a credit to the bank as cash is spent and a corresponding debit to the creditors' control account.

credit note A document expressing the indebtedness of the organization issuing it, usually to a customer. When goods are supplied to a customer an invoice is issued; if the customer returns all or part of the goods the invoice is wholly or partially cancelled by a credit note.

creditor–days ratio A ratio that gives an estimate of the average number of days' credit taken by an organization before the creditors are paid. It is calculated by the formula:

(trade creditors × 365)/annual purchases on credit.

creditors Businesses or individuals to whom an organization owes money, for example unpaid suppliers of raw materials. The balance on the *creditors' ledger control account is included in the balance sheet: creditors whose payments are due in less than one year are classed as current liabilities; creditors whose payments are due after more than one year are long-term liabilities. The payment of creditors should be tightly controlled to ensure that full credit periods are taken and that any prompt-payment discounts are received.

creditors' buffer The fixed capital of a company, which cannot be reduced or distributed (except with special permission). The knowledge that there is this fixed capital base gives creditors the confidence to invest in the company in the short term (for example as suppliers) or in the longer term (for example as debenture holders).

creditors' ledger (purchases ledger) A memorandum ledger account in which individual creditors' accounts are recorded; it is additional to the nominal ledger and forms part of the internal control system. In each individual creditor's account there is a record of the purchases made (credit), payments made (debit), discounts received (debit), and returns outwards (debit). The total sum of all the creditors' ledger accounts is periodically extracted and compared to the total on the *creditors' ledger control account as part of the internal control system. The total of the individual creditors' ledger accounts should always equal the creditors' ledger control accounts; any differences that do occur must be investigated.

creditors' ledger control account (purchases ledger control account) The nominal (or general) ledger control account recording the totals of the entries made to the individual *creditors' ledgers from the purchases journal and the cash payments journal. The total on the creditors' ledger control account is periodically compared to the sum total of individual creditors' ledger accounts as part of the internal control system. The creditors' ledger control account should always equal the total of the individual creditors' ledger amounts; any differences that do occur must be investigated.

creditors' voluntary liquidation (creditors' voluntary winding-up) The winding-up of a company by special resolution of the members when it is insolvent. A **meeting of creditors** must be held within 14 days of such a resolution and the creditors must be given seven days' notice of the meeting. Notices must also be posted in the *London Gazette* and two local newspapers. The creditors also have certain rights to information before the meeting. A *liquidator may be appointed by the members before the meeting of creditors or at the meeting by the creditors. If two different liquidators are appointed, an application may be made to the court to resolve the matter.

credit rating An assessment of the creditworthiness of an individual or a firm, i.e. the extent to which they can safely be granted credit. Traditionally, banks have provided confidential trade references, but recently **credit-reference agencies** (also known as **rating agencies**) have grown up, which gather information from a wide range of sources, including the county courts, bankruptcy proceedings, hire-purchase companies, and professional debt collectors. This information is then provided, for a fee, to interested parties. The consumer was given some protection from such activities in the Consumer Credit Act (1974), which allows an individual to obtain a copy of all the information held by such agencies relating to that individual, as well as the right to correct any discrepancies. There are also agencies that specialize in the corporate sector, giving details of a company's long-term and short-term debt. This can be extremely important to the price of the company's shares on the market, its ability to borrow, and its general standing in the business community.

credit reporting agency (credit reference agency) An organization that gathers data on the creditworthiness of businesses and individuals from various sources and supplies the data to interested parties in return for a fee.

credit risk (commercial credit risk) The risk taken when a loan is made that the borrower will not be able to repay the principal or the interest. *Compare* political credit risk; transfer credit risk.

credit sale A sale made on terms in which cash is to be paid at an agreed future date. As the debtors, who are customers to whom credit sales have been made, pay, the debtors' control account balance will be reduced.

creditworthiness An assessment of a person's or a business's ability to pay for goods purchased or services received. Creditworthiness may be presented in the form of a *credit rating from a *credit reporting agency.

CREST The paperless share settlement system used by the *London Stock Exchange. A Bank of England system, it replaced the earlier Taurus system, which failed to function. Part of CREST began operation in 1995.

critical event In *critical-path analysis, an event – i.e. the start and/or completion of an activity – that lies on a critical path (*see* critical-path analysis).

critical-path analysis (CPA; critical-path method; CPM; network analysis; programme evaluation and review technique; PERT)
A decision-making technique to determine the minimum time needed to complete a project by establishing the time taken to complete the longest path (i.e. the **critical path**) through a network of activities. The network diagram is drawn up by arranging each activity sequentially, bounded by the events that record the start and/or completion of each activity. Estimated activity times allow the earliest and latest start times for each event to be established, and from this information the critical path can be determined.

cross-default clause The most onerous clause in a loan agreement, stating that if the borrower defaults on one loan, any other loans may become repayable. The cross-default clause is activated when another lender is in a position to call a default on its loan or an event occurs which, with the passage of time, is capable of giving any lender the right to call a default. *See* event of default.

crossed cheque *See* cheque.

cross rate An exchange rate between two currencies based upon the rate of each of them with a third currency, often the US dollar.

crown jewel option A form of *poison pill in which a company, defending itself against an unwanted *takeover bid, writes an *option that would allow a partner or other friendly company to acquire one or more of its best businesses at an advantageous price if control of the defending company is lost to the unwelcome predator. The granting of such an option may not always be in the best interests of the shareholders of the defending company.

CT Abbreviation for *corporation tax.

CTT Abbreviation for *capital transfer tax.

CULS Abbreviation for *convertible unsecured loan stock.

cum rights *See* ex-.

cumulative preference share A type of *preference share that entitles the owner to receive any dividends not paid in previous years. Companies are not obliged to pay dividends on preference shares if there are insufficient earnings in any particular year. Cumulative preference shares guarantee the eventual payment of these dividends in arears before the payment of dividends on ordinary shares, provided that the company returns to profit in subsequent years.

cumulative preferred stock In the USA, stock in which the dividends accumulate if not paid out in a particular financial period.

currency **1.** Any kind of money that is in circulation in an economy.
2. Anything that functions as a medium of exchange, including coins, banknotes, cheques, *bills of exchange, promissory notes, etc. **3. (legal tender)** The money in use in a particular country. *See* foreign exchange. **4.** The time that has to elapse before a bill of exchange matures.

currency exposure The effect on the net worth of a business of changes in exchange rates in relation to its *functional currency.

current account 1. An active account at a bank or building society into which deposits can be paid and from which withdrawals can be made by cheque. The bank or building society issues cheque books free of charge and supplies regular statements listing all transactions and the current balance. Banks sometimes make charges for current accounts, based on the number of transactions undertaken, but modern practice is to waive these charges if a certain credit balance has been maintained for a given period. Building societies usually make no charges and pay interest on balances maintained in a current account. Banks, in order to remain competitive, are following this practice, although they have traditionally not paid interest on current-account balances. 2. The part of the *balance of payments account that records non-capital transactions. 3. An account in which intercompany or interdepartmental balances are recorded. 4. An account recording the transactions of a partner in a partnership that do not relate directly to that partner's capital in the partnership (*see* capital account).

current-asset investment An investment (e.g. shares) intended to be held for less than one year. *See also* fixed-asset investment.

current assets *See* circulating assets.

current cash equivalent (CCE) In *continuously contemporary accounting, the measure of assets and liabilities.

current cost 1. A cost calculated to take into consideration current circumstances of cost and performance levels. 2. The sum that would be required at current prices to purchase or manufacture an asset. This may be the replacement cost or the historical cost adjusted for inflation by means of an appropriate price index. 3. (**constant dollar**) In the USA, the method of converting historical cost to current cost and then adjusting to constant purchasing power by using the average *Consumer Price Index for the current year.

current cost accounting (CCA) A form of accounting in which the approach to capital maintenance is based on maintaining the operating capability of a business. Assets are valued at their value to the business, also known as their **deprival value**. The deprival value of an asset is the loss that a business would suffer if it were to be deprived of the use of the asset. This may be the *replacement cost of the asset, its *net realizable value, or its *economic value to the business. Current cost accounting ensures that a business maintains its operating capacity by separating *holding gains from *operating profits to prevent them being distributed to shareholders. The current cost accounting profit figure is derived by making a number of adjustments to the *historical cost accounting profit and loss account: these are the *cost of sales adjustment, *depreciation adjustment, monetary *working-capital adjustment, and the *gearing adjustment. The current-cost reserve in the balance sheet is used to 'collect' the current cost adjustments. *Statement of Standard Accounting Practice 16, 'Current Cost Accounting', was issued in March 1980 but withdrawn in April 1988 after much criticism.

current-cost depreciation A *depreciation charge that is calculated on the *current cost of assets.

current-cost operating profit Using *current cost accounting, the amount remaining after the cost of sales adjustment, depreciation adjustment, and monetary working-capital adjustment have been made to the conventional accounting profit.

current liabilities Amounts owed by a business to other organizations and individuals that should be paid within one year from the balance-sheet date. These generally consist of trade creditors, *bills of exchange payable, amounts owed to group and related companies, taxation, social-security creditors, proposed dividends, accruals, deferred income, payments received on account, bank overdrafts, and short-term loans. Any long-term loans repayable within one year from the balance-sheet date should also be included. Current liabilities are distinguished from long-term liabilities on the balance sheet.

current purchasing power accounting (constant purchasing power accounting; CPP accounting) A form of accounting that measures profit after allowing for the maintenance of the purchasing power of the shareholders' capital. The *Retail Price Index is used to adjust for general price changes to ensure that the shareholders' capital maintains the same monetary purchasing power. There is no requirement to allow for the maintenance of the purchasing power of the loan creditors' capital. Current purchasing power accounting was covered by the provisional *Statement of Standard Accounting Practice 7, issued in May 1974; however, it was withdrawn in October 1978.

current ratio (working-capital ratio) The ratio of the current assets of a business to the current liabilities, expressed as x:1 and used as a test of liquidity. For example, if the current assets are £25,000 and the current liabilities are £12,500 the current ratio is 2:1. There is no simple rule of thumb, but a low ratio, e.g. under 1:1, would usually raise concern over the liquidity of the company. Too high a ratio, e.g. in excess of 2:1, may indicate poor management of working capital; this would be established by calculating the *stock turnover ratio and *debtor collection period ratio. Care must be taken when making comparisons between companies to ensure that any industry differences are recognized. The *acid-test ratio is regarded as a more rigorous test of liquidity.

current replacement cost The cost of replacing an asset, or the services provided by the asset, estimated at the balance-sheet date. Current replacement costs may be difficult to establish if, for example, the asset cannot be replaced as a result of obsolescence.

current standard A cost, income, or *performance standard used in *standard costing; it is based on current operating conditions and is established for use over a short period of time. *Compare* basic standard.

current-value accounting An accounting method that takes account of changes in specific prices rather than changes in the general price level. Assets can be valued at their *net realizable value, *current replacement cost, or net present value – or a combination of these.

current-year basis Tax charged in a *fiscal year on profits arising in the accounts for the period ending in that tax year. The profits arising in the year to 30 April 1998 will be assessed, under the current-year basis, in the tax year 1998–99.

curvilinear cost function Any cost relationship that results in a curved line when plotted on a graph.

customs duty A levy on the importation of certain goods and on some goods manufactured from the imported goods. Customs duties are also charged on some exports.

customs invoice An invoice for goods imported or exported, which is prepared especially for the customs authorities.

cut-off date The date on which an accounting period ends and the accounts of a business are ruled off. It is important that this should happen on the correct date to ensure that a true and fair view of the performance and position of a business is given. An *auditor will pay particular attention to the cut-off date as accounts can be manipulated for purposes of *window dressing.

CVP analysis *See* breakeven analysis.

cwmni cyfyngedig cyhoeddus (c.c.c.) Welsh for *public limited company.

cycle billing The method sometimes adopted in large organizations for invoicing their customers at different time intervals. Often using the alphabet as a basis, customers starting with the letter A may be invoiced on the first day, B on the second day, and so on. This method has the advantage of spreading the work load in the organization and ensuring a steady inflow of cash – providing that there are many customers with comparable accounts.

daisy chain The buying and selling of the same items several times over, for example *stocks and *shares. This may be done to 'inflate' trading activity (that is, the sale of the same items are being included in the sales figure more than once).

damages Compensation, in monetary form, for a loss or injury, breach of contract, tort, or infringement of a right. Damages refers to the compensation awarded, as opposed to damage, which refers to the actual injury or loss suffered. The legal principle is that the award of damages is an attempt, as far as money can, to restore the position of the injured party to what it was before the event in question took place; i.e. the object is to provide restitution rather than profit. Damages are not assessed in an arbitrary fashion but are subject to various judicial guidelines. In general, damages capable of being quantified in monetary terms are known as **liquidated damages**. In particular, liquidated damages include instances in which a genuine pre-estimate can be given of the loss that will be caused to one party if a contract is broken by the other party. If the anticipated breach of contract occurs this will be the amount, no more and no less, that is recoverable for the breach. However, liquidated damages must be distinguished from *penalties. Another form of liquidated damages is that expressly made recoverable under a statute. These may also be known as **statutory damages** if they involve a breach of statutory duty or are regulated or limited by statute. **Unliquidated damages** are those fixed by a court rather than those that have been estimated in advance.

General damages represents compensation for general damage, which is the kind of damage the law presumes to exist in any given situation. It is recoverable even without being specifically claimed and is awarded for the usual or probable consequences of the wrongful act complained of. For example, in an action for medical negligence, pain and suffering is presumed to exist, therefore if the action is successful, general damages would be awarded as compensation even though not specifically claimed or proved. Loss of earnings by the injured party, however, must be specifically claimed and proved, in which case they are known as **specific damages**.

Nominal and **contemptuous damages** are those awarded for trifling amounts. These are awarded either when the court is of the opinion that although the plaintiff's rights have been infringed no real loss has been suffered, or, although actual loss has resulted, the loss has been caused by the conduct of the plaintiff. The prospect of receiving only nominal or contemptuous damages prevents frivolous actions being brought. The award is usually accompanied by an order that each party bears their own legal costs. **Exemplary damages**, on the other hand, are punitive damages awarded not merely as a means of compensation but also to punish the party responsible for the loss or injury. This usually occurs when the party causing the damage has done so wilfully or has received financial gain from the wrongful conduct. Exemplary damages will be greater than the amount that would have been payable purely as compensation. **Prospective damages** are awarded to a plaintiff, not as compensation for any loss suffered at the time of a legal action but in respect of a loss it is reasonably anticipated will be suffered at some future time. Such an injury or loss may sometimes be considered to be too remote and therefore not recoverable.

dandy note A delivery order issued by an exporter and countersigned by HM Customs and Excise, authorizing a bonded warehouse to release goods for export.

dangling debit A practice in which companies write off *goodwill to *reserves and create a goodwill account, which is deducted from the total of shareholders' funds. This treatment is permitted by *Statement of Standard Accounting Practice 22.

data The information that is processed, stored, or produced by a computer.

database An organized collection of information held on a computer. A special computer program, called a **database management system (DBMS)**, is used to organize the information held in the database according to a specified schema, to update the information, and to help users find the information they seek. There are two kinds of DBMS: simple DBMS, which are the electronic equivalents of a card index; and programmable DBMS, which provide a programming language that allows the user to analyse the data held in the database. On large computer systems, other programs can generally communicate with the DBMS and use its facilities. The term **data bank** is used for a collection of databases.

database management system (DBMS) *See* database.

data capture The insertion of information into a computerized system. For example, information about the sale of an item (the item sold, the sales price, and discount given, date and location of sale, etc.) is taken into the accounting system either at the point of sale in a retail organization by an electronic till or by keyboarding into the system when the invoice is prepared. This information is then readily available and up-to-date; it can also be used to adjust stock levels.

data file A file on a computer system that contains *data, contrasted with one that contains a program. A data file is usually subdivided into records and fields.

data flow chart (data flow diagram) A chart that illustrates the way in which specified data is handled by a computer program. It concentrates on the functions performed rather than upon the detailed logic or programming instructions necessary for performing the functions. Its purpose is to specify the data, to show where it is used or changed, where it is stored, and which reports use it.

Datapost A Royal Mail fast service for packages weighing up to 27.5 kg. The same-day door-to-door service by radio-controlled motorcycles and vans is more expensive than the overnight service, which guarantees next-day delivery to any point in the UK. There is also a Datapost International Service, which operates to many countries.

data processing (DP) The class of computing operations that manipulate large quantities of information. In business, these operations include book-keeping, printing invoices and mail shots, payroll calculations, and general record keeping. Data processing forms a major use of computers in business, and many firms have full-time data-processing departments.

data protection Safeguards relating to personal data in the UK, i.e. personal information about individuals that is stored on a computer. The principles of data protection, the responsibilities of data users, and the rights of data subjects are governed by the Data Protection Act (1984).

The principles of data protection include the following:

(1) The information to be contained in personal data shall be obtained, and personal data shall be processed, fairly and lawfully.

(2) Personal data shall be held only for specified and lawful purposes and shall not be used or disclosed in any manner incompatible with those purposes.

(3) Personal data held for any purpose shall be relevant to that purpose.

(4) Personal data shall be accurate and, where necessary, kept up to date.

(5) Personal data held for any purpose shall not be kept longer than necessary for that purpose.

(6) Appropriate security measures shall be taken against unauthorized access to, or alteration, disclosure, or destruction of personal data and against accidental loss or destruction of personal data.

Data users must register their activities with the **Data Protection Registrar** by means of a registration form obtained from a post office. This requires the data user to give: a description of the personal data it holds and the purposes for which the data is held; a description of the sources from which it intends or may wish to obtain the data or the information to be contained in the data; a description of any persons to whom it intends or may wish to disclose the data; the names or a description of any countries or territories outside the UK to which it intends or may wish directly or indirectly to transfer from data subjects for access to the data. A data user who fails to register is guilty of the offence of failing to register.

An individual is entitled to be informed by any data user whether that data user holds personal data of which the individual is the subject. The data subject is also entitled to obtain a printout from a registered data user of any personal data held and to demand that any inaccurate or misleading information is corrected or erased. If a court is satisfied on the application of a data subject that personal data held by a data user concerning the data subject is inaccurate it may order the rectification or erasure of the data. Additionally it may order the rectification or erasure of any data held by the data user that contains an expression of opinion that appears to the court to be based on the inaccurate data.

dawn raid An attempt by one company or investor to acquire a significant holding in the equity of another company by instructing brokers to buy all the shares available in that company as soon as the stock exchange opens, usually before the target company knows that it is, in fact, a target. The dawn raid may provide a significant stake from which to launch a *takeover bid. The conduct of dawn raids is now restricted by the *City Code on Takeovers and Mergers.

day book A specialized *journal or book of prime entry recording specific transactions. For example, the *sales day book records invoices for sales, the *purchase day book records invoices received from suppliers. Day-book entries are transferred to memorandum *ledgers, such as the *debtors' ledger and the *creditors' ledger, while totals of entries are transferred to the *nominal ledger control accounts, such as the *debtors' ledger control account and the *creditors' ledger control account.

days' sales in inventory The amount of inventory (stock) expressed in days of sales. For example, if 2 items a day are sold and 20 items are held in inventory, this represents 10 days' (20/2) sales in inventory.

days' sales in receivables The amount of *receivables (i.e. debtors) expressed in days of sales. For example, if £5000 worth of sales are made each day and the total debtors' balance outstanding is £500,000, this represents 100 (£500,000/£5000) days' sales.

days' sales outstanding The amount of sales outstanding expressed in days. For example, if £5000 worth of sales were made per day and £50,000 worth of sales were outstanding, this would represent 10 days' (£50,000/£5000) of sales outstanding.

DBMS Abbreviation for database management system. *See* database.

DCF Abbreviation for *discounted cash flow.

DCV Abbreviation for *direct charge voucher.

Dearing Report The report of a committee to examine the setting of accountancy standards, established in the UK under the chairmanship of Sir Ronald Dearing. The report, 'The Making of Accounting Standards', was published in 1988; this led to the replacement of the *Accounting Standards Committee by the *Accounting Standards Board and to the establishment of the *Financial Reporting Council, the Review Panel, and the *Urgent Issues Task Force.

death duty (estate duty) A tax levied on the estate of a person who has died; the amount of the tax is calculated by assessing the estate of the deceased person in accordance with the appropriate tax regulations. In the UK, estate duty was replaced in 1975 by *capital transfer tax, which in turn was replaced by *inheritance tax in 1986.

debenture 1. The most common form of long-term loan taken by a company. It is usually a loan repayable at a fixed date, although some debentures are irredeemable securities; these are sometimes called perpetual debentures. Most debentures also pay a fixed rate of interest, and this interest must be paid before a *dividend is paid to shareholders. Most debentures are also secured on the borrower's assets, although some, known as **naked debentures** or unsecured debentures, are not. In the USA debentures are usually unsecured, relying only on the reputation of the borrower. In a secured debenture, the bond may have a *fixed charge (i.e. a charge over a particular asset) or a *floating charge. If debentures are issued to a large number of people (for example in the form of **debenture stock** or **loan stock**) trustees may be appointed to act on behalf of the debenture holders. There may be a premium on redemption and some debentures are *convertible, i.e. they can be converted into ordinary shares on a specified date, usually at a specified price. The advantage of debentures to companies is that they carry lower interest rates than, say, overdrafts and are usually repayable a long time into the future. For an investor, they are usually saleable on a stock exchange and involve less risk than *equities. **2.** A deed under seal setting out the main terms of such a loan.

debenture redemption reserve A capital reserve into which amounts are transferred from the *profit and loss account for *debentures that are redeemable at a future date. The aim is to limit the profits available for distribution, although the reserve does not provide the actual funds for redeeming the debentures. To provide these funds a periodic *sinking-fund payment needs to be made to a debenture-redemption reserve fund, matched with investments earmarked for the fund.

debit An entry on the left-hand side of an account in *double-entry book-keeping, showing an amount owed by the organization keeping the book. In the case of a bank account, a debit shows an outflow of funds from the account.

debit balance The balance of an account whose total *debit entries exceed the total of the *credit entries. Debit balances represent expenditure and *assets.

debit card A plastic card issued by a bank or building society to enable its customers with cheque accounts to pay for goods or services at certain retail outlets by using the telephone network to debit their cheque accounts directly. The retail outlets, such as petrol stations and some large stores, need to have the necessary computerized input device, into which the card is inserted; the customer may be required to tap in a personal identification number before entering the amount to be debited. Some debit cards also function as cheque cards and cash cards.

debit entry An entry made in *double-entry book-keeping on the left-hand side of an account. It records either an increase in an asset or expense or a decrease in a liability, revenue, or equity item. For example, cash paid into the bank from a debtor will increase the asset of cash. The entries to be made are debiting the bank and crediting the *debtors' ledger control account.

debit note A document sent by an organization to a person showing that the recipient is indebted to the organization for the amount shown in the debit note. Debit notes are rare as invoices are more regularly used; however, a debit note might be used when an invoice would not be appropriate, e.g. for some form of inter-company transfer other than a sale of goods or services.

debt **1.** A sum owed by one person or organization to another. In commerce, it is usual for debts to be required to be settled within one month of receiving an invoice, after which *interest may be incurred. A long-term debt may be covered by a *bill of exchange, which can be a *negotiable instrument. *See also* debenture. **2.** In the USA, the long-term borrowings of an organization, such as debentures, *mortgage debentures, or long-term loans.

debt capital *See* loan capital.

debt collection agency An organization that specializes in collecting the outstanding debts of its clients, charging a commission for doing so.

debt–equity ratio A ratio used to examine the financial structure or *gearing of a business. The long-term debt, normally including *preference shares, of a business is expressed as a percentage of its equity. A business may have entered into an agreement with a bank that it will maintain a certain debt–equity ratio; if it breaches this agreement the loan may have to be repaid. A highly geared company is one in which the debt is higher than the equity, compared to companies in a similar industry. A highly geared company offers higher returns to shareholders when it is performing well but should be regarded as a speculative investment. The debt–equity ratio is now sometimes expressed as the ratio of the debt to the sum of the debt and the equity.

debt instrument A formal document setting out the terms and conditions attached to a short-term loan.

debtor collection period (average collection period) The period, on average, that a business takes to collect the money owed to it by its trade debtors. If a company gives one month's credit then, on average, it should collect its debts within 45 days. The **debtor collection period ratio** is calculated by dividing the amount owed by trade debtors by the annual sales on credit and multiplying by 365. For example if debtors are £25,000 and sales are £200,000, the debtors collection period ratio will be:

(£25,000 × 365)/£200,000 = 46 days approximately.

debtors Those who owe money to an organization, for example for sales of goods. The balance on the *debtors' ledger control account is included in the balance sheet (subject to any *provision for bad or doubtful debts) under *circulating assets. Amounts due from debtors in more than one year should be disclosed separately. A memorandum listing of the individual account of each debtor is also kept, this is known as the *debtors' ledger. The total of the debtors' ledger is periodically checked with the total on the debtors' control account as a form of internal control.

debtors' ledger (sales ledger; sold ledger) A memorandum *ledger account in which individual *debtors' accounts are recorded. Each account records sales made (debit), payments received (credit), discounts given (credit), and *returns inwards (credit). The total sum of all individual debtors' ledgers is periodically extracted and compared to the total on the *debtors' ledger control account as part of the internal control system. The total of the individual debtors' ledger accounts should always equal the debtors' ledger control account.

debtors' ledger control account (sales ledger control account) A *nominal ledger (or general ledger) control account that records the totals of entries made to the individual *debtors' ledgers from the *sales day book and the cash receipts journal. The total on the debtors' ledger control account is periodically compared with the sum total of individual *debtors' ledger accounts as part of the internal control system. The debtors' ledger control account should always equal the total of the individual debtors' ledger amounts.

debt restructuring The adjustment of a debt, either as a result of legal action or by agreement between the interested parties, to give the debtor a more feasible arrangement with the creditors for meeting the financial obligations. The management may also voluntarily restructure debt, for example by replacing long-term debt with short-term debt.

decision making The act of deciding between two or more alternative courses of action. In the running of a business, accounting information and techniques are used to facilitate decision making, especially by the provision of decision models, such as *discounted cash flow, *critical-path analysis, *marginal costing, and *breakeven analysis.

decision model A model that simulates the elements or variables inherent in a business decision, together with their relationships to each other and the constraints under which they operate; the purpose of the model is to enable a solution to be arrived at in keeping with the objectives of the organization. For example, a *linear programming decision model may arrive at a particular production mix that, having regard to the constraints that exist, either minimizes costs or maximizes the contribution. Other decision models include *decision trees, *discounted cash flow, *breakeven analysis, and *budgets.

decision support system (DSS) A computer system specifically designed to assist managers in making unstructured decisions, i.e. the nature of the problem requiring a decision is not known in advance. A language subsystem will need to be included in the DSS to allow managers to communicate easily with the system. A problem processing subsystem, such as a *spreadsheet, will be required. The system should have a store of internal data and be able to access external data.

decision table A table used to aid decision making. The table shows the problems requiring actions to be considered and estimated probabilities of outcomes. Where probabilities are difficult to estimate, the maximax and maximin criteria are often used, the former leading to the selection of the option with the greatest maximum outcome, the latter to the selection of the action with the greatest minimum outcome.

decision trees Diagrams that illustrate the choices available to a decision maker and the estimated outcomes of each possible decision. Each possible decision is shown as a separate branch of the tree, together with each estimated outcome for each decision and the subjective *probabilities of these outcomes actually occurring. From this information the *expected values for each outcome can be determined, which can provide valuable information in decision making.

declaration of dividend A statement in which the directors of a company announce that a *dividend of a certain amount is recommended to be paid to the shareholders. The *liability should be recognized as soon as the declaration has been made and the appropriate amount is included under *current liabilities on the *balance sheet. The company pays the dividend net of income tax to the shareholders and pays the tax due in the form of *advance corporation tax.

declining balance method *See* diminishing-balance method.

deed of arrangement A document drawn up and registered with the Department of Trade and Industry within seven days of a *scheme of arrangement being agreed.

deed of covenant *See* covenant.

deed of partnership A *partnership agreement drawn up in the form of a deed. It covers the respective *capital contributions of the partners, their entitlement to interest on their capital, their profit-sharing percentages, agreed salary, etc.

deed of variation A written deed that identifies the specific provisions of a will to be varied. It must be signed by any person who would otherwise have benefited from the will as originally drawn. No payment or inducement must pass between the *beneficiaries in order to encourage them to enter into the variation. In order to apply, the deed must have been executed within two years of the testator's death and must have been filed within six months of the deed being executed.

deep discount A loan stock issued at a discount of more than 15% of the amount on redemption or, if less, at a discount of more than 1/2% for each completed year between issue and redemption. The discount will be treated as income accruing over the life of the stock. For example, a **deep-discount bond** might be a four-year loan stock issued at £95 for every £100 nominal (the discount exceeds 1/2% per annum) or a 25-year loan stock issued at £75 for every £100 nominal (the discount exceeds 15% in total). On **deep-discount securities** the discount is normally chargeable to tax. There are new proposals to tax all discounts.

deep-gain security A security issued at a *deep discount or redeemed at a premium. The terms of the issue mean that the amount of discount or premium cannot be allocated evenly over the life of the bond. From 14 March 1989 the whole of the excess of the proceeds over the cost became assessable for income tax.

deep market A market in which a large number of transactions can take place without moving the price of the underlying commodity, currency, or financial instrument. *Compare* thin market.

deep pocket A description of a person or company who appears to have an apparently endless supply of money and would, therefore, be worth suing. The big accountancy firms are protected by professional-liability insurance and can therefore be said to have deep pockets.

defalcation Embezzlement of property belonging to another party.

default A failure to fulfil a contractual or other legal obligation. Defaults include failure to settle a debt, failure to defend legal proceedings, failure to submit a *value added tax (VAT) return on time or to make a VAT payment on the appropriate date. In the case of a VAT default, a *surcharge liability notice is served on the *taxable person.

defeasance Irrevocably committing specific assets to meet long-term obligations. It provides a method of eliminating from a company's balance sheet liabilities that carry no appropriate right of early repayment. *See* sinking fund.

defective accounts Accounts that do not comply with legislation or *accounting standards. By the terms of the Companies Act (1989) a company producing such accounts may be called on to issue revised accounts. Although an apparently modest legislative change, it has done much to enhance the authority of the *Financial Reporting Review Panel.

defended takeover bid A *takeover bid for a company in which the directors of the target company oppose the bid.

defensive interval ratio A ratio that demonstrates the ability of a business to satisfy its current debts by calculating the time for which it can operate on current liquid assets, without needing revenue from the next period's sales. Current assets less stock is divided by the projected daily operational expenditure less non-cash charges. Projected daily operational expenditure is calculated by dividing by 365 the total of the cost of goods sold, operating expenses, and other cash expenses.

deferred annuity An *annuity in which payments do not start at once but either at a specified later date or when the policyholder reaches a specified age.

deferred asset *See* deferred debit.

deferred consideration agreement An agreement in which payment of the consideration is delayed either until a certain date or until a specified and certain event has occurred.

deferred credit (deferred liability) Income received or recorded before it is earned, under the *accruals concept. The income will not be included in the *profit and loss account of the period but will be carried forward on the *balance sheet until it is matched with the period in which it is earned. A common example of a deferred credit is a government grant. The grant is shown as a separate item or under *creditors in the balance sheet, and an annual amount is transferred to the profit and loss account until the deferred credit balance is brought to nil.

deferred debit (deferred asset; deferred expense) An item of expenditure incurred in an accounting period but, under the *accruals concept, not matched with the income it will generate. Instead of being treated as an operating cost for that period, it is treated as an *asset with the intention of treating it as an operating cost to be charged against the income it will generate in a future period.

deferred income A payment received in advance of the period to which it relates. Under the *accruals concept credit will not be taken for it in the *profit and loss account of the period; instead it will be shown as a deferred *credit balance in the *balance sheet. Amounts are transferred from the deferred credit balance to the profit and loss account of future periods until the deferred credit balance in the balance sheet is brought to nil.

deferred liability *See* deferred credit.

deferred ordinary share 1. A type of ordinary share, formerly often issued to founder members of a company, in which dividends are paid only after all other types of ordinary share have been paid. Such shares often entitle their owners to a large share of the profit. 2. A type of share on which little or no dividend is paid for a fixed number of years, after which it ranks with other ordinary shares for dividend.

deficit A loss that results when expenditure exceeds income.

defined-benefit pension scheme An occupational pension scheme in which the rules specify the benefits to be received on retirement and the scheme is funded accordingly. The benefits are normally calculated on a formula incorporating years of service and salary levels. Accounting for pension costs poses a number of difficulties for accountants; *Statement of Standard Accounting Practice 24 provides the regulations. *Compare* defined-contribution pension scheme.

defined-contribution pension scheme A pension scheme in which the benefits are based on the value of the contributions paid in by each member. The rate of contribution is normally specified; the amount of pension an individual will receive will depend on the size of the fund accumulated and the annuity that can be obtained from it at the date of retirement. *Compare* defined-benefit pension scheme.

deflation The opposite of *inflation, in which there is a general decrease in prices.

defunct company A company that has been wound up and has therefore ceased to exist.

delivery lead time The delay between the time at which an order is placed to replenish an item of *stock and the receipt of the item ordered.

Delphi technique A technique for predicting a future event or outcome, in which a group of experts are asked to make their forecasts, initially independently, and subsequently by consensus in order to discard any extreme views. In some circumstances subjective *probabilities can be assigned to the possible future outcomes in order to arrive at a conclusion.

demerger A business strategy in which a large company or group of companies splits up so that its activities are carried on by two or more independent companies. Alternatively, subsidiaries of a group are sold off. Demerging was popular in the late 1980s when large conglomerates became unfashionable.

department A discrete section of an organization under the responsibility of a **department manager**; separate costs and, where appropriate, income are allocated or apportioned to the department for the purposes of costing, performance appraisal, and control.

departmental accounting The process of providing accounting information analysed by department, so that each department of an organization can be treated as a separate *cost centre, *revenue centre, or *profit centre (as appropriate) and the department manager can have access to the department's performance.

departmental budget A budget for a particular department of an organization for a budget period. Ideally, it will be produced either by, or in consultation with, the department manager concerned in accordance with the procedures set out in the *budget manual; coordinated with other budgets on which it may have an impact; and agreed with the *budget committee for integration into the master budget, which is submitted to the board of directors for approval.

depletion The using up of an *asset, especially a mineral asset. For example, a quarry is depleted by the extraction of stone. *See also* depletion accounting; wasting asset.

depletion accounting A method of calculating the *depreciation of a *wasting asset, based on the rate at which it is being used. For example, a coal mine could be depreciated on the basis of the rate at which coal is extracted from it.

deposit 1. A sum of money paid by a buyer as part of the sale price of something in order to reserve it. Depending on the terms agreed, the deposit may or may not be returned if the sale is not completed. 2. A sum of money left with an organization, such as a bank, for safekeeping or to earn interest or with a broker, dealer, etc., as a security to cover any trading losses incurred. 3. A sum of money paid as the first instalment on a *hire-purchase agreement. It is usually paid when the buyer takes possession of the goods.

depository receipt A certificate issued by a depository, bank, or other company stating what has been deposited for safekeeping.

deposits in transit Cash receipts that have arrived at a company's bank too late in the current month to be credited to the depositor's bank statement. An adjustment will therefore be required to the *bank reconciliation statement.

depreciable amount The value of a *fixed asset used as the basis for calculating the *depreciation charge for the period. When using the *diminishing-balance method of depreciation, the depreciable amount is the book value of the asset at the end of the previous financial period. However, when the *straight-line method of depreciation is used, the depreciable amount is based on cost, or alternatively on valuation, if the asset has been subject to revaluation at some prior stage.

depreciable asset A fixed asset that is to be the subject of *depreciation.

depreciated cost (depreciated value) *See* net book value.

depreciation 1. The diminution in value of a *fixed asset due to *wear and tear or *obsolescence over an accounting period. A **provision for depreciation** can be computed by means of a number of generally accepted techniques, including the *straight-line method, the *diminishing-balance method, the *sum-of-the-digits method, the *production-unit method, and the *revaluation method. The depreciation reduces the book value of the asset and is charged against income of an organization in the income statement or *profit and loss account. In the UK, Statement of Standard Accounting Practice 12 deals with the subject of depreciation in the accounts. 2. The reduction in value of one currency in relation to other currencies.

depreciation rate The percentage rate used in the *straight-line method and *diminishing-balance method of *depreciation in order to determine the amount of depreciation that should be written off a *fixed asset and charged against income or the profit and loss account.

deprival value *See* current cost accounting; value to the business.

depth of market *See* deep market; thin market.

depth tests Tests of the different control features of an internal-control system, which are linked together to become a *walk-through test. Depth tests differ from walk-through tests in that the sample tested must be representative of the population in order to achieve the compliance objectives. *See* compliance tests.

deputy special commissioner A person appointed by the Lord Chancellor to assist the *Special Commissioners.

deregistration Ceasing to be registered for *value added tax. When a *taxable person ceases to make *taxable supplies, deregistration is compulsory and notification is required within 30 days. Failure to give the required notification may result in a penalty being charged.

deregulation The removal of controls imposed by governments on the operation of markets. Many economists and politicians believe that during this century governments have imposed controls over markets that have little or no justification in economic theory; some have even been economically harmful. For example, in the post-war era, as a result of the Bretton Woods agreements, many governments imposed controls on the flow of capital between countries. In the belief that this was harmful to economic growth, many governments have recently eliminated these restrictions. However, most economists still argue that certain markets should be regulated, particularly if a monopoly is involved.

derivative A financial instrument, the price of which has a strong correlation with a related or underlying commodity, currency, or financial instrument. The most common derivatives are *futures and *options. These standard products can be customized with regard to maturity, quantity, or pricing structure for a particular client. A **derivative market** is a futures or options market derived from a cash market. For example, the market for traded options in shares (the *London International Financial Futures and Options Exchange) is a derivative market of the London Stock Exchange.

derivative action A legal action brought by a shareholder on behalf of a company, when the company cannot itself decide to sue. A company will usually sue in its own name but if those against whom it has a cause of action are in control of the company (i.e. directors or majority shareholders) a shareholder may bring a derivative action. The company will appear as defendant so that it will be bound by, and able to benefit from, the decision. The need to bring such an action must be proved to the court before it can proceed.

desktop evaluation The process of deciding whether a computer system or program can perform a particular task by testing it in realistic, or desktop, circumstances. This contrasts with evaluation on a theoretical basis, using technical data supplied by the manufacturer.

desktop publishing (DTP) An application of computers that enables small companies and individuals to produce reports, advertising, magazines, etc., to near-typeset quality. A typical system comprises a microcomputer, using DTP software, and a laser printer. The capabilities of the software vary with price, although all offer basic page formatting and the ability to use several founts. More elaborate systems enable graphics to be incorporated into the text and simulate many of the functions of professional typesetting systems. A common feature is the ability to preview each page on the computer's screen before it is printed; many DTP systems therefore require a computer with a superior graphics capability. The laser printer is usually capable of printing text and graphics at a resolution of 300 dots per inch, although some programs are capable also of driving typesetting machines, which use resolutions of over 1000 dots per inch.

detection risk The risk that an *auditor will fail to detect any misstatements that have occurred. Unlike the *control risk and the inherent risk, the level of the detection risk can be directly controlled by the auditor, who can modify his programme of testing. *See* audit risk.

devaluation A fall in the value of a currency relative to gold or to other currencies. Governments engage in devaluation when they feel that their currency has become overvalued, for example through high rates of inflation making exports uncompetitive or because of a substantially adverse balance of trade. The intention is that devaluation will make exports cheaper and imports dearer, although the loss of confidence in an economy forced to devalue invariably has an adverse effect. Devaluation is a measure that need only concern governments with a *fixed exchange rate for their currency. With a *floating exchange rate, devaluation or revaluation takes place continuously and automatically (*see* depreciation).

development costs The expenditure incurred by an organization in improving a product or process. The treatment of development costs in the accounts of the organization is determined by the UK Statement of Standard Accounting Practice 13, which deals with the treatment of *research and development costs. If there is a reasonable expectation that the product or process on which the development expenditure is being spent is likely to create future income, the organization may capitalize the expenditure in the balance sheet, to be written off against the income when it arises. In all other circumstances development expenditure must be written off to the profit and loss account as soon as it is incurred.

development gains tax A former UK tax charged on the sale of land subject to development potential. It was abolished in 1976 when the **development land tax** replaced it. This was abolished in 1985.

development-state enterprise In the USA, a business that is employing all its resources to establish itself. Either the planned sales phase has not commenced or no significant revenues have yet been generated.

diary panel A group of shops and shoppers who keep a regular record of all purchases or purchases of selected products, for the purpose of marketing research.

dies non (Latin: short for *dies non juridicus*, a non-juridical day) A day on which no legal business can be transacted; a non-business day.

different costs for different purposes The principle in *management accounting that the management of an organization is likely to need different information, and thus different costs, for the various activities it carries out, especially when making decisions. For example, when calculating the price of a product on a *cost-plus basis, management would need to ensure that all costs, both fixed and variable, are charged to the product. On the other hand, in determining whether or not additional units of a product should be produced, only the variable costs would be relevant to that decision.

differential analysis An assessment of the impact on costs and revenues of specific management decisions.

differential cost A cost that changes as a result of making a specific decision. In *decision making, management is often concerned to know the differential costs as they represent part of the impact on profit of a particular decision. For example, a decision to increase production may in the short term cause total variable costs to increase, in which case the variable costs are the differential costs. In the longer term, an increase in production may only be achieved by an increase in both fixed and variable costs, in which case both fixed and variable costs are differential costs. In every case, differential costs must be compared with *differential revenue to determine whether a decision is profitable.

differential income *See* differential revenue.

differential pricing A method of pricing a product in which the same product is supplied to different customers, or different market segments, at different prices. This approach is based on the principle that to achieve maximum market penetration the price charged should be what a particular market will bear. For example, the prices charged for similar motor vehicles in the UK market have been higher than those charged in the rest of Europe.

differential revenue (differential income) Income that changes in total as the result of a specific decision. *Compare* differential cost.

differentiated marketing Marketing in which provision is made to meet the special needs of consumers. For example, weight watchers require diet drinks and left-handed people require left-handed scissors.

diffusion of innovation The process by which the sale of new products and services spreads among customers. Initially, only those with confidence in the new product or who like taking risks will try it out. Once the innovators have accepted the product, a larger group of early adopters will come into the market. These **opinion leaders** will in turn bring about a wider acceptance by consumers. The diffusion process can be speeded up by making new products more attractive, for example by giving away free samples or by special introductory prices.

dilapidations Disrepair of leasehold premises. The landlord may be liable to repair certain parts of domestic premises (e.g. the structure and exterior, and the sanitary appliances) under the Landlord and Tenant Act (1985) if the lease is for less than seven years. Otherwise, the lease will usually contain a covenant by either the landlord or the tenant obliging them to keep the premises in repair. Under the Landlord and Tenant Act (1985), a landlord cannot enforce a repairing covenant against a tenant by ending the lease prematurely except by first serving a notice on the tenant specifying the disrepair and giving time for the repairs to be carried out. If there is no covenant in the lease, the tenant is under a common-law duty not to damage the premises and must keep them from falling down.

diminishing-balance method (reducing-balance method) A method of computing the *depreciation of a *fixed asset in an accounting period, in which the percentage to be charged against income is based on the depreciated value at the beginning of the period (*see* net book value). This has the effect of reducing the annual depreciation charge against profits year by year. The annual percentage to be applied to the annual depreciated value is determined by the formula:

$$\text{rate of depreciation} = 1 - (S/C)^{1/N},$$

where N = estimated life in years, S = estimated scrap value at the end of its useful life, and C = original cost.

direct charge voucher (DCV) A *prime document that records the purchases of parts and material directly chargeable to a job or process, without passing through the organization's stores. The document gives a description of the items, the commodity codes, the value of the items, and the accounting or cost code to which the items are chargeable.

direct costing *See* marginal costing.

direct cost of sales (direct production cost of sales) The cost of goods sold, expressed as *direct materials, *direct labour, and *direct expenses only. The direct cost of sales excludes any *overhead.

direct costs **1.** Product costs that can be directly traced to a product or *cost unit. They are usually made up of *direct materials (which can be charged directly to the product by means of *materials requisitions), direct labour (charged by means of time sheets, time cards, or computer *direct data entries), and *direct expenses (which are subcontract costs charged by means of an invoice from the subcontractor). The total of direct materials, direct labour, and direct expenses is known as the *prime cost. **2.** Departmental or *cost centre overhead costs that can be traced directly to the appropriate parts of an organization, without the necessity of *cost apportionment. They can therefore be allocated to the cost centres. For example, the costs of a maintenance section that serves only one particular cost centre should be charged directly to that cost centre. *Compare* indirect costs.

direct data entry The process of recording accounting and other transactions directly onto a computer system from individual department terminals. For example, direct labour times spent on jobs or processes can be entered directly into the computer system through a terminal in the operating department. Usually the entry is subjected to tests and constraints to ensure that it complies with certain parameters and to ensure that the system is not corrupted by the inputs from a remote terminal.

direct expense Expenditure that would not be incurred unless a particular *cost unit were produced. Direct expenses are included in the *direct cost of an item.

direct financing lease In the USA, a method used by lessors in *capital leases, in which the lessor has purchased the asset solely for the purpose of leasing it. The minimum lease payments must be collectable and no significant uncertainties should attach to the amount of unreimbursable costs yet to be incurred.

direct hour An hour spent working on a product, service, or *cost unit of an organization. It is usually expressed as a *direct labour hour, *machine hour, or *standard hour.

direct labour Workers directly concerned with the production of a product, service, or *cost unit, such as machine operators, assembly and finishing operators, etc. *Compare* indirect labour.

direct labour cost (direct wages) Expenditure on wages paid to those operators who are directly concerned with the production of a product, service, or *cost unit. It is one of the *cost classifications making up the *prime cost of a cost unit; it is quantified as the product of the time spent on each activity (collected by means of time sheets or job cards) and the rate of pay of each operator concerned. A percentage of the direct labour cost is sometimes used as a basis for absorbing production overheads to the cost unit in *absorption costing.

direct labour efficiency variance (labour efficiency variance) The *expenditure variance arising in a *standard costing system as part of the total direct labour cost variance. It compares the actual labour time taken to carry out an activity with the standard time allowed and values the difference at the *standard direct labour rate per hour. The resultant adverse or favourable variance is the amount by which the budgeted profit is affected by virtue of labour efficiency. The formula for this variance is:

(standard hours allowed for production – actual hours taken) × standard rate per *direct labour hour.

See also efficiency variances.

direct labour hour An hour spent working on a product, service, or *cost unit produced by an organization by those operators whose time can be directly traced to the production. The direct labour hour is sometimes used as a basis for absorbing *production overheads to the cost unit in *absorption costing.

direct labour hour rate (labour hour rate) **1.** The individual rate of pay per hour paid to operators categorized as *direct labour. **2.** An *absorption rate used in *absorption costing. It is obtained by the following formula:

(budgeted cost centre overheads)/(budgeted direct labour hours).

direct labour rate of pay variance (labour rate variance) The *expenditure variance arising in a *standard costing system as part of the *direct labour total cost variance. It compares the actual rate paid to direct labour for an activity with the *standard rate of pay allowed for that activity for the actual hours worked. The resultant adverse or favourable variance is the amount by which the budgeted profit is affected by differences in direct labour rates of pay. The formulae for this variance are:

(standard rate per hour – actual rate per hour) × actual hours worked, or alternatively:

(standard rate per hour × actual hours worked) – actual wages paid.

direct labour total cost variance The combination of the *direct labour rate of pay variance and the *direct labour efficiency variance; it compares the actual cost and the standard cost of the direct labour incurred in carrying out the actual production. The formula for this variance is:

(standard rate per hour × actual hours worked) – actual labour cost.

direct materials Materials that are directly incorporated in the final *product or *cost unit of an organization. For example, in the production of furniture, direct materials would include wood, glue, and paint. *Compare* indirect materials.

direct materials cost Expenditure on *direct materials. It is one of the *cost classifications that make up the *prime cost of a *cost unit and is ascertained by collecting together the quantities of each material used on each product by means of *materials requisitions and multiplying the quantities by the cost per unit of each material. A percentage on direct materials cost is sometimes used as a basis for absorbing production overheads to the cost unit in *absorption costing.

direct materials inventory *See* direct materials stocks.

direct materials mix variance Part of the *direct materials usage variance arising in *standard costing, the difference between the total material used in standard proportions and the material used in actual proportions, valued at standard prices (*see* standard purchase price; standard selling price).

direct materials price variance The *expenditure variance arising in a *standard costing system as part of the *direct materials total cost variance. There are two alternative points at which the materials price variance may be established, either when the material is purchased or when it is issued to production. When established on issue to production, it compares the actual price paid for direct material used in a product with the *standard purchase price of the material consumed. When established on purchase, it compares the actual price paid for the direct material purchased with the standard price allowed for the purchased material. The resultant adverse or favourable variance is the amount by which the budgeted profit is affected by differences in direct material prices. The formulae for this variance are:
(standard price per unit of material − actual price per unit of material) × actual units consumed or purchased,
or alternatively:
(standard price per unit of material × actual units consumed or purchased) − actual material cost.

direct materials stocks (direct materials inventory) The list of raw materials in store awaiting transfer to production, after which the materials are incorporated into *work in progress.

direct materials total cost variance A combination of the *direct materials price variance and the *direct materials usage variance; it compares the actual cost and the standard cost of the direct material consumed in carrying out the actual production. The formula for this variance is:
(standard price per unit of material × actual units of material consumed) − actual material cost.

direct materials usage variance The *expenditure variance arising in a *standard costing system as part of the *direct materials total cost variance. It compares the actual quantity of material used to carry out production with the standard quantity allowed, and values the difference at the standard material price per unit. The resultant adverse or favourable variance is the amount by which the budgeted profit is affected by virtue of material usage. The formula for this variance is:

(standard quantity of material allowed for production – actual quantity used) × standard price per unit of material.

direct materials yield variance Part of the *direct materials usage variance arising in *standard costing; it is the difference between the total standard quantity of material allowed for a process in standard proportions and the total actual material used, also in standard proportions, valued at standard prices (*see* standard purchase price; standard selling price).

direct method A method of preparing a *cash-flow statement under Financial Reporting Standard 1, in which operating cash receipts and payments are aggregated to show the net cash flow from operating activities.

director A person appointed to carry out the day-to-day management of a company. A public company must have at least two directors, a private company at least one. The directors of a company, collectively known as the **board of directors**, usually act together, although power may be conferred (by the *articles of association) on one or more directors to exercise executive powers; in particular there is often a managing director with considerable executive power.

The first directors of a company are usually named in its articles of association or are appointed by the subscribers; they are required to give a signed undertaking to act in that capacity, which must be sent to the *Registrar of Companies. Subsequent directors are appointed by the company at a general meeting, although in practice they may be appointed by the other directors for ratification by the general meeting. Directors may be discharged from office by an ordinary resolution with special notice at a general meeting, whether or not they have a *service contract in force. They may be disqualified for fraudulent trading or *wrongful trading or for any conduct that makes them unfit to manage the company.

Directors owe duties of honesty and loyalty to the company (fiduciary duties) and a duty of care; their liability in negligence depends upon their personal qualifications (e.g. a chartered accountant must exercise more skill than an unqualified man). Directors need no formal qualifications. Directors may not put their own interests before those of the company, may not make contracts (other than service contracts) with the company, and must declare any personal interest in work undertaken by the company. Their formal responsibilities include: presenting to members of the company, at least annually, the *accounts of the company and a *directors' report; keeping a register of directors, a register of directors' shareholdings, and a register of shares; calling an *annual general meeting; sending all relevant documents to the Registrar of Companies; and submitting a statement of affairs if the company is wound up (*see* liquidator).

*Directors' remuneration consists of a salary and in some cases **directors' fees**, paid to them for being a director, and an expense allowance to cover their expenses incurred in the service of the company. Directors' remuneration must be disclosed in the company's accounts and shown separately from any pension payments or *compensation for loss of office. *See also* Cadbury Report; directors or higher-paid employees; executive director; non-executive director; shadow director.

directors' interests The interests held by *directors in the shares and debentures of the company of which they are a director. The directors' interests can also include options on shares and debentures of the company. These interests must be disclosed to comply with the *Companies Acts.

directors or higher-paid employees A higher-paid employee is defined in the UK as one earning more than £8500 per annum. This amount includes remuneration together with benefits and reimbursed expenses. The £8500 limit was set in 1979. For directors there is no earnings limit. The employer must account to the Inland Revenue, on form P11D, for all the benefits received by the employee or director. These benefits are assessed at the cost to the employer, although special rules apply to certain benefits, e.g. company cars.

directors' remuneration (directors' emoluments) The amounts received by directors from their office or employment, including all salaries, fees, wages, perquisites, and other profit as well as certain expenses and benefits paid or provided by the employer, which are deemed to be remuneration or emoluments.

directors' report An annual report by the directors of a company to its shareholders, which forms parts of the company's *accounts required to be filed with the Registrar of Companies under the Companies Act (1985). The information that must be given includes the principal activities of the company, a fair review of the developments and position of the business with likely future developments, details of research and development, significant issues on the sale, purchase, or valuation of assets, recommended dividends, transfers to reserves, names of the directors and their interests in the company during the period, employee statistics, and any political or charitable gifts made during the period. *See also* medium-sized company; small company.

direct production cost of sales *See* direct cost of sales.

direct wages *See* direct labour cost.

direct worker An operator in an organization whose time is spent working on the product or *cost unit produced to such an extent that the operator's time is traceable to the product as a *direct cost. *See also* direct labour cost.

direct write-off method In the USA, the procedure of writing off bad debts as they occur instead of creating a provision for them. Although this practice is unacceptable for financial reporting purposes, as it ignores the *matching concept and *prudence concept, it is the only method allowed for tax purposes.

disbursement A payment made by a professional person, such as a solicitor or banker, on behalf of a client. This is claimed back when the client receives an account for the professional services.

disclaimer of opinion The opinion expressed by an *auditor when the *audit report is being qualified as a result of the effect of a limitation on the scope of an audit. If the limitation of scope is so material that the auditor has not been able to obtain sufficient evidence to support an opinion on the financial statements, he or she must express a disclaimer of opinion. *See also* qualified audit report.

disclosure The provision of financial and non-financial information, on a regular basis, to those interested in the economic activities of an organization. The information is normally given in an *annual report and accounts (*see* annual accounts), which includes *financial statements and other financial and non-financial information. The annual report and accounts of a limited company is regulated by company legislation, *accounting standards, and, in the case of a quoted company, by stock exchange regulations.

discontinued operations The operations of a reporting entity that has been sold or permanently closed down in a period or before the earlier of three months after the commencement of the subsequent period and the date on which the financial statements are approved. According to *Financial Reporting Standard 3, if the sale or termination has a material effect on the reporting entity's operations and the assets, liabilities, and results are clearly distinguishable, the *profit and loss account should show the results of these operations separately.

discount 1. A deduction from a *bill of exchange when it is purchased before its maturity date. The party that purchases (discounts) the bill pays less than its face value and therefore makes a profit when it matures. The amount of the discount consists of interest calculated at the *bill rate for the length of time that the bill has to run. 2. A reduction in the price of goods below list price, for buyers who pay cash (*see* cash discount), for members of the trade (*see* trade discount), for buying in bulk (**bulk** or **quantity discount**), etc. 3. The amount by which the market price of a security is below its *par value. A £100 par value loan stock with a market price of £95 is said to be at a 5% discount.

discount allowed A discount granted by a company to a client, for example for a bulk purchase or a prompt payment. It is shown as an expense in the *profit and loss account.

discounted cash flow (DCF) A method of *capital budgeting or *capital expenditure appraisal that predicts the stream of cash flows, both inflows and outflows, over the estimated life of a project and discounts them, using a *cost of capital or *hurdle rate, to *present values or discounted values in order to determine whether the project is likely to be financially feasible. A number of appraisal approaches use the DCF principle, namely the *net present value, the *internal rate of return, and the *profitability index. Most computer spreadsheet programs now include a DCF appraisal routine.

discounted value *See* present value.

discount factor (present-value factor) A factor that, when multiplied by a particular year's predicted cash flow, brings the cash flow to a *present value. The factor takes into consideration the number of years from the inception of the project and the *hurdle rate that the project is expected to earn before it can be regarded as feasible. The factor is computed using the formula:
$$\text{discount factor} = 1/(1 + r)^t,$$
where r = hurdle rate required and t = the number of years from project inception.

In practice there is little necessity to compute discount factors when carrying out appraisal calculations as they are readily available in discount tables. Most computer spreadsheet programs now include a *discounted cash flow routine, which also obviates the need for using discount factors.

discounting 1. The application of *discount factors to each year's cash flow projections in a *discounted cash flow appraisal calculation. **2.** The process of selling a *bill of exchange before its maturity at a price below its face value.

discount rate The *hurdle rate of interest or *cost of capital rate applied to the *discount factors used in a *discounted cash flow appraisal calculation. The discount rate may be based on the cost-of-capital rate adjusted by a risk factor based on the risk characteristics of the proposed investment in order to create a hurdle rate that the project must earn before being worthy of consideration. Alternatively, the discount rate may be the interest rate that the funds used for the project could earn elsewhere.

discount received A discount granted to a supplier, for example for a bulk purchase or a prompt payment. It is shown as a credit in the *profit and loss account.

discovery value accounting In the USA, the method of accounting used for extractive enterprises, such as oil and gas.

discretionary costs (managed costs) Costs incurred as a result of a managerial decision; the extent of these costs is consequently subject to managerial discretion. A characteristic of such costs is that they are often for a specified amount or subject to a specific formula, such as a percentage of sales revenue. Examples include advertising and research expenditure.

discretionary trust A trust in which the shares of each beneficiary are not fixed by the settlor in the trust deed but may be varied at the discretion of some person or persons (often the trustees). In an **exhaustive discretionary trust** all the income arising in any year must be paid out during that year, although no beneficiary has a right to any specific sum. In a **nonexhaustive discretionary trust** (or **accumulation trust**), income may be carried forward to subsequent years and no beneficiary need receive anything. Such trusts are useful when the needs of the beneficiaries are likely to change, for example when they are children.

discussion memorandum In the USA, a document published by the *Financial Accounting Standards Board before issuing a *Statement of Financial Accounting Standard. The document specifies the topic under consideration, describes the alternative accounting treatments, and explains the perceived advantages and disadvantages of each treatment.

dishonour 1. To fail to pay a cheque when the account of the drawer does not have sufficient funds to cover it. When a bank dishonours a cheque it marks it 'refer to drawer' and returns it to the payee through his or her bank. **2.** To fail to accept a *bill of exchange (**dishonour by non-acceptance**) or to fail to pay a bill of exchange (**dishonour by non-payment**).

disintermediation Cutting out such middlemen as brokers and bankers. For example, individuals or companies with spare cash, instead of depositing it with a bank, lend it direct to an end-user. *Commercial paper is an example of disintermediation, in which companies borrow from each other. The improvement in cost has to be offset by the increase in the *credit risk.

disposals account An account used to record the disposal of a fixed *asset. The original cost (a debit entry), *accumulated depreciation (a credit entry), and the amount received (credit entry) are transferred to the account, the balancing figure being any profit (debit entry) or loss (credit entry) on disposal.

disposal value *See* net residual value.

disproportionate expense and undue delay A reason for excluding an individual subsidiary undertaking from the *consolidated financial statements of a group. It concerns a situation in which there would be a relatively high cost and an excessive time lag in obtaining the information necessary for the preparation of the consolidated accounts. *Financial Reporting Standard 2, 'Accounting for Subsidiary Undertakings', seeks to narrow this exclusion by stating that disproportionate expense and undue delay cannot justify the exclusion from consolidation of subsidiary undertakings that are individually or collectively material in the context of the group. *See also* exclusion of subsidiaries from consolidation.

dissimilar activities A situation in which the activities of one undertaking in a group are so different from those of the other group undertakings that its inclusion in *consolidated financial statements would be incompatible with the obligation to give a true and fair view of the activities of the group. This exclusion may not be used merely because some of the undertakings are industrial, some commercial, and some provide services, for example. Nor is exclusion permitted merely because the industrial or commercial activities involve different products or provide different services. *Financial Reporting Standard 2, 'Accounting for Subsidiary Undertakings', states that it would be unusual for activities to be so different that the exclusion of the subsidiary undertakings would be appropriate. In the unlikely case that it were appropriate to use this exclusion, the excluded subsidiary should be recorded in the consolidated financial statements, using the *equity method of accounting. *See also* exclusion of subsidiaries from consolidation.

dissolution The ending of a business entity, for example the breaking up of a *partnership on the death of one of the partners.

distributable profits The profits of a company that are legally available for distribution as *dividends. They consist of a company's accumulated realized profits after deducting all realized losses, except for any part of these net realized profits that have been previously distributed or capitalized. Public companies, however, may not distribute profits to such an extent that their net assets are reduced to less than the sum of their called-up capital (*see* share capital) and their undistributable reserves (*see* capital reserves).

distributable reserves The retained profits of a company that it may legally distribute by way of *dividends. *See* distributable profits.

distributed logic A computer system that supplements the main computer with remote terminals capable of doing some of the computing, or with electronic devices capable of making simple decisions, distributed throughout the system. *See also* distributed processing.

distributed processing A system of processing data in which several computers are used at various locations within an organization instead of using one central computer. The computers may be linked to each other in a network, allowing them to cooperate, or they may be linked to a larger central computer, although a significant amount of the processing is done without reference to the central computer.

distribution 1. A payment by a company from its *distributable profits, usually by means of a *dividend. 2. A dividend or quasi-dividend on which *advance corporation tax is payable. For UK tax purposes a distribution includes, in addition to dividends, any payment, whether in cash or kind, out of the assets of a company in respect of shares of that company, except repayments of capital. 3. The allocation of goods to consumers by means of wholesalers and retailers. 4. The division of property and assets according to law, e.g. of a bankrupt person or a deceased person. *See also* qualifying distribution.

distribution centre A warehouse, usually owned by a manufacturer, that receives goods in bulk and despatches them to retailers.

distribution channel The network of firms necessary to distribute goods or services from the manufacturers to the consumers; it therefore primarily consists of wholesalers and retailers.

distribution overhead (distribution cost; distribution expense) The *cost classification that includes the costs incurred in delivering a product to the customers. Examples include postage, transport, packaging, and insurance.

distribution to owners In the USA, a payment of a *dividend to shareholders (stockholders).

distributor An intermediary, or one of a chain of intermediaries (*see* distribution channel), that specializes in transferring a manufacturer's goods or services to the consumers.

diversification 1. Movement by a manufacturer or trader into a wider field of products. This may be achieved by buying firms already serving the target markets or by expanding existing facilities. It is often undertaken to reduce reliance on one market, which may be diminishing (e.g. tobacco), to balance a seasonal market (e.g. ice cream), or to provide scope for general growth. 2. The spreading of an investment portfolio over a wide range of companies to avoid serious losses if a recession is localized to one sector of the market.

divestment 1. The act of realizing the value of an asset by selling or exchanging it. It is the opposite of investment. 2. The selling of or closing down of one or more of a business's operating activities.

dividend The distribution of part of the earnings of a company to its shareholders. The dividend is normally expressed as an amount per share on the *par value of the share. Thus a 15% dividend on a £1 share will pay 15p. However, investors are usually more interested in the **dividend yield** (or **gross dividend yield**), i.e. the dividend expressed as a percentage of the share value; thus if the market value of these £1 shares is now £5, the dividend yield would be $1/5 \times 15\% = 3\%$. The size of the dividend payment is determined by the board of directors of a company, who must decide how much to pay out to shareholders and how much to retain in the business; these amounts may vary from year to year. In the UK it is usual for companies to pay a dividend every six months, the largest portion (the **final dividend**) being announced at the company's AGM together with the annual financial results. A smaller **interim dividend** usually accompanies the interim statement of the company's affairs, six months before the AGM. Dividends are paid by *dividend warrant in the UK. This is accompanied by a **tax voucher** stating that the *advance corporation tax will be paid to the Inland Revenue for the amount shown on the voucher as a *tax credit. In the USA dividends are usually paid quarterly by **dividend check**. *See also* dividend cover; yield.

Interest payments on *gilt-edged securities are also sometimes called dividends although they are fixed.

dividend control (dividend limitation) Regulations limiting the amount of dividend that may be paid to shareholders, which have been imposed by the UK government on a number of occasions, usually as part of a prices and incomes policy as a counterpart to a wage freeze.

dividend cover The number of times a company's *dividends to ordinary shareholders could be paid out of its *net profits after tax in the same period. For example, a net dividend of £400,000 paid by a company showing a net profit of £1M is said to be covered 2   times. Dividend cover is a measure of the probability that dividend payments will be sustained (low cover might make it difficult to pay the same level of dividends in a bad year's trading) and of a company's commitment to investment and growth (high cover implies that the company retains its earnings for investment in the business). Negative dividend cover is unusual, and is taken as a sign that a company is in difficulties. In the USA, the dividend cover is expressed as the **pay-out ratio**, the total dividends paid as a percentage of the net profit. *See also* price–dividend ratio.

dividend-growth model A method for calculating the cost of capital for a company, using the dividends paid and likely to be paid by the company.

dividend limitation *See* dividend control.

dividend policy A company's policy on the extent to which *profits should be distributed by way of *dividends to shareholders and on the extent to which profits should be retained in the business.

dividends in arrears Dividends that are due but have not been paid. Dividends in arrears must be disclosed in the notes to the *financial statements of a company. *See* preference dividend.

dividends payable Any *dividends that have been declared by a company but not yet paid. They are shown as an *appropriation in the *profit and loss account and a *current liability in the *balance sheet.

dividend waiver A decision by a major shareholder in a company not to take a dividend, usually because the company cannot afford to pay it.

dividend warrant The cheque issued by a company to its shareholders when paying *dividends. It states the tax deducted and the net amount paid. This document must be sent by non-taxpayers to the Inland Revenue when claiming back the tax.

dividend yield (gross dividend yield) *See* dividend.

division A part of an organization, usually an *investment centre or *profit centre, which, although ultimately responsible to head office, enjoys a degree of autonomy in terms of decisions. Divisions usually operate in clearly defined product, market, or geographical areas, and are formed to facilitate decision making and control in large organizations.

divisional performance measurement The way in which the central management of an organization measures the performance of each of the individual divisions in a divisionalized structure. Methods used include *return on capital employed, *residual income, and profit-to-sales ratio.

documentary credit *See* letter of credit.

documentary draft Any order in writing requiring the recipient to pay the amount specified on the face of the document, either on presentation of the document (**sight draft**) or at a fixed future date (**time draft**).

dollar value LIFO In the USA, a method of expressing the value of an *inventory in monetary values rather than units. Each homogeneous group of inventory items is converted into base-year prices by using the appropriate price indices. The difference between opening and closing inventories is a measure in monetary terms of the change in the financial period.

domestic corporation A corporation (company) established in the USA under federal or state law.

domicile (domicil) 1. The country or place of a person's permanent home, which may differ from that person's nationality or place where they are a *resident. Domicile is determined by both the physical fact of residence and the continued intention of remaining there. For example, a citizen of a foreign country who is resident in the UK is not necessarily domiciled there unless there is a clear intention to make the UK a permanent home. Under the common law, it is domicile and not residence or nationality that determines a person's civil status, including the capacity to marry. A corporation may also have a domicile, which is determined by its place of registration. Under English law a child normally takes the domicile of its father unless the child is illegitimate or the parents divorce, when the child takes its mother's domicile. The **domicile of choice** is the domicile an individual chooses to take up. It involves taking up permanent residence in a country other than the **domicile of origin** with the intention of never returning to live in the original country. The domicile of origin is acquired at birth and is usually that of the father except in the case of illegitimate children or those of divorced parents, when the child takes the mother's domicile. In order to prove that the domicile of origin has been relinquished in favour of the domicile of choice, tangible changes have to be made. Links with the country of origin must be severed and active steps taken to become involved with the country that is the domicile of choice, e.g. by making a will under the laws of the domicile of choice. The status of domicile of choice will be kept under review and if actions are subsequently taken to re-establish links with the domicile of origin, the individual's domicile could revert to the domicile of origin. The **domicile of dependency** was a concept that applied to women whose marriage took place prior to 1 January 1974. In these circumstances the woman acquired the domicile of her husband. For marriages since 31 December 1973 the position is determined under the provisions of the Domicile and Matrimonial Proceedings Act (1973), which allows a woman to retain her own domicile of origin or domicile of choice on marriage, if it differs from that of her husband.

2. In banking, an account is said to be domiciled at a particular branch and the customer treats that branch as his or her main banking contact. Customers may be charged for using other branches as if they were their own. Computer technology, however, now allows customers to use many branches as if their account was domiciled there.

dominant influence An influence that can be exercised over a company to achieve the operating and financial policies desired by the holder of the influence, notwithstanding the rights or influence of any other party. If one organization exerts such a dominant influence over a company, this company should be treated as a subsidiary of the organization and consolidated into the *group accounts of the organization. This principle is made clear in *Financial Reporting Standard 2, 'Accounting for Subsidiary Undertakings'.

donated capital In the USA, a gift of an asset to a company. The value is credited to a donated-capital account, which is a stockholders' equity account.

dormant company A company that has had no significant accounting transactions for the accounting period in question. Such a company need not appoint auditors.

double account system A now outdated way of presenting *financial statements, used by railways and public utilities prior to privatization.

double declining balance method A method of *depreciation in which the historical cost (or revalued amount) of an *asset less its estimated residual value (*see* net residual value) is divided by the number of years of its estimated useful life and the resulting amount is multiplied by two to give the depreciation figure. For example, in the first year an asset costing £12,000 with an estimated residual value of £2000 and an estimated useful life of 10 years would have a depreciation charge of £2000, i.e. $2 \times [(£12,000 - £2000)/10]$.

double-entry book-keeping A method of recording the transactions of a business in a set of *accounts, such that every transaction has a dual aspect and therefore needs to be recorded in at least two accounts. For example, when a person (debtor) pays cash to a business for goods he has purchased, the cash held by the business is increased and the amount due from the debtor is decreased by the same amount; similarly, when a purchase is made on credit, the stock is decreased and the amount owing to creditors is increased by the same amount. This double aspect enables the business to be controlled because all the *books of accounts must balance.

double-entry cost accounting The maintenance of *cost accounting records using the principles of *double-entry book-keeping.

double taxation agreement An agreement made between two countries identifying the relief available to companies or individuals that are subject to tax in both countries.

double taxation relief Relief available when income or gains are liable to tax in more than one country. Double taxation relief is given under the provisions of a *double taxation agreement between the UK and the country concerned, if one exists, or it can be given unilaterally.

doubtful debts Money owed to an organization, which it is unlikely to receive. A provision for doubtful debts may be created, which may be based on specific debts or on the general assumption that a certain percentage of debtors' amounts are doubtful. As the doubtful debt becomes a *bad debt, it may be written off to the provision for doubtful debts or alternatively charged to the *profit and loss account if there is no provision. *See* provision for bad debts.

DP Abbreviation for *data processing.

draft **1.** *See* bank draft. **2.** Any order in writing to pay a specified sum, e.g. a *bill of exchange. **3.** A preliminary version of a document, before it has been finalized.

dragon bond A US dollar *bond issued in the Asian bond markets.

drawback The refund of import duty by the Customs and Excise when imported goods are re-exported. Payment of the import duty and claiming the drawback can be avoided if the goods are stored in a bonded warehouse immediately after unloading from the incoming ship or aircraft until re-export.

drawdown The drawing of funds against a bank loan, especially a *revolving bank facility.

drawee **1.** The person on whom a *bill of exchange is drawn (i.e. to whom it is addressed). The drawee will accept it and pay it on maturity. **2.** The bank on whom a cheque is drawn, i.e. the bank holding the account of the individual or company that wrote it. **3.** The bank named in a *bank draft. *Compare* drawer.

drawer **1.** A person who signs a *bill of exchange ordering the *drawee to pay the specified sum at the specified time. **2.** A person who signs a cheque ordering the drawee bank to pay a specified sum of money on demand.

drawings *Assets (cash or goods) withdrawn from an unincorporated business by its owner. If a business is incorporated, drawings are usually in the form of *dividends or *scrip dividends. Drawings are shown in a **drawings account**, which is used, for example, by the partners in a *partnership.

drop lock A new form of issue in the bond market that combines the benefits of a bank loan with the benefits of a bond. The borrower arranges a variable-rate bank loan on the understanding that if long-term interest rates fall to a specified level, the bank loan will be automatically refinanced by a placing of fixed-rate long-term bonds with a group of institutions.

DSS Abbreviation for *decision support system.

dual aspect The principle that every financial event has an aspect that gives rise to a *debit entry and an aspect that gives rise to a *credit entry.

dual-capacity system A system of trading on a stock exchange in which the functions of stockjobber and stockbroker are carried out by separate firms. In a **single-capacity system** the two functions can be combined by firms known as *market makers. Dual capacity existed on the *London Stock Exchange prior to

October, 1986 (*see* Big Bang), since when a single-capacity system has been introduced, bringing London into line with most foreign international stock markets. The major advantage of single capacity is that it cuts down on the costs to the investor, although it can also create more opportunity for unfair dealing (*see* Chinese wall).

dual pricing A method of pricing transfers of goods and services when trading takes place between the divisions of an organization. The dual prices method charges a low price, say a price based on the *marginal cost, to the buying division, while at the same time crediting a high price, say a price based on *full cost pricing, to the selling division. The benefit is said to arise by encouraging a buying division to buy within the organization without penalizing a selling division. However, this is only likely to be beneficial to the organization as a whole if the selling division has sufficient spare capacity to supply the buying division's needs. A compensating entry to eliminate unrealized profits is required in the books of the head office when *consolidation of the divisional results takes place.

Du Pont formula A formula for breaking down return on investment into two parts: margin and turnover (*see* return on capital employed). The return on investment = net income/invested capital. This can be restated as:

$$(\text{net income/sales}) \times (\text{sales/invested capital}),$$

i.e. margin × turnover.

duration The average life of the discounted values of the cash flows associated with a *bond.

early repayment tax clause A clause in a loan agreement that allows the loan to be repaid if changes occur to any relevant tax legislation that would have the effect of increasing the amount of interest payable.

earned income The following types of income are treated as earned income:
• income from employment,
• income from trades, professions, and vocations,
• foreign business profits,
• patent and copyright income received by the creator,
• a proportion of the annuity paid to a retired partner.
There is little difference in the tax treatment of earned and unearned income under the present UK taxation system. Previously, however, investment (unearned) income was subject to an additional tax (the investment-income surcharge).

earnings The net income or *profit of a business. Because of the importance of earnings in calculating the *earnings per share, there has been considerable debate as to its definition. Under *Statement of Standard Accounting Practice 6 (SSAP 6) earnings excluded *extraordinary items; this permitted some companies to use *creative accounting to ensure that they reported a high earnings figure. The introduction of *Financial Reporting Standard 3 by the *Accounting Standards Board removed SSAP 6 and amended SSAP 3, concerned with earnings, so that any extraordinary items are now included in the calculation. This has led to a greater volatility in the earnings per share figure.

earnings available for ordinary shareholders The *profit of a company that is available for distribution in the form of a *dividend to the holders of ordinary shares.

earnings before interest and tax (EBIT) The *profit of a company as shown on the *profit and loss account, before deducting the variables of interest and tax. This figure, which is used in calculating many ratios, enables better comparisons to be made with other companies.

earnings per share (eps) The *profit in pence attributable to each *ordinary share in a company, based on the *consolidated profit for the period, after tax and after deducting *minority interests and *preference dividends. This profit figure is divided by the number of equity shares in issue that rank for dividend in respect of the period. The eps may be calculated on a **net basis** or a **nil basis**. Using the net basis, the tax charge includes any irrecoverable *advance corporation tax and any unrelieved overseas tax arising from the payment or proposed payment of dividends (*see* overseas-income taxation). The nil basis excludes both these items from the tax charge. *Statement of Standard Accounting Practice 3, 'Earnings per Share', requires the use of the net basis; the nil basis should also be disclosed if it produces a figure that is materially different from the net basis. The eps should be shown on the face of the *profit and loss account on the net basis, both for the period under review and for the corresponding previous period. The basis of calculating the earnings per share should be disclosed on the face of the profit and loss account or in the notes to the accounts. *See also* fully diluted earnings per share.

earnings retained The *profit of a company after the distribution of *dividends; the earnings retained in the business are used to fund future operations.

earnings yield The ratio of the *earnings per share of a company to the market price of the share, expressed as a percentage. *See also* price–earnings ratio.

earn-out agreement (contingent contract) An agreement to purchase a company in which the purchaser pays a lump sum at the time of the acquisition, with a promise to pay more (a *contingent consideration) if certain criteria, usually specified earnings levels, are met for a specified number of years. This method of acquisition has been popular in 'people' businesses, in particular advertising agencies.

EBIT Abbreviation for *earnings before interest and tax.

ECGD Abbreviation for *Export Credits Guarantee Department.

economic appraisal A method of *capital budgeting that makes use of *discounted cash flow techniques to determine a preferred investment. However, instead of using annual projected cash flows in the analysis, the technique discounts over the project's life the expected annual *economic costs and *economic benefits. It is mainly used in the assessment of governmental or quasi-governmental projects, such as road, railway, and port developments.

economic batch quantity A refinement of the *economic order quantity to take into account circumstances in which the goods are produced in batches. The formula is:
$$Q = [2cdr/h(r - d)]^{1/2},$$
where Q = quantity to be purchased or manufactured, c = cost of processing an order for delivery, d = demand in the period for that stock item, h = cost of holding a unit of stock, and r = rate of production.

economic benefits The projected benefits revealed by an *economic appraisal. Economic benefits are usually gains that can be expressed in financial terms as the result of an improvement in facilities provided by a government, local authority, etc. For example, the economic benefits arising from the construction of a new or improved road might include lower vehicle operating costs, time savings for the road users, and lower accident costs as a result of fewer accidents. In each case the savings would be in economic terms, that is, excluding the effect of taxes and subsidies within the economy. *See also* economic costs.

economic costs The projected costs revealed by an *economic appraisal. Economic costs differ from financial costs in that they exclude the transfer payments within the economy, which arise when an investment is made. In the construction of a road, for example, the economic costs exclude taxes and import duties on the materials and plant used in its construction, while any subsidies made are added back to the costs.

economic exposure The impact on the value of a business of future movements in exchange rates. Nearly all companies have some economic exposure because even if they themselves are not involved in foreign currency transactions, some of their competitors almost certainly are.

economic income Income calculated by comparing the *net present value of future *cash flows at the beginning and end of a period.

economic order quantity (EOQ) A decision model, based on differential calculus, that determines the optimum order size for purchasing (sometimes called the **economic purchase quantity**) or manufacturing (**economic manufacturing quantity**) an item of stock. The optimum order quantity is that which equates the total ordering and total holding costs. The formula used is:
$$Q = \sqrt{(2cd/h)},$$
where Q = quantity to be purchased or manufactured, c = cost of processing an order for delivery, d = demand in the period for that stock item, and h = cost of holding a unit of stock. *See also* economic batch quantity.

economic value The *present value of expected future *cash flows. For example, the economic value of a fixed *asset would be the present value of any future revenues it is expected to generate, less the present value of any future costs related to it.

economies of scale (scale effect) Reductions in the average cost of production, and hence in the unit costs, when output is increased. If the average costs of production rise with output, this is known as **diseconomies of scale**. Economies of scale can enable a producer to offer his product at more competitive prices and thus to capture a larger share of the market. **Internal economies of scale** occur when better use is made of the factors of production and by using the increased output to pay for a higher proportion of the costs of marketing, financing, and development, etc. Internal diseconomies can occur when a plant exceeds its optimum size, e.g. requiring a disproportionate unwieldy administrative staff. **External economies** and diseconomies arise from the effects of a firm's expansion on market conditions and on technological advance.

ECP Abbreviation for *euro-commercial paper.

ECU Abbreviation for *European Currency Unit.

EDI Abbreviation for *electronic data interchange.

EDP Abbreviation for *electronic data processing.

effective annual rate The total interest paid or earned in a year expressed as a percentage of the principal amount at the beginning of the year.

effective units *See* equivalent units.

effective yield *See* gross redemption yield.

efficiency A measure of the ability of an organization to produce and distribute its product. In accounting terms it is quantified by a comparison of the *standard hours allowed for a given level of production and the actual hours taken. This represents the gain or loss due to efficiency, which is usually expressed as a direct labour or overheads *efficiency variance. *See also* efficiency ratio.

efficiency ratio A ratio that measures the efficiency of labour or an activity over a period by dividing the *standard hours allowed for the production by the actual hours taken. It is usually expressed as a percentage, using the formula:

(standard hours allowed × 100)/actual hours worked.

efficiency variances The *expenditure variances that arise in a *standard costing system as part of the total direct labour cost variance and the total production overhead variable cost variance. It compares the actual time taken to carry out an activity with the standard time allowed, and values the difference at either the standard labour rate per hour or the variable overhead recovery rate. The resultant adverse or favourable variance is the amount by which the budgeted profit is affected by either direct labour efficiency or the amount of variable overhead over- or under-recovered due to efficiency. The formulae for this variance are:

Direct labour: (standard hours allowed for production − actual hours taken) × standard rate per *direct labour hour.

Variable overhead: (standard hours allowed for production − actual hours taken) × standard variable overhead *absorption rate.

See also direct labour efficiency variance; overhead efficiency variance.

EFTPOS Abbreviation for *electronic funds transfer at point of sale.

EGM Abbreviation for *extraordinary general meeting.

eighth directive A directive approved by the Council of the EC (now the EU) in 1984. The directive concerns auditing and the regulation of *auditors. The provisions were implemented in the UK by the *Companies Act (1989).

EIS Abbreviation for *enterprise investment scheme.

EITF Abbreviation for *Emerging Issues Task Force.

election to waive exemption *See* option to tax.

elective resolution A form of resolution for private *companies introduced by the Companies Act (1989). It can be passed by the members in general meeting, if at least 21 days' notice in writing has been given, providing the terms of the resolution, and it is passed by all members entitled to attend and vote, whether in person or by proxy. A copy of the resolution must be filed at Companies House; its effect ceases if the company is re-registered as a public company. An *ordinary resolution can be passed to revoke an elective resolution and such a resolution must also be filed at Companies House. An elective resolution may be used in five specified situations concerning:
(1) the directors' authority to allot shares;
(2) dispensing with the laying of accounts in a general meeting;
(3) dispensing with the *annual general meeting;
(4) the appointment of *auditors;
(5) the holding of *extraordinary general meetings.

electronic data interchange (EDI) The exchange of data between organizations by electronic means rather than by paper. Its principal benefit is that it is faster.

electronic data processing (EDP) The processing of data by electronic means rather than manually or by mechanical means. Most organizations are now computerized and keep their accounts on EDP systems.

electronic funds transfer at point of sale (EFTPOS) The automatic debiting of a purchase price from the customer's bank or credit-card account by a computer link between the checkout till and the bank or credit-card company. The system is used in the UK by most large reputable UK retailers and also operates in Scandinavia and many parts of Europe. The system depends on a magnetic strip on the customer's plastic card, which is 'swiped' through a terminal reader machine at the point of sale. This gives authorization and prints a voucher for the customer to sign. Transfer of funds to the retailer can take place within 48 hours.

electronic mail The transfer of correspondence, such as letters and memos, from one computer to another. The computers are connected by cables or telephone lines (using a modem). Often a central computer acts as a post office, providing each user with a space in its memory, called a **mailbox**, where messages can be left. The users periodically contact the mailbox to check for messages.

electronic office (paperless office) An office that has been computerized; i.e. traditional methods have been replaced by electronic ones. For example, wordprocessing packages have replaced typewriters, *spreadsheet packages have replaced manual accounts, and *electronic mail has replaced paper mail.

electronic transfer of funds (ETF) The transfer of money from one bank account to another by means of computers and communications links. Banks routinely transfer funds between accounts using computers; another variety of ETF is the telebanking service enabling the Viewdata network to be used for banking in a customer's home. In the USA, the Electronic Transfer of Funds Act (1978) limits customer liability for unauthorized transfers to $50M. *See also* electronic funds transfer at point of sale.

elements of cost The classification of costs in a production process into the primary elements of material, labour, and expenses.

eligible paper 1. Treasury bills, short-dated gilts, and any first-class security, accepted by a British bank or an accepting house and thus acceptable by the Bank of England for rediscounting, or as security for loans to discount houses. The Bank of England's classification of eligible paper influences portfolios because of the ability to turn them into quick cash, and thus reinforces the Bank's role as lender of last resort. 2. Acceptances by US banks available for rediscounting by the Federal Reserve System.

embedded audit facility A *computer-assisted audit technique in which the program and additional data are provided by the *auditor and incorporated into the computerized accounting system of the client. This facility enables a continuous review of a client's computerized accounting system to be made. The two most common types of embedded audit facility are an *integrated test facility and the use of a *systems control and review file.

emergency tax code An income tax code issued by the Inland Revenue in the event of an employee not having the correct code available for the employer to apply to earnings under *PAYE. The code gives the basic *personal allowance, but does not allow for any further allowance, e.g. the married-couples allowance. This code is used until the correct code has been notified to the employer by the Inland Revenue.

Emerging Issues Task Force (EITF) In the USA, the body responsible to the *Financial Accounting Standards Board for suggesting appropriate treatment for new accounting problems and practices, without the delays involved in issuing a *Statement of Financial Accounting Standard. The comparable body in the UK is the *Urgent Issues Task Force.

emoluments Amounts received from an office or employment including all salaries, fees, wages, perquisites, and other profits as well as certain expenses and benefits paid or provided by the employer, which are deemed to be emoluments. *See also* directors' remuneration.

emphasis of matter An optional paragraph in an *auditor's report referred to by the *Auditing Practices Committee in their standard 'The Audit Report' issued in April 1980. This paragraph was to be used if the auditor considered that information was adequately disclosed in the *financial statements but that the reader's attention should be drawn to important matters in the financial statements to ensure that they would not be overlooked. The use of such a paragraph was intended to be rare and to be restricted to matters of emphasis in a separate paragraph. In May 1993 the *Auditing Practices Board issued a new *Statement of Auditing Standard, 'Auditors' Reports on Financial Statements', which does not include the option of an emphasis-of-matter paragraph.

employee report A simplified version of the statutory annual report and accounts of a company prepared for the employees of the company (*see* annual accounts). Although this is a voluntary practice, such documents should comply with section 240 of the Companies Act relating to non-statutory accounts. Employee reports have been published by some companies since the beginning of the century; the 1930s and 1970s were periods during which employee reports were very popular.

employee share ownership plan (ESOP) A method of providing the employees of a company with shares in the company. The ESOP buys shares in its sponsoring company, usually with assistance from the company concerned. The shares are ultimately made available to the employees, usually directors, who satisfy certain performance targets. The advantage claimed for ESOPs is that they do not involve dilution of the sponsoring company's share capital by the creation of new shares. In the USA these are known as **employee stock option plans**. *See also* employee share ownership trust.

employee share ownership trust (ESOT) A trust set up by a UK company, under the provisions introduced in 1989, to acquire shares in the company and distribute them to the employees. The company's payments to the trust are tax-deductible. The trust deed sets out the specified period of employment and all those employees who fulfil the requirements must be included in the class of beneficiaries of the trust. *See also* employee share ownership plan.

employment costs The expenditure incurred in employing personnel. It includes salaries, wages, bonuses, incentive payments, employer's National Insurance contributions, and employer's pension scheme contributions.

employment report A report that was recommended to be included with the annual *financial report of a company in the 1970s. The report should include details of numbers of employees, their age and sex, where they are based, the costs of employing them, and the health and safety measures undertaken.

EMS Abbreviation for *European Monetary System.

EMV Abbreviation for *expected monetary value.

encryption The coding of text when it cannot be transmitted in plain language for security reasons. On receipt it must be decoded to its original form.

ending inventory In the USA, the stock held at the end of a financial period. It appears on the *profit and loss account in the calculation of *cost of sales and on the *balance sheet.

end-of-day sweep An automatic transfer of funds from one bank account held by a company to another of its bank accounts, usually one that pays interest on deposits. The sweep takes place at the end of every day, or at the end of the day when certain conditions are met, for instance that the *cleared value exceeds £50,000 in one of the accounts.

endorsement (indorsement) 1. A signature on the back of a *bill of exchange or cheque, making it payable to the person who signed it. A bill can be endorsed any number of times, the presumption being that the endorsements were made in the order in which they appear, the last named being the holder to receive payment. If the bill is **blank endorsed,** i.e. no endorsee is named, it is payable to the bearer. In the case of a **restrictive endorsement** of the form 'Pay X only', it ceases to be a *negotiable instrument. A **special endorsement,** when the endorsee is specified, becomes payable **to order,** which is short for 'in obedience to the order of'. **2.** A signature required on a document to make it valid in law. **3.** An amendment to an insurance policy or cover note, recording a change in the conditions of the insurance.

energy cost The expenditure on all the sources of energy required by an organization; these can include electricity, gas, solid fuels, oil, and steam.

engagement letter (letter of engagement) A letter used by an *auditor to define clearly the scope of the auditors' responsibilities in an engagement. It provides written confirmation of the auditors' acceptance of the appointment, the scope of the *audit, the form of the report, and details of any non-audit services to be provided. It is usual to discuss the contents of the letter with the management of the business to be audited before sending it.

engineered costs The building up of the levels of costs likely to be incurred by a production process by means of constructing synthetic costs, based on a logical consideration of the make-up of each cost item. For example, the expected labour cost for a particular product may be obtained by using time studies to determine the labour times likely to be required and multiplying the result by the expected rates of pay. The method is used for *standard costing, budgeting, and planning purposes in which estimated unit costs are likely to be required before production takes place.

enrolled agents In the USA, agents recognized by the Treasury Department for representing the taxpayer when dealing with the *Internal Revenue Service.

enterprise fund In the USA, an organization, such as a government-owned utility, that provides goods or services to the public for a fee that makes the organization self-supporting.

enterprise investment scheme (EIS) An investment scheme in the UK that replaced the *business expansion scheme (BES) on 1 January 1994. Relief is available under the scheme when eligible shares are issued to an individual on subscription. The company issuing the shares must be engaged in a qualifying business activity and the money raised through the EIS must be used wholly for that purpose. The tax relief available on a qualifying EIS investment is 20% of the amount subscribed. This contrasts with the relief given under the BES, in which a higher-rate taxpayer received full tax relief. *See also* capital gains tax.

entity An organization for which the annual report and accounts is prepared (*see* annual accounts). There may be some difficulty in defining the boundaries of an accounting entity and the determination of its extent will influence the amount and nature of the information prepared.

entity view The view of an accounting entity that emphasizes the importance of the business or the organization and its separateness from its owners. It is based on the *accounting equation, in which the sum of the assets is equal to the claims on these assets by owners and others. *Compare* proprietary view; residual equity theory.

entry A record made in a book of account, register, or computer file of a financial transaction, event, proceeding, etc. *See also* double-entry book-keeping.

entry value The current *replacement cost of an asset. This value may be used in *current-value accounting. *Compare* exit value.

environmental accounting *See* green reporting.

environment audit (green audit) An *audit of the impact of the activities of an organization on the environment. Its purpose is usually to ensure that the organization has clear environmental policies, that its operations comply with the stated environmental policies, and that its policies are subject to regular review. Environmental audits may be conducted internally or externally by environmental consultants.

EOQ Abbreviation for *economic order quantity.

eps Abbreviation for *earnings per share.

equal-instalment depreciation *See* straight-line method.

equipment trust certificate In the USA, a document setting out the details of a loan used to fund the purchase of equipment. The holder of the certificate has a secured interest in the asset in the event of a corporate default.

equitable apportionment The process of sharing common costs between *cost centres in a fair manner, using a *basis of apportionment that reflects the way in which the costs are incurred by the cost centres.

equity 1. A beneficial interest in an asset. For example, a person having a house worth £100,000 with a mortgage of £20,000 may be said to have an equity of £80,000 in the house. **2.** The net assets of a company after all creditors (including the holders of *preference shares) have been paid off. **3.** The amount of money returned to a borrower in a mortgage or hire-purchase agreement, after the sale of the specified asset and the full repayment of the lender of the money. **4.** The ordinary share capital of a company.

equity accounting The practice of showing in a company's accounts a share of the undistributed profits of another company in which it holds a share of the *equity (usually a share of between 20% and 50%). The share of profit shown by the equity-holding company is usually equal to its share of the equity in the other company. Although none of the profit is actually paid over, the company has a right to this share of the undistributed profit.

equity dilution A reduction in the percentage of the *equity owned by a shareholder as a result of a new issue of shares in the company, which rank equally with the existing voting shares.

equity dividend cover A ratio that shows how many times the *dividend to ordinary shareholders can be paid out of the profits of a company available for distribution. The higher the cover, the greater the certainty that dividends will be paid in the future.

equity finance Finance raised from shareholders in the form of *ordinary shares and reserves, as opposed to *non-equity shares and to *debt finance.

equity gearing *See* gearing.

equity share Any *share in a company, other than a *non-equity share.

equity share capital The *share capital of a company that consists of its equity shares as opposed to its *non-equity shares.

equity shareholder The owner of *equity shares.

equivalent units (effective units) Unfinished units of production that remain in a process at the end of a period as *work in progress (or process). Degrees of completion are assigned to each cost classification, which, when applied to the number of units in work in progress, give an equivalent number of completed units. For example, if the number of units of work in progress is, say, 3000 units to the following degrees of completion, the equivalent units are given as follows:

Equivalent units	Cost classification	Work in progress (units)	Degrees of completion (%)
3000	direct materials	3000	100
1500	direct labour	3000	50
1500	overheads	3000	50

The equivalent units have an impact on the valuation of opening and closing work in process.

ERM Abbreviation for Exchange Rate Mechanism. *See* European Monetary System.

error or mistake A claim by the taxpayer that there has been an overpayment of tax. A formal claim has to be made within six years against the overassessment to income tax or capital gains tax resulting from an error or mistake in, or omission from, any return or statement.

ESOP Abbreviation for *employee share ownership plan (or, in the USA, employee stock option plan).

ESOT Abbreviation for *employee share ownership trust.

estate duty See death duty.

estimated assessment A *tax assessment raised by the *Board of Inland Revenue based on the estimated profits or income of a taxpayer. The level of profits from the assessment of the previous period is often used as a rough indication of the expected profits for the assessment under consideration. The taxpayer has 30 days to appeal against the assessment. An estimated assessment will be revised once the actual profits or income for the *fiscal year in question are known.

ETF Abbreviation for *electronic transfer of funds.

ethical investment (socially responsible investment) An investment made in a company not engaged in an activity that the investor considers to be unethical, such as armaments or tobacco, or an investment in a company of which the investor approves on ethical grounds, e.g. one having a good environmental or employment record.

Eurobanks Financial intermediaries that deal in the *eurocurrency market.

eurobond A *bond issued in a *eurocurrency, which is now one of the largest markets for raising money (it is much larger than the UK stock exchange). The reason for the popularity of the eurobond market is that *secondary market investors can remain anonymous, usually for the purpose of avoiding tax. For this reason it is difficult to ascertain the exact size and scope of operation of the market. Issues of new eurobonds normally take place in London, largely through syndicates of US and Japanese investment banks; they are *bearer securities, unlike the shares registered in most stock exchanges, and interest payments are free of any *withholding taxes. There are various kinds of eurobonds. An ordinary bond, called a **straight**, is a fixed-interest loan of 3 to 8 years duration; others include **floating-rate notes**, which carry a variable interest rate based on the *London Inter Bank Offered Rate; and perpetuals, which are never redeemed. Some carry *warrants and some are *convertible. See also Centrale de Livraison de Valeurs Mobilières; Euroclear; note issuance facility; swap; zero coupon bond.

Euroclear One of two settlement houses for the clearance of *eurobonds. Based in Brussels, it was set up in 1968 by a number of banks. The other settlement house is *Centrale de Livraison de Valeurs Mobilières.

euro-commercial paper (ECP) *Commercial paper issued in a *eurocurrency, the market for which is centred in London. It provides a quick way of obtaining same-day funds by the issue of unsecured notes, for example in Europe for use in New York.

eurocurrency A currency held in a European country other than its country of origin. For example, dollars deposited in a bank in Switzerland are *eurodollars, yen deposited in Germany are **euroyen**, etc. Eurocurrency is used for lending and borrowing; the **eurocurrency market** often provides a cheap and convenient form of liquidity for the financing of international trade and investment. The main borrowers and lenders are the commercial banks, large companies, and the central banks. By raising funds in eurocurrencies it is possible to secure more favourable terms and rates of interest, and sometimes to avoid domestic regulations and taxation. Most of the deposits and loans are on a short-term basis but increasing use is being made of medium-term loans, particularly through the raising of *eurobonds. This has to some extent replaced the syndicated loan market, in which banks lent money as a group in order to share the risk. *Euromarkets emerged in the 1950s.

eurodollars Dollars deposited in financial institutions outside the USA. The eurodollar market evolved in London in the late 1950s when the growing demand for dollars to finance international trade and investment coincided with a greater supply of dollars. The prefix 'euro' indicates the origin of the practice but it now refers to all dollar deposits made anywhere outside the USA. *See also* eurocurrency.

euromarket 1. A market that emerged in the 1950s for financing international trade. Its principal participants are *commercial banks, large companies, and the *central banks of members of the EU. Its main business is in *eurobonds, *euro-commercial paper, *euronotes, and euroequities issued in *eurocurrencies. The largest euromarket is in London, but there are smaller ones in Paris, Brussels, and Frankfurt. **2.** The European Union, regarded as one large market for goods.

euronote A form of *euro-commercial paper consisting of short-term negotiable *bearer notes. They may be in any currency but are usually in dollars or ECUs. The **euronote facility** is a form of *note issuance facility set up by a syndicate of banks, which underwrites the notes.

European Currency Unit (ECU) A currency medium and unit of account created in 1979 to act as the reserve asset and accounting unit of the *European Monetary System. The value of the ECU is calculated as a weighted average of a basket of specified amounts of European Union (EU) currencies; its value is reviewed periodically as currencies change in importance and membership of the EU expands. It also acts as the unit of account for all EU transactions. It has some similarities with the Special Drawing Rights of the *International Monetary Fund; however, ECU reserves are not allocated to individual countries but are held in the European Monetary Cooperation Fund. Private transactions using the ECU as the denomination for borrowing and lending have proved popular. It is planned that the ECU will be the basis for a future European currency to replace all or most national currencies.

European Monetary System (EMS) A European system of exchange-rate stabilization involving the countries of the European Union. There are two elements: the **Exchange Rate Mechanism (ERM)**, under which participating countries commit themselves to maintaining the value of their currencies within agreed narrow limits, and a *balance of payments support mechanism, organized through the European Monetary Cooperation Fund. The ERM is generally regarded as having helped to maintain exchange-rate stability and to have encouraged the coordination of macroeconomic policy. It operates by giving each currency a value in ECUs and drawing up a **parity grid** giving exchange values in ECUs for each pair of currencies. If market rates differ from this parity by more than a permitted percentage (currently 2.25%), the relevant governments have to take action to correct the disparity. The ultimate goal of the EMS is controversial: to some its function is to facilitate monetary cooperation; to others, it is the first step towards a single European currency and European Monetary Union (EMU) with a European *central bank. In 1992 the ERM failed and the Italian, British, and Spanish governments were unable to support their currencies above their floor values; they then had to be allowed to float, enabling critics of the EMS to claim that the system was flawed and that EMU was therefore unattainable. *See also* European Currency Unit.

European option An *option that can only be exercised on its expiry date. *Compare* American option.

EV Abbreviation for *expected value.

event of default A critical clause in a loan agreement, the breaching of which will make the loan repayable immediately. The breaching of any *covenant clause will be an event of default. Events of default also include failure to pay, failure to perform other duties and obligations, false *representation and warranty, *material adverse change, bankruptcy, and *alienation of assets. *See also* cross-default clause.

events accounting A method of accounting in which data is stored and reported in respect of particular events rather than being classified chronologically or in any other way.

ex- (Latin: without) A prefix used to exclude specified benefits when a security is quoted. A share is described as **ex-dividend** (xd or ex-div) when a potential purchaser will no longer be entitled to receive the company's current dividend, the right to which remains with the vendor. Government stocks go ex-dividend 36 days before the interest payment. Similarly, **ex-rights**, **ex-scrip**, **ex-coupon**, **ex-capitalization** (**ex-cap**), and **ex-bonus** mean that each of these benefits belongs to the vendor rather than the buyer. **Ex-all** means that all benefits belong to the vendor. **Cum-** (Latin: with) has exactly the opposite sense, meaning that the dividend or other benefits belong to the buyer rather than the seller. The price of a share that has gone ex-dividend will usually fall by the amount of the dividend, while one that is **cum-dividend** will usually rise by this amount. However, in practice market forces usually mean that these falls and rises are often slightly less than expected.

ex ante (Latin) Before the event. The phrase is used, for example, of a budget that is prepared as an estimate and subsequently compared with actual figures. *Compare* ex post.

except for (with the exception of) A qualification by an *auditor stating that the *financial statements of the company audited give a *true and fair view except for the effects of any adjustments that might have been found necessary, had a **limitation of scope** not affected the evidence available to them. This limitation is not so significant that a *disclaimer of opinion is required.

The auditor may also use the 'except for' opinion if there is a disagreement with the treatment or disclosure of a matter in the financial statements but concludes that the effect of the disagreement is not so significant that an *adverse opinion is required. An opinion is expressed, which is qualified by stating that the financial statements give a true and fair view except for the effects of the matter giving rise to the disagreement. *See also* qualified audit report.

exceptional items It is generally believed that the users of the accounts of an organization should be informed of any events or transactions of an exceptional nature. It has been difficult, however, to reach agreement on how to define and report exceptional items; Financial Reporting Standard 3, 'Reporting Financial Performance', sets out the rules. Exceptional items are material in nature and fall within the ordinary activities of the reporting entity, but need to be disclosed because of their size or incidence if the *financial statements are to give a *true and fair view. *Compare* extraordinary items.

exchange control Restrictions on the purchase and sale of foreign exchange. It is operated in various forms by many countries, in particular those who experience shortages of *hard currencies; sometimes different regulations apply to transactions that would come under the capital account of the *balance of payments. There has been a gradual movement towards dismantling exchange controls by many countries in recent years. The UK abolished all form of exchange control in 1979.

exchange gain or loss A gain or loss resulting from an exchange-rate fluctuation arising from the conversion of other currencies into the domestic currency.

exchange rate The number of units of one currency, usually the home currency, expressed in terms of a unit of another currency. The UK is exceptional in expressing exchange rates as the number of units of a foreign currency that £1 sterling will buy.

Exchange Rate Mechanism (ERM) *See* European Monetary System.

excise duty A tax charged in the UK on the production of certain items, the most popular being petrol, alcoholic drinks, and tobacco products. It is also charged on betting and gaming and on certain activities requiring an excise licence, such as using a motor vehicle.

exclusion of subsidiaries from consolidation Subsidiary undertakings may be excluded from *consolidation on the following grounds:
(1) an individual subsidiary may be excluded from consolidation if its inclusion is not *material for the purpose of giving a *true and fair view;
(2) an individual subsidiary may be excluded from consolidation for reasons of disproportionate expense in respect of its value (*see* disproportionate expense and undue delay);
(3) if *severe long-term restrictions substantially hinder the exercise of the rights of a parent company over the assets or the management of an undertaking, it may be excluded from consolidation;
(4) if the interest in a subsidiary undertaking is held with a view to resale, and has not previously been included in the consolidated accounts prepared by the parent company, that subsidiary may be excluded from consolidation;
(5) a subsidiary undertaking may be excluded from consolidation if its activities are so different from those of the other group undertakings that its inclusion would be incompatible with the obligation to give a *true and fair view. Such

exclusion does not arise merely because some of the undertakings are industrial, some commercial, and some provide different services (*see* dissimilar activities).

executive director A *director of a company who has management responsibilities for the day-to-day activities of the business. *Compare* non-executive director.

executive share option scheme An approved share option scheme that entitles a specified class of directors or employees to purchase shares in the company in which they are employed. Strict conditions need to be met in order to receive Inland Revenue approval for such a scheme. Once achieved there are no income tax charges on the grant or exercise of the option or on the growth in value of the shares. The only charge will be to *capital gains tax when the shares are sold.

executor A person named in a will of another person to gather in the assets of that person's estate, paying any outstanding liabilities and distributing any residue to the beneficiaries in accordance with the instructions contained in the will.

exemptions from preparing consolidated financial statements Under the *Companies Act a parent company is not required to prepare *group accounts for a financial year in which the group headed by that company qualifies as a *small company or a *medium-sized company. A group is not eligible for exemption if any member of the group is a public company or a body corporate that has power under its constitution to offer its shares or debentures to the public and may lawfully exercise that power; an authorized institution under the Banking Act (1987); an insurance company; or an authorized person under the Financial Services Act (1986). Under the Companies Act and *Financial Reporting Standard 2, 'Accounting for Subsidiary Undertakings', a parent undertaking is exempt from preparing group accounts when it is itself a subsidiary of a parent company in the European Union and consolidated financial statements are prepared at the highest level. Also, a parent undertaking is exempt from preparing group accounts when all of its subsidiaries are excluded. *See* exclusion of subsidiaries from consolidation.

exempt private company A family company that was exempt from filing its *financial statements with the *Registrar of Companies. The exempt private company was created by the Companies Act (1948) and abolished by the Companies Act (1967). The *small companies and *medium-sized companies' filing exemptions replace it to some extent.

exempt supplies Supplies of goods or services in the categories of items that are identified as exempt from *value added tax, as given in the Value Added Tax Act (1994). The main categories are: land (including rent), financial services, postal services, betting, charities (except on their business activities), education (non-profitmaking), health services, burial and cremation.

exempt transfers Transfers resulting in no liability to *inheritance tax. These are:
• gifts to a spouse,
• normal expenditure out of income,
• small gifts, up to £250, to any number of individuals,

- a gift of up to £3000,
- marriage gifts, up to £5000 for each parent of the parties to the marriage, but limited to £1000 for other gifts in consideration of marriage,
- gifts to charities,
- gifts for national purposes,
- gifts for public benefit,
- gifts to political parties,
- certain transfers to employee trusts.

See also potentially exempt transfer.

exercise price (strike price) The price at which an *option can be exercised.

ex gratia pensions A pension paid by an employer although there is no legal, contractual, or implied commitment to provide it.

exit charge The charge to *inheritance tax made when an asset is taken out of a *discretionary trust. The inheritance tax liability is calculated by taking the rate of inheritance tax charged at the most recent *ten-year charge before the asset leaves the trust and applying the fraction:

number of completed quarters since the ten-year charge/40.

exit value The *net realizable value of an asset, i.e. its market price at the date of a balance sheet less the selling expenses. Exit values are effectively *break-up values and are not consistent with the *going-concern concept, which assumes that a business is continuing to trade. *Compare* entry value.

expected deviations rate The extent of non-compliance with recognized control procedures that an *auditor expects to find when performing *compliance tests on a population or a sample of it.

expected error The extent of the errors that an *auditor expects to find when performing *substantive tests on a population or a sample of it.

expected monetary value (EMV) In decision making, the sum of the products of the outcomes in monetary terms and the probabilities of these outcomes arising. In *decision trees subjective probability estimates are assigned to each possible outcome. In the EMV, the outcomes are expressed in terms of money. In the example given in the table below, the EMV is 3900. *Compare* expected value.

Possible outcomes (£)	Subjective probability (p)	Product (£ × p)
3000	0.5	1500
4000	0.3	1200
6000	0.2	1200
	1.0	EMV = 3900

expected standard A cost, income, or performance standard set in *standard costing at a level that is expected to be achieved by the actual result.

expected value (EV) In decision making, the sum of the products of the outcomes in quantitative terms, such as units of output or sales, weights, or volumes, and the probabilities of these outcomes arising. *Compare* expected monetary value.

expenditure The costs or expenses incurred by an organization. They may be *capital expenditure or *revenue expenditure. Although expenditure is usually incurred by an outlay of money, expenditure may also arise in accounting by the acknowledgment of a liability, for example rent accrued due, which is regarded as expenditure in the period accrued although it will not be paid until a later date.

expenditure code *See* accounting code.

expenditure variance (overhead expenditure variance) An *overhead variance arising in *standard costing equal to the difference between the budgeted overhead allowance and the actual expenditure incurred. This overhead variance can be analysed into fixed overhead expenditure variance and variable overhead expenditure variance; it represents the amount by which the budgeted profits should be adjusted to account for the over- or under-spending on overheads.

expense account **1.** An account, opened in either the cost ledger or the nominal ledger, for each *expenditure heading in which the costs of an organization are recorded before being totalled and transferred to the *profit and loss account at the end of an accounting period. **2.** The amount of money that certain staff members are allowed to spend on personal expenses in carrying out their activities for an organization.

Export Credits Guarantee Department (ECGD) A UK government department that offers credit insurance to UK exporters. Certain sections of the ECGD were privatized in 1991, including short-term credit insurance.

ex post (Latin) Short for *ex post facto*: after the event. This abbreviation is used, for example, to refer to the collection of financial data for transactions after they have been effected. *Compare* ex ante.

exposure draft Generally, a draft issued as a discussion document prior to the release of a final document. Specifically, it refers to a draft issued for discussion by the *Accounting Standards Committee before issuing an *accounting standard.

ex rights *See* ex-.

extended trial balance A *trial balance that gives a vertical listing of all the *ledger account balances with three additional columns for adjustments, *accruals, and *prepayments, and a final two columns (each containing a debit and a credit side) that show the entries in the *profit and loss account and the *balance sheet.

extendible bond issue A *bond, the maturity of which can be extended at the option of all the parties.

external audit An *audit of an organization carried out by an *auditor who is external to, and independent of, the organization. An example would be a *statutory audit carried out on behalf of the shareholders of a limited company. *Compare* internal audit.

extraordinary general meeting (EGM) Any general meeting of a company other than the *annual general meeting. Most company's articles give the directors the right to call an EGM whenever they wish. Members have the right to requisition an EGM if they hold not less than 10% of the paid-up share capital; a resigning auditor may also requisition a meeting. Directors must call an EGM when there has been a serious loss of capital. The court may call an EGM if it is impracticable to call it in any other way. Those entitled to attend must be given 14 days' notice of the meeting (21 days if a special resolution is to be proposed).

extraordinary items Costs or income affecting a company's *profit and loss account that do not derive from the *ordinary activities of the company and, if undisclosed, would distort the normal trend of profits. Such items are therefore disclosed after the normal trading profit or loss has been shown. Extraordinary items are to be distinguished from *exceptional items, which arise from the normal activities of the company but are of exceptional magnitude.

extraordinary resolution A resolution submitted to a general meeting of a company; 14 days' notice of such a resolution is required, and the notice should state that it is an extraordinary resolution. 75% of those voting must approve the resolution for it to be passed.

extrapolation Estimating unknown quantities that lie outside a series of known values. *Compare* interpolation.

extra-statutory concession A concession made by the *Board of Inland Revenue to taxpayers, which is usually followed in practice but which is not specified in the tax legislation.

F

face value *See* par value.

facility An agreement between a bank and a company that grants the company a line of credit with the bank. This can either be a *committed facility or an *uncommitted facility.

facility fee *See* agency fee.

factoring The buying of the trade debts of a manufacturer, assuming the task of debt collection and accepting the credit risk, thus providing the manufacturer with working capital. A firm that engages in factoring is called a **factor. With service factoring** involves collecting the debts, assuming the credit risk, and passing on the funds as they are paid by the buyer. **With service plus finance factoring** involves paying the manufacturer up to 90% of the invoice value immediately after delivery of the goods, with the balance paid after the money has been collected. This form of factoring is clearly more expensive than with service factoring. In either case the factor, which may be a bank or finance house, has the right to select its debtors. In the UK, the High-Street banks have well over 60% of the factoring market, run by factoring subsidiary companies owned by the banks.

factors of production The resources required to produce economic goods. They are land (including all natural resources), labour (including all human work and skill), capital (including all money, assets, machinery, raw materials, etc.), and entrepreneurial ability (including organizational management skills, inventiveness, and the willingness to take risks). For each of these factors there is a price, i.e. rent for land, wages for labour, interest for capital, and profit for the entrepreneur.

factory burden The US name for *factory overhead.

factory costs (factory expenses) The expenditure incurred by the manufacturing section of an organization. Factory costs include *direct materials, *direct labour, *direct expenses, and *production overheads but not mark-up or profit.

factory overhead (indirect manufacturing costs) Those manufacturing costs of an organization that cannot be traced directly to the product. Examples are factory rent, maintenance wages, and depreciation of general production machinery. In the USA factory overhead is known as **factory burden**.

fair value The amount of money for which it is assumed an asset or liability could be exchanged in an arm's length transaction between informed and willing parties. The concept is essential in *acquisition accounting and is covered in *Financial Reporting Standard 3, 'Fair Value in Acquisition Accounting'.

FAPA Abbreviation for Fellow of the *Association of Authorized Public Accountants.

FASB Abbreviation for *Financial Accounting Standards Board.

favourable variance In *standard costing and *budgetary control, the differences between actual and budgeted performance of an organization if the differences create an addition to the budgeted profit. For example, this may occur if the actual sales revenue is greater than that budgeted or if actual costs are less than budgeted costs.

FCA Abbreviation for Fellow of the *Institute of Chartered Accountants.

FCCA Abbreviation for Fellow of the *Chartered Association of Certified Accountants.

FCIS Abbreviation for Fellow of the *Institute of Chartered Secretaries and Administrators.

FCMA Abbreviation for Fellow of the *Chartered Institute of Management Accountants.

FCT Abbreviation for Fellow of the *Association of Corporate Treasurers.

feasibility study An investigation to determine which of a range of decisions is likely to give a satisfactory return in a *financial appraisal or *economic appraisal of the alternatives.

fellow subsidiary One of two or more of the subsidiary undertakings in a group of companies that consists of a parent company and at least two subsidiaries.

FIAB Abbreviation for Fellow of the *International Association of Book-keepers.

FIFO cost Abbreviation for *first-in-first-out cost.

FII Abbreviation for *franked investment income.

filing of accounts The lodging of the *financial statements of a company with the *Registrar of Companies. There are penalties for late filing. Companies that meet the statutory definition of a *small company or a *medium-sized company are permitted to file *abbreviated accounts.

FIMBRA Abbreviation for *Financial Intermediaries, Managers and Brokers Regulatory Association.

final dividend A *dividend recommended by the directors of a company to be paid to the shareholders, subject to the shareholders giving approval at the *annual general meeting. It is an *appropriation of profits in the *profit and loss account and, until paid, is shown as a current liability in the *balance sheet. *See also* interim dividend.

finance **1.** The practice of manipulating and managing money. **2.** The capital involved in a project, especially the capital that has to be raised to start a new business. **3.** A loan of money for a particular purpose, especially by a *finance house.

Finance Act The annual act of parliament in the UK that sets out the taxation legislation for the coming year. The draft of the Act is the **Finance Bill**.

finance charge A charge levied for the benefit of being able to delay payment of a sum due.

finance company A company that provides finance, normally in the form of loans. As it tends to finance ventures with a high risk factor, the cost of borrowing is likely to be higher than that made by a clearing bank.

finance house An organization, many of which are owned by *commercial banks, that provides finance for *hire-purchase agreements. A consumer, who buys an expensive item (such as a car) from a trader and does not wish to pay cash, enters into a hire-purchase contract with the finance house, who collects the deposit and instalments. The finance house pays the trader the cash price in full, borrowing from the commercial banks in order to do so. The finance house's profit is the difference between the low rate of interest it pays to the commercial banks to borrow and the high rate it charges the consumer. Most finance houses are members of the Finance Houses Association.

finance lease A lease that transfers substantially all the risks and rewards of ownership of an *asset to the lessee. Under *Statement of Standard Accounting Practice 21, 'Accounting for Leases and Hire Purchase Contracts', the lessee should record the finance lease as an asset in the *balance sheet.

financial accounting The branch of *accounting concerned with classifying, measuring, and recording the transactions of a business. At the end of a period, usually a year but sometimes less, a *profit and loss account and a *balance sheet are prepared to show the performance and position of the business. Financial accounting is primarily concerned with providing a *true and fair view of the activities of a business to parties external to it. To ensure that this is done correctly considerable attention will be paid to *accounting concepts and to any requirements of legislation, *accounting standards, and (where appropriate) the regulations of the *stock exchange. Financial accounting can be separated into a number of specific activities, such as conducting *audits, taxation, *book-keeping, and *insolvency. **Financial accountants** need not be qualified, in that they need not belong to an *accountancy body, although the majority of those working in public practice will be. *Compare* management accounting.

Financial Accounting Foundation In the USA, the funding body of the *Financial Accounting Standards Board; it appoints its members and reviews the process of setting standards and accounting principles.

Financial Accounting Standards Board (FASB) In the USA, a non-government body founded in 1973 with the responsibility of promulgating *generally accepted accounting principles (GAAP). This is achieved by the issue of *Statements of Financial Accounting Standards, which practising *certified public accountants are expected to follow. The *American Institute of Certified Public Accountants and the *Securities and Exchange Commission officially recognize the Statements of Financial Accounting Standards.

financial analysis The use of *financial statements and the calculation of ratios, to monitor and evaluate the financial performance and position of a business.

financial appraisal The use of financial evaluation techniques to determine which of a range of possible alternatives is preferred. Financial appraisal usually refers to the use of *discounted cash flow techniques but it may also be applied to any other approaches used to assess a business problem in financial terms, such as *ratio analysis or *profitability index.

financial budget *See* cash-flow budget.

financial capital maintenance *See* capital maintenance concept.

financial control (financial management) The actions of the management of an organization taken to ensure that the costs incurred and revenue generated are at acceptable levels. Financial control is assisted by the provision of financial information to management by the accountant and by the use of such techniques as *budgetary control and *standard costing, which highlight and analyse any *variances.

financial expense An item of expenditure recorded in the financial records rather than the cost records. Examples include interest paid and directors' fees.

financial futures A *futures contract in currencies or interest rates. Unlike simple forward contracts, futures contracts themselves can be bought and sold on specialized markets. In the UK financial futures and options are traded on the *London International Financial Futures and Options Exchange (LIFFE). *See also* hedging; portfolio insurance.

financial gearing *See* gearing; debt–equity ratio.

financial institution Any organization, such as a bank, building society, or finance house, that collects funds from individuals, other organizations, or government agencies and invests these funds or lends them on to borrowers. Some financial institutions are non-deposit-taking, e.g. brokers and life insurance companies, who fund their activities and derive their income from selling securities or insurance policies, or undertaking brokerage services. At one time there was a clear distinction and regulatory division between deposit-taking and non-deposit-taking financial institutions. This is no longer the case; brokers and other companies now often invest funds for their clients with banks and in the money markets.

financial instrument *See* instrument.

Financial Intermediaries, Managers and Brokers Regulatory Association (FIMBRA) A *Self-Regulating Organization set up under the Financial Services Act (1986). It regulated the provision of services by independent intermediaries, such as insurance brokers, before being amalgamated into the *Personal Investment Authority, which came into effect from October 1994. The costs of being a FIMBRA member were high compared to those of the *Life Assurance and Unit Trust Regulatory Organization (LAUTRO); during the recession of the 1980s–1990s this led to a high level of defection to LAUTRO.

financial leverage *See* gearing.

financial management *See* financial control.

financial modelling The construction and use of planning and decision models based on financial data to simulate actual circumstances in order to facilitate decision making within an organization. The financial models used include *discounted cash flow, *economic order quantity, *decision trees, *learning curves, and *budgetary control.

financial period The period falling between two successive *balance sheets for which *financial statements are prepared. For statutory accounts the period is normally 12 months, although it may be less.

financial planning The formulation of short-term and long-term plans in financial terms for the purposes of establishing goals for an organization to achieve, against which its actual performance can be measured.

financial ratio The use of two or more figures taken from the *financial statements in order to calculate a ratio that provides an indication of the financial performance and position of a company. Ratios may be expressed as a percentage (e.g. *return on capital employed), in days (e.g. *debtor collection period), or as a multiple (e.g. *stock turnover).

financial report The *financial statements of a company.

Financial Reporting Council (FRC) A body set up in 1990, following the recommendations contained in the *Dearing Report to promote good financial reporting. The FRC makes appointments to the *Accounting Standards Board and other operational bodies concerned with standards setting; it also provides guidance to the Accounting Standards Board and ensures that it is adequately funded.

Financial Reporting Exposure Draft (FRED) A document issued by the *Accounting Standards Board for discussion and debate prior to the issue of a *Financial Reporting Standard.

Financial Reporting Release (FRR) In the USA, policy pronouncements made by the *Securities and Exchange Commission.

Financial Reporting Review Panel (FRRP) A panel established following company legislation in respect of the revision of *defective accounts. It is authorized by the Secretary of State for Trade and Industry to examine the accounts of companies that depart from the requirements of company legislation or from accounting standards. If the Panel considers a company's accounts are defective it can seek the company's agreement to revise them or it can apply to the courts to compel the company to revise them.

Financial Reporting Standard (FRS) A standard issued by the *Accounting Standards Board. The first such standard issued was FRS 1, 'Cash Flow Statements'.

Financial Services Act (1986) A UK act of parliament that came into force in April 1988. Its purpose was to regulate investment business in the UK by means of the *Securities and Investment Board and its *Self-Regulating Organizations. It provided legislation for many of the recommendations of the *Gower Report.

financial stability measures Quantitative measures that help to determine whether a company or group is likely to be able to meet its financial obligations, including interest, dividends, and capital repayments. The measures include the *gearing ratio and *interest cover.

financial statement analysis An analysis designed to assess the financial performance and position of a business. It is used by investors, creditors, analysts, and others. Ratios are normally calculated from the *financial statements to assess the profitability, solvency, working capital management, liquidity, and financial structure of an organization. They may also be calculated over a period to enable an analysis of trends to be formulated or compared to other similar companies or industry averages. In conducting the analysis, regard will need to be paid to the *accounting policies of the company and the extent to which any *creative accounting may have taken place.

financial statements The annual statements summarizing a company's activities over the last year. They consist of the *profit and loss account, *balance sheet, statement of total recognized gains and losses, and, if required, the *cash-flow statement, together with supporting notes.

financial structure *See* capital structure.

Financial Times Share Indexes A number of share indexes published by the *Financial Times*, daily except Sundays and Mondays, as a barometer of share prices on the London Stock Exchange. The **Financial Times Actuaries Share Indexes** are calculated by the Institute of Actuaries and the Faculty of Actuaries as weighted arithmetic averages for 54 sectors of the market (capital goods, consumer goods, etc.) and divided into various industries. They are widely used by investors and portfolio managers. The widest measure of the market comes from the **FTA All-Share Index** of some 800 shares and fixed-interest stocks (increased from 657 in October 1992), which includes a selection from the financial sector. Calculated after the end of daily business, it covers 98% of the market and 90% of turnover by value. The **FTA World Share Index** was introduced in 1987 and is based on 2400 share prices from 24 countries. The **Financial Times Industrial Ordinary Share Index** (or FT-30) represents the movements of shares in 30 leading industrial and commercial shares, chosen to be representative of British industry rather than of the Stock Exchange as a whole; it therefore excludes banks, insurance companies, and government stocks. The index is an unweighted geometric average, calculated hourly during the day and closing at 4.30 pm. The index started from a base of 100 in 1935 and for many years was the main day-to-day market barometer. It continues to be published but it has been superseded as the main index by the **Financial Times-Stock Exchange 100 Share Index** (FT-SE 100 or **Footsie**), a weighted arithmetic index representing the price of 100 securities with a base of 1000 on 3 January 1984. This index is calculated minute-by-minute and its constituents, whose membership is by market capitalization, above £1 billion, are reviewed quarterly. The index was created to help to support a UK equity-market base for a futures contract. In 1992 the index series was extended to create two further real-time indexes, the **FT-SE Mid 250**, comprising companies capitalized between £150 million and £1 billion, and the **FT-SE Actuaries 350**, both based on 31 December 1985. These indexes are further broken down into Industry Baskets, comprising all the shares of the industrial sectors, to provide an instant view of industry performance across the market, and corresponding roughly to sectors defined by markets in New York and Tokyo. A **FT-SE Small Cap Index** covers 500–600 companies capitalized between £20 million and £150 million, calculated at the end of the day's business, both including and excluding investment trusts. The **Financial Times Government Securities Index**

measures the movements of Government stocks (gilts). The newest indexes measure the performance of securities throughout the European market. The **Financial Times-Stock Exchange Eurotrack 100 Index** (FT-SE Eurotrack 100) is a weighted average of 100 stocks in Europe, which started on 29 October 1990, with a base of 1000 at the close of business on 26 October 1990. Quoted in Deutschmarks, the index combines prices from *SEAQ and SEAQ International with up-to-date currency exchange rates. On 25 February 1991 the **Financial Times-Stock Exchange Eurotrack 200 Index** was first quoted, with the same base as the Eurotrack 100 to combine the constituents of the FT-SE 100 and the Eurotrack 100.

financial year 1. Any year connected with finance, such as a company's accounting period or a year for which budgets are made up. 2. A specific period relating to corporation tax, i.e. the year beginning 1 April (the year beginning 1 April 1995 is the financial year 1995). Corporation-tax rates are fixed for specific financial years by the Chancellor in the Budget; if a company's accounting period falls into two financial years the profits have to be apportioned to the relevant financial years to find the rates of tax applicable. *Compare* fiscal year.

finished goods Products that have completed the manufacturing process and are available for distribution to customers.

finished goods inventory *See* finished goods stock.

finished goods stock (finished goods inventory) The value of goods that have completed the manufacturing process and are available for distribution to customers. In any accounting period there will be *opening stock of finished goods at the beginning of the period and *closing stock of finished goods at the end of the period. Methods of valuing finished goods stock are covered by Statement of Standard Accounting Practice 9 and may include *first-in-first-out cost or *average cost methods.

finished goods stocks budget A budget that expresses in both financial and quantitative terms the planned levels of *finished goods at various times during the budget period.

firm 1. Any business organization. 2. A business partnership.

firm offer An offer to sell goods that remains in force for a stated period. For example, an 'offer firm for 24 hours' binds the seller to sell if the buyer accepts the offer within 24 hours. If the buyer makes a lower *bid during the period that the offer is firm, the offer ceases to be valid. An offer that is not firm is usually called a quotation in commercial terms.

firm order An order to a broker (for securities, commodities, currencies, etc.) that remains firm for a stated period or until cancelled. A broker who has a firm order from a principal does not have to refer back if that broker can execute the terms of the order in the stated period.

firmware Computer programs or data that are stored in a memory chip. These are often built into a computer to make it unnecessary to load the programs or data from disk or from the keyboard. Wordprocessing programs, for example, on read-only memory (ROM) chips are built into some business computer systems. Firmware is also used where absolute reliability is required, for example in air-traffic control.

first-in-first-out cost (FIFO cost) A method of valuing units of *raw material or *finished goods issued from stock based on using the earliest unit value for pricing the issues until all the stock received at that price has been used up. The next latest price is then used for pricing the issues, and so on. Because the issues are based on a FIFO cost, the valuation of closing stocks is described as being on the same FIFO basis. The method may also be used in *process costing to value the work in process at the end of an accounting period. *Compare* last-in-first-out cost.

first mortgage debenture A *debenture with the first charge over property owned by a company. Such debentures are most commonly issued by property companies.

first-year allowance A *capital allowance, at a rate of 40%, available during the period 1 November 1992 to 31 October 1993 in place of the *writing-down allowance. It was also available before 1986 at varying rates. The allowance was given for the *basis period provided the expenditure was incurred between 1 November 1992 and 31 October 1993.

fiscal policy The use of government spending to influence macroeconomic conditions. Fiscal policy was actively pursued to sustain full employment in the post-war years; however, monetarists and others have claimed that this set off the inflation of the 1970s. Fiscal policy has remained 'tight' in most western countries since the 1980s, with governments actively attempting to reduce the level of public expenditure.

fiscal year (tax year) The year beginning on 6 April in one year and ending on 5 April in the next year. The 1995–96 fiscal year runs from 6 April 1995 to 5 April 1996. In the UK, *income tax, *capital gains tax, and *inheritance tax are all computed for fiscal years. The budget, in November, covers the provisions for the coming fiscal year, beginning on the following 6 April.

fixed asset (capital asset) An asset of a business intended for continuing use, rather than a short-term *circulating asset (such as stock). Fixed assets must be classified in a company's *balance sheet as intangible, tangible, or investments. Examples of intangible assets include *goodwill, *patents, and *trademarks. Examples of tangible fixed assets include land and buildings, plant and machinery, fixtures and fittings. Fixed assets must be written off to the *profit and loss account over their useful economic life; this is effected by the *amortization of intangible fixed assets and the *depreciation of tangible fixed assets. An investment included as a fixed asset is shown at its purchase price, market value, or directors' valuation, or using the equity method of accounting (*see* equity accounting).

fixed-asset investment Expenditure on tangible assets that are likely to have a life of more than one year.

fixed-assets register (assets register; plant register) A listing of the *fixed assets of a company. It records a description of the asset, its location, cost, revaluation, estimated *net residual value, estimated useful economic life, *depreciation method, accumulated provision for depreciation, and *net book value.

fixed-asset to equity-capital ratio A ratio used to calculate a business's ability to satisfy long-term debt. The value of the fixed assets is divided by the equity capital; a ratio greater than 1 means that some of the fixed assets are financed by debt.

fixed-asset–turnover ratio A ratio that measures an organization's activity over a period by calculating the number of times the sales are a multiple of the balance-sheet value of the *fixed assets. The fixed-asset values may be taken either at the beginning or the end of the period or an average of the two.

fixed budget (static budget) A budget that does not take into account any circumstances resulting in the actual levels of activity achieved being different from those on which the original budget was based. Consequently, in a fixed budget the *budget cost allowances for each cost item are not changed for the variable items. *Compare* flexible budget.

fixed charge **1. (specific charge)** A *charge in which a creditor has the right to have a specific asset sold and applied to the repayment of a debt if the debtor defaults on any payments. The debtor is not at liberty to deal with the asset without the charge-holder's consent. *Compare* floating charge. **2.** The part of an expense that remains unchanged, irrespective of the amount of the commodity or service used or consumed. For example, in the UK both the electricity and gas industries operate tariffs consisting of a fixed charge, which remains unchanged irrespective of the consumption of energy, and a variable charge, based on the energy consumed.

fixed-charge–coverage ratio *See* interest cover.

fixed cost (fixed expense) An item of expenditure that remains unchanged, in total, irrespective of changes in the levels of production or sales. Examples are business rates, rent, and some salaries. *Compare* semi-variable cost; variable cost.

fixed exchange rate A rate of exchange between one currency and another that is fixed by government and maintained by that government buying or selling its currency to support or depress its currency. *Compare* floating exchange rate.

fixed overhead absorption rate The budgeted fixed overheads divided by the budgeted *standard hours or the budgeted fixed overheads divided by the budgeted production in units.

fixed overhead capacity variance *See* idle capacity variance.

fixed overhead cost The elements of the *indirect costs of an organization's product that, in total, remain unchanged irrespective of changes in the levels of production or sales. Examples include administrative salaries, sales personnel salaries, and factory rent.

fixed overhead expenditure variance The difference arising in a system of *standard costing between the fixed overhead budgeted and the fixed overhead incurred.

fixed overhead total variance The difference arising in a system of *standard costing between the fixed overhead absorbed and that incurred for a period.

fixed overhead volume variance *See* overhead volume variance.

fixed production overhead The elements of an organization's *factory overheads that, in total, remain unchanged irrespective of changes in the level of production or sales. Examples include factory rent, depreciation of machinery using the *straight-line method, and the factory manager's salary.

fixed-rate loan A loan in which the interest rate is fixed at the start of the loan. It is standard for *bond issues, but unusual for bank borrowing.

flash report In the USA, a management report that highlights key data for corrective action.

flexed allowance (flexed budget allowance) The budgeted expenditure level for each of the variable cost items adjusted to the level of activity actually achieved. *See* budget cost allowance.

flexed budget A budget that has been adjusted to take into consideration the levels of activity actually achieved.

flexed budget allowance *See* flexed allowance.

flexible budget A budget that takes into account circumstances resulting in the actual levels of activity achieved being different from those on which the original budget was based. Consequently, in a flexible budget the *budget cost allowances for each cost item are changed for the variable items to allow for the actual levels of activity achieved. *Compare* fixed budget.

float *See* bank float; cash float.

floating assets *See* circulating assets.

floating charge A *charge over the assets of a company; it is not a legal charge over its fixed assets but floats over the charged assets until crystallized by some predetermined event. For example, a floating charge may be created over all the assets of a company, including its trading stock. The assets may be freely dealt with until a crystallizing event occurs, such as the company going into liquidation. Thereafter no further dealing may take place but the debt may be satisfied from the charged assets. Such a charge ranks in priority after legal charges and after preferred creditors in the event of a winding-up. It must be registered (*see* register of charges).

floating exchange rate A rate of exchange between one currency and others that is permitted to float according to market forces. Most major currencies and countries now have floating exchange rates but governments and central banks intervene, buying or selling currencies when rates become too high or too low. *Compare* fixed exchange rate.

floating-rate loan A loan that does not have a fixed interest rate throughout its life. Floating-rate loans can take various forms but they are all tied to a short-term market indicator; in the UK this is usually the *London Inter Bank Offered Rate.

floating-rate note (FRN) A *eurobond with a floating-rate interest, usually based on the *London Inter Bank Offered Rate. They first appeared in the 1970s and are usually issued as negotiable *bearer bonds. A **perpetual FRN** has no *redemption. A **capped FRN** is one with a maximum rate of interest. *Compare* variable-rate note.

floor *See* collar.

flotation The process of launching a public company for the first time by inviting the public to subscribe for its shares (also known as 'going public'). It applies both to private and nationalized share issues, and can be carried out by means of an *introduction, *issue by tender, *offer for sale, *placing, or *public issue. After flotation the shares can be traded on a stock exchange. Flotation allows the owners of the business to raise new capital or to realize their investments. In the UK, flotation can be either on the main market through a full listing or on the *unlisted securities market, where less stringent regulations apply. Some countries allow flotation on *over-the-counter markets.

flotation costs Costs arising on the *flotation of a company.

flowchart A diagram representing the sequence of logical steps required to solve a problem. It is a useful tool for the computer programmer, being used to plan a program. There are a number of conventional symbols used in flowcharts. The important ones are the process box, which indicates a process taking place, and the decision lozenge, which indicates where a decision is needed.

FMCG Abbreviation for fast-moving consumer goods.

Footsie *See* Financial Times Share Indexes.

forecast reporting The inclusion of projected figures in the *financial report of a company. For example, forecast sales figures may be included.

foreclosure The legal right of a lender of money if the borrower fails to repay the money or part of it on the due date. The lender must apply to a court to be permitted to sell the property that has been held as security for the debt. The court will order a new date for payment in an order called a **foreclosure nisi**. If the borrower again fails to pay, the lender may sell the property. This procedure can occur when the security is the house in which the mortgagor lives and the mortgagor fails to pay the mortgagee (bank, building society, etc.) the mortgage instalments. The bank, etc., then forecloses the mortgage, dispossessing the mortgagor.

foreign currency The currency of another country, which is not used in the preparation of an organization's domestic accounts. However, the existence of foreign subsidiaries or branches or overseas transactions may mean that an organization must translate these foreign currencies into the domestic currency to prepare its *financial statements. The rules for doing so are contained in *Statement of Standard Accounting Practice 20, 'Foreign Currency Translation'.

foreign emoluments Earnings received by a person domiciled outside the UK (*see* domicile), who is employed by a *non-resident employer.

foreign exchange (FX) The currencies of foreign countries, which are bought and sold on a **foreign-exchange market**. The foreign-exchange spot market caters for transactions in which the two currencies are exchanged usually within two business days. The *forward market in foreign exchange caters for situations in which the exchange does not take place until a specified date in the future.

foreign-exchange dealer A person who buys and sells *foreign exchange on a foreign-exchange market, usually as an employee of a *commercial bank. Banks charge fees or commissions for buying and selling foreign exchange on behalf of their customers; dealers may also be authorized to speculate in forward exchange rates.

forensic accounting Accounting that involves litigation. In such circumstances accountants may be called on to provide expert investigations and evidence.

forfaiting A form of *debt discounting for exporters in which a forfaiter accepts at a discount, and without recourse, a *promissory note, *bill of exchange, *letter of credit, etc., received from a foreign buyer by an exporter. Maturities are normally from one to three years. Thus the exporter receives payment without risk at the cost of the discount.

forfeited share A partly paid share in a company that the shareholder has to forfeit because of a failure to pay a subsequent part or final payment. Such shares must be sold or cancelled by a public *company but a private company is not regulated in this respect.

forgery The legal offence of making a false instrument in order that it may be accepted as genuine, thereby causing harm to others. Under the Forgery and Counterfeiting Act (1981), an instrument may be a document or any device (e.g. magnetic tape) on which information is recorded. An instrument is considered false, for example, if it purports to have been made or altered by someone who did not do so, on a date or at a place when it was not, or by someone who does not exist.

for information only Denoting a quotation given to provide a client with a guide to current market prices. It cannot be treated as a firm offer either to buy or to sell at the quoted price.

Form 10-K In the USA, the form filed annually with the *Securities and Exchange Commission by public traded companies. Audited financial statements and supporting detail are included; it normally provides more information than the annual report to stockholders.

Form 10-Q In the USA, the form filed quarterly with the *Securities and Exchange Commission by public traded companies. The form contains interim financial statements and may be for a single quarter or it may be cumulative. Comparative figures are provided for the same period in the previous year.

Form 20-F In the USA, the form required by the *Securities and Exchange Commission for the filing of annual results by non-US companies.

format The method of presenting financial statements chosen by an organization. Incorporated bodies must use the formats prescribed by the Companies Act for their *balance sheet and *profit and loss account. The profit and loss format is also regulated by *Financial Reporting Standard 3, 'Reporting Financial Performance'. *See* balance-sheet format; profit and loss account format.

formation expenses The expenses incurred on setting up a company. According to the Companies Act, these expenses must not be treated as an asset of the company.

forward differential *See* forward points.

forward forward interest rate The rate of interest that will apply to a loan or deposit beginning on a future date and maturing on a second future date.

forward margin *See* forward points.

forward market in foreign exchange A foreign-exchange market (*see* foreign exchange) in which currencies are traded for exchange at a future date. If an importer has an obligation to pay for goods in a foreign currency at some time in the future and does not wish to accept the risk that a currency fluctuation may lead to that obligation increasing, the importer can cover the risk by buying the foreign currency for delivery at a future date. Rates for standard periods for one, two, three, six, and twelve months can be obtained, while for other forward periods the price may have to be negotiated. The three most common forward-exchange contracts are forward *swaps, forward outrights (direct purchases), and maturity *option contracts.

forward points (forward differential; forward margin) The amount to be added to or deducted from the spot foreign-exchange rate to calculate the forward exchange rate.

forward-rate agreement (FRA) 1. A contract between two parties that determines the rate of interest that will apply to a future loan or a deposit, which may or may not materialize. **2.** A specified amount of a specified currency to be exchanged on an agreed future date at a specified rate of exchange.

founders' shares The shares issued to the founders of a company. These shares sometimes carry special *dividend rights and voting rights.

FRA Abbreviation for *forward-rate agreement.

fragmentation A situation that arises when two transactions, especially foreign-exchange transactions, offset each other commercially but not in terms of taxation.

franked investment income (FII) Dividends and other distributions from UK companies that are received by other companies. The principle of the *imputation system of taxation is that once one company has paid corporation tax, any dividends it pays can pass through any number of other companies without carrying a further corporation-tax charge, hence the term 'franked'. The amount of tax credit included in the franked investment income can reduce the amount of *advance corporation tax that the recipient company has to pay on its own dividends. Where franked investment income exceeds franked payments, the excess is carried forward to future accounting periods and can be set off against future franked payments (e.g. dividends). If the company has unused trading losses that could be carried back, a terminal loss, unused capital allowances, or a deduction for charges on income (e.g. debenture interest) then a claim can be made for the repayment of any unused tax credit.

franked payment A *dividend or other *distribution from a UK company together with the *advance corporation tax (ACT) attributable to that dividend. The shareholder will receive the dividend with the associated tax credit, which for 1995–96 will equate to the ACT paid by the company. For the company the ACT payable to the *Collector of Taxes will be the ACT attributable to the dividend less the ACT attributable to any *franked investment income received.

franked SORPs *See* Statements of Recommended Practice.

FRC Abbreviation for *Financial Reporting Council.

FRED Abbreviation for *Financial Reporting Exposure Draft.

free asset ratio The ratio of the market value of an insurance company's assets to its liabilities.

freehold An estate in land that is now usually held in fee simple. Land that is not freehold will be *leasehold.

free in and out Denoting a selling price that includes all costs of loading goods (into a container, road vehicle, ship, etc.) and unloading them (out of the transport).

free issue *See* scrip issue.

Friendly Society A UK non-profitmaking association registered as such under the Friendly Society Acts (1896–1955). Mutual insurance societies, dating back to the 17th century, were widespread in the 19th and 20th centuries, until many closed in 1946 after the introduction of National Insurance. Some developed into trade unions and some large insurance companies are still registered as Friendly Societies. They now offer tax-free investment plans normally over a 10-year period, with the policies including a life-assurance element. Investment in the tax-free plans are limited by government regulations.

fringe benefits 1. Non-monetary benefits offered to the employees of a company in addition to their wages or salaries. They include company cars, expense accounts, the opportunity to buy company products at reduced prices, private health plans, canteens with subsidized meals, luncheon vouchers, cheap loans, social clubs, etc. Some of these benefits, such as company cars, do not escape the tax net. 2. Benefits, other than dividends, provided by a company for its shareholders. They include reduced prices for the company's products or services, Christmas gifts, and special travel facilities.

FRN Abbreviation for *floating-rate note.

front-end fee A fee payable by a company that has borrowed a sum of money. It is paid shortly after signing the loan agreement and relates to the full amount of the loan, regardless of usage, subsequent cancellation, or early repayment. It is usually made up of four components: a lead management fee; general management fee; underwriting fee; and the participation fee.

front-end loading The initial charge to cover administrative expenses and commission included in the first payment of a loan instalment, unit trust investment, or insurance premium. The effect of this is to increase the first payment in relation to subsequent payments. Therefore, if an investment is being made on behalf of a client, the investment is the initial payment made by the client less the front-end load.

frozen assets Assets that for one reason or another cannot be used or realized. This may happen when a government refuses to allow certain assets to be exported.

FRR Abbreviation for *Financial Reporting Release.

FRRP Abbreviation for *Financial Reporting Review Panel.

FRS Abbreviation for *Financial Reporting Standard.

frustration of contract The termination of a contract as a result of an unforeseen event that makes its performance impossible or illegal. A contract to sell an aircraft could be frustrated if it crashed before the contract was due to be implemented. Similarly an export contract could be frustrated if the importer was in a country that declared war on the country of the exporter.

FSA Abbreviation for *Financial Services Act (1986).

FTII Abbreviation for Fellow of the *Chartered Institute of Taxation. In order to achieve this qualification a thesis on an aspect of UK taxation has to be submitted and accepted as being of the appropriate standard.

FT-SE 100 Index (Footsie) *See* Financial Times Share Indexes.

full absorption costing A costing method that charges all the production costs to the units produced. Production overhead costs are initially charged to *cost centres by allocation and apportionment; *absorption rates are then calculated using the total cost centre overheads by which the production overheads are charged to the *cost units. The method provides costs for product pricing and valuation of work in progress and finished goods, as well as profit measurement.

full consolidation The method of *consolidation in which 100% of each item of all subsidiary undertakings is brought into the *consolidated financial statements of a group. This will include *assets, *liabilities, income, and expenses. If a subsidiary undertaking is less than 100% owned, the percentage pertaining to the *minority interest must be adjusted for. This method of consolidation is generally adopted in the UK. *Compare* proportional consolidation.

full costing method (full costs) A method of costing a product or service that charges all the costs of an organization, both *direct costs and *overheads, to the *cost unit. The full costing method usually takes the total absorption cost approach to the costing of products and services.

full cost pricing A method of setting the selling prices of a product or service that ensures the price is based on all the costs likely to be incurred in its supply. *Compare* marginal cost pricing.

fully diluted earnings per share The *earnings per share for a company that takes into account the number of shares in actual issue as well as those that may be issued as a result of such factors as convertible loans and options or warranties.

fully paid capital *See* paid-up share capital.

fully paid share A *share in a company in which all calls for payment have been paid. The total paid will be the *par value plus any premium.

function A section or department of an organization that carries out a discrete activity, under the control of a manager or director. It is the section of the business for which *functional budgets are produced. Examples of separate functions are production, sales, finance, and personnel.

functional budget A financial or quantitative statement prepared for a *function of an organization; it summarizes the policies and the level of performance expected to be achieved by that function for a *budget period.

functional currency The currency of the economic environment in which a business operates. It is usually, although not necessarily, the currency in which the business will produce its audited accounts.

function costing The technique of collecting the costs of an organization by *function and presenting them to the functional management in operating statements on a regular basis.

fund 1. A resource managed on behalf of a client by a *financial institution. 2. A separate pool of monetary and other resources used to support designated activities.

fundamental accounting concepts *See* accounting concepts.

fundamental analysis A detailed analysis of the annual reports and accounts, as well as other information pertaining to a company, to assess whether its shares are incorrectly valued on the market (*see* annual accounts).

fundamental error A material mistake in, or omission from, the accounts of a business; it is not a recurring adjustment or the correction of an accounting estimate made in a prior period. When a fundamental error is discovered applying to a prior period, a *prior-period adjustment should be made.

funded pension scheme An occupational pension scheme in which the future liabilities for benefits are provided for by the accumulation of a fund of assets, held externally to the business of the employer.

funds flow statement A former *financial statement required by *Statement of Standard Accounting Practice 10, 'Source and Application of Funds', which showed the differences between two successive balance sheets. It has now been replaced by the *cash-flow statements required by *Financial Reporting Standard 1.

fungible issue A *bond issued on the same terms and conditions as a bond previously issued by the same company. It has the advantage of having paperwork consistent with the previous bond and of increasing the depth of the market of that particular bond (*see* deep market; thin market). The *gross redemption yield on the fungible issue will probably be different from that of the original issue, which is achieved by issuing the bond at a discount or a premium.

fungibles 1. Interchangeable goods, securities, etc., that allow one to be replaced by another without loss of value. Bearer bonds and banknotes are examples. 2. Perishable goods the quantity of which can be estimated by number or weight.

Future Development of Auditing (McFarlane Report) The title of a report published by the *Auditing Practices Board in November 1992. The report, which was published for public debate, was headed by John McFarlane. It examined the role and scope of *audits, the independence of the auditor, and how audit reports could include greater disclosure. Since this report was published, a new audit report with greater disclosure has been introduced in *Statement of Auditing Standards 600, 'Auditors' Reports on Financial Statements'.

futures contract An agreement to buy or sell a fixed quantity of a particular commodity, currency, or security for delivery at a fixed date in the future at a fixed price. Unlike an *option, a futures contract involves a definite purchase or sale and not an option to buy or sell; it therefore may entail a potentially unlimited loss. However, **futures** provide an opportunity for those who must purchase goods regularly to hedge against changes in price. For *hedging to be possible there must be speculators willing to offer these contracts; in fact trade between speculators usually exceeds the amount of hedging taking place by a considerable amount. In London, futures are traded in a variety of markets. *Financial futures are traded on the *London International Financial Futures and Options Exchange; the Baltic Exchange deals with shipping and agricultural products; *London FOX deals with cocoa, coffee, and other foodstuffs; the London Metal Exchange with metals; and the International Petroleum Exchange with oil. In these **futures markets**, in many cases actual goods (*see* actuals) do not pass between dealers, a bought contract being cancelled out by an equivalent sale contract, and vice versa; money differences arising as a result are usually settled through a *clearing house. In some futures markets only brokers are allowed to trade; in others, both dealers and brokers are permitted to do so.

FX Abbreviation for *foreign exchange.

G

GAAP Abbreviation for *generally accepted accounting principles.

GAAS Abbreviation for *generally accepted auditing standards.

gamma stocks Formerly, stocks that were less frequently traded on the London Stock Exchange than alpha and beta stocks.

Gantt chart A chart presenting a planned activity as horizontal bands against a background of dates. Planned production may also be compared to actual production.

Garner vs Murray A case (1904) cited in the determination of the dissolution of a *partnership. If any partners have a debit balance on their capital accounts at the end of the dissolution of a partnership, they must make the necessary contribution to the partnership. However, if a partner is insolvent, the other partners will have to bear the loss (*see* insolvency). In the event of the insolvency of a partner any losses should be shared in the ratio of the last agreed capital balances before the dissolution took place. This is known as the **Garner vs Murray rule**. Many *partnership agreements specifically exclude this rule, however, and agree instead that any such deficit will be borne in the *profit-sharing ratio.

GDP Abbreviation for *gross domestic product.

gearing (capital gearing; equity gearing; financial gearing; leverage) The relationship between the funds provided to a company by *ordinary shareholders and the long-term funds with a fixed interest charge, such as *debentures and *preference shares. A company is said to be highly geared when its fixed charges, either in terms of capital or income, are significantly higher than those for other companies. A highly geared company is considered to be a speculative investment for the ordinary shareholder and will be expected to show good returns when the company is doing well. The US word **leverage** is increasingly used in the UK.

gearing adjustment In *current cost accounting, an adjustment that reduces the charge to the owners for the effect of price changes on *depreciation, *stock, and *working capital. It is justified on the grounds that a proportion of the extra financing is supplied by the *loan capital of the business.

gearing ratios (leverage ratios) Ratios that express a company's capital *gearing. There are a number of different ratios that can be calculated from either the *balance sheet or the *profit and loss account. Ratios based on the balance sheet usually express *debt as a percentage of *equity, or as a percentage of debt plus equity. **Income gearing** is normally calculated by dividing the *profit before interest and tax by the gross interest payable to give the *interest cover.

General Commissioners An unpaid local body of persons of good standing appointed by the Lord Chancellor or, in Scotland, by the Secretary of State for

Scotland, to hear appeals against income tax, corporation tax, and capital gains tax assessments or matters of dispute arising from them. General Commissioners can appoint their own clerk, often a lawyer, who can advise them on procedure and legal matters. *Compare* Special Commissioners.

general controls Controls, other than *application controls, that relate to the environment within which computer-based accounting systems are developed, maintained, and operated; they are therefore applicable to all the applications. The objectives are to ensure the proper development and implementation of applications and the integrity of program and data files.

general expenses Those expenses of an organization that cannot easily be placed in any other cost classification.

general ledger *See* nominal ledger.

generally accepted accounting principles (GAAP) In the USA, the rules, *accounting standards, and *accounting concepts followed by accountants in measuring, recording, and reporting transactions. There is also a requirement to state whether *financial statements conform with GAAP. In the UK the concept is more loosely used but is normally taken to mean accounting standards and the requirements of company legislation and the *stock exchange. There is an argument that compliance with these requirements places an undue burden on small companies, which should be exempt from certain accounting standards.

generally accepted auditing standards (GAAS) In the USA, the broad rules and guidelines set down by the *Auditing Standards Board of the *American Institute of Certified Public Accountants (AICPA). In carrying out work for a client, a certified public accountant would apply the *generally accepted accounting principles; if they fail to do so, they can be held to be in violation of the AICPA's code of professional ethics.

general meeting A meeting that all the members of an association may attend.

general obligation bond In the USA, a security in which the government department with the authority to levy taxes has unconditionally promised payment.

general partner A member of a *partnership who has unlimited liability for any debts of that partnership. *Compare* limited partner.

general price level An index that gives a measure of the purchasing power of money. In the UK, the best-known measure is the *Retail Price Index; in the USA it is the *Consumer Price Index.

general purpose financial statements The *annual accounts and report prepared by companies; they are intended to serve the needs of many users and are therefore regarded as general purpose documents. Specific purpose statements are sometimes prepared to meet the needs of a particular group of users. However, as many annual report and accounts are over 80 pages in length it would not be practical to extend them further in an attempt to meet more closely the needs of the special groups of users. Therefore general purpose financial statements are often regarded as compromise documents designed to satisfy to a large extent the information needs of a number of different groups. Recent changes in legislation and the increasing complexity of *accounting standards have resulted in statements that are likely to be understood only by the financially sophisticated.

geographic segment A geographical area consisting of an individual country or group of countries in which a company or group operates. Under *Statement of Standard Accounting Practice 25, 'Segmental Reporting', companies are required to disclose certain financial information in respect of the geographic segments in which they operate or to which they supply products or services. The information is normally given in the notes to the financial statements in the *annual accounts and report.

geometric mean An average obtained by calculating the nth root of a set of n numbers. For example the geometric mean of 7, 100, and 107 is $\sqrt[3]{74\,900}$ = 42.15, which is considerably less than the *arithmetic mean of 71.3.

gifts inter vivos Gifts made during an individual's lifetime. The treatment of such gifts, for *inheritance tax purposes, depends on the amount of the gift, the occasion of the gift, and the recipient of the gift. Small gifts can be covered by the small gifts exemption (if less than £250) or by the individual's annual exemption (if less than £3000). Additional gifts are exempt if they are given on the occasion of marriage. Any gift from one individual to another individual is a *potentially exempt transfer and only becomes liable to tax if the donor dies within seven years of making the gift. Gifts to some *discretionary trusts are chargeable to inheritance tax at lifetime rates, which is half the death rate. The level of charge is dependent on the size of the transfer to the discretionary trust and the amount of previous *chargeable transfers within the preceding seven years. *See also* exempt transfers.

gifts with reservation of benefit A gift in which the donor retains some benefit from the asset given away. Examples include:
• shares given away in which the donor continues to receive the dividends;
• property given by a parent to a child, although the parent continues to live in the property, rent-free.

gilt-edged security (gilt) A fixed-interest security or stock issued by the British government in the form of **Exchequer stocks** or **Treasury stocks**. Gilts are among the safest of all investments, as the government is unlikely to default on interest or on principal repayments. They may be irredeemable or redeemable. **Redeemable gilts** are classified as: **long-dated gilts** or **longs** (not redeemable for 15 years or more), **medium-dated gilts** or **mediums** (redeemable in 5 to 15 years), or **short-dated gilts** or **shorts** (redeemable in less than 5 years).

Like most fixed-interest securities, gilts are sensitive not only to interest rates but also inflation rates. This led the government to introduce *index-linked gilts in the 1970s, with interest payments moving in a specified way relative to inflation.

Most gilts are issued in units of £100. If they pay a high rate of interest (i.e. higher than the current rate) a £100 unit may be worth more than £100 for a period of its life, even though it will only pay £100 on *redemption. Gilts bought through a stockbroker or bank are entered on the Bank of England Stock Register. Gilts can, however, be bought direct by post through the National Savings Stock Register.

giro A banking arrangement for settling debts that has been used in Europe for many years. In 1968 the Post Office set up the UK **National Girobank** (now Girobank plc) based on a central office in Bootle, Merseyside. Originally a system for settling debts between people who did not have bank accounts, it now offers many of the services provided by *commercial banks, with the advantage that there are many more post offices, at which Girobank services are provided, than there are bank branches. Also the post offices are open for longer hours than banks. Girobank also offers banking services to businesses, including an **automatic debit transfer** system, enabling businesses to collect money from a large number of customers at regular intervals for a small charge.

The **Bank Giro** is a giro system operated in the UK, independently of Girobank, by the clearing banks. It has no central organization, being run by bank branches. The service enables customers to make payments from their accounts by credit transfer to others who may or may not have bank accounts.

Bancogiro is a giro system in operation in Europe, enabling customers of the same bank to make payments to each other by immediate book entry.

global bond A single bond for the total amount of a new issue of bonds, issued on a temporary basis to the bank (normally the *paying agent) that has responsibility for distributing the actual bonds to investors. In due course the global bond, sometimes referred to as a **global bearer bond**, is exchanged for the actual bonds.

global custody Safekeeping, usually by banks, of securities held on behalf of clients. It can include full portfolio services, with valuation and reporting, settlement of trades, registration of ownership, use of specialized nominee companies, collection of domestic and foreign income, and tax accounting.

GNP Abbreviation for *gross national product.

goal congruency The circumstances in which the objectives of individual managers coincide with those of the organization as a whole.

going-concern concept A principle of accounting practice that assumes businesses to be going concerns, unless circumstances indicate otherwise. It assumes that an enterprise will continue in operation for the foreseeable future, i.e. that the accounts assume no intention or necessity to liquidate or significantly curtail the scale of the enterprise's operation. The implication of this principle is that assets are shown at cost, or at cost less depreciation, and not at their break-up values; it also assumes that liabilities applicable only on liquidation are not shown. The **going-concern value** of a business is higher than the value that would be achieved by disposing of its individual assets, since it is assumed that the business has a continuing potential to earn profits. The concept is assumed in the preparation of *financial statements. If an *auditor thinks otherwise the *audit report should be qualified.

golden handcuffs Financial incentives offered to key staff to persuade them to remain with an organization.

golden handshake (golden good-bye) An ex gratia payment or payment for loss of office made by an employer to an employee if the contract of employment is terminated; for example, in the case of a takeover. It is possible, under certain circumstances, for the compensation payment to be paid wholly or partly tax-free. The payment must not be made as a result of a contractual obligation to make such a payment nor should the employee be entitled to the payment. If it can be shown that the payment complies with the regulations then the first £30,000 is tax-free, with only the balance chargeable to tax.

golden hello A payment made to induce an employee to take up employment. The tax treatment depends on the nature of the payment; in some cases the taxpayer has successfully argued that the payment should be tax-free. However, in 1991 the House of Lords ruled that a payment made to a well-known footballer by a football club, as an inducement to join a new club, was taxable.

golden key The key that unlocks the *golden handcuffs; it usually consists of a single payment to an employee who has not lived up to expectations or who is no longer considered worth retaining.

golden parachute A clause in the employment contract of a senior executive in a company that provides for financial and other benefits if the executive is sacked or decides to leave as the result of a takeover or change of ownership.

golden share A share in a company that controls at least 51% of the voting rights. A golden share has been retained by the UK government in some *privatization issues to ensure that the company does not fall into foreign or other unacceptable hands.

good output In *process costing, the sound and flawless output from a process either to a succeeding process or to finished goods stock, the *normal loss and the *abnormal loss having been accounted for in the process costing procedures.

goods received note (GRN) A form completed by the recipient of ordered goods confirming the specification of the goods received. The form includes a description of the goods, the quantity, the *commodity code, the date received, and the order number.

goodwill The difference between the value of the separable net *assets of a business and the total value of the business. Purchased goodwill is the difference between the *fair value of the price paid for a business and the aggregate of the fair values of its separable net assets. It may be written off to *reserves or recognized as an *intangible fixed asset in the balance sheet and written off by *amortization to the *profit and loss account over its useful economic life. Internally generated goodwill should not be recognized in the financial statements of an organization. The treatment of goodwill is governed by *Statement of Standard Accounting Practice 22, 'Accounting for Goodwill'.

goodwill write-off reserve A special reserve against which to place a goodwill write-off, in accordance with *Statement of Standard Accounting Practice 22, 'Accounting for Goodwill'. The reserve has a debit balance and is referred to as the *dangling debit.

Government Accounting Standards Board In the USA, the organization responsible for *accounting standards for government units. It is under the control of the *Financial Accounting Foundation.

government grant An amount paid to an organization to assist it to pursue activities considered socially or economically desirable. Grants may be revenue-based, i.e. made by reference to a specified category of revenue expenditure. Revenue-based grants should be credited to the *profit and loss account in the same period as the revenue expenditure to which they relate. Capital-based grants are made by reference to specified categories of capital expenditure and should be credited to the profit and loss account over the useful *economic life of the asset to which they relate. *Statement of Standard Accounting Practice 4, 'Accounting for Government Grants', gives guidance with respect to the treatment of grants.

Gower Report A report on the protection of investors delivered to the UK government in 1984 by Professor J. Gower. Many of its recommendations were adopted in the subsequent *Financial Services Act (1986).

grace and notice provision The provision in a loan agreement that a borrower who fails on the due date to meet either an interest obligation or capital repayment obligation or who fails to comply with an undertaking is not initially in default. This prevents the *cross-default clause being invoked. The grace and notice provision is inserted into a loan agreement to avoid problems arising because of administrative mistakes, such as payments not being made on the correct day.

grace period *See* callable bonds.

green audit *See* environment audit.

greenmail The purchase of a large block of shares in a company, which are then sold back to the company at a premium over the market price in return for a promise not to launch a bid for the company. This practice is not uncommon in the USA, where companies are much freer than in the UK to buy their own shares. Although the morality of greenmail is dubious, it can be extremely profitable.

green reporting (environmental accounting) A report by the directors of a company that attempts to quantify the costs and benefits of that company's operations in relation to the environment. Although there are a number of advocates of the practice, few companies disclose in their *annual accounts and report information on the impact their activities have had on the environment.

grey knight In a takeover battle, a counterbidder whose ultimate intentions are undeclared. The original unwelcome bidder is the *black knight, the welcome counterbidder for the target company is the *white knight. The grey knight is an ambiguous intervener whose appearance is unwelcome to all.

grey market 1. Any market for goods that are in short supply. It differs from a black market in being legal; a black market is usually not. 2. A market in shares that have not been issued, although they are due to be issued in a short time. Market makers will often deal with investors or speculators who are willing to trade in anticipation of receiving an allotment of these shares or are willing to cover their deals after flotation. This type of grey market provides an indication of the market price (and premium, if any) after flotation. An investor who does not receive the anticipated allocation has to buy the shares on the open market, often at a loss.

GRN Abbreviation for *goods received note.

gross corporation tax The total *corporation tax payable on the profits chargeable to corporation tax for an accounting period, before deduction of any *advance corporation tax paid on distributions or income tax suffered on taxed income.

gross dividend The amount of a *dividend prior to the deduction of tax. Gross dividend is therefore equal to the dividend payable plus the *tax credit. *See* advance corporation tax.

gross dividend per share The total of the *gross dividends paid by a company in a year divided by the total number of ordinary shares on which the dividend is paid.

gross dividend yield *See* dividend.

gross domestic product (GDP) The monetary value of all the goods and services produced by an economy over a specified period. It is measured in three ways:
(i) on the basis of expenditure, i.e. the value of all goods and services bought, including consumption, capital expenditure, increase in the value of stocks, government expenditure, and exports less imports;
(ii) on the basis of income, i.e. income arising from employment, self-employment, rent, company profits (public and private), and stock appreciation;
(iii) on the basis of the value added by industry, i.e. the value of sales less the costs of raw materials.
In the UK, statistics for GDP are published monthly by the government on all three bases, although there are large discrepancies between each measure. Economists are usually interested in the real rate of change of GDP to measure the performance of an economy, rather than the absolute level of GDP. *See also* gross national product (GNP).

gross margin (gross profit; gross profit margin) The difference between the sales revenue of a business and the cost of goods sold. It does not include finance costs, administration, or the cost of distributing the goods. *Compare* net margin.

gross margin ratio (gross profit percentage) A ratio of financial performance calculated by expressing the *gross margin as a percentage of sales. With retailing companies in particular, it is regarded as a prime measure of their trading success. The only ways in which a company can improve its gross margin ratio are to increase selling prices and/or reduce its cost of sales.

gross national product (GNP) The *gross domestic product (GDP) with the addition of interest, profits, and dividends received from abroad by UK residents. The GNP better reflects the welfare of the population in monetary terms, although it is not as accurate a guide to the productive performance of the economy as the GDP.

gross profit *See* gross margin; profit.

gross profit percentage *See* gross margin ratio.

gross redemption yield (effective yield; yield to maturity) The internal rate of return of a bond bought at a specified price and held until maturity; it therefore includes all the income and all the capital payments due on the bond. The tax payable on the interest and the capital repayments is ignored.

gross up To convert a net amount into its equivalent gross amount. For example, an amount payable net of 17.5% *value added tax would be grossed up to the amount payable including 17.5% value added tax, i.e. by multiplying the net amount by 1.175.

group A parent undertaking and its subsidiary or subsidiaries. *See* consolidation; consolidated financial statements.

group accounts (group financial statements) *See* consolidated financial statements.

group company A company that is a *subsidiary undertaking or a *holding company.

group income A *dividend paid by one *group company to another, which is exempt from *advance corporation tax. The dividends received are not *franked investment income of the receiving company and are not subject to *corporation tax.

group registration Registration for *value added tax for a group of companies under common control. The business carried on by any group member is treated as that of the *representative member. VAT is not charged on supplies between group members.

group relief Relief available to companies within a 75% group as a result of which *qualifying losses can be transferred to other group companies. The losses transferred are available to set against the other group members' profits chargeable to corporation tax, thus reducing the overall tax liability for the group. A 75% group, for group relief, exists if one company holds 75% or more of:
• the ordinary share capital, and
• the distributable income rights, and
• the rights to the net assets in a winding-up.

group undertaking *See* subsidiary undertaking.

growth rate The amount of change over a period in some of the financial characteristics of a company, such as sales revenue or profits. It is normally measured in percentage terms and can be compared to the *Retail Price Index, or some other measure of inflation, to assess the real performance of the company.

guarantee A promise made by a third party (**guarantor**), who is not a party to a contract between two others, that the guarantor will be liable if one of the parties fails to fulfil the contractual obligations. For example, a bank may make a loan to a person, provided that a guarantor is prepared to repay the loan if the borrower fails to do so. The banker may require the guarantor to provide some *security to support the guarantee.

guaranteed bond In the USA, a *bond issued by one party with payment

guaranteed by another party. A common example is a bond issued by a
*subsidiary undertaking, which is guaranteed by the *holding company.

guaranteed minimum pension The earnings-related component of a state
pension that a person would have been entitled to as an employee of a
company, had that person not contracted out of the *State Earnings-Related
Pension Scheme (SERPS). Any private pension contract must pay at least the
guaranteed minimum pension if it is to be an acceptable replacement of a
SERPS pension.

hacker A person who uses a computer system without authorization, generally gaining access by means of a telephone connection.

hard currency A currency that is commonly accepted throughout the world; they are usually those of the western industrialized countries although other currencies have achieved this status, especially within regional trading blocs. Holdings of hard currency are valued because of their universal purchasing power. Countries with *soft currencies go to great lengths to obtain and maintain stocks of hard currencies, often imposing strict restrictions on their use by the private citizen.

hardware The electronic and mechanical parts of a computer system; for example, the central processing unit, disk drive, screen, and printer. *Compare* software package.

harmonization 1. The harmonization of financial reporting internationally, especially within the European Union. 2. *See* tax harmonization.

harvesting strategy Making a short-term profit from a particular product shortly before withdrawing it from the market. This is often achieved by reducing the marketing support it enjoys, such as advertising, on the assumption that the effects of earlier advertising will still be felt and the product will continue to sell.

haulage The charge made by a **haulier (haulage contractor)** for transporting goods, especially by road. If the goods consist of a large number of packages (e.g. 100 tonnes of cattlefood packed in 2000 bags each weighing 50 kilograms) there will be a separate charge for loading and unloading the vehicle.

head lease The main or first *lease, out of which **sub-leases** may be created. For example, if A grants a 99-year lease to B and B then grants a 12-year lease of the same property to C, the 99-year lease is the head lease and the 12-year lease is a sub-lease.

Health and Safety Commission A commission appointed by the Secretary of State for Employment to look after the health, safety, and welfare of people at work; to protect the public from risks arising from work activities; and to control the use and storage of explosives and other dangerous substances. It is composed of representatives from trade unions, employers, and local authorities with a full-time chairman. The **Health and Safety Executive** is a statutory body that advises the Commission and carries out its policies through 20 area offices. It includes HM Factory Inspectorate and a Medical Division, which itself includes the Employment Medical Advisory Service.

hedged funds Funding in which the managers invest in liquid instruments, such as currency and interest rate *derivatives, with the aim of making profits from movements in foreign-exchange or bond markets.

hedging An operation undertaken by a trader or dealer who wishes to protect an *open position, especially a sale or a purchase of a commodity, currency, security, etc., that is likely to fluctuate in price over the period that the position remains open. For example, a manufacturer may contract to sell a large quantity of a product for delivery over the next six months. If the product depends on a raw material that fluctuates in price, and if the manufacturer does not have sufficient raw material in stock, an open position will result. This open position can be hedged by buying the raw material required on a *futures contract; if it has to be paid for in a foreign currency the manufacturer's currency needs can be hedged by buying that foreign currency forward or on an *option. Operations of this type do not offer total protection because the prices of spot goods and futures do not always move together, but it is possible to reduce the vulnerability of an open position substantially by hedging.

Buying futures or options as a hedge is only one kind of hedging; it is known as **long hedging**. In **short hedging**, something is sold to cover a risk. For example, a fund manager may have a large holding of long-term fixed income investments and is worried that an anticipated rise in interest rates will reduce the value of the *portfolio. This risk can be hedged by selling interest-rate futures on a *financial futures market. If interest rates rise the loss in the value of the portfolio will be offset by the profit made in covering the futures sale at a lower price.

herd basis An election to treat a *production herd as a capital asset. The election is irrevocable and must be made within two years from the end of the first year of assessment or company accounting period for which the tax liability will be affected by the purchase of the herd.

higher-rate tax A higher rate of *income tax than the *basic rate. For 1995–96 higher-rate tax is payable on taxable income, after *personal allowances and other allowances, of £24,300 and over. The rate of tax is 40%.

highlights Brief summaries of financial information often given some prominence in the *annual accounts and report of a company. As there are no regulations covering their form and content there is considerable variety in the information they disclose. However, it is normal practice to show at the least the sales revenue, *profits, *earnings per share, and *dividend for the current and previous financial year.

high-low method A method used to predict *cost behaviour in which the observations of the cost levels for various activity levels are plotted on a graph; a straight line is drawn through the plots recording costs at the highest and lowest activity levels. This line then purports to represent the cost behaviour characteristics of that cost item. The method suffers from the major drawback that the line drawn has no particular mathematical characteristics, making the technique weak at cost prediction.

High-Street bank *See* commercial bank.

HIP Abbreviation for *human-information processing.

hire purchase (HP) A method of buying goods in which the purchaser takes possession of them as soon as an initial instalment of the price (a **deposit**) has been paid; ownership is obtained when all the agreed number of subsequent instalments have been completed. A **hire-purchase agreement** differs from a **credit-sale agreement** and **sale by instalments** (or a **deferred payment**

agreement) because in these transactions ownership passes when the contract is signed. It also differs from a contract of hire, because in this case ownership never passes. Hire-purchase agreements in the UK were formerly controlled by government regulations stipulating the minimum deposit and the length of the repayment period. These controls were removed in 1982. Hire-purchase agreements were also formerly controlled by the Hire Purchase Act (1965), but most are now regulated by the Consumer Credit Act (1974). In this Act a hire-purchase agreement is regarded as one in which goods are bailed in return for periodical payments by the bailee; ownership passes to the bailee if the terms of the agreement are complied with and the option to purchase is exercised.

A hire-purchase agreement often involves a *finance company as a third party. The seller of the goods sells them outright to the finance company, which enters into a hire-purchase agreement with the hirer.

historical cost A method of valuing units of stock or other assets based on the *original cost incurred by the organization. For example, the issue of stock using *first-in-first-out cost or *average cost charge the original cost against profits. Similarly, the charging of depreciation to the *profit and loss account, based on the original cost of an asset, is writing off the historical cost of the asset against profits. An alternative approach is the use of *current cost accounting.

historical cost accounting A system of accounting based primarily on the original costs incurred in a transaction. It is relaxed to some extent by such practices as the valuation of *stock at the lower of cost and *net realizable value and, in the UK, revaluation of *fixed assets. The advantages of historical cost accounting are that it is relatively objective, easy to apply, difficult to falsely manipulate, suitable for *audit verification, and fulfils the *stewardship function. In times of high inflation, however, the results of historical cost accounting can be misleading as profit can be overstated, assets understated in terms of current values, and *capital maintenance is only concerned with the nominal amount of the capital invested rather than its purchasing power. Because of these defects it is argued that historical cost accounting is of little use for decision making, but attempts to replace it with such other methods as *current cost accounting have failed.

Company legislation sets out the rules for the application of historical cost accounting to *financial statements. Companies may also choose to use alternative accounting rules based on current cost accounting.

historical-cost convention A convention under which *assets are carried in the *books of account at their historical cost.

historical summary A voluntary statement appearing in the *annual accounts and report of some companies in which the main financial results are given for the previous five to ten years.

holding company (parent company; parent undertaking) A company that has *subsidiary undertakings, forming part of a *group of companies.

holding gain A gain that results from the length of time an asset has been held rather than its use in the operations of a business. A holding gain is realized when the asset is sold but remains unrealized when the asset is still held. *See also* current cost accounting; cost of sales adjustment.

horizontal form The presentation of a *financial statement in which the debits are given on one side of the statement and the credits on the other. In the case of a *balance sheet, the *fixed assets and *circulating assets would be shown on the left-hand side of the statement and the *capital and *liabilities on the right-hand side. *Compare* vertical form.

horizontal integration The combination of two or more companies in the same business, carrying out the same process or production, usually to reduce competition and gain *economies of scale. *Compare* vertical integration.

hostile bid *See* agreed bid.

human-information processing (HIP) A study of the processes involved in decision making. The importance to the accountant is that an understanding of the way in which an individual uses information in the decision-making process should make it possible to determine the most appropriate information to be provided and the most suitable form.

human-resource accounting (human-asset accounting) An attempt to recognize the human resources of an organization, quantify them in monetary terms, and show them on the *balance sheet. A value is placed on such factors as the age and experience of employees as well as their future earnings power for the company. Although this approach has aroused some interest, in practice considerable difficulty has been met in quantifying the value of human resources. As a result human-resource accounting has failed to develop.

hurdle rate The rate of interest in a *capital budgeting study that a proposed project must exceed before it can be regarded worthy of consideration. The hurdle rate is often based on the *cost of capital or the *weighted average cost of capital, adjusted by a factor to represent the risk characteristics of the projects under consideration.

hybrid A synthetic financial instrument formed by combining two or more individual financial instruments, such as *bonds with warrants.

hyperinflation A very high rate of increase in the general price level. What constitutes hyperinflation is described in International Accounting Standard 29. The appropriate accounting treatment in the UK is explained in *Urgent Issues Task Force Abstract 9 and in the USA *Financial Accounting Standard 52.

hypothecation **1.** An authority given to a banker, usually as a **letter of hypothecation**, to enable the bank to sell goods that have been pledged to them as security for a loan. It applies when the bank is unable to obtain the goods themselves. The goods have often been pledged as security in relation to a documentary bill, the banker being entitled to sell the goods if the bill is dishonoured by non-acceptance or non-payment. **2.** A mortgage granted by a ship's master to secure the repayment with interest, on the safe arrival of the ship at her destination, of money borrowed during a voyage as a matter of necessity (e.g. to pay for urgent repairs). The hypothecation of a ship itself, with or without cargo, is called **bottomry** and is effected by a **bottomry bond**; that of its cargo alone is **respondentia** and requires a **respondentia bond**. The bondholder is entitled to a maritime lien.

IAPC Abbreviation for *International Auditing Practices Committee.

IAS Abbreviation for *International Accounting Standard.

IASC Abbreviation for *International Accounting Standards Committee.

IBRD Abbreviation for *International Bank for Reconstruction and Development.

ICAEW Abbreviation for *Institute of Chartered Accountants in England and Wales.

ICAI Abbreviation for *Institute of Chartered Accountants in Ireland.

ICAS Abbreviation for *Institute of Chartered Accountants of Scotland.

ICQ Abbreviation for *internal control questionnaire.

ICSA Abbreviation for *Institute of Chartered Secretaries and Administrators.

ideal standard (ideal standard cost) A cost, income, or performance standard set in *standard costing at such a level that it is only likely to be achieved under the most favourable conditions possible.

idle capacity The part of the budgeted capacity within an organization that is unused. It is measured in hours using the same measure as production. Idle capacity can arise as a result of a number of causes in all of which the actual hours worked is less than the budgeted hours available. The reasons can include non-delivery of raw materials, shortage of skilled labour, or lack of sales demand.

idle capacity ratio The ratio, sometimes expressed as a percentage, of the production capacity idle during a specified period to the capacity as expressed in the budget. Capacity can be measured in machine hours or labour hours and idle capacity is measured in the same way. The formula is:

(budgeted hours − actual hours worked × 100)/budgeted hours.

idle capacity variance (capacity usage variance; fixed overhead capacity variance) A variance in *standard costing that forms part of the *fixed overhead total variance; it measures the gain or loss arising in an accounting period due to the actual hours worked being greater or less than those budgeted.

idle time The time, usually measured in labour hours or machine hours, during which a production facility is unable to operate. *See also* idle capacity; waiting time.

IFA Abbreviation for *independent financial adviser.

IFAC Abbreviation for *International Federation of Accountants.

if-converted method In the USA, the method used for determining the dilution of *convertible securities that are not common *stock equivalents in the calculation of *fully diluted earnings per share. The assumption is made that the securities are converted at the beginning of the year or the issue date if later.

IHT Abbreviation for *inheritance tax.

IMA Abbreviation for *Institute of Management Accountants.

IMF Abbreviation for *International Monetary Fund.

immaterial Denoting any item or transaction that is not significant in the context of the whole of which it forms a part.

immediate holding company A company that has a *controlling interest in another company, even though it is itself controlled by a third company, which is the *holding company of both companies.

impersonal account A *ledger account that does not bear the name of a person. These accounts normally comprise the *nominal accounts, having such names as motor vehicles, heat and light, and stock in trade.

implicit contract theory The theory, introduced by several economists in the 1970s, that wage contracts contain an element of insurance for workers. Thus firms provide an implicit contract guaranteeing stable wages and employment in return for lower average pay, much as an insurance company charges a premium. This theory explains why, even in a recession, employers are reluctant to reduce wages creating the possibility of *involuntary unemployment. Unfortunately it has subsequently been shown that overemployment is just as likely an outcome as underemployment as a result of implicit contracts. However, the theory has provided many new insights into the operation of labour markets.

imprest account A means of controlling petty-cash expenditure in which a person is given a certain sum of money (float or imprest). When some of it has been spent, that person provides appropriate vouchers for the amounts spent and is then reimbursed so that the float is restored. Thus at any given time the person should have either vouchers or cash to a total of the amount of the float.

imputation system The system in which the *advance corporation tax paid by a company making *qualifying distributions is available to set against the *gross corporation tax for the company. The shareholder receiving the *dividend is treated as having suffered tax on the dividend and the *tax credit is available to set against his or her own liability to tax.

imputed cost A cost that is not actually incurred by an organization but is introduced into the management accounting records in order to ensure that the costs incurred by dissimilar operations are comparable. For example, if rent is not payable by an operation it will be introduced as an imputed cost so that the costs may be compared with an operation that does pay rent.

IMRO Abbreviation for Investment Management Regulatory Organization. *See* Self-Regulating Organization.

incentive stock option In the USA, the right given to employees to purchase a specified number of company shares at a specified price during a specified period. Only when the stock is sold by employees is it subject to tax.

income and expenditure account An account, similar to a *profit and loss account, prepared by an organization whose main purpose is not the generation of profit. It records the income and expenditure of the organization and results in either a surplus of income over expenditure or of expenditure over income. Such an organization's accounts do not use the *accrual concept.

income code *See* accounting code.

income gearing *See* gearing ratios.

income smoothing The manipulation by companies of certain items in their *financial statements so that they eliminate large movements in profit and are able to report a smooth trend over a number of years. The practice is pursued because of the belief that investors have greater confidence in companies that are reporting a steady increase in profits year by year. It is doubtful if any regulations can totally prevent this form of *creative accounting.

income standard In *standard costing, a predetermined level of income expected to be generated by an item to be sold. An income standard is often applied to a budgeted quantity in order to determine the *budgeted revenue.

income statement In the USA, the equivalent of a UK *profit and loss account.

income tax (IT) A direct tax on income. Income is not defined in UK tax legislation; amounts received are classified under various headings or *schedules and these schedules are subdivided into cases. In order to be classed as income an amount received must fall into one of these schedules. There are some specific occasions when the legislation requires capital receipts to be treated as income for taxation purposes, e.g. when a landlord receives a lump sum on the granting of a lease. In the UK the importance of the distinction between income and capital has diminished since income and capital have been charged at the same rate. Prior to 6 April 1988 capital was charged at 30%, whereas the top rate of income tax was 60%. The tax is calculated on the taxpayer's taxable income, i.e. gross income less any *income tax allowances and deductions. If the allowances and deductions exceed the gross income in a *fiscal year, no income tax is payable. In the UK, from 6 April 1995 the first £3200 of taxable income is charged at a reduced rate of 20%, after which tax at the *basic rate applies. For those on high incomes, *higher-rate tax is also charged. *See also* pay as you earn.

income tax allowances Allowances that may be deducted from a taxpayer's gross income before calculating the liability to *income tax. Every individual who is a UK resident is entitled to a *personal allowance. The level of allowance will depend on the age of the individual. For 1995–96 married couples are entitled to a married couple's allowance of £1720 if the elder spouse is under 65. This increases to £2995 when the elder spouse is aged between 65 and 74, and to £3035 when the elder spouse is aged 75 and over. There is an additional personal allowance for single parents equal to the married couple's allowance. A widow's bereavement allowance, equal to the married couple's allowance, is available to a widow for the year of her husband's death and the year following, if she does not remarry during that time. A blind person's relief is available to a blind person, which amounted to £1200 for 1995–96.

income tax code A code number issued by the *Board of Inland Revenue that takes account of the *personal allowance available to the taxpayer together with any other additional allowances to which he or she is entitled, e.g. married couple's allowance. The code is used by the employer through the *pay as you earn scheme to calculate the taxable pay using tables supplied by the Inland Revenue. The income tax code can also be used to tax *benefits in kind, such as company cars, by reducing the code number and so collecting more tax each tax week or month. The code provides a means of ensuring that the tax due for the *fiscal year is deducted from the employee's earnings in equal weekly or monthly amounts.

income tax month Under the UK taxation system, the month running from the 6th day of one month until the 5th day of the following month. This ensures that there are 12 complete tax months within the *fiscal year.

income tax schedules *See* schedule.

incomplete records Accounting records from which some details are missing. For example, some transactions may not have been recorded at all or some may have been partially recorded. To complete the records the cash book must be examined and, with the other information available, the missing items deduced.

incorporated company *See* company.

incorporation The process by which a *company is registered under the Companies Act, by act of parliament, or by Royal Charter.

incremental analysis A form of analysis used in decision making in which increases in the costs and revenues arising as the result of a decision are used to determine whether or not the decision is justified. For example, a decision further to process a product would only be justifiable if the incremental revenue is likely to exceed the incremental cost. Because costs and revenues may also fall as a result of a decision, *differential analysis, which considers *differential costs and revenues, is often preferred.

incremental budget A budget prepared using a previous period's budget or actual performance as a basis, with incremental amounts added for the new budget period. This approach to budget preparation is not recommended as it often fails to take into account the changed operating conditions for the new budget period, which will not necessarily replicate those for the previous period. *Compare* zero-base budget.

incremental cost The additional cost incurred as the result of a particular decision or set of circumstances.

independence of auditors The fundamental principle that *auditors must be, and must be seen to be, independent to enable them to behave with integrity and make objective professional and business judgments. Specific threats to independence include:
(1) an overdependence upon the fees paid by an audit client, especially if fees are overdue;
(2) any family or personal relationship between auditor and client;
(3) any beneficial interest held by the auditor or the staff of the practice in shares or other investments or trusts involving the client;

(4) any loan between an auditor and the client;
(5) any services or hospitality offered by an audit client to the auditors;
(6) any services other than the audit provided by the auditor to the client.

The independence of the auditor is strengthened by the *Companies Act regulation of the qualification of auditors and by conferring certain rights on the auditor. The professional audit bodies give ethical guidance designed to deal with each of the above situations.

independent financial adviser (IFA) A person defined under the *Financial Services Act (1986) as an adviser who is not committed to the products of any one company or organization. Such a person is licensed to operate by one of the *Self-Regulating Organizations or *recognized professional bodies. With no loyalties except to the customer, the IFA must offer **best advice** from the whole market place. Eight categories of IFA exist, grouped into four main areas: advising on investments; arranging and transacting life assurance, pensions, and unit trusts; arranging and transacting other types of investments; and management of investments. All licensed independent financial advisers contribute to a compensation fund for the protection of their customers.

independent projects Projects that are independent of each other in a comparative *appraisal. Such projects are not *mutually exclusive projects, as it is possible to pursue all of them if circumstances permit.

independent taxation A system in which married women are taxed separately from their husbands. Prior to 1990 in the UK, the income of a married woman was added to the income of her husband and taxed accordingly. There was some relief for earned income, which if the taxpayer elected could be treated as the income of the married woman and taxed as such, but when this occurred the personal allowance available for the husband was reduced.

index *See* Financial Times Share Indexes; Retail Price Index.

indexation 1. The policy of connecting such economic variables as wages, taxes, social-security payments, annuities, or pensions to rises in the general price level (*see* inflation) This policy is often advocated by economists in the belief that it mitigates the effects of inflation. In practice, complete indexation is rarely possible, so that inflation usually leaves somebody worse off (e.g. lenders, savers) and somebody better off (borrowers). *See* Retail Price Index.
2. An adjustment to take account of the rise in the *Retail Price Index over the period of ownership of an asset. In the UK, indexation is applied to the cost, or 31 March 1982 value, of an asset. The indexed cost, or indexed 31 March 1982 value, is deducted from the proceeds of sale on disposal of the asset, in order to establish the *chargeable gain for *capital gains tax purposes. Indexation was introduced to eliminate the part of the gain arising from inflation. *See* indexation allowance.

indexation allowance An allowance used to accommodate a rise in the *Retail Price Index (RPI) over the period of ownership of an asset, when calculating gains or losses for *capital gains tax. The indexation allowance is the product of the cost of the asset and the **indexation factor**. This factor is calculated as:

$$(R_2 - R_1)/R_1,$$

where R_2 is the RPI in the month of disposal and R_1 is the RPI in the month of acquisition.

Thus, if an asset cost £1000 in June 1984, when the RPI was 89.2, and was sold for £1900 in March 1995, when the RPI was 147.5, the indexation factor would have been:

$$(147.5 - 89.2)/89.2 = 0.654.$$

The indexation allowance was therefore:

$$£1000 \times 0.654 = £654.$$

The profit of £900 is therefore reduced to a chargeable gain for capital gains tax of £900 − £654 = £246. For an asset acquired before 31 March 1982, its *open-market value on this date can be used instead of cost.

index-linked gilt A *gilt-edged security in which the UK government has an obligation to increase both interest and redemption payments pro rata to increases in the *Retail Price Index. Interest payments are calculated using the ratio of the RPI for the start date to RPI for the end date of the interest period.

indirect cost centre *See* service cost centre.

indirect costs (indirect expenses) Expenses that cannot be traced directly to a *product or *cost unit and are therefore *overheads (*compare* direct costs). As some indirect product costs may, however, be regarded as *cost centre direct costs, the indirect cost centre costs are usually those costs requiring *apportionment to cost centres in an *absorption costing system.

indirect labour Personnel not directly engaged in the production of a product or *cost unit manufactured by an organization. Examples of indirect labour include maintenance personnel, cleaning staff, and senior supervisors, such as foremen. *Compare* direct labour.

indirect labour cost The wages, bonuses, and other remuneration paid to *indirect labour.

indirect manufacturing costs *See* factory overhead.

indirect materials Those materials that do not feature in the final product but are necessary to carry out the production, such as machine oil, cleaning materials, and consumable materials. *Compare* direct materials.

indirect materials cost The expenses incurred in providing *indirect materials.

indirect method The method used for a *cash-flow statement in which the operating profit is adjusted for non-cash charges and credits to reconcile it with the net cash flow from operating activities.

indirect taxation Taxation that is intended to be borne by persons or organizations other than those who pay the tax. The principal indirect tax in the UK is *value added tax, which is paid by traders as goods or services enter into the chain of production, but which is ultimately borne by the consumer of the goods or services. One of the advantages of indirect taxes is that they can be collected from comparatively few sources while their economic effects can be widespread.

industrial buildings Factories and ancillary premises used for manufacturing a product or for carrying on a trade in which goods are subjected to any process. For qualifying buildings there is a special category of capital allowance, known as **industrial-buildings allowance**. From 1 November 1993 this was restricted to a *writing-down allowance of 4% on a *straight-line basis. The allowance is based on the cost of the building including the cost of preparing the land, but excluding the cost of the land itself and the cost of the non-industrial parts, e.g. offices. If the cost of any non-industrial parts is less than 25% of the total cost of the building, the costs of the non-industrial parts are included for the purpose of calculating the industrial-buildings allowance. For qualifying industrial buildings an **initial allowance** was available until 31 March 1986 and for the year 1 November 1992 to 31 October 1993. During the year to 31 October 1993 the initial allowance was 20%, and both the initial and the writing-down allowance could be claimed in the year of purchase, provided the building was brought into use.

industrial development bond In the USA, a *debt issued by a municipality to finance *assets, which are then leased to private industrial businesses in order to promote local economic development.

industry segment A distinguishable component of an organization that provides a separate product or service or a separate group of related products or services.

ineligible group A *group of companies that does not qualify for an exemption (e.g. a *medium-sized company filing exemption) because a member of the group is a non-qualifying company for that particular exemption. For example, if a *public limited company or a bank is a member of a group all the companies in the group are ineligible for medium-sized company filing exemption.

inflation A general increase in prices in an economy and consequent fall in the purchasing value of money. *See also* Retail Price Index.

inflation accounting A method of accounting that, unlike *historical cost accounting, attempts to take account of the fact that a monetary unit (e.g. the pound sterling) does not have a constant value; because of the effects of inflation, successive accounts expressed in that unit do not necessarily give a fair view of the trend of profits. The principal methods of dealing with inflation have been *current cost accounting and *current purchasing power accounting.

information inductance The extent to which a person's behaviour is affected by the information they are required to communicate. For example, the directors of a company required to produce an *annual accounts and report (*see* annual accounts) may emphasize the favourable aspects of the *financial statements and may even adopt *creative accounting.

information intermediaries Individuals and groups who obtain, analyse, and interpret information, communicating their findings to others. An example is the analyst who uses the *financial statements and other information relating to a company to advise clients whether to buy, hold, or sell the company's shares. The information intermediary will make use of not only the *annual accounts and report, *preliminary announcements of profits, and *interim financial statements but also any other financial or non-financial information that is available, including that not on the public record, although this could lead to the accusation of *insider dealing.

information overload The increasing amount of financial information that companies are required to provide, some of which is beyond the user's ability to assimilate, analyse, and interpret. Because it was considered that full *annual accounts and reports may present an information overload, the Department of Trade and Industry have introduced *summary financial statements.

information system A system that gathers information. It may process the information and present it in a format suitable for decision making.

information technology (IT) The use of computers and other electronic means to process and distribute information. Information can be transferred between computers using cables, satellite links, or telephone lines. Networks of connected computers can be used to send *electronic mail or to interrogate *databases, using such systems as Viewdata and Teletext. These systems also enable *electronic transfer of funds to be made between banks, as well as telebanking and teleshopping from the home. The same technology is used in the entertainment industry to provide cable and satellite television and videotape and laser disk films.

infrastructure (social overhead capital) The goods and services, usually requiring substantial investment, considered essential to the proper functioning of an economy. For example, roads, railways, sewerage, and electricity supply constitute essential elements of a community's infrastructure. Since the infrastructure often possesses many of the characteristics of public goods, it is often argued that they should be funded, partly if not wholly, by the government by means of taxation.

inherent vice A defect or weakness of an item, especially of a cargo, that causes it to suffer some form of damage or destruction without the intervention of an outside cause. For example, certain substances, such as jute, when shipped in bales, can warm up spontaneously, causing damage to the fibre. Damage by this cause is excluded from most cargo insurance policies as an excepted peril.

inheritance tax (IHT) A tax introduced in the budget of 1986 to replace *capital transfer tax. Inheritance tax is chargeable on the death of an individual domiciled in the UK on all property, wherever it is situated. It is also charged on *potentially exempt transfers made within seven years of death. A non-UK domiciled individual is charged on death to inheritance tax on all UK property. Inheritance tax arises on lifetime *chargeable transfers at a lifetime rate, which is half the death rate of inheritance tax (*see also* exempt transfers).

initial yield The gross initial annual income from an asset divided by the initial cost of that asset. *Compare* gross redemption yield.

input tax *Value added tax paid by a *taxable person on purchasing goods or services from a VAT-registered trader. The input tax, excluding *irrecoverable input VAT, is set against the *output tax in order to establish the amount of VAT to be paid to the tax authorities.

inside director In the USA, an employee of a company who has been appointed to the board of directors.

insider dealing (insider trading) Dealing in company securities with a view to making a profit or avoiding a loss while in possession of information that, if generally known, would affect their price. Under the Companies Securities (Insider Dealing) Act (1985) those who are or have been connected with a company (e.g. the directors, the company secretary, employees, and professional advisers) are prohibited from such dealing on or, in certain circumstances, off the stock exchange if they acquired the information by virtue of their connection and in confidence. The prohibition extends to certain unconnected persons to whom the information has been conveyed.

insolvency The inability to pay one's debts when they fall due. In the case of individuals this may lead to *bankruptcy and in the case of companies to *liquidation. In both of these cases the normal procedure is for a specialist, a trustee in bankruptcy or a liquidator, to be appointed to gather and dispose of the assets of the insolvent and to pay the creditors. Insolvency does not always lead to bankruptcy and liquidation, although it often does. An insolvent person may have valuable assets that are not immediately realizable.

insolvency administration order A court order for the administration of the insolvent estate of a deceased debtor in *bankruptcy.

insolvency practitioner A person authorized to undertake insolvency administration as a *liquidator, provisional liquidator, *administrator, *administrative receiver, or nominee or supervisor under a *voluntary arrangement. Insolvency practitioners are members of the Insolvency Practitioners Association.

inspector general In the USA, the federal office that performs audit and investigative activities on federal agencies, making periodic reports to Congress.

Inspector of Taxes A civil servant responsible to the *Board of Inland Revenue for issuing tax returns and assessments, the conduct of appeals, and agreeing tax liabilities with taxpayers.

instability index of earnings A measure of the deviation between actual profits of a company and trend profit. The higher the index, the greater the instability of a company's profitability.

instalment sale In the USA, the equivalent of a UK retail sale by hire purchase.

Institute of Certified Public Accountants A body of accountants established in 1903 and amalgamated in 1932 with the Central Association of Accountants; in 1941 this body amalgamated with the *Chartered Association of Certified Accountants.

Institute of Chartered Accountants in England and Wales (ICAEW) An institute formed in 1880 from the following five bodies: the Incorporated Society of Liverpool Accountants (1870); the Institute of Accountants in London (1870); the Manchester Institute of Accountants (1871); the Society of Accountants in England (1872); the Sheffield Institute of Accountants (1877). The ICAEW was established by Royal Charter in 1880 and merged with the Society of Incorporated Accountants and Auditors (1885) in 1957. The members of the

ICAEW are prominent in public practice and tend to concentrate in areas of *financial accounting. *See also* accountancy bodies.

Institute of Chartered Accountants in Ireland (ICAI) An institute established in 1888 before the partition of Ireland. The Institute operates in both the Republic of Ireland and the province of Northern Ireland. *See also* accountancy bodies.

Institute of Chartered Accountants of Scotland (ICAS) A body of accountants that originated with the Edinburgh Society of Accountants (1854), the Glasgow Institute of Accountants and Actuaries (1854), and the Aberdeen Society of Accountants (1867), which merged in 1951. It is the longest established professional accountancy body in the world. *See also* accountancy bodies.

Institute of Chartered Secretaries and Administrators (ICSA) A professional body established in 1891 to safeguard the interests of company secretaries and administrators.

Institute of Internal Auditors An institute founded in 1945 in the USA; it was established in the UK in 1948 as part of the US-based international body. Its journal is *The Internal Auditor*.

Institute of Management Accountants (IMA) A US accountancy body established in 1919 as the National Association of Cost Accountants.

Institute of Taxation *See* Chartered Institute of Taxation.

institutional investor An organization, such as a bank, insurance company, or pension fund, that trades in very large volumes of securities. Institutional investors tend to dominate stock exchanges in many countries.

instrument (financial instrument) An agreement in the form of a document that sets out the terms and conditions of an order to pay or promise to pay, or a certificate of indebtedness. In company accounts it is essential to distinguish between capital instruments and *equity; the regulations are given in *Financial Reporting Standard 4, 'Capital Instruments'. *See also* negotiable instrument.

intangible fixed assets *Fixed assets of a non-monetary nature that have no physical substance. This definition is based on that contained in the *Accounting Standards Committee Exposure Draft 52, 'Accounting for Intangible Assets'. Excluded from this definition are development expenditure, leases relating to tangible assets, *goodwill, and investments. The accounting treatment for intangible assets has been a controversial topic and assets, such as *brands and publication titles, have appeared on the balance sheets of a number of well-known companies. By identifying such items as intangible assets, separate from goodwill, they do not fall under the requirements of *Statement of Standard Accounting Practice 22, in which goodwill has either to be written off immediately to *reserves or *amortized over a period of years to the *profit and loss account. The *Accounting Standards Board has issued a discussion document, which has received a number of criticisms because of its simplistic treatment of intangible assets. Under the Companies Act (1985) intangible assets is a main heading, which should appear on the face of the *balance sheet. The following subheadings are required but may be shown either on the face of the balance sheet or in the notes: *development costs;

concessions, patents, licences, trademarks, and similar rights and assets; goodwill; payments on account.

intangible property A property that cannot be possessed physically but that confers on its owner a legally enforceable right to receive a benefit, for example money. *See also* intangible fixed assets.

integrated accounts Accounting records kept in one set of books that contains both the *financial accounts and the *cost accounts of an organization in an integrated form. This avoids the necessity of reconciling separate financial and cost books and at the same time ensures that both records are based on the same data.

integrated test facility (ITF) An *embedded audit facility consisting of program, code, or additional data provided by the *auditor and incorporated into the computer element of the client's accounting system. Using ITF, a fictitious entity is created, for example a customer, within the context of the regular application. Transactions are then posted to the fictitious entity together with regular transactions and the results produced by the normal processing cycle are then compared with predetermined results. Such entries should be reversed at defined cut-off dates to ensure that they are not included in the financial reports. ITF enables an auditor and the client's management to check continuously on the internal processing functions. *See also* computer-assisted audit techniques; systems control and review file.

Inter-American Accounting Association A professional organization concerned with the technical aspects of accounting in the Americas; it meets once every two to three years.

interbank market **1.** The part of the London *money market in which banks lend to each other and to other large financial institutions. The *London Inter Bank Offered Rate (LIBOR) is the rate of interest charged on interbank loans. Trading is over-the-counter and usually through brokers and dealers. The sums are large but the periods of the loans are very short, often overnight. **2.** The market between banks in foreign currencies, including spot currencies and forward *options.

intercompany transactions (intragroup transactions) Transactions between the companies in a *group. These may be in the form of charges or the transfer of goods or services. It is important in the preparation of *consolidated financial statements that such transactions are eliminated or suitable adjustments made as they do not reflect transactions between the group and external parties. *See also* consolidation adjustments.

interest The charge made for borrowing a sum of money. The *interest rate is the charge made, expressed as a percentage of the total sum loaned, for a stated period of time (usually one year). Thus, a rate of interest of 15% per annum means that for every £100 borrowed for one year, the borrower has to pay a charge of £15, or a charge in proportion for longer or shorter periods. In **simple interest**, the charge is calculated on the sum loaned only, thus $I = Prt$, where I is the interest, P is the principal sum, r is the rate of interest, and t is the period. In **compound interest**, the charge is calculated on the sum loaned plus any interest that has acrued in previous periods. In this case $I = P[(1 + r)^n - 1]$, where n is the number of periods for which interest is separately calculated. Thus, if £500 is loaned for two years at a rate of 12% per annum, compounded quarterly, the value of n will be $4 \times 2 = 8$ and the value of r will be $12/4 = 3\%$. Thus, $I = 500 \left[(1.03)^8 - 1 \right] = £133.38$, whereas on a simple-interest basis it would be only £120. These calculations of interest apply equally to deposits that attract income in the form of interest.

In general, rates of interest depend on the money supply, the demand for loans, government policy, the risk of nonrepayment as assessed by the lender, the period of the loan, and relative levels of foreign-exchange rates into other currencies.

interest cover (fixed-charge–coverage ratio) A ratio showing the number of times interest charges are covered by *earnings before interest and tax. For example, a company with interest charges of £12 million and earnings before interest and tax of £36 million would have its interest covered three times. The ratio is one way of analysing *gearing and reflects the vulnerability of a company to changes in interest rates or profit fluctuations. A highly geared company, which has a low interest cover, may find that an increase in the interest rate will mean that it has no earnings after interest charges with which to provide a dividend to shareholders. *Compare* financial stability measures.

interest-in-possession trust A type of fixed-interest *trust in which there is an entitlement to the income generated by the trust assets. The *beneficiaries of an interest-in-possession trust, the life tenants, are entitled to the income arising for a fixed period or until their death. The capital in the trust then passes absolutely to the *remainderman.

interest rate The amount charged for a loan, usually expressed as a percentage of the sum borrowed. Conversely, the amount paid by a bank, building society, etc., to a depositor on funds deposited, again expressed as a percentage of the sum deposited. *See* annual percentage rate; base rate; London Inter Bank Bid Rate; London Inter Bank Offered Rate.

interest-rate guarantee An indemnity sold by a bank, or similar financial institution, that protects the purchaser against the effect of future movements in interest rates. It is similar to a *forward-rate agreement, but the terms are specified by the customer.

interest-rate risk The risk that the value of an asset or liability can vary during its life as a result of movements in interest rates.

interest receivable account A ledger account that is credited with interest receivable (double entry to *debtors until received and then to the bank). It is credited to the *profit and loss account for the period.

interfirm comparison The process carried out by some independent bodies and trade associations in which the accounts and statistical data of comparable organizations are subjected to a *ratio analysis in order to compare the ranges of performance in various areas of operation of the different organizations.

interim accounts *See* interim financial statements.

interim audit **1.** The conduct by *auditors of certain phases of the *audit of a company during the course of a financial year, rather than leaving all the work until after the year has ended. **2.** An audit of the *interim financial statements of a company.

interim dividend A *dividend paid midway through a *financial year. *See also* dividend policy.

interim financial statements (interim accounts; interim report)
*Financial statements issued for a period of less than a financial year. Although there are provisions under the Companies Act (1985) that refer to interim accounts in certain circumstances relating to the distribution of *dividends, there are no legal requirements obliging companies to produce interim accounts on a regular basis. However, *listed companies on the *London Stock Exchange are required to prepare a half-yearly report on their activities and *profit and loss during the first six months of each financial year. The interim financial statement must be either sent to the holders of the company's listed *securities or advertised in at least one national newspaper not later than four months after the end of the period to which it relates. A copy of the interim financial statements must also be sent to the Company Announcements Office and to the competent authority of each other state in which the company's shares are listed. The vast majority of companies choose to send the interim statement to shareholders with a brief announcement of the headline figures reported in the press. There is no requirement for the interim statements to be audited. Although the stock-exchange regulations require mainly profit information, there is a trend for the larger companies to also provide *balance sheets and *cash-flow statements. In the UK, the requirements only call for six-monthly financial statements, but some of the larger companies with interests in the USA follow the US practice of issuing reports quarterly.

interlocking accounts An accounting system that keeps *cost accounting and *financial accounting information separately, regularly reconciling the two by use of *control accounts.

intermediate holding company A company that is both a *holding company of one group and a *subsidiary undertaking of a larger group. It may qualify for exemption from publishing *consolidated financial statements as a holding company of the smaller group. *See* exemption from preparing consolidated financial statements.

intermediation The activity of a bank, similar financial institution, broker, etc., in acting as an intermediary between the two parties to a transaction; the intermediary can accept all or part of the credit risk or the other commercial risks. *Compare* disintermediation.

internal audit An *audit that an organization carries out on its own behalf, normally to ensure that its own internal controls are operating satisfactorily. Whereas an external audit is almost always concerned with financial matters, this may not necessarily be the case with an internal audit; internal auditors may also concern themselves with such matters as the observation of the safety and health at work regulations or of the equal opportunities legislation. It may also be used to detect any theft or fraud (*see also* internal control).

internal auditor An auditor who is a member of an *internal audit department of a company.

internal control The measures an organization employs to ensure that opportunities for fraud or misfeasance are minimized. Examples range from requiring more than one signature on certain documents, security arrangements for stock-handling, division of tasks, keeping of *control accounts, use of special passwords, handling of computer files, etc. It is one of the principal concerns of an *internal audit to ensure that internal controls are working properly so that the external auditors can have faith in the accounts produced by the organization. Internal control should also reassure management of the integrity of its operations.

internal control questionnaire (ICQ) A document used by an *auditor to assess the *internal control system of an organization. Questions will be tailored to the cycle being audited; for example, the sales or revenue cycle will check that sales are authorized, goods are invoiced, invoices are properly prepared, recorded, and supported, and payment is received at the correct time. The questionnaire will be used by the auditor to identify strengths and weaknesses in the system, which can be used to predict the errors or irregularities that could occur. These predictions enable the auditors to design *substantive tests to discover and quantify errors. *See also* internal control risk; audit risk.

internal control risk The risk that material errors will neither be prevented or detected by the *internal control system of a company. *See also* audit risk.

internal control system A system of controls, both financial and non-financial, set up by the management of a company to carry out the business of the company in an orderly and efficient manner. The system should ensure that management policies are adhered to, assets are safeguarded, and the records of the company's activities are both complete and accurate. The individual components of an internal control system are the individual internal controls. *See also* internal control risk.

internal rate of return (IRR) An interest rate that gives a *net present value of zero when applied to a projected cash flow. This interest rate, where the *present values of the cash inflows and outflows are equal, is the internal rate of return for a project under consideration, and the decision to adopt the project would depend on its size compared with the *cost of capital. The approximate IRR can be computed manually by *linear interpolation but most computer *spreadsheet programs now include a routine enabling the IRR to be computed quickly and accurately. The IRR technique suffers from the possibility of *multiple solution rates in some circumstances.

Internal Revenue Code The federal tax law of the USA, which comprises the regulations applied to taxpayers.

Internal Revenue Service (IRS) In the USA, the branch of federal government responsible for collecting most types of taxes. The IRS administers the *Internal Revenue Code, investigates tax abuses, and makes criminal prosecution for tax fraud through the US tax court.

International Accounting Standards (IAS) Accounting standards issued by the *International Accounting Standards Committee. Some of the advantages claimed for international standards are that *financial statements prepared in different countries will be more comparable, multinational companies will find preparation of their accounts easier, listing on different stock exchanges can be achieved more simply, and financial statements will be of greater use to users. However, international standards are not mandatory; moreover, some permit such a degree of flexibility in accounting treatments that comparability is impaired. Countries in which the setting of accounting standards is well established have national accounting standards that usually deal with the same topics as international standards. Some countries, with a less well-developed procedure for setting standards, adopt international accounting standards or use them as a model for preparing their own.

International Accounting Standards Committee (IASC) A committee that came into existence in 1973 as a result of an agreement by accounting bodies in a number of countries; there are now 95 member organizations from all major countries. The IASC has as its objectives the formulation and publication of accounting standards, the promotion of their worldwide acceptance, and the harmonization of regulations, accounting standards, and procedures relating to the presentation of *financial statements. The IASC has a small full-time secretariat and has published some 29 *International Accounting Standards. Although critics would argue that the standards issued to date have been too flexible and are often a compromise between UK and US standards, the influence of the IASC has been growing; it has succeeded in reducing the number of alternative accounting treatments permitted in its standards.

International Association of Book-keepers A professional association of book-keepers. Members must have passed, or be exempt from, the Association's exams and have completed a period working in a book-keeping position. There are three levels of membership: Licentiate (LIAB), Associate (AIAB), and Fellow (FIAB).

International Auditing Practices Committee (IAPC) A standing committee of the *International Federation of Accountants. It has a specific responsibility to issue exposure drafts and guidelines on auditing and related services. It also issues *International Standards on Auditing (ISA). The members of the committee are nominated by the member bodies in the countries selected by the Council of the International Federation of Accountants. The representatives designated by the member body or bodies to serve on the IAPC must be members of one of the bodies. To obtain a broad spectrum of views, whenever possible, the subcommittees of IAPC include representatives from countries that are not members of IAPC.

International Bank for Reconstruction and Development (IBRD) A specialized agency working in coordination with the United Nations, established in 1945 to help finance post-war reconstruction and to help raise standards of living in developing countries, by making loans to governments or guaranteeing outside loans. It lends on broadly commercial terms, either for specific projects or for more general social purposes; funds are raised on the international capital markets. The Bank and its affiliates, the International Development Association and the International Finance Corporation, are often known as the **World Bank**; it is owned by the governments of 151 countries. Members must also be members of the *International Monetary Fund. The headquarters of the Bank are in Washington, with a European office in Paris and a Tokyo office.

International Federation of Accountants (IFAC) A body formed in 1977 with the objective of developing an international accountancy profession with harmonized standards. Based in the USA, it has a membership of accounting bodies representing some 80 countries. It works through a number of committees responsible for education, ethics, financial and management accounting, and public-sector and international auditing practices. Although it does not issue standards, the Federation supports *International Accounting Standards and makes a significant contribution to the annual running costs of the *International Accounting Standards Committee.

International Monetary Fund (IMF) A specialized agency of the United Nations established in 1945 to promote international monetary cooperation and expand international trade, stabilize exchange rates, and help countries experiencing short-term balance of payments difficulties to maintain their exchange rates. The Fund assists members by supplying the amount of foreign currency it wishes to purchase in exchange for the equivalent amount of its own currency. The member repays this amount by buying back its own currency in a currency acceptable to the Fund, usually within three to five years. The Fund is financed by subscriptions from its members, the amount determined by an estimate of their means. Voting power is related to the amount of the subscription – the higher the contribution the higher the voting rights. The head office of the IMF is in Washington.

International Organization for Securities Commissions (IOSCO) A body formed in 1987 with the objective of establishing internationally agreed accounting standards to aid in multinational share offering by companies. Formerly critical of *Accounting Standards issued by the *International Accounting Standards Committee, it is now actively cooperating in the improvement of these standards.

International Securities Market Association The *eurobond market's trade association.

International Standards on Auditing (ISA) Standards issued by the *International Auditing Practices Committee; they do not override the local regulations of countries. To the extent that the international standards on auditing conform with local regulations on a particular subject, the audit of financial information in that country will automatically comply with the international regulations. *See also* International Federation of Accountants.

International Stock Exchange of the UK and Republic of Ireland Ltd *See* London Stock Exchange.

interpolation Estimating unknown quantities that lie between two of a series of known values. *Compare* extrapolation.

intestate A person who dies without having made a will. The estate, in these circumstances, is divided according to the rules of **intestacy**. The division depends on the personal circumstances of the deceased. If there is a spouse then there is a fixed statutory legacy, with the remainder being split between an *interest-in-possession trust for the remaining spouse and the children's absolute entitlement to the other half, if they are over 18. Where there is no surviving spouse the estate is divided between the children or their issue. Where there are no children then the split is rather more complicated and can include parents, brothers and sisters, grandparents, uncles, and aunts.

intragroup transactions *See* intercompany transactions.

in transit Denoting goods or cash that have been sent by one part of an entity to another. Funds or goods in transit need to be accounted for. For example, if a branch of a company has remitted a cheque to its Head Office, which has not been received by the end of the accounting year, the accounts will need to be adjusted for cash in transit to ensure that they balance.

introduction A method of issuing shares on the *London Stock Exchange in which a broker or issuing house takes small quantities of the company's shares and issues them to clients at opportune moments. It is also used by existing public companies that wish to issue additional shares. *Compare* issue by tender; offer for sale; placing; public issue.

inventoriable costs Costs that can be included in the valuation of *stocks, *work in progress, or *inventories according to Statement of Standard Accounting Practice 9. Stocks should be valued at the lower of cost or *net realizable value and the costs incurred up to the stage of production reached. This effectively means that inventoriable costs for finished goods and work in progress include both fixed and variable production costs but exclude the selling and distribution costs.

inventory In the USA, the equivalent of the UK *stock, i.e. the products or supplies of an organization on hand or in transit at any time. For a manufacturing company the types of inventory are raw materials, work in progress, and finished goods. An inventory count usually takes place at the end of the *financial year to confirm that the actual quantities support the figures given in the *books of account. The differences between the inventories at the beginning and the end of a period are used in the calculation of *cost of sales for the *profit and loss account and the end inventory is shown on the *balance sheet as a *circulating asset.

inventory accounting The accounting records and systems used for the ordering, receipt, issuing, and valuation of materials bought by an organization for stock. It includes the recording of the entries on *bin cards and in the stock ledger as well as the procedures adopted to carry out an effective *stocktaking.

inventory control (stock control) A control system to ensure that adequate but not excessive levels of stocks are maintained by an organization, having regard to consumption levels, delivery lead times, reorder levels, and reorder quantities of each commodity.

inventory turnover (stock turnover) A ratio that measures the number of times items of stock are used annually. To obtain an accurate measure of stock turnover the following formula is used for each commodity:

number of units used per annum/number of units in stock.

The number of units in stock may be taken at the start or the end of the year or may be the average of both. Because the information required for this ratio is only likely to be available from the internal management accounts, a different formula using final accounts figures is often used as an overall measure of inventory turnover:

sales or cost of sales per annum/value of stocks.

Again the value of stocks may be taken at the start or the end of the period or may be an average of both. The second formula tends to be inaccurate and is an average of the turnover of all stocks.

inventory valuation (stock valuation) The valuation of stocks of raw material, work in progress, and finished goods. According to Statement of Standard Accounting Practice 9, stocks should be valued at the lower of cost or *net realizable value and the costs incurred up to the stage of production reached. This effectively means that finished goods and work in progress should include both fixed and variable production costs but exclude the selling and distribution costs. In the UK valuing stocks at cost, the *first-in-first-out cost, or the *average cost may be used, but not the *last-in-first-out cost or the *next-in-first-out cost. *Marginal cost may be used as a basis of stock valuation for *management accounting purposes but is unacceptable by Statement of Standard Accounting Practice 9 for *financial accounting.

investing activities A heading required in the cash-flow statement of an organization by *Financial Reporting Standard 1, 'Cash Flow Statements', which shows the cash flows related to the acquisition or disposal of any asset held by the organization as a *fixed asset or as a *current-asset investment, other than assets included within *cash equivalents.

investment analyst A person employed by stockbrokers, banks, insurance companies, unit trusts, pension funds, etc., to give advice on the making of investments, especially investments in securities, commodities, etc. Many pay special attention to the study of *equities in the hope of being able to advise their employers to make profitable purchases of ordinary shares. To do this they use a variety of techniques, including a comparison of a company's present profits with its future trading prospects; this enables the analyst to single out the companies likely to outperform the general level of the market. This form of **technical analysis** is often contrasted with **fundamental analysis**, in which predicted future market movements are related to the underlying state of an economy and its expected trends. Analysts who rely on past movements to predict the future are called *chartists.

investment appraisal *See* capital budgeting.

investment centre A section of an organization in which *capital expenditure is made under the instructions of the management controlling that investment centre. The size and nature of investment centres are determined by individual organizations; they may be a *division, *subsidiary undertaking, *function, *department, or section, or any group of these.

investment company *See* investment trust.

investment costs *See* capital expenditure.

investment expenditure *See* capital expenditure.

Investment Management Regulatory Organization (IMRO) *See* Self-Regulating Organization.

investment properties Properties owned by a company that holds investments as part of its business, such as an *investment trust or a property-investment company. Investment properties may also include properties owned by a company whose main business is not the holding of investments. Such properties are strictly defined by *Statement of Standard Accounting Practice 19, 'Accounting for Investment Properties', as being an interest in land and/or buildings:

(1) in respect of which construction work and development have been completed; and

(2) that is held for its investment potential, any rental income being negotiated at arm's length.

However, a property owned and occupied by a company for its own purposes is not an investment property, and a property let to and occupied by another company in the same group is not an investment property for the purposes of its own accounts or the *group accounts. Investment properties should not be depreciated annually unless they are held on a lease. If they are leased they should be depreciated on the basis set out in *Statement of Standard Accounting Practice 12, 'Accounting for Depreciation', at least over the period, when the unexpired term is 20 years or less. Investment properties should be included in the *balance sheet at their open-market value, movements being taken to the *investment revaluation reserve unless it is insufficient to cover a deficit, in which case it should be taken to the *profit and loss account.

investment revaluation reserve A *reserve created by a company with *investment properties, if these properties are included in the *balance sheet at open-market value. Changes in the value of investment properties should be disclosed as movements on the investment revaluation reserve, unless the total of the investment revaluation reserve is insufficient to cover a deficit, in which case the amount by which the deficit exceeds the amount in the investment revaluation reserve should be charged to the *profit and loss account. In the case of investment *trust companies and property *unit trusts it may not be appropriate to deal with these deficits in the profit and loss account; in these circumstances they should be shown prominently in the *financial statements.

investment tax credit In the USA, an incentive to investment in which part of the cost of an asset subject to depreciation is used to offset income tax falling due in the year of purchase.

investment trust (investment company) A company that invests the funds provided by shareholders in a wide variety of securities. It makes its profits from the income and capital gains provided by these securities. The investments made are usually restricted to securities quoted on a stock exchange, but some will invest in unquoted companies. The advantages for shareholders are much the same as those with *unit trusts, i.e. spreading the risk of investment and making use of professional managers. Investment trusts, which are not usually *trusts in the usual sense, but private or public limited companies, differ from unit trusts in that in the latter the investors buy units in the fund but are not shareholders. Some investment trusts aim for high capital growth (**capital shares**), others for high income (**income shares**).

invisible asset *See* intangible fixed assets.

invisible earnings Earnings from international transactions involving such services as insurance, banking, shipping, tourism, and accountancy.

invoice A document stating the amount of money due to the organization issuing it for goods or services supplied. A **commercial invoice** will normally give a description of the goods and state how and when the goods were dispatched by the seller, who is responsible for insuring them in transit, and the payment terms.

invoice discounting A form of debt discounting in which a business sells its invoices to a *factoring house at a discount for immediate cash. The service does not usually include sales accounting and debt collecting.

involuntary unemployment Unemployment in which workers who would be willing to work for lower wages than those in employment are still unable to find work. J M Keynes (1883–1946) argued that recessions are characterized by involuntary unemployment because firms may be unwilling or unable to cut the wages of workers they employ. Although neoclassical economists have found difficulty accepting this concept in recent years, a number of theories (including the *implicit contract theory and the efficiency wage theory) have been suggested to explain it. The emergence of these theories reflects the need to explain the high and persistent levels of unemployment that began in the 1980s.

IOSCO Abbreviation for *International Organization for Securities Commissions.

IRR Abbreviation for *internal rate of return.

irrecoverable advance corporation tax *Advance corporation tax paid that cannot be set against the current year's *gross corporation tax (GCT) or carried back against GCT arising on profits for the *accounting periods beginning in the preceding six years, as it exceeds the maximum set-off available. The advance corporation tax is carried forward to set against future GCT liabilities arising on profits in future accounting periods. If profits are not expected in the foreseeable future or if future *dividends are expected to be paid up to the maximum available for future years, the current advance corporation tax surplus is considered to be irrecoverable advance corporation tax.

irrecoverable input VAT VAT *input tax paid on items acquired in order to produce *exempt supplies.

irrevocable letter of credit *See* letter of credit.

IRS Abbreviation for *Internal Revenue Service.

ISA Abbreviation for *International Standards on Auditing.

issue by tender (sale by tender) A method of issuing shares on the *London Stock Exchange in which an issuing house asks investors to tender for them. The stocks or shares are then allocated to the highest bidders. It is usual for the tender documents to state the lowest price acceptable. This method may be used for a new issue or for loan stock (*see* debenture), but is not frequently employed. *Compare* introduction; offer for sale; placing; public issue.

issued share A *share that has been allotted by the directors of a company to an applicant and paid for in full by that applicant.

issued share capital (subscribed share capital) The amount of the *authorized share capital for which shareholders have subscribed. *See also* called-up share capital.

issue price The price at which a new issue of shares is sold to the public. Once the issue has been made the securities will have a market price, which may be above (at a premium on) or below (at a discount on) the issue price (*see also* stag). In an *introduction, *offer for sale, or *public issue, the issue price is fixed by the company on the advice of its stockbrokers and bankers; in an *issue by tender the issue price is fixed by the highest price that can be obtained for the whole issue; in a *placing the issue price is negotiated by the issuing house or broker involved.

IT 1. Abbreviation for *income tax. **2.** Abbreviation for *information technology.

ITF Abbreviation for *integrated test facility.

J

JDS Abbreviation for *Joint Disciplinary Scheme.

JIT techniques Abbreviation for *just-in-time techniques.

job An identifiable discrete piece of work carried out by an organization. For costing purposes a job is usually given a *job number.

job card (job ticket) Traditionally, a card containing the written instructions for the operations to be carried out for the completion of a job. The instructions are now likely to be in the form of a computer printout.

job cost The costs incurred in carrying out a *job. These are usually analysed into the constituent costs, for example *direct materials costs, *direct labour costs, and *overheads.

job costing (job order costing; specific order costing) A costing process to assess the individual costs of performing each *job. It is important in organizations in which the production of different products is carried out, and also in service organizations, in which the cost is required of each service provided.

job number A number assigned to each job where *job costing is in operation; it enables the costs to be charged to this number so that all the individual costs for a job can be collected.

job ticket *See* job card.

joint and several liability A liability that is entered into by a group, on the understanding that if any of the group fail in their undertaking the liability must be shared by the remainder. Thus, if two people enter into a joint and several guarantee for a bank loan, if one becomes bankrupt the other is liable for repayment of the whole loan.

joint audit An *audit carried out by two or more firms and in which the *audit report is prepared jointly.

joint costs In *process costing, the costs incurred prior to the separation point after which the *joint products are treated individually. The joint costs are therefore common to the joint products; in order to determine individual product costs, the joint costs need to be apportioned between the joint products. The joint costs may be apportioned on the basis of the number of units, weights, or volumes of each product or their *sales values at the *separation point. *See also* common costs.

Joint Disciplinary Scheme (JDS) A scheme established in 1979 by the *Institute of Chartered Accountants in England and Wales, the *Institute of Chartered Accountants of Scotland, and the *Chartered Association of Certified Accountants. Its aim is to investigate and regulate the professional and business conduct of members and the efficiency and competence of members in matters of public concern. Each participating body appoints two of its members to an executive committee as well as a further two members who are not accountants. The chariman is appointed by agreement between the participating bodies. The executive committee has responsibility for administering the scheme and for setting up committees of inquiry to look into matters referred to it and to report on its findings. If the committee finds against a firm it may decide on the sanction to be imposed. If an individual is involved the matter is referred to the body to which that individual belongs.

joint products The output of a process in which there is more than one product and all the products have similar or equal economic importance. *Compare* main product; by-product.

joint-stock company A *company in which the members pool their stock and trade on the basis of their joint stock. This differs from the earliest type of company, the merchant corporations or regulated companies of the 14th century, in which members traded with their own stock, subject to the rules of the company. Joint-stock companies originated in the 17th century and some still exist, although they are now rare.

joint venture A commercial undertaking entered into by two or more parties, usually in the short term. Joint ventures are generally governed by the Partnership Act (1890) but they differ from *partnerships in that they are limited by time or by activity. Separate books are not usually kept and the joint venturers will have a profit- or loss-sharing ratio for the purpose of the joint venture only. Joint venturers often carry on their principal businesses independently of, and at the same time as, the joint venture.

journal A book of prime entry in which transfers to be made from one *account to another are recorded. It is used for transfers not recorded in any other of the books of prime entry, such as the sales *day book or the *cash book.

joystick A computer input device resembling a small aircraft control stick that is used with computer games, and some computer-aided design programs, to move graphics symbols on the screen.

judgmental sampling (non-statistical sampling) A form of sampling in which the *auditor selects his sample from a population based on his own experience and assessment of the situation, rather than using *statistical sampling techniques.

junk bond A *bond that offers a high rate of interest because it carries a higher than usual probability of default. The issuing of junk bonds to finance the takeover of large companies in the USA is a practice that has developed rapidly over recent years and has spread elsewhere. *See* leveraged buyout.

just-in-time techniques (JIT techniques) The approach to manufacturing designed to match production to demand by only supplying goods to order. This has the effect of reducing stocks of raw material and finished goods, encouraging those production activities that add value to the output, and minimizing levels of scrap and defective units.

Keogh plan A US savings scheme to create a pension plan for self-employed people, in which tax is deferred until withdrawals are made. It can be held at the same time as a corporate pension or individual retirement account. Keogh plans originated with the Self-Employment Individuals Retirement Act (1982).

kite An informal name for an *accommodation bill. **Kite-flying** or **kiting** is the discounting of a kite (accommodation bill) at a bank, knowing that the person on whom it is drawn will dishonour it.

know-how Industrial information and techniques that assist in manufacturing or processing goods or materials. Allowances are given for expenditure that qualifies as know-how. The expenditure for the year is added to the *written-down value brought forward and a *writing-down allowance of 25% of the total is available.

labour costs (wages costs) Expenditure on wages paid to those operators who are both directly and indirectly concerned with the production of the product, service, or *cost unit. *See also* direct labour cost; indirect labour cost.

labour efficiency variance *See* direct labour efficiency variance.

labour hour rate *See* direct labour hour rate.

labour rate variance *See* direct labour rate of pay variance.

lapping In the USA, the fraudulent practice of concealing a shortage of cash by delaying the recording of cash receipts. In the UK it is referred to as **teeming and lading**. There are a number of variations, but essentially the cashier conceals the theft of cash received from the first customer by recording the cash received from the second customer as attributable to the first, and so on with subsequent customers. The cashier hopes to be in a position to replace the cash before the dishonesty is discovered. As such hopes are frequently based on attempts at gambling, the deception is often discovered.

last-in-first-out cost (LIFO cost) A method of valuing units of raw material or finished goods issued from stock by using the latest unit value for pricing the issues until all the quantity of stock received at that price is used up. The next earliest price is then used for pricing the issues, and so on. Because the issues are based on a LIFO cost, the valuation of closing stocks is described as being on the same LIFO basis. The method may also be used in *process costing to value the work in process at the end of an accounting period. This method of costing is not normally acceptable for stock valuation in the UK. *Compare* first-in-first-out cost.

LAUTRO Abbreviation for Life Assurance and Unit Trust Organization. *See* Self-Regulating Organization.

LBO Abbreviation for *leveraged buyout.

leading and lagging Techniques often used at the end of a financial year to enhance a cash position and reduce borrowing. This is achieved by arranging for the settlement of outstanding obligations to be accelerated (leading) or delayed (lagging).

lead managers Banks that launch a new issue, usually a *eurobond. They are usually chosen either because they have a close relationship with the borrower or because they have been successful in a *competitive bought deal contest.

learning curve A technique that takes into account the reduction in time taken to carry out production as the cumulative output rises. The concept is based on a doubling of output, so that a 70% learning curve means that the cumulative average time taken per unit falls to 70% of the previous cumulative average time as the output doubles. The cumulative average time per unit is measured from the very first unit produced. The formula is:

$$y = ax^{-b},$$

where y = cumulative average time per unit of production, a = the time taken to produce the first unit, x = cumulative number of units manufactured to date, and b = the learning coefficient.

lease A contract between the owner of a specific asset, the **lessor**, and another party, the **lessee**, allowing the latter to hire the asset. The lessor retains the right of ownership but the lessee acquires the right to use the asset for a specific period of time in return for the payment of specific rentals or payments. *Statement of Standard Accounting Practice 21, 'Accounting for Leases and Hire Purchase Contracts', classifies leases into *operating leases and *finance leases with differing accounting treatments.

leaseback (renting back) An arrangement in which the owner of an *asset (such as land or buildings) sells it to another party but immediately enters into a *lease agreement with the purchaser to obtain the right to use the asset. Such a transaction is a method for raising funds and can affect the *financial statements of a company, depending on whether a *finance lease or an *operating lease is entered into.

leasehold The right acquired under a *lease to use land and buildings for a specified period in return for the payment of a specific rental.

least-squares line *See* linear regression.

ledger A collection of *accounts of a similar type. Traditionally, a ledger was a large book with separate pages for each account. In modern systems, ledgers may consist of separate cards or computer records. The most common ledgers are the *nominal ledger containing the *impersonal accounts, the *debtors' (or sales) ledger containing the accounts of an organization's customers, and the *creditors' (or purchases) ledger containing the accounts of an organization's suppliers.

ledger account An *account in a ledger that holds the records for all the transactions relating to that particular person (e.g. a *debtor), thing (e.g. *stock item), or activity (e.g. sales).

legal capital In the USA, the amount of *stockholders' equity, which cannot be reduced by the payment of dividends.

legal tender Money that must be accepted in discharge of a debt. It may be **limited legal tender**, i.e. it must be accepted but only up to specified limits of payment; or **unlimited legal tender**, i.e. acceptable in settlement of debts of any amount. Bank of England notes and the £2 and £1 coins are unlimited legal tender in the UK. Other Royal Mint coins are limited legal tender; i.e. debts up to £10 can be paid in 50p and 20p coins; up to £5 by 10p and 5p coins; and up to 20p by bronze coins.

lessee *See* lease.

lessor *See* lease.

letter of awareness A formal letter written by a parent company to a lender, acknowledging its relationship with another group company and its awareness of a loan being made to that company. It is weakest form of a *letter of comfort.

letter of comfort A letter to a bank from the parent company of a subsidiary that is trying to borrow money from the bank. The letter gives no guarantee for the repayment of the projected loan but offers the bank the comfort of knowing that the subsidiary has made the parent company aware of its intention to borrow; the parent also usually supports the application, giving, at least, an assurance that it intends that the subsidiary should remain in business and that it will give notice of any relevant change of ownership. *See also* letter of awareness.

letter of credit (documentary credit) A letter from one banker to another authorizing the payment of a specified sum to the person named in the letter on certain specified conditions. Commercially, letters of credit are widely used in the international import and export trade as a means of payment. In an export contract, the exporter may require the foreign importer to open a letter of credit at the importer's local bank (the issuing bank) for the amount of the goods. This will state that it is to be negotiable at a bank (the negotiating bank) in the exporter's country in favour of the exporter; often, the exporter (who is called the beneficiary of the credit) will give the name of the negotiating bank. On presentation of the shipping documents (which are listed in the letter of credit) the beneficiary will receive payment from the negotiating bank.

An **irrevocable letter of credit** cannot be cancelled by the person who opens it or by the issuing bank without the beneficiary's consent, whereas a **revocable letter of credit** can. In a **confirmed letter of credit** the negotiating bank guarantees to pay the beneficiary, even if the issuing bank fails to honour its commitments (in an **unconfirmed letter of credit** this guarantee is not given). A confirmed irrevocable letter of credit therefore provides the most reliable means of being paid for exported goods. However, all letters of credit have an expiry date, after which they can only be negotiated by the consent of all the parties.

A **circular letter of credit** is an instruction from a bank to its correspondent banks to pay the beneficiary a stated sum on presentation of a means of identification. It has now been replaced by traveller's cheques.

Although the term 'letter of credit' is still widely used, in 1983 the International Chamber of Commerce recommended **documentary credit** as the preferred term for these instruments.

letter of engagement *See* engagement letter.

letter of representation A formal written record of representations made by the management of an organization to the *auditors. The letter is prepared by the auditor and signed by management on a date as near as possible to the date of the *audit report and after all audit work has been completed, including the review of events occurring after the *balance sheet date, for example. The information referred to in the letter is material to the *financial statements for which the auditor is unable to obtain independent corroborative evidence. These matters might include any future legal claims and *adjusting events.

leverage *See* gearing.

leveraged buyout (LBO) The acquisition of one company by another through the use of borrowed funds. Usually the acquiring company or individuals use their own assets as security for the funds. The intention is that the loans will be repaid from the cash flow of the acquired company.

leverage ratios *See* gearing ratios.

LIAB Abbreviation for Licentiate of the *International Association of Book-keepers.

liability An obligation to transfer economic benefits (generally money) as a result of past transactions (e.g. the purchase of a *fixed asset or a *circulating asset). *See also* contingent liability; current liabilities; deferred credit; long-term liability; secured liability.

LIBID Abbreviation for *London Inter Bank Bid Rate.

LIBOR Abbreviation for *London Inter Bank Offered Rate.

life assurance An insurance policy that pays a specified amount of money on the death of the life assured or, in the case of an endowment assurance policy, on the death of the life assured or at the end of an agreed period, whichever is the earlier. Life assurance grew from a humble means of providing funeral expenses to a means of saving for oneself or one's dependants, with certain tax advantages.

Life Assurance and Unit Trust Regulatory Organization (LAUTRO) *See* Self-Regulating Organization.

life-cycle costing The approach to determining the total costs of a fixed asset that takes into account all the costs likely to be incurred both in acquiring it and in operating it over its effective life. For example, the initial cost to an airline of an aircraft is only part of the costs relevant to the decision to purchase it. The operating costs over its effective life are also relevant and would therefore be part of the decision – making data. This is an aspect of *terotechnology.

LIFFE Abbreviation for *London International Financial Futures and Options Exchange.

LIFO cost Abbreviation for *last-in-first-out cost.

LIMEAN Abbreviation for *London Inter Bank Mean Rate.

limitation of scope *See* except for.

limited company A *company in which the liability of the members in respect of the company's debts is limited. It may be **limited by shares**, in which case the liability of the members on a winding-up is limited to the amount (if any) unpaid on their shares. This is by far the most common type of registered company. The liability of the members may alternatively be **limited by guarantee**; in this case the liability of members is limited by the memorandum to a certain amount, which the members undertake to contribute on winding-up. These are usually societies, clubs, or trade associations. Since 1980 it has not been possible for such a company to be formed with a share capital, or converted to a company limited by guarantee with a share capital. *See also* public limited company.

limited liability *See* limited company.

limited partner A *partner whose liability is limited to his or her investment in the *partnership. A partnership in which one or more (but not all) of the partners are limited partners is called a **limited partnership** and is governed by the Limited Partnership Act (1907). *Compare* general partner.

limited recourse finance A loan made to a company specifically set up by a developer to manage a particular property. In case of default, the lender has no recourse to the other assets of the developer. *See also* non-recourse finance.

limiting factor (principal budget factor) A *constraint in budgetary control and decision making, the existence of which limits an organization from achieving higher levels of performance and profitability. On identifying the limiting factor, resources are deployed in order to eliminate or reduce its effect, at which point it may be replaced by a different limiting factor. Examples of limiting factors are sales volume, skilled labour, and productive capacity.

linear cost function *Cost behaviour that, when plotted on a graph against activity levels, results in a straight line. For example, total fixed cost levels and variable costs per unit of activity will both result in a straight line horizontal to the x-axis when activity, production, or sales is plotted on the x-axis. Total variable costs will also result in a straight line and is thus a linear cost function.

linear depreciation *Depreciation charges that, when plotted on a graph against time on the x-axis, result in a straight line, as a constant amount per annum is written off the assets concerned. Both the *straight-line method of depreciation and the *rate per unit of production method, when the depreciation charge is plotted against production levels, result in linear depreciation.

linear interpolation A technique used in *discounted cash flow for calculating the approximate *internal rate of return of a project. The cash flows for the project are discounted at two *discount rates to obtain a small positive and a small negative *net present value. A linear relationship is assumed between the two results in order to calculate the discount rate that would give a net present value of zero.

linear programming A modelling technique that determines an optimal solution for attaining an objective by taking into consideration a number of *constraints. The *objective function, often to optimize profits or minimize costs, is expressed as an equation and the constraints are also expressed in mathematical terms. Where only two products and few constraints are involved a solution may be obtained graphically. More than two products requires the *simplex method to be used or alternatively a computer program.

linear regression (least-squares line) The process of finding a **line of best fit** to a graph on which the values of two variables are plotted in pairs. The line of best fit is computed mathematically, so that the sum of the squares of the divergence of the plots from the line are minimized. For example, a line of best fit through plots of cost levels incurred for levels of production can be used to determine the *cost behaviour characteristics of the selected cost.

line of best fit *See* linear regression.

linked presentation The presentation in a balance sheet of an *asset that is in substance a financing; the item can be shown gross on the face of the balance sheet with the finance deducted from it within a single asset caption. To make a linked presentation there are a number of criteria to be met and it must be intended that the financing will be repaid from the proceeds of the asset and the company must not be able to keep the asset on repayment of the financing or be able to re-acquire it at any time. This is the procedure recommended in *Financial Reporting Standard 5, 'Reporting Financial Transactions'.

liquid assets (liquid capital; quick assets; realizable assets) Assets held in cash or in something that can be readily turned into cash (e.g. deposits in a bank current account, trade debts, marketable investments). The ratio of these assets to current liabilities provides an assessment of an organization's *liquidity or solvency. *See also* liquid ratio.

liquidation (winding-up) The distribution of a company's assets among its creditors and members prior to its dissolution. This brings the life of the company to an end. The liquidation may be voluntary (*see* creditors' voluntary liquidation; members' voluntary liquidation) or by the court (*see* compulsory liquidation). *See also* liquidator.

liquidator A person appointed by a court, or by the members of a company or its creditors, to regularize the company's affairs on a *liquidation (winding-up). In the case of a *members' voluntary liquidation, it is the members of the company who appoint the liquidator. In a *creditors' voluntary liquidation, the liquidator may be appointed by company members before the **meeting of creditors** or by the creditors themselves at the meeting; in the former case the liquidator can only exercise his or her powers with the consent of the court. If two liquidators are appointed, the court resolves which one is to act. In a *compulsory liquidation, the court appoints a provisional liquidator after the winding-up petition has been presented; after the order has been granted, the court appoints the *official receiver as liquidator, until or unless another officer is appointed.

The liquidator is in a relationship of trust with the company and the creditors as a body; a liquidator appointed in a compulsory liquidation is an officer of the court, is under statutory obligations, and may not profit from the position. A liquidator must be a qualified **insolvency practitioner**, according to the Insolvency Act (1986). Under this act, insolvency practitioners must meet certain statutory requirements, including membership of an approved professional body (such as the Insolvency Practitioners' Association or the Institute of Chartered Accountants). On appointment, the liquidator assumes control of the company, collects the assets, pays the debts, and distributes any surplus to company members according to their rights. In the case of a compulsory liquidation, the liquidator is supervised by the court, the *liquidation committee, and the Department of Trade and Industry. The liquidator receives a *statement of affairs from the company officers and must report on these to the court.

liquid instrument A *negotiable instrument that the purchaser is able to sell before maturity.

liquidity The extent to which an organization's assets are liquid (*see* liquid assets), enabling it to pay its debts when they fall due and also to move into new investment opportunities.

liquidity index A measure of a company's liquidity assessed by calculating the number of days it would take for current assets to be converted into cash.

liquidity management A combination of day-to-day operations carried out by the financial management of an organization with the objective of optimizing its *liquidity so that it can make the best use of its liquid resources.

liquidity risk The risk, in lending operations, that an investment cannot be liquidated during its life without significant costs.

liquid ratio (acid-test ratio; quick ratio) A ratio used for assessing the *liquidity of a company; it is the ratio of the *liquid (quick) assets, i.e. the *circulating assets less the *stock, to the *current liabilities. The answer is expressed either as a percentage or as *x*:1. For example, a company with current assets of £25,000 including stock of £15,000 and liabilities of £12,000 will have a liquid ratio of:

$$(£25,000 - £15,000)/£12,000 = 0.83,$$

i.e. 83% or 0.83:1. This may be interpreted as the company having 83 pence of liquid or current assets for every £1 of current liabilities. If, for some reason, the company is obliged to repay the current liabilities immediately there would be insufficient liquid assets to allow it to do so. The company may therefore be forced into a hurried sale of stock at a discount to raise finance. Although there is no rule of thumb, and there are industry differences, a liquid ratio significantly below 1:1 will give rise to concern. The liquid ratio is regarded as an acid test of its solvency and is therefore sometimes called the acid-test ratio.

listed company A company that has a **listing agreement** (*see* listing requirements) with the London Stock Exchange and whose shares therefore have a quotation on the main market. These companies were formerly called **quoted companies**.

listed security 1. In general, a security that has a quotation on a recognized *stock exchange. **2.** On the *London Stock Exchange, a security that has a quotation in the Official List of Securities of the main market, as opposed to the unlisted securities market or the third market. *See also* flotation; listing requirements.

listing requirements The conditions that must be satisifed before a security can be traded on a stock exchange. To achieve a quotation in the Official List of Securities of the main market of the *London Stock Exchange, the requirements contained in a **listing agreement** must be signed by the company seeking quotation. The two main requirements of such a listing are usually:
(i) that the value of the company's assets should exceed a certain value;
(ii) that the company publish specific financial information, both at the time of *flotation and regularly thereafter (*see* accounts; directors' report).

Listing requirements are generally more stringent the larger the market. For example, the main market in London demands considerably more information from companies than the unlisted securities market (*see* unlisted securities). The listing requirements are set out in the *Yellow Book.

little GAAP The *generally accepted accounting principles applied to small companies. Some argue that with small companies, which are primarily owner-managed, compliance with GAAP imposes a heavy burden in relation to the value the owners receive from the information in the *annual accounts. There are difficulties in determining, however, the criteria that should be used to exempt companies as well as widespread concern that accounts that do not comply with accounting standards would not present a *true and fair view of a company's activities. *Compare* big GAAP.

loan capital (borrowed capital; debt capital) Capital used to finance an organization that is subject to payment of interest over the life of the loan, at the end of which the loan is normally repaid. There are different categories of loan capital: *mortgage debentures are secured on specific assets of the organization, while convertible debentures may be converted into equity according to the terms of the issue.

loan creditor A person or institution that has lent money to a business. For example, when a bank loan is obtained the bank becomes a loan creditor.

loan stock *See* debenture.

local taxation A tax applicable to those living in a particular area. In the UK the council tax and business rates are the main local taxes.

lockbox In the USA, a Postal Service box used for the collection of customer payments. The recipient's bank will arrange collection from these boxes throughout the day, deposit the funds, and provide a computer listing of the payments with the daily total. This method is effective for a small number of payments with a high value as the bank's charges per item are relatively high.

Lombard rate The *interest rate used by the Bundesbank, the German central bank.

Lombard Street The street in the City of London that is the centre of the money market. Many commercial banks have offices in or near Lombard Street, as do many bill brokers and discount houses. The Bank of England is round the corner.

London approach The approach adopted by London banks to customers facing a cash-flow crisis. The key feature is that the banks remain supportive for as long as possible, decisions are made collectively, and all information and any money paid is shared between the lending banks on an equitable basis.

London code of conduct A code issued by the Bank of England, that is applicable to all wholesale dealings not regulated by the rules of a recognized exchange. It is considered the best practice for company treasurers by the *Association of Corporate Treasurers.

London FOX (Futures and Options Exchange) A commodity exchange formed in 1987 from the **London Commodity Exchange**, which itself emerged after World War II as a successor to the London Commercial Sale Rooms. London FOX is located in a purpose-built exchange in St Katharine Dock, which it shares with the International Petroleum Exchange. The commodities dealt in on the exchange are cocoa, coffee, raw sugar, and white sugar as well as the agricultural products potatoes, soya-bean meal, wheat, barley, pigs, and lamb. The market also includes the **Baltic International Freight Futures Market** (BIFFEX). The market is in futures and traded options and it makes use of the services provided by the London Clearing House.

London Inter Bank Bid Rate (LIBID) The rate of interest at which banks bid for funds to borrow from each other. *See* London Inter Bank Offered Rate.

London Inter Bank Mean Rate (LIMEAN) The median average between the London Inter Bank Offered Rate (LIBOR) and the London Inter Bank Bid Rate (LIBID).

London Inter Bank Offered Rate (LIBOR) The rate of interest in the short-term wholesale market (*see* interbank market) in which banks offer to lend money to each other. The loans are for a minimum of £250,000 for periods from overnight up to five years. The importance of the market is that it allows individual banks to adjust their liquidity positions quickly, covering shortages by borrowing from banks with surpluses. This reduces the need for each bank to hold large quantities of liquid assets, thus releasing funds for more profitable lending transactions. LIBOR is the most significant interest rate for international banks. It is officially fixed at 11 a.m. each day by five major London banks, but fluctuates during the day. It is also used as a benchmark for lending to bank customers. *See also* London Inter Bank Bid Rate.

London International Financial Futures and Options Exchange (LIFFE) A *financial futures market opened in 1982, in London's Royal Exchange, to provide facilities within the European time zone for dealing in options and futures contracts, including those in government bonds, stock-and-share indexes, foreign currencies, and interest rates. In 1991 LIFFE moved into its own premises in the City of London. A client wishing to buy or sell options or futures telephones a LIFFE broker, who instructs the booth run by that broker on the floor of the exchange. The booth clerk hands a slip to the broker's trader in the pit of the market who executes the transaction with another trader. The bargain details are passed to the London Clearing House, which acts as guarantor. Automated (electronic) pit trading was introduced in 1989, though this only operates after the close of live pit trading. The London Traded Options Market merged with LIFFE in 1992, when the words 'and Options' was added to its name, although the acronym remains unchanged.

London Stock Exchange The market in London that deals in securities. Dealings in securities began in London in the 17th century. The name Stock Exchange was first used for New Jonathan's Coffee House in 1773, although it was not formally constituted until 1802. The development of the industrial revolution encouraged many other share markets to flourish throughout the UK, all the remnants of which amalgamated in 1973 to form The Stock Exchange of Great Britain and Ireland. After the *Big Bang in 1986 this organization became the **International Stock Exchange of the UK and Republic of Ireland Ltd** (**ISE**) in an attempt to stress the international nature of the main UK securities market, although it is still widely known as the London Stock Exchange. Its major reforms included:
(i) allowing banks, insurance companies, and overseas securities houses to become members and to buy existing member firms;
(ii) abolishing scales of commissions, allowing commissions to be negotiated;
(iii) abolishing the division of members into jobbers and brokers, enabling a member firm to deal with the public, to buy and sell shares for their own account, and to act as *market makers;
(iv) the introduction of the *Stock Exchange Automated Quotations System, a

computerized dealing system that has virtually abolished face-to-face dealing on the floor of exchange.

In merging with members of the international broking community in London, the International Stock Exchange became a registered investment exchange and The Securities Association Ltd became a *Self-Regulating Organization (SRO) complying with the Financial Services Act (1986). In 1991 The Securities Association Ltd merged with the Association of Futures Brokers and Dealers Ltd to form the *Securities and Futures Authority Ltd (SFA), which is now the Self-Regulating Organization responsible for the Stock Exchange.

The International Stock Exchange provides two markets for companies: the main market for *listed companies and the *unlisted securities market (USM). A third market, formed in 1987, merged with the USM in 1990. The International Stock Exchange formerly offered a market in traded options in equities, currencies, and indexes but this has now moved to the *London International Financial Futures and Options Exchange.

long-form report A detailed report made by an *auditor on a client's financial statements.

long lease A lease that has more than 50 years to run, as defined by the Companies Act (1985). *Compare* short lease.

long position A position held by a dealer in securities (*see* market maker), commodities, currencies, etc., in which holdings exceed sales, because the dealer expects prices to rise enabling a profit to be made by selling at the higher levels. *Compare* short position.

long-term contract A contract that falls into two or more accounting periods before being completed. Such a contract may be for the design, manufacture, or construction of a single substantial asset, for example in the construction or civil engineering industries. From an accounting point of view, there is a problem in determining how much profit can be reasonably allocated to each accounting period, although the contract is not complete. *Statement of Standard Accounting Practice 9, 'Stocks and Long Term Contracts', requires contracts to be assessed on an individual basis and shown in the *profit and loss account by recording turnover and related activity as the contract progresses. Where the outcome of the contract can be assessed with reasonable certainty, even though it is not complete, the part of the profit that can be attributed to the work performed by an accounting date may be recognized in the profit and loss account. Attributable profit is that part of the total profit currently estimated to arise over the duration of the contract, after allowing for estimated remedial costs, maintenance costs, and increases in costs not recoverable under the contract agreement.

long-term debtors *Debtors who are not expected to pay what they owe in the near future. The debtors of an organization shown on the face of a *balance sheet under *circulating assets may be assumed by some readers to be expected to pay within 12 months, thus being comparable to *current liabilities. The legal definition of *fixed assets, however, means that current assets are merely those assets that an organization does not mean to keep in the business and there are no time implications. In some cases, possibly by mutual agreement, it may be many years before a company is able to recover money from certain debtors. The *Urgent Issues Task Force requires that if the size of the debt due after more than one year is material, the amounts should be disclosed on the face of the balance sheet.

long-term liability A sum owed that does not have to be repaid within the next accounting period of a business. In some contexts a long-term liability may be regarded as one not due for repayment within the next three, or possibly ten, years.

loss The amount by which the expenses of a transaction or operation exceed the income produced.

loss on manufacture *See* profit on manufacture.

loss reliefs Relief available to sole traders, partnerships, and companies making losses, as adjusted for tax purposes. *Capital allowances can create a trading loss or can enhance it. Trading losses can be carried forward to set against future trading profits. For sole traders and partnerships, trading losses can be set against other income for the year of the loss and for the previous year. Partners can decide individually how to use their share of the losses. Special rules apply to trading losses in the early years of a trade. These losses can be carried back three years to a period before the trade commenced. From 1991–92 it has been possible to set trading losses against capital gains if the loss cannot be used first by setting against other income during the year. *Terminal-loss relief is available when a trade is permanently discontinued and a loss is made during the last 12 months. For companies, a trading loss can be set off against profits of the three previous accounting periods, provided the company was carrying on the same trade during that period. Terminal-loss relief is available for companies. *Capital losses can be set against capital gains in the same period. Any surplus capital loss that cannot be utilized during the current year must be carried forward to set against future capital gains. Capital losses cannot be set against other income, unlike trading losses.

lowballing An alleged practice in which *auditors compete for clients by reducing their fees for statutory *audits. The lower audit fees would be compensated by the auditor carrying out highly lucrative non-audit work, such as consultancy and tax advice, for the client. It is difficult to assess how widespread the practice is in an economic climate in which competition has pushed down audit fees, but a number of well-publicized examples suggest that it has been taking place since the 1980s.

lower of cost and net realizable value rule The method of valuing stocks and work in progress, recommended by Statement of Standard Accounting Practice 9, in which they should be valued at the lower of either cost or *net realizable value, for published accounts purposes.

lower rate of income tax A rate of *income tax below the *basic rate. It was re-introduced in the UK in 1992–93 at 20%; for 1995–96 the lower rate applied to the first £3200 of taxable income.

low-level language A computer-programming language closely related to the machine code. Low-level languages are not as user-friendly as high-level languages.

McFarlane Report *See* Future Development of Auditing.

machine hour A measurement of production in terms of the time taken for a machine operation to complete a given amount of production.

machine hour rate An *absorption rate used in *absorption costing, obtained by the formula:

> budgeted *cost centre overheads/budgeted machine hours.

mad dog An informal name for a company with the potential to grow quickly, providing it can obtain substantial capital; risks are likely to be high. The computer industry is an example of a sector that has included a number of mad dogs.

main product The product of a process that has the greatest economic significance. Other products of secondary economic importance are regarded as *by-products; however, if all products have equal economic significance they are regarded as *joint products. *See also* process costing.

mainstream corporation tax (MCT) The *gross corporation tax less the *advance corporation tax and income tax suffered by deduction at source on *unfranked investment income.

maintenance expense The costs incurred in carrying out the **maintenance function**. Factory maintenance would be classified as a *manufacturing overhead, office maintenance as an *administration overhead, salesmen's car maintenance as a *selling overhead, and distribution vehicle maintenance as a *distribution overhead.

make or buy decision A decision to make a product or component internally or to buy it in from a subcontractor. If the decision is based on cost terms alone, the *relevant costs of manufacture compared to purchase should be considered and if there is no spare capacity then *opportunity costs of manufacture may also be relevant. This decision often has to be made in the course of planning a manufacturing process.

malpractice insurance In the USA, liability insurance taken out by an *accountant against legal action in connection with professional services. There have been a number of very high awards made to plaintiffs and this has greatly increased the cost to the accountant of obtaining insurance cover. One solution to this may be for accountants to form *corporate bodies rather than *partnerships, thus reducing their exposure to personal liability.

managed costs *See* discretionary costs.

management accounting The techniques used to collect, process, and present financial and quantitative data within an organization to enable effective *scorekeeping, *cost control, *planning, *pricing, and *decision making to take place. The major professional body of **management accountants** in the UK is the *Chartered Institute of Management Accountants (CIMA).

management audit An independent review of the management of an organization, carried out by a firm of management consultants specializing in this type of review. The review will cover all aspects of running the organization, including the control of production, marketing, sales, finance, personnel, warehousing, etc.

management buyout (MBO) The acquisition of a company by its managers, often in the face of closure, after the acquisition of the company by another group that wishes to dispose of it, or occasionally as a result of its owners wishing to dispose of the business through a trade sale. In some cases a management buyout occurs when a large corporate group of companies wishes to divest itself of an operating division. Financial backers tend to like managers who know the company's business intimately, staking their own assets and taking full control of the company with the aim of boosting its profitability. Popularized in the early 1980s, management buyouts have occasionally failed, but many have continued to profit and a few have been sold on to major groups. In a highly **leveraged buyout**, funding will usually consist of a small amount of equity, allowing the management team to obtain and retain control, considerable straight debt, and a certain amount of *mezzanine finance. *See also* BIMBO.

management by exception **1.** A principle of management in which a management decision that cannot be made at one level is passed up to the next level for a decision; i.e. exceptional decisions are passed up the management tree. **2.** The principle used in budgetary control in which items of income or expenditure that show no variances or small variances require no action, whereas exceptional items showing adverse variances to an unacceptable degree require action to be taken.

management by objectives (MBO) A management technique in which all levels of management are encouraged to specify and agree quantitative and/or qualitative objectives to be achieved within a set period and to answer to higher levels of management for the actual performance achieved against these objectives.

management discussion and analysis (MD&A) In the USA, the section in the annual report to stockholders (*see* annual accounts) and in *Form 10-K that is required by the *Securities and Exchange Commission. The purpose of the MD&A is to assist investors to understand the impact of changes in accounting and business activity that have affected comparisons with the results of previous years. Management should summarize and discuss, among other matters, the reasons for changes in the results of operations, capital resources, and liquidity. In the UK, the *operating and financial review is modelled on the MD&A.

management information system (MIS) An information system designed to provide financial and quantitative information to all the levels of management in an organization. Most modern management information systems provide the data from an integrated computer database, which is constantly updated from all areas of the organization in a structured way. Access to the data is usually restricted to the areas regarded as useful to particular managers; access to confidential information is limited to top management.

management letter A letter written by an *auditor to the management of a client company at the end of the annual *audit to suggest any possible improvements that could be made to the company's accounting and internal control system or to communicate any other such information that the auditor believes would be of benefit to the client.

mandate 1. A written authority given by one person (the **mandator**) to another (the **mandatory**) giving the mandatory the power to act on behalf of the mandator. It comes to an end on the death, mental illness, or bankruptcy of the mandator. 2. A document instructing a bank to open an account in the name of the mandator (customer), giving details of the way it is to be run, and providing specimen signatures of those authorized to sign cheques, etc.

mandatory liquid assets (MLA) The Bank of England's requirement that clearing banks maintain with the Bank liquid reserves not used for loans or other transactions, which must be cleared at the end of each working day. The banks usually pass on the cost of this reserve (which earns them no interest) to its customers as a part of the facility cost (*see* committed facility). The cost may be between 5 and 10 *basis points. This cost is sometimes called the **reserve asset cost.**

manufacturing account (manufacturing statement) An accounting statement forming part of the internal final accounts of a manufacturing organization; for a particular period, it is constructed to show, inter alia, *prime cost of production, *manufacturing overhead, total *production cost, and *manufacturing cost of finished goods. In some cases a *manufacturing profit is also computed.

manufacturing cost of finished goods (total production cost of finished goods) An item computed in a *manufacturing account by the addition of *prime cost and *manufacturing overhead, adjusted by the opening and closing *work in progress for the period.

manufacturing costs (manufacturing expenses) Items of expenditure incurred to carry out the manufacturing process in an organization. They include *direct material, *direct labour, *direct expenses (such as subcontract costs), and *manufacturing overhead.

manufacturing expenses *See* manufacturing costs.

manufacturing lead time The elapsed time between placing a *production order and the receipt of the completed production.

manufacturing overhead (production overhead) The costs of production that cannot be traced directly to the product or *cost unit. Apart from the *direct costs, all other costs incurred in the manufacturing process are the manufacturing overhead; examples include depreciation of machinery, factory rent and business rates, cleaning materials, and maintenance expenses.

manufacturing profit (or **loss)** The difference between the value of the goods transferred from a *manufacturing account to a *trading account at a price other than the *production cost of finished goods, and the production cost of finished goods.

manufacturing requisition *See* production order.

manufacturing statement *See* manufacturing account.

manufacturing time The time taken to produce a specified quantity of production.

margin 1. The difference between the sales revenue and cost of goods or services expressed as a percentage of revenue. *See* contribution; gross margin; net margin. 2. The difference between the prices at which a *market maker or commodity dealer will buy and sell. This is often known colloquially as a **haircut** 3. In banking, the price added to a market rate of interest or subtracted from a market rate of deposit to provide a return for the bank. 4. In commodity and currency dealing, the amount advanced by a speculator or investor to a broker or dealer, when buying futures. 5. Money or securities deposited with a stockbroker to cover any possible losses a client may make.

marginal cost The variable costs per unit of production. The variable costs are usually regarded as the *direct costs plus the variable overheads. Marginal cost represents the additional cost incurred as a result of the production of one additional unit of production.

marginal costing (direct costing; variable costing) A costing and decision-making technique that charges only the *marginal costs to the *cost units and treats the *fixed costs as a lump sum to be deducted from the total *contribution in obtaining the profit or loss for the period. In some cases, *inventory valuation is also at marginal cost, although this approach does not conform to Statement of Standard Accounting Practice 9 and is used for internal reporting purposes only. *Compare* absorption costing.

marginal cost pricing The setting of product selling prices based on the charging of *marginal costs only to the product. The approach is only likely to be used in exceptional circumstances, such as when competition is intensive, as its application to the complete range of products is likely to cause the business to make losses by its failure to cover its *fixed costs. *Compare* full cost pricing.

marginal rate of tax The rate of *corporation tax that applies to the profits of a company between the lower limit for corporation tax (£300,000 for *financial year 1995) and the upper limit (£1,500,000 for that year).

marginal relief (small companies relief) Relief available when the profits chargeable to corporation tax (PCTCT) of a company plus its *franked investment income (FII) fall between the upper and lower limits for the *financial year (between £300,000 and £1,500,000 for 1995). The full rate of *corporation tax is applied to the PCTCT and the marginal relief is deducted from this total. Marginal relief is calculated as:
$$PCTCT[HRA - (PCTCT + FII)]/50(PCTCT + FII),$$
where HRA is the higher relevant amount, i.e. the upper limit, £1,500,000, for the financial year 1995 for companies with no *associated companies. For companies in a group the HRA is divided by the number of active members in the group.

marginal revenue The additional income that accrues to an organization as the result of selling an extra unit of sales.

margin of safety The difference between the level of activity at which an organization breaks even and a given level of activity greater than the *breakeven point. The margin of safety may be expressed in the same terms as the breakeven point, i.e. sales value, number of units, or percentage of capacity.

margin of safety ratio The *margin of safety expressed as a percentage of a given level of activity. For example, if the sales level achieved is £500,000 and the sales level breakeven point is £400,000, the margin of safety is £100,000 and the margin of safety ratio will be:

$$(£100,000 \times 100)/£500,000 = 20\%.$$

marker rate The base interest rate defined in the loan agreement, to which the spread is added in order to establish the interest rate payable on a variable-rate loan.

market capitalization (market valuation) The value of a company obtained by multiplying the number of its issued ordinary shares by their *market price.

marketing costs The costs incurred by an organization in carrying out its marketing activities. These would include sales promotion costs, salesmen's salaries, advertising, and point-of-sale promotional material, such as display stands.

marketing cost variance The difference between the budgeted *marketing cost for a period and the actual marketing cost incurred for the same period.

market maker A dealer in securities on the *London Stock Exchange who undertakes to buy and sell securities as a principal and is therefore obliged to announce buying and selling prices for a particular security at a particular time. Before October 1986 (see Big Bang) this function was performed by a stockjobber, who was then obliged to deal with the public through a stockbroker. However since October 1986, when the rules changed, market makers attempt to make a profit by dealing in securities as principals (selling at a higher price than that at which they buy; see margin) as well as acting as agents, working for a commission. While this dual role may create a conflict of interest for market makers (see Chinese wall), it avoids the restrictive trade practice of the former system and reduces the cost of dealing in the market.

market price 1. The price of a raw material, product, service, security, etc., in an open market. In a formal market, such as a stock exchange, commodity market, foreign-exchange market, etc., there is often a *margin between the buying and selling price; there are, therefore, two market prices. In these circumstances the market prices often quoted are the average of the buying and selling price. **2.** The economic concept of the price at which commodities are exchanged in a market, either for money or for each other.

market report The report on the daily activities of the *stock exchange or – less commonly – of some other market.

market-risk premium *See* risk premium.

market valuation *See* market capitalization.

mark-up The amount by which the cost of a service or product has been increased to arrive at the selling price. It is calculated by expressing the profit as a percentage of the cost or service. For example, if a product cost £8 and is sold for £12, the mark-up would be:

$$£4/£8 \times 100 = 50\%.$$

Note that the margin (see gross margin; net margin) is calculated by expressing the profit as a percentage of the selling price; in this case it would be:

$$£4/£12 \times 100 = 33.3\%.$$

The mark-up is widely used in retailing, both for setting prices and as a ratio for control and decision making.

marriage value The latent value released by the merger of two or more interests in land. Often the merger consists of the freehold and a long leasehold on the same property.

master budget The final coordinated overall *budget for an organization as a whole, which brings together the *functional budgets, the *capital budget, and the *cash-flow budget, as well as the budgeted profit and loss account and balance sheet for the period.

master file A computer file that holds standing data, such as clients' names and addresses.

matched bargain A transaction in which a sale of a particular quantity of stock is matched with a purchase of the same quantity of the same stock. Transactions of this kind are carried out on the *London Stock Exchange by **matching brokers**.

matching concept A fundamental concept in accounting and an essential element of *accrual accounting in which revenue and expenditure are not allocated to *financial periods on the basis of cash received or paid, but matched within one particular period so that the *profit for the period can be determined. The revenue to be recognized for a particular period is determined and the costs incurred in achieving that revenue matched against it. This process involves some arbitrary decisions involving, for example, *depreciation; it can lead to *creative accounting or profits that are determined subjectively.

material The production supplies of an organization that feature as revenue expenditure purchased from a third party. Materials may be classed as either *direct materials, which feature in the final product produced (such as wood and metal in furniture), or *indirect materials, which are necessary to carry out production but do not feature in the final product (such as maintenance and cleaning materials). Materials are not necessarily *raw materials, but can include components and sub-assemblies used in the finished product.

material adverse change A clause in a loan agreement or bank facility stating that the loan will become repayable if there should a material change in the borrower's credit standing. The clause can be contentious because it is not always clear what constitutes a material change.

material control The control of the materials required in a production process. It includes seeing that they are available in the required place, at the required time, and in the required quantities, as well as ensuring that the materials are properly accounted for. While it is clearly imperative that a production process should not be delayed by lack of materials, it is also important that overstocking of inventories should be avoided.

materiality The extent to which an item of accounting information is material. Information is considered material if its omission from a *financial statement could influence the decision making of its users. Materiality is therefore not an absolute concept but is dependent on the size and nature of an item and the particular circumstances in which it arises.

materials cost The expenditure incurred by an organization on *direct materials or *indirect materials. The expenditure on direct materials is part of *prime cost and that on indirect materials is a *manufacturing overhead.

materials oncost *See* oncost.

materials requisition (stores issue note; stores requisition) A form requiring that a specified item be issued from an organization's stores for a specified use. Such a requisition is usually a *prime document, which must be properly completed and authorized. It will contain a description of the material, *commodity code, *job number or *expenditure code, and the value of the material transferred from store to expenditure. The material requisition is used to credit stock and debit expenditure.

materials returns note (MRN; stores returns note; SRN) A form that records the return of material to store. A *prime document, it contains similar information to a *materials requisition and is used to debit stock and credit expenditure.

materials variances *See* direct materials total cost variance.

material transfer note A form that records the transfer of material from one *accounting code to another. A *prime document, it will contain a description of the material, *commodity code, *job number or accounting code to be credited, job number or accounting code to be debited, and the value of material transferred.

matrix accounting The use of a matrix (an array of figures arranged in rows or columns) to record accounting transactions and events, rather than a *T-account.

maturity date The date on which a document, such as a *bond, *bill of exchange, or insurance policy, becomes due for payment. In some cases, especially for redeemable government stocks, the maturity date is known as the **redemption date**. *See also* redemption.

maximum stock level The highest level of stock planned to be held; any amounts above the maximum would be considered excess stock.

MBO 1. Abbreviation for *management buyout. 2. Abbreviation for *management by objectives.

MCT 1. Abbreviation for Member of the *Association of Corporate Treasurers. 2. Abbreviation for *mainstream corporation tax.

MD&A Abbreviation for *management discussion and analysis.

medium-sized company A company that may claim certain filing exemptions if it meets two out of three of the following criteria for the current and preceding year, or the two preceding financial years:
• the *balance-sheet total (total assets) should not exceed £5,600,000;
• the *turnover should not exceed £11,200,000;
• the average number of employees should not exceed 250.

In a company's first *financial year it need only meet the conditions for that year; in its second financial year it may claim the filing exemptions of a medium-sized company if it met the conditions in its first financial year. A public *company, a banking or insurance company, an authorized person under the Financial Services Act (1986), or a member of an *ineligible group may not claim medium-sized company filing exemptions.

A medium-sized company must prepare full audited *financial statements for distribution to its shareholders but it may file *abbreviated accounts instead of full accounts with the *Registrar of Companies. *See also* exemptions from preparing consolidated financial statements. *Compare* small company.

medium-term note (MTN) An unsecured note issued in a eurocurrency with a maturity of about three to six years.

member of a company A shareholder of a company whose name is entered in the *register of members. Founder members (*see* founders' shares) are those who sign the memorandum of association; anyone subsequently coming into possession of the company's shares becomes a member.

members' voluntary liquidation (members' voluntary winding-up) The winding-up of a company by a special resolution of the members in circumstances in which the company is solvent. Before making the winding-up resolution, the directors must make a declaration of solvency. It is a criminal offence to make such a declaration without reasonable grounds for believing that it is true. When the resolution has been passed, a *liquidator is appointed; if, during the course of the winding-up, the liquidator believes that the company will not be able to pay its debts, a meeting of creditors must be called and the winding-up is treated as a members' *compulsory liquidation.

memorandum entry An entry in a *ledger that does not form part of the *double-entry system. For example, individual debtors' ledgers are memorandum ledgers.

memorandum of association An official document setting out the details of a *company's existence. It must be signed by the first subscribers and must contain the following information (as it applies to the company in question): the company name; a statement that the company is a public company; the address of the registered office; the objects of the company (called the **objects clause**); a statement of limited liability; the amount of the guarantee; and the amount of authorized share capital and its division.

merchant bank A bank that formerly specialized in financing foreign trade, an activity that often grew out of its own merchanting business. This led them into accepting *bills of exchange and functioning as accepting houses. More recently they have tended to diversify into the field of *hire-purchase finance, the granting of long-term loans (especially to companies), providing venture capital, advising companies on flotations and *takeover bids, underwriting new issues, and managing investment portfolios and unit trusts. Many of them are old-established and some offer a limited banking service. Their knowledge of international trade makes them specialists in dealing with the large multinational companies. They are most common in Europe, but some merchant banks have begun to operate in the USA. Several UK merchant banks were taken over in the 1990s either by the commercial banks or by large overseas banks.

merger A combination of two or more businesses on an equal footing that results in the creation of a new reporting entity formed from the combining businesses. The shareholders of the combining entities mutually share the risks and rewards of the new entity and no one party to the merger obtains control over another. Under *Financial Reporting Standard 6, 'Acquisitions and Mergers', to qualify as a merger a combination must satisfy four criteria:

• no party is the acquirer or acquired;

• all parties to the combination participate in the management structure of the new entity;

• the combining entities are relatively equal in terms of size;

• the consideration received by the equity shareholders of each party consists primarily of equity shares in the combined entity, any other consideration received being relatively immaterial.

In the UK, approval of the *Monopolies and Mergers Commission may be required and the merger must be conducted on lines sanctioned by the City Code on Takeovers and Mergers.

merger accounting A method of accounting that treats two or more businesses as combining on an equal footing. It is usually applied without any restatement of *net assets to fair value and includes the results of each of the combined entities for the whole of the *accounting period, as if they had always been combined. It does not reflect the issue of shares as an application of resources at fair value. The difference that arises on *consolidation does not represent *goodwill but is deducted from, or added to, *reserves. *Compare* acquisition accounting.

merger relief Relief from adding to, or setting up, a *share premium account when issuing shares at a premium if an issuing company has secured at least a 90% equity holding in another company. This relief applies if the issuing company is providing for the allotment of equity shares in the issuing company in exchange for the equity shares (or non-equity shares) in the other company or by the cancellation of any such shares not held by the issuing company. This relief is given under section 131 of the Companies Act (1985). *See* merger reserve.

merger reserve A *reserve credited in place of a *share premium account when *merger relief is made use of. *Goodwill on consolidation may be written off against a merger reserve (unlike the share premium account).

Metcalf Report A report published by a subcommittee of the US Senate chaired by Senator Metcalf in 1976; it was critical of the accounting profession's structure and independence. Although it encouraged debate, no legislation resulted from the report.

mezzanine finance Finance, usually provided by specialist financial institutions, that is neither pure equity nor pure debt. It can take many different forms and can be secured or unsecured; it usually earns a higher rate of return than pure debt but less than equity. Conversely, it carries a higher risk than pure debt, although less than equity. It is often used in *management buyouts.

minimum subscription The minimum sum of money, stated in the prospectus of a new company, that the directors consider must be raised if the company is to be viable.

minority interest The interest of individual shareholders in a company more than 50% of which is owned by a holding company. For example, if 60% of the ordinary shares in a company are owned by a holding company, the remaining 40% will represent a minority interest. These **minority shareholders** will receive their full share of profits in the form of dividends although they will be unable to determine company policy as they will always be outvoted by the majority interest held by the holding company.

minority shareholders *See* minority interest.

MIRAS Abbreviation for *mortgage interest relief at source.

MIS Abbreviation for *management information system.

misdeclaration penalty A penalty of 15% of the *value added tax lost in understating the VAT liability or overstating the VAT refund due on the VAT return, when the amounts involved are material. The penalty will apply if the inaccuracy equals the lesser of £1 million and 30% of the total amount of tax due for the period of the VAT return. The penalty can be avoided if the *taxable person can show that there was reasonable excuse, that there had been a voluntary disclosure, or that the taxable person had reason to believe that their VAT affairs were under investigation by Customs and Excise.

mix variance **1.** A variance that arises in *standard costing as a direct materials variance, when a number of raw materials are used in production. It measures the loss or gain arising when the actual mix of materials used is different from the *standard mix of materials specified. **2.** A *sales margin mix variance for an organization that sells a number of alternative products. It measures the loss or gain that arises from the actual mix of sales volumes being different from the standard mix of sales volumes specified.

MLA Abbreviation for *mandatory liquid assets.

MMC Abbreviation for *Monopolies and Mergers Commission.

modified accounts The original name for what are now called *abbreviated accounts.

modified historical-cost convention A modification of the *historical-cost convention in which certain assets are included at revalued amounts rather than their original cost. Modified historical cost accounting is permitted by the Companies Act. *See* alternative accounting rules.

monetary assets *Assets, such as *cash and *debtors, that have a fixed monetary exchange value and are not affected by a change in the price level. If there are no regulations requiring companies to account for changing price levels, monetary assets remain in the *financial statements at their original amounts. If the principle of accounting for changes in price levels is applied, the monetary assets will be indexed.

monetary measurement convention The accounting convention that transactions are only recognized in *financial statements if they can be measured in monetary terms. This means that some assets, such as a highly trained workforce or a sound customer base, will not be shown. It is also assumed, when preparing current statutory accounts, that money is a stable unit of measurement; in times of price changes, therefore, financial statements can be misleading. This is a major disadvantage of *historical cost accounting.

monetary working-capital adjustment *See* working-capital adjustment.

money A medium of exchange that functions as a unit of account and a store of value. Originally it enhanced economic development by enabling goods to be bought and sold without the need for barter. However, throughout history money has been beset by the problem of its debasement as a store of value as a result of *inflation. Now that the supply of money is a monopoly of the state, most governments are committed in principle to stable prices. The central debate in economics over the past 50 years has been whether *fiscal policy and monetary policy can have any effect other than to create inflation. The word *money* is derived from the Latin *moneta*, which was one of the names of Juno, the Roman goddess whose temple was used as a mint.

money market 1. The UK market for short-term loans in which money brokers arrange for loans between the banks, the government, the discount houses, and the accepting houses, with the Bank of England acting as lender of last resort. The main items of exchange are *bills of exchange, Treasury bills, and trade bills. The market takes place in and around Lombard Street in the City of London. Private investors, through their banks, can place deposits in the money market at a higher rate of interest than bank deposit accounts, for sums usually in excess of £10,000. **2.** The foreign-exchange market and the bullion market in addition to the short-term loan market.

money market line An agreement between a bank and a company that entitles the company to borrow up to a certain limit each day in the money markets, on a short-term basis (often overnight or in some cases up to one month). *See* uncommitted facility.

Monopolies and Mergers Commission (MMC) A commission established in 1948 as the Monopolies and Restrictive Practices Commission and reconstructed under its present title by the Fair Trading Act (1973). It investigates questions referred to it on unregistered monopolies relating to the supply of goods in the UK, the transfer of newspapers, mergers qualifying for investigation under the Fair Trading Act, and uncompetitive practices and restrictive labour practices, including public-sector monopolies as laid down in the provisions of the Competition Act (1980).

moratorium 1. An agreement between a creditor and a debtor to allow additional time for the settlement of a debt. **2.** A period during which one government permits a government of a foreign country to suspend repayments of a debt. **3.** A period during which all the trading debts in a particular market are suspended as a result of some exceptional crisis in the market. In these circumstances, not to call a moratorium would probably lead to more insolvencies than the market could stand. The intention of such a moratorium is, first, that firms should be given a breathing space to find out exactly what their liabilities are and, secondly, that they should be given time to make the necessary financial arrangements to settle their liabilities.

mortgage An interest in property created as a security for a loan or payment of a debt and terminated on payment of the loan or debt. The borrower, who offers the security, is the **mortgagor**; the lender, who provides the money, is the **mortgagee**. *Building societies and banks are the usual mortgagees for house purchasers, although there are other providers. A mortgage is generally repaid by monthly instalments, usually over a period of 25 years. Repayments may consist of capital and interest (**repayment mortgage**) or of interest only, with arrangements being made to repay the capital, generally from the proceeds of an endowment assurance policy (**endowment mortgage**) or a pension policy (**pension mortgage**). Business uses of the mortgage include using property to secure a loan to start a business. Virtually any property may be mortgaged (though land is the most common).

Under the Law of Property Act (1925), which governs mortgage regulations in the UK, there are two types of mortgage, legal and equitable. A **legal mortgage** confers a legal estate on the mortgagee; the only valid mortgages are (a) a lease granted for a stated number of years, which terminates on repayment of the loan at or before the end of that period; and (b) a deed expressed to be a *charge by way of legal mortgage. An **equitable mortgage** can be created if the mortgagee has only an equitable interest in the property (for example, when the mortgagee is a beneficiary under a trust of the property). Provided that this is done by deed, the rights of the parties are very similar to those under a legal mortgage. An equitable mortgage can also be created of a legal or equitable interest by an informal agreement, e.g. the mortgagor hands the title deeds to the mortgagee as security for a loan. Such a mortgagee has the remedies of possession and foreclosure only (see below). A second or subsequent mortgage may be taken out on the same property, provided that the value of the property is greater than the amount of the previous mortgage(s). All mortgages of registered land are noted in the *register of charges on application by the mortgagee, and a charge certificate is issued. When mortgaged land is unregistered, a first legal mortgagee keeps the title deeds. A subsequent legal mortgagee and any equitable mortgagee who does not have the title deeds should protect their interests by registration.

If the mortgaged property is the mortgagor's main residence, the mortgagor is entitled to **mortgage interest relief**, an income tax allowance on the value of the interest paid on mortgages up to a specified figure (currently £30,000). For mortgages made on or after 1 August 1988, the limit of mortgage relief applies to the property rather than to the borrower. Thus when two or more people share a residence, the relief is allocated between them in equal shares. Previously, each occupant (except when couples were married) was entitled to the full relief. Under the MIRAS (*mortgage interest relief at source) scheme, interest payments made by a borrower to a bank, building society, etc., are made after deduction of an amount equivalent to the relief of income tax due at the basic rate, and therefore no other relief is necessary, unless the person paying the mortgage pays tax at a higher rate.

Under the **equity of redemption**, the mortgagor is allowed to redeem the property at any time on payment of the loan together with interest and costs; any provisions in a mortgage deed to prevent redemption (known as **clogs**) are void.

In theory, the mortgagee always has the right to take possession of mortgaged property even if there has been no default. This right is usually excluded by building-society mortgages until default, and its exclusion may be implied in any instalment mortgage. Where residential property is concerned, the court has power to delay the recovery of possession if there is a realistic possibility that the default will be remedied in a reasonable time. In case of default, the mortgagor has a statutory right to sell the property, but this will normally be exercised after obtaining possession first. Any surplus left after the debt and the mortgagee's expenses have been met must be paid to the mortgagor. The mortgagee also has a statutory right to appoint a *receiver to manage mortgaged property in the event of default; this power is useful where business property is concerned. As a final resort, a mortgage may be brought to an end by *foreclosure, in which the court orders the transfer of the property to the mortgagee. This is not common in times of rising property prices, as the mortgagor would lose more than the value of the debt, so the court will not order foreclosure where a sale would be more appropriate. However, when property values are falling the mortgagor may have negative equity and the only recourse of the courts is foreclosure.

mortgage bond In the USA, a bond in which a debt is secured by a real *asset. **Senior mortgage bonds** have first claim on assets and **junior mortgage bonds** are subordinate. A mortgage bond may have a closed-end provision, which prevents an organization issuing further bonds of a similar nature on the same asset or open-end provision, which permits further issues with the same status.

mortgagee *See* mortgage.

mortgage interest relief at source (MIRAS) An arrangement allowing income tax relief to be given to a mortgagor on the first £30,000 of a loan taken out to purchase a main residence. From 6 April 1994 the relief was reduced to 20%, from the previous *basic rate tax relief of 25%. For 1995–96 the relief was reduced to 15%.

mortgagor *See* mortgage.

MRN Abbreviation for *materials returns note.

MTN Abbreviation for *medium-term note.

multicolumn reporting The presentation of financial information prepared on different bases (e.g. *historical-cost convention, *modified historical-cost convention, *replacement cost, etc.) in column form, each column representing a different basis. It is designed to facilitate understanding by the user.

multilateral netting A method of reducing bank charges in which the subsidiaries of a group offset their receipts and payments with each other, usually monthly, resulting in a single net intercompany payment or receipt made by each subsidiary to cover the period concerned. This saves both on transaction costs and paperwork. *See also* bilateral netting; netting.

multiple breakeven points Two or more activity levels at which an organization breaks even. They can occur on *breakeven charts when the cost and revenue functions are not linear and the total cost curve and the total revenue curve cross each other more than once.

multiple solution rates The several rates of return that can in some circumstances be computed in an *appraisal based on *discounted cash flow using the *internal rate of return method. These circumstances may arise when the projected cash flows change from positive to negative and back to positive again, causing an internal rate of return at each change of sign in the stream of cash flows.

mutually exclusive projects A number of alternative projects being considered for *appraisal, in which no one project can be pursued in conjunction with any of the other projects. For example, a parcel of land may be used to build a factory, an office block, or a mixture of the two. Each alternative is mutually exclusive because the choice of one alternative automatically excludes the others. Mutually exclusive projects arise when there is a scarce resource, in this case land. *Compare* independent projects.

NAA Abbreviation for *National Association of Accountants.

naked position *See* open position.

NAO Abbreviation for *National Audit Office.

NASD Abbreviation for *National Association of Securities Dealers.

NASDAQ Abbreviation for *National Association of Securities Dealers Automated Quotations System.

National Association of Accountants (NAA) In the USA, a body of accountants whose members are mostly not *certified public accountants. It has made a significant contribution to the development of *management accounting.

National Association of Securities Dealers (NASD) In the USA, a self-regulating organization whose members are *brokers and dealers operating in the *over-the-counter market for securities. The association has a written code of practice, standards procedures for its practitioners, and arbitration and disciplinary mechanisms, and it comments on impending legislation on *securities. *See also* National Association of Securities Dealers Automated Quotations System.

National Association of Securities Dealers Automated Quotations System (NASDAQ) In the USA, a computerized system that provides quotations for *over-the-counter market and some *stock exchange securities. It is owned and operated by the *National Association of Securities Dealers.

National Audit Office (NAO) A body set up in 1983 to be responsible for auditing the appropriation accounts of government departments and also to examine the economy, efficiency, and effectiveness with which government departments have used their resources. The NAO reports to the parliamentary Committee of Public Accounts and is under the control of the Comptroller and Auditor General.

National Insurance contribution (NIC) Payments made by those with *earned income that contribute to the National Insurance Fund, from which benefits are paid. These benefits include retirement pensions, unemployment pay, widow's benefits, invalidity benefit, and certain sickness and maternity benefits. There are five different classes of National Insurance contributions; the class applicable to a person depends on the type of earned income received by that person. Class 1 is paid by those with earnings from employment. There are two parts to class 1, primary contributions paid by the employee and secondary contributions paid by the employer. The rates of contributions depend on the level of earnings and also whether or not the employee is a member of a contracted-out occupational pension scheme. Class 2 is a flat-rate contribution paid by the self-employed; it is £5.75 for 1995–96. Class 3 is voluntary, and is also at a flat rate – £5.65 for 1995–96. It is paid by those wishing to maintain their contribution record even though their level of earnings is below that for mandatory contributions. Class 4 is paid by the self-employed at a fixed rate, on income between a lower limit and an upper limit. For 1995–96 the class 4 rate is 7.3%; for 1995–96 the lower limit is £6640 and the upper limit is £22,880. Class 1A was introduced in 1991 and is payable by employers who provide cars for private as well as business use for their employees. The level of payment depends on the cost and age of the car and the number of business miles travelled. It is based on the income tax car scale rates. *See also* State Earnings-Related Pension Scheme (SERPS).

National Savings A wide range of schemes for personal savers, administered by the UK Department for National Savings (established in 1969 and previously known as the Post Office Savings Department). They include premium bonds, income bonds, capital bonds, and yearly savings plans. In addition the department has offered a range of **National Savings Certificates (NSC)**, costing either £10 (up to 1985), £25 (1985–92), or £100 (from 1992), some of which have been index-linked (*see* indexation). The income they pay is income-tax free and the element of capital gain is free of capital gains tax.

NAV Abbreviation for *net asset value.

NBV Abbreviation for *net book value.

near money An asset that is immediately transferable and may be used to settle some but not all debts, although it is not as liquid as banknotes and coins. *Bills of exchange are examples of near money. Near money is not included in the money supply indicators.

negative cash flow Cash paid out by an organization.

negative consolidation difference A *consolidation difference showing a credit balance. In *acquisition accounting this will represent *negative goodwill.

negative goodwill on consolidation The *goodwill consolidation in which the price paid for an acquisition is less than the fair value of its net *tangible assets. According to *Statement of Standard Accounting Practice 22, 'Accounting for Goodwill', the amount of negative goodwill must be credited directly to *reserves.

negative income tax (NIT) A suggested means of targeting social security benefits to those most in need. The payments would be made through the income tax system by granting personal allowances to taxpayers so that the *basic rate of income tax on these allowances would constitute a minimum amount required for living. Those with high incomes would obtain that amount as an income tax relief, while those with incomes lower than the allowance would have a negative income tax liability and be paid the appropriate sums. The principal objection to the system is that to cover the needs of the disadvantaged the wealthier would obtain excessively high allowances.

negative pledge A *covenant in a loan agreement in which a borrower promises that no secured borrowings will be made during the life of the loan or will ensure that the loan is secured equally and ratably with any new borrowings as specifically defined.

negative yield curve A graph in which interest rates for deposits or securities are plotted against different maturities when short-term interest rates are higher than longer rates. The result is a graph that starts at a high level and curves downwards.

negligible value Denoting an asset of little or no value. For *capital gains tax, if an asset is determined to have negligible value it can be treated as having been sold and immediately re-acquired at the current negligible value (nil), resulting in an allowable *capital loss for capital gains tax purposes.

negotiability The ability of a document to change hands thereby entitling its owner to some benefit, so that legal ownership of the benefit passes by delivery or endorsement of the document. For a document to be negotiable it must also entitle the holder to bring an action in law if necessary. *See* negotiable instrument.

negotiable instrument A document of title that can be freely negotiated (*see* negotiability). Such documents are *cheques and *bills of exchange, in which the stated payee of the instrument can negotiate the instrument by either inserting the name of a different payee or by making the document 'open' by endorsing it (signing one's name), usually on the reverse. Holders of negotiable instruments cannot pass on a better title than they possess. Bills of exchange, including cheques, in which the payee is named or that bear a restrictive endorsement, such as 'not negotiable', are **non-negotiable instruments**.

net Denoting an amount remaining after specific deductions have been made. For example, **net profit before taxation** is the profit made by an organization after the deduction of all business expenditure but before the deduction of the *taxation charge.

net assets The difference between the *assets of a company and its *liabilities.

net asset value (NAV) The value of a share in a company calculated by dividing the amount for the *net assets of the company by the number of shares in issue. The net asset value is frequently below the *market price of a share because *financial statements do not reflect the present values of all assets because of the *monetary measurement convention and the *historical-cost convention, whereas the market price may reflect them.

net basis The basis upon which the *earnings per share of a company is calculated, taking into account both constant and variable elements in the company's tax charge. According to *Statement of Standard Accounting Practice 3, 'Earnings per Share', a *listed company must show the earnings per share on the net basis on the face of the *profit and loss account. *Compare* nil basis.

net book value (NBV; depreciated cost; depreciated value) The value at which an asset appears in the books of an organization (usually as at the date of the last balance sheet) less any depreciation that has been applied since its purchase or its last revaluation.

net cash flow The difference between the cash coming into an organization and that going out of it in a financial period. The difference may be positive, in which case there is a surplus of cash, or negative, in which case there is a deficit.

net cash investment in a lease (net investment in a lease) The amount of funds invested in a lease by a lessor. It comprises the cost of the leased asset, together with grants received, rentals received, taxation payments and receipts, residual values, interest payments, interest received on cash surplus, and any profit taken out of the lease. *See* finance lease.

net current assets *See* working capital.

net dividend The dividend paid by a company to its shareholders, after excluding the *tax credit received by the shareholders.

net investment in a lease *See* net cash investment in a lease.

net margin The *gross margin less all the other costs of an organization in addition to those included in the *cost of goods sold.

net present value (NPV) In *discounted cash flows, the difference between the *present values of the cash outflows and the present values of the cash inflows. The NPV is the application of *discount factors, based on a *required rate of return to each year's projected cash flow, both in and out, so that the cash flows are discounted to *present values. If the NPV is positive, the required rate of return is likely to be earned and the project should be considered; if it is negative, the project should be rejected.

net profit The amount of income earned by an organization after deducting all expenses. It is shown before and after *taxation in the *profit and loss account.

net profit ratio The net profit for a *financial period expressed as a percentage of the turnover.

net realizable value (NRV) The sales value of the stock of an organization less the additional costs likely to be incurred in getting the stocks into the hands of the customer. It is the value placed on the closing stock according to the requirements of *Statement of Standard Accounting Practice 9, when the NRV is lower than cost.

net residual value (disposal value) The expected proceeds from the sale of an asset, net of the costs of sale, at the end of its estimated useful life. It is used for computing the *straight-line method and *diminishing-balance method of depreciation, and also for inclusion in the final year's cash inflow in a *discounted cash flow appraisal.

netting A method of reducing bank charges in which the number of payments and receipts between connected parties is reduced by offsetting transactions between them. *See* bilateral netting; multilateral netting.

netting off The deduction of one amount from another. For example, debtors are usually shown in a *balance sheet after netting off (deducting) a provision for *bad debts and *doubtful debts.

network analysis *See* critical-path analysis.

net worth The value of an organization when its liabilities have been deducted from the value of its assets. Often taken to be synonymous with *net asset value (i.e. the total assets as shown by the balance sheet less the current liabilities), net worth so defined can be misleading in that balance sheets rarely show the real value of assets; in order to arrive at the true net worth it would normally be necessary to assess the true market values of the assets rather than their book values. It would also be necessary to value *goodwill, which may not even appear in the balance sheet.

New York Stock Exchange (NYSE) The main US stock exchange. It was founded in 1792 under the Buttonwood Agreement (the name of the tree under which 24 merchants agreed to give each other preference in their dealings); it moved to Wall Street in 1793. The New York Stock & Exchange Board was formally established in 1817; it was renamed the New York Stock Exchange in 1983.

next-in-first-out cost (NIFO cost) A method of valuing units of *raw material or *finished goods issued from stock by using the next unit price at which a consignment will be received for pricing the issues. It is effectively using *replacement cost as a stock valuation method, which is not normally acceptable as a stock valuation system in the UK when computing profits for taxation purposes.

NIC Abbreviation for *National Insurance contribution.

NIF Abbreviation for *note issuance facility.

NIFO cost Abbreviation for *next-in-first-out cost.

nil basis The basis upon which the *earnings per share of a company is calculated taking into account only the constant elements in the company's tax charge. *Compare* net basis.

nil paid shares *Shares issued without payment, usually as the result of a *rights issue.

nil-rate band The first slice of a *chargeable transfer or the estate on death that is subject to a nil rate of *inheritance tax. The nil rate band for 1995–96 is £154,000. For example, on an estate of £200,000, where there have been no lifetime transfers, the first £154,000 is at nil rate while the remaining £46,000 attracts duty at 40%, giving an inheritance-tax liability for the estate of £18,400.

NIT Abbreviation for *negative income tax.

nominal account A *ledger account that is not a *personal account in that it bears the name of a concept, e.g. light and heat, bad debts, investments, etc., rather than the name of a person. These accounts are normally grouped in the *nominal ledger. *See also* impersonal account; real account.

nominal capital *See* authorized share capital.

nominal ledger (general ledger) The *ledger containing the *nominal accounts and *real accounts necessary to prepare the accounts of an organization. This ledger is distinguished from the personal ledgers, such as the *debtors' ledger and *creditors' ledger, which contain the accounts of customers and suppliers respectively.

nominal price 1. A minimal price fixed for the sake of having some consideration for a transaction. It need bear no relation to the market value of the item. **2.** The price given to a security when it is issued, also called the **face value**, **nominal value**, or *par value. For example, XYZ plc 25p ordinary shares have a nominal price of 25p, although the market value may be quite different. The nominal value of a share is the maximum amount the holder can be required to contribute to the company.

nominal share capital *See* authorized share capital.

nominal value *See* par value.

nominee A person named by another (the **nominator**) to act on his or her behalf, often to conceal the identity of the nominator. *See* nominee shareholding.

nominee shareholding A shareholding held in the name of a bank, stockbroker, company, individual, etc., that is not the name of the beneficial owner of the shares. A shareholding may be in the name of nominees to facilitate dealing or to conceal the identity of the true owner. Although this cover was formerly used in the early stages of a takeover, to enable the bidder clandestinely to build up a substantial holding in the target company, this is now prevented by the Companies Act (1981), which makes it mandatory for anyone holding 5% or more of the shares in a public company to declare that interest to the company. The earlier Companies Act (1967) made it mandatory for directors to openly declare their holdings, and those of their families, in the companies of which they are directors.

non-adjusting events Any events, either favourable or unfavourable, that occur between the *balance-sheet date and the date on which the *financial statements of an organization are approved by the board of directors, but which concern conditions that did not exist at the balance-sheet date. If they are sufficiently *material for their non-disclosure to affect a user's understanding of the financial statements, non-adjusting events should be disclosed in the notes to the accounts. If a non-adjusting event suggests that the *going-concern concept is no longer applicable to the whole, or a material part, of the company, changes in the amounts to be included in the financial statements should be made.

non-contributory pension scheme An *occupational pension scheme in which all the contributions to the scheme are made by the employer.

non-controllable costs *See* uncontrollable costs.

non-cumulative preference share A *preference share not having the right to *dividends that were not paid in previous years. *Compare* cumulative preference share.

non-domiciled Having a *domicile in a country other than the country in question.

non-equity share A *share in a company having any of the following characteristics:

• any of the rights of the share to receive payments are for a limited amount that is not calculated by reference to the company's assets or profits or the dividends on any class of equity share;

• any of the rights of the share to participate in a surplus on *liquidation are

limited to a specific amount that is not calculated by reference to the company's assets or profits;
• the share is redeemable either according to its terms or because the holder, or any party other than the issuer, can require its redemption.
This definition is based on that contained in *Financial Reporting Standard 4, 'Capital Instruments'.

non-executive director A director of a company who is not involved in the day-to-day management of the business but who is appointed to bring independent judgment on issues of strategy, performance, resources, and standards of conduct. The *Cadbury Report on corporate governance recommended the appointment of non-executive directors.

non-participating preference share A *preference share that does not carry a right to participate in the profits of a company beyond a fixed rate of *dividend. This is the most common type of preference share.

non-production overhead costs The *indirect costs of an organization that are not classified as *manufacturing overhead. They include *administration overheads, *selling overhead, *distribution overhead, and (in some cases) *research and development costs.

non-purchased goodwill *Goodwill that has been internally generated by an organization rather than purchased on the acquisition of another business.

non-ratio covenant A form of *covenant in a loan agreement that includes conditions relating to the payment of dividends, the granting of guarantees, disposal of assets, change of ownership, and a *negative pledge. Breaching such a covenant will usually empower the lender to request repayment of any of the loan then outstanding, and the loan then becomes null and void. *Compare* ratio covenant.

non-recourse finance A bank loan in which the lending bank is only entitled to repayment from the profits of the project the loan is funding and not from other resources of the borrower. *See also* limited recourse finance.

non-resident Being *resident in a country other than the country in question. Some taxpayers take active steps to ensure that they are considered non-resident for UK tax purposes as this will affect their exposure to UK tax.

non-revolving bank facility A loan from a bank to a company in which the company has a period (often several years) in which to make its *drawdowns, as well as flexibility with regard to the amount and timing of the drawdowns, but once drawn an amount takes on the characteristics of a *term loan. *Compare* revolving bank facility.

non-statistical sampling *See* judgmental sampling.

non-statutory accounts Any *balance sheet or *profit and loss account dealing with a *financial period of a company that does not form part of the *statutory accounts. Prior to the Companies Act (1989) they were known as *abridged accounts.

non-taxable income Income that is specifically exempt from tax. This includes the first £70 of interest from a National Savings Bank ordinary account, increase in value of National Savings Certificates, premium bond prizes, the capital part of the yearly amount received from a purchased life annuity, some social security benefits, prizes and betting winnings (including the National Lottery), *savings related share option scheme (SAYE) account bonuses, shares allotted by an employer under an approved profit-sharing scheme, *profit-related pay up to £4000, statutory redundancy pay, and maintenance payments made under arrangements after 14 March 1988.

non-voting ordinary shares *See* A shares.

no par value capital stock In the USA, stock (shares) that have no par value or assigned value printed on the stock certificate. An advantage of this stock is that it avoids a *contingent liability to stockholders in the event of a stock discount. For accounting purposes, on the issue of no par value capital stock, cash is debited and a capital stock account credited with the total proceeds received. No premium account is required.

normal capacity The production capacity level budgeted for a period, expressed in *direct labour hours, *machine hours, or *standard hours.

normal loss The loss arising from a manufacturing or chemical process through waste, seepage, shrinkage, or spoilage that can be expected, on the basis of historical studies, to be part of that process. It may be expressed as a weight or volume or in other units appropriate to the process. It is usually not valued but if it is, a notional scrap value is used. It is axiomatic in costing that normal losses are part of the normal *manufacturing cost, whereas the cost of *abnormal losses should not be borne by the good output. *See also* waste.

normal shrinkage *See* normal loss.

normal spoilage *See* normal loss.

normal standard An average standard, used in *standard costing, set to be applied over a future period during which conditions are unlikely to change.

normal volume The volume of activity used to determine the overhead *absorption rate in a system of *absorption costing. It is usually the budgeted volume of production for a period.

normal waste *See* normal loss.

normative theories of accounting Theories of accounting, often based on deductive reasoning, that prescribe the accounting procedures and policies to be implemented.

note issuance facility (NIF; note purchase facility) A means of enabling short-term borrowers in the *eurocurrency markets to issue euronotes, with maturities of less than one year, when the need arises rather than having to arrange a separate issue of euronotes each time they need to borrow. A **revolving underwriting facility (RUF)** achieves the same objective.

note of historical cost profits and losses A memorandum item in the *annual accounts and report of a company giving an abbreviated restatement of the profit and loss account, showing the reported profit or loss as if no revaluations had been made. The statement need not be made where the difference is not material. *Financial Reporting Standard 3, 'Reporting Financial Performance', states that such a note should be published.

notes to the accounts (notes to financial statements) Information supporting that given on the face of a company's *financial statements. Many notes are required to be given by law, including those detailing *fixed assets, investments, *share capital, *debentures, and *reserves. Other information may be required by accounting standards or be given to facilitate the users' understanding of the company and its current and future performance; social and environmental information, for example, falls into this category.

not for profit organization In the USA, an organization that provides goods or services with a policy that no individual or group will share in any profits or losses. Examples are government and charity organizations.

not negotiable Words marked on a *bill of exchange indicating that it ceases to be a *negotiable instrument, i.e. although it can still be negotiated, the holder cannot obtain a better title to it than the person from whom it was obtained, thus providing a safeguard if it is stolen. A cheque is the only form of bill that can be crossed 'not negotiable'; other forms must have it inscribed on their faces.

novation A cancellation of the rights and obligations under one loan agreement and their replacement by new ones under another agreement. The principal effect is to change the identity of the lender.

NPV Abbreviation for *net present value.

NRV Abbreviation for *net realizable value.

number of days' stock held A ratio that measures the average number of days' stock held by an organization. To obtain an accurate measure the following formula should be used for each commodity:

(number of units in stock × 365)/stock usage in units per annum.

The number of units in stock may be taken at the start or the end of the year or may be the average of both. Because the information required for the above ratio is only likely to be available from the internal management accounts, a different formula using final accounts figures is often used as an overall measure of stock levels:

(value of stocks × 365)/sales or cost of sales per annum.

Again, the value of stocks may be taken at the start or the end of the period or may be an average of both. The second formula tends to be inaccurate and is an average of the turnover of all stocks.

NYSE Abbreviation for *New York Stock Exchange.

objective function In *linear programming, a statement that gives the aim of a decision in the form of an equation. For example, the objective function may be either to maximize the *contribution or to minimize the costs, based on a relationship between the factors of production.

objectives of financial statements The purposes for which the *financial statements in the *annual accounts and report have been made. It is essential to identify these purposes because they are needed to determine what information should be provided in financial statements. The current thinking is that the objective is to provide information useful in economic decision making. It is debatable whether present disclosures are appropriate for this purpose; there is some uncertainty as to the users of financial statements, the purposes they use them for, and how they process the information. The issues are addressed by the *Accounting Standards Board's *Statement of Principles in the UK, and by the *Financial Accounting Standards Board's Statement of Financial Accounting Concepts No. 1, 'Objectives of Financial Statements', in the USA.

objectivity An accounting concept attempting to ensure that any subjective actions taken by the preparer of *accounts are minimized. The aim of the rules and regulations required to achieve objectivity is that users should be able to compare *financial statements for different companies over a period with some confidence that the statements have been prepared on the same basis. One of the major advantages claimed for *historical cost accounting is that it is objective, but necessarily some subjective decisions will have been made.

objects clause A clause contained in the *memorandum of association of a company setting out the objects for which the company has been formed. If the activities undertaken by a company are not included in the objects clause, the company is said to be acting beyond its powers, i.e. *ultra vires.

obligation A commitment given to comply with the terms of a contract or to pay a debt.

OBSF Abbreviation for *off balance sheet finance.

obsolescence A fall in the value of an asset as a result of its age or decline in its usefulness for other reasons. Obsolescence is an important factor both for *depreciation and *stock. In respect of depreciation, changes in technology or markets may mean a *fixed asset becomes obsolete before the end of its predicted useful life. In respect of stocks, obsolescence may mean that the total cost of outdated items held in stock has to be charged against the *profit and loss account immediately, as the rule is that stocks must be shown at the lower of cost or market value.

occupational pension scheme A pension scheme run by a company or other organization for its employees.

off balance sheet finance (OBSF) A method of financing a company's activities so that some or all of the finance and the corresponding assets do not appear on the *balance sheet of the company. By making use of OBSF a company can enhance its *accounting ratios, such as the *gearing ratio and *return on capital employed, and also avoid breaking any agreements it has made with the banks in respect of the total amount it may borrow. It has been possible for companies, by drawing up complex legal agreements, to conduct off balance sheet finance and thus mislead the user of the accounts. The accounting profession has attempted to counter these practices by emphasizing that accounting should reflect the commercial reality of transactions and not simply their legal form. The recent *Financial Reporting Standard 5, 'Reporting the Substance of Transactions', provides specific guidance for certain transactions, such as *factoring and *consignment stock, for which companies have previously used off balance sheet finance.

offer The price at which a seller is willing to sell something. If there is an acceptance of the offer a legally binding *contract has been entered into. In law, an offer is distinguished from an **invitation to treat**, which is an invitation by one person or firm to others to make an offer. An example of an invitation to treat is to display goods in a shop window. *See also* offer price.

offer by prospectus An offer to the public of a new issue of shares or debentures made directly by means of a prospectus, a document giving a detailed account of the aims, objects, and capital structure of the company, as well as its past history. The prospectus must conform to the provisions of the Companies Act (1985). *Compare* offer for sale.

offer for sale An invitation to the general public to purchase the stock of a company through an intermediary, such as an issuing house or *merchant bank (*compare* offer by prospectus); it is one of the most frequently used means of *flotation. An offer for sale can be in one of two forms: at a fixed price (the more usual), which requires some form of balloting or rationing if the demand for the shares exceeds supply; or an *issue by tender, in which case individuals offer to purchase a fixed quantity of stock at or above some minimum price and the stock is allocated to the highest bidder. In the USA an offer for sale is called a **public offering**. *Compare* introduction; placing; public issue.

offer price The price at which a security is offered for sale by a *market maker and also the price at which an institution will sell units in a unit trust. *Compare* bid.

Office of Fair Trading (OFT) A government department that, under the Director General of Fair Trading, reviews commercial activities in the UK and aims to protect the consumer against unfair practices. Established in 1973, it is responsible for the administration of the Fair Trading Act (1973), the Consumer Credit Act (1974), the Restrictive Trade Practices Act (1976), the Estate Agents Act (1979), the Competition Act (1980), the Financial Services Act (1986), and the Control of Misleading Advertisements Regulations (1988). Its five main areas of activity are: consumer affairs, consumer credit, monopolies and mergers, restrictive trade practices, and anti-competitive practices.

officers of a company The *directors of a company and the *company secretary. An officer of a company may not be appointed as the *auditor of that company.

Official List 1. A list of all the securities traded on the main market of the *London Stock Exchange. *See* listed security; listing requirements; Yellow Book. 2. A list prepared daily by the London Stock Exchange, recording all the bargains that have been transacted in listed securities during the day. It also gives dividend dates, rights issues, prices, and other information.

official receiver (OR) A person appointed by the Secretary of State for Trade and Industry to act as a *receiver in *bankruptcy and winding-up cases. The High Court and each county court that has jurisdiction over insolvency matters has an official receiver, who is an officer of the court. Deputy official receivers may also be appointed. The official receiver commonly acts as the *liquidator of a company being wound up by the court.

offset account An account that reduces the gross amount of another account to derive a net balance. An example is a *fixed asset that remains in the *books of account at cost as a *debit balance and is offset by a provision for *depreciation account, which accumulates the annual charge for depreciation as a *credit balance.

offshore company 1. A company not registered in the same country as that in which the persons investing in the company are resident. 2. A company set up in a foreign country or *tax haven by a financial institution with the object of benefiting from tax laws or exchange control regulations in that country.

OFT Abbreviation for *Office of Fair Trading.

OMV Abbreviation for *open-market value.

oncost 1. The additional costs incurred as a consequence of employing personnel, i.e. **wages oncost**, or the additional costs incurred by storing and handling direct materials, i.e. **materials oncost** or **stores oncost**. 2. A rarely used alternative name for *overheads.

opening balance The balance *brought forward at the beginning of an *accounting period. Opening balances may be on the *debit or the *credit side of a *ledger. *See also* brought down.

opening entries *Journal entries made to open a business. All the *assets and *liabilities must be entered into the accounts, together with the owners' capital.

opening stock The stock held by an organization at the beginning of an accounting period as *raw materials, *work in progress, or *finished goods. The *closing stocks of one period become the opening stocks of the succeeding period and it is necessary to establish the level of closing stocks so that the cost of their creation is not charged against the profits of that period but brought forward as opening stocks to be charged against the profits of the succeeding period.

open-market value (OMV) The value of an asset equal to the amount that a willing purchaser would be prepared to pay a willing vendor. For *capital gains tax purposes, the open-market value refers to such a valuation made on 31 March 1982, the date from which *indexation is calculated for assets acquired before 31 March 1982.

open position (naked position) A trading position in which a dealer has commodities, *securities, or currencies bought but unsold or unhedged (*see* hedging), or sales that are neither covered nor hedged. In the former position the dealer has a **bull position**; in the latter, a **bear position**. In either case the dealer is vulnerable to market fluctuations until the position is closed or hedged. *See also* option.

operating and financial review A discussion paper issued by the *Accounting Standards Board, which recommends that companies should publish in their *annual accounts and report a statement similar to the *management discussion and analysis statement issued by US companies. The operating and financial review gives directors the opportunity to interpret the *financial statements and discuss the business, the structure of its finance, and any risks that can be foreseen. The review should give both positive and negative points.

operating budget *See* production budget.

operating costing The form of costing applied both to the provision of services within an organization and to the costing of continuous operating processes, such as electricity generation.

operating expenses and revenues The costs and revenues incurred or generated by an organization in the ordinary course of business. *See also* revenue expenditure.

operating lease A lease under which an asset is hired out to a lessee or lessees for a period that is substantially shorter than its useful economic life. Under an operating lease, the ownership of the leased asset remains with the lessor. *Statement of Standard Accounting Practice 21, 'Accounting for Leases and Hire Purchase Contracts', defines an operating lease as a lease other than a *finance lease.

operating performance ratios Various ratios used to analyse the financial performance of a company in terms of the return generated by the sales for a *financial period. The higher the ratios, the higher the profitability of the organization. Examples are *net profit margin and *gross margin.

operating profit (or loss) The profit (or loss) made by a company as a result of its principal trading activity. This is arrived at by deducting its **operating expenses** from its *trading profit, or adding its operating expenses to its trading loss; in either case this is before taking into account any extraordinary items.

operating risk The inherent risk that a plant, once started, will not continue to produce at the levels achieved to meet the completion definition.

operating statement A financial and quantitative statement provided for the management of an organization to record the performance achieved by that area of the operation for which the management is responsible, for a selected budget period. An operating statement may include production levels, costs incurred, and (where appropriate) revenue generated, all compared with budgeted amounts and the performance in previous periods.

operational audit A review of an organization's activities to assess whether they are being carried out efficiently and effectively.

operational variances The variances arising in *standard costing that measure the difference between the standards set for the current operating conditions and the actual performance achieved. *Compare* revision variance.

opinion shopping A colloquial name for the activity of seeking an *auditor who will approve a company's accounting policies.

opportunity cost The income or benefit foregone as the result of carrying out a particular decision, when resources are limited or when *mutually exclusive projects are involved. For example, the opportunity cost of building a factory on a piece of land is the income foregone by not constructing an office block on this particular site. Similarly, the income foregone by not constructing a factory if an office block is constructed represents the opportunity cost of an office block. Opportunity cost is an important factor in decision making (*see* cost-benefit analysis), although it represents costs that are not recorded in the accounts of the relevant organization.

option The right to buy or sell a fixed quantity of a commodity, currency, *security, etc., at a particular date at a particular price (the *exercise price). Unlike futures, the purchaser of an option is not obliged to buy or sell at the exercise price and will only do so if it is profitable; the purchaser may allow the option to lapse, in which case only the initial purchase price of the option (the option money or *premium) is lost. In London, options in commodity futures are bought and sold on *London FOX, and options on share indexes, foreign currencies, equities, and interest rates are dealt with through the *London International Financial Futures and Options Exchange (LIFFE).

An option to buy is known as a **call option** and is usually purchased in the expectation of a rising price; an option to sell is called a **put option** and is bought in the expectation of a falling price or to protect a profit on an investment. Options, like futures, allow individuals and firms to hedge against the risk of wide fluctuations in prices; they also allow dealers and speculators to gamble for large profits with limited liability.

Professional traders in options make use of a large range of potential strategies, often purchasing combinations of options that reflect particular expectations or cover several contingencies.

Traded options can be bought and sold on an exchange, at all times, i.e. there is a trade in the options themselves. Traded options are dealt in on London FOX and LIFFE. **Traditional options**, however, once purchased, cannot be resold. Traditional options in equities are dealt in on the London Stock Exchange, but traded options in equities are now dealt in on LIFFE. In a **European option** the buyer can only exercise the right to take up the option or let it lapse on the expiry date, whereas with an **American option** this right can be exercised at any time up to the expiry date. European options are therefore cheaper than American options. *See also* hedging.

option to tax (election to waive exemption) An irrevocable election made by a landlord to charge *value added tax on *exempt supplies of buildings (rents). This enables the otherwise *irrecoverable input VAT on costs relating to the property to be reclaimed by the landlord against the *output tax charged on the rents. The decision to opt to tax often depends on whether the tenant's business is fully subject to VAT. If the tenant makes *taxable supplies the VAT charged by the landlord can be set off in full against the total output tax of the tenant's business. In the case of tenants providing financial services (exempt supply) the VAT charged by the landlord under the option to tax cannot be set off and will result in the rent charge being increased by the additional VAT charged.

OR Abbreviation for *official receiver.

ordinary activities Any activities undertaken by an organization as part of its business and any related activities in which it engages in furtherance of, incidental to, or arising from, these activities. This definition is based on that given in *Financial Reporting Standard 3, 'Reporting Financial Performance'. Ordinary activities include the effects on the reporting entity of any event in the various environments in which it operates, including the political, regulatory, economic, and geographical environments, irrespective of the frequency or unusual nature of the events. *See also* extraordinary items.

ordinary resolution A resolution that is valid if passed by a majority of the votes cast at a general meeting of a British company. No notice that the resolution is to be proposed is required.

ordinary share A *share in a company that carries the right to a share of the company's *profits without limit. Ordinary shares generally carry the right to vote. *See also* A shares; equity share; non-equity share.

ordinary share capital The total *share capital of a company consisting of *ordinary shares.

ordinary shareholders' equity (ordinary shareholders' funds)
The value of the *assets of a company net of its *liabilities and any amounts of capital due to holders of shares other than *ordinary shares (e.g. *preference shares). If the company were to go into liquidation this would be the equity available for distribution to the ordinary shareholders.

organization chart A chart illustrating the structure of an organization; in particular it will show for which function of the business each manager is responsible and the chain of responsibility throughout the organization. Some organization charts include managers by name; others show the management positions in the structure.

original cost The cost of an item at the time of purchase or creation. This applies particularly to *fixed assets in which depreciation by the *straight-line method uses the original cost as a basis for the calculation. *See also* historical cost.

original entry error A mistake made in a *book of prime entry; for example, a purchase incorrectly entered in the purchases *journal. Original entry errors are not revealed by the *trial balance.

originating timing difference A difference between profits or losses computed for tax purposes on a receipts-and-payments basis and profits presented in the *financial statements on an *accruals basis. These differences arise as a result of items of income and expenditure in tax computations being included in different periods from those in which they are included in financial statements. An originating timing difference is described as originating in the period in which it arises; it is capable of reversal in subsequent periods. These differences are dealt with in *Statement of Standard Accounting Practice 15, 'Accounting for Deferred Tax'. *Compare* permanent difference.

origin of turnover The geographical segment from which products or services are supplied to a third party or another segment of the same organization, as defined by *Statement of Standard Accounting Practice 25, 'Segmental Reporting'. The standard requires certain companies to disclose this information in their *annual accounts and report.

OTC market Abbreviation for *over-the-counter market.

outlay cost The expenditure incurred as the initial cost of a project or activity. The outlay cost may include both *capital expenditure and expenditure on working capital, such as stocks of raw material.

out-of-pocket costs The *incremental costs incurred as the result of a particular decision being pursued. For example, an organization with limited cash resources may make a decision to pursue an investment alternative that would not have been the first choice had it not offered the lowest level of out-of-pocket costs.

output tax *Value added tax charged on total *taxable supplies by a trader registered for VAT. The standard rate (since 1991) is 17.5%.

outside director In the USA, a person who is a member of the board of directors of a company but is not an employee of the company and has no executive responsibilities. Such directors are appointed because they offer either wide business experience or specialist knowledge not available from the *executive directors.

overabsorbed overhead The circumstance in *absorption costing in which the *absorbed overhead is greater than the overhead costs incurred for a period. The difference, known as a favourable variance, represents an addition to the budgeted profits of the organization. *Compare* underabsorbed overhead.

overcapitalization A condition in which an organization has too much *capital for the needs of its business. If a business has more capital than it needs it is likely to be overburdened by interest charges or by the need to spread profits too thinly by way of dividends to shareholders. Businesses can now reduce overcapitalization by repaying long-term debts or by buying their own shares.

overdraft A loan made to a customer with a cheque account at a bank or building society, in which the account is allowed to go into debit, usually up to a specified limit (the **overdraft limit**). Interest is charged on the daily debit balance. This is a less costly way of borrowing than taking a *bank loan (providing the interest rates are the same) as, with an overdraft, credits are taken into account.

overhead (overhead cost) The *indirect costs of an organization, usually classified as *manufacturing overhead, *administration overheads, *selling overhead, *distribution overhead, and *research and development costs.

overhead absorption *See* absorption.

overhead absorption rate *See* absorption rate.

overhead analysis sheet (overhead distribution summary) A form on which the *manufacturing overhead is charged to the *cost centres of an organization by using appropriate allocation or apportionment techniques for each item of overhead cost.

overhead cost *See* overhead.

overhead cost absorbed (overhead cost recovered) The actual production for a period multiplied by the overhead *absorption rate budgeted for that period.

overhead distribution summary *See* overhead analysis sheet.

overhead efficiency variance (productivity variance, overhead productivity variance) That part of the variable overhead total cost variance that arises in a *standard costing system; it is due to the more efficient use of the time available to carry out the actual production. It compares the actual time taken to carry out an activity with the standard time allowed and values the difference at the standard variable overhead *absorption rate per hour. The resultant adverse or favourable variance is the amount by which the budgeted profit is affected by virtue of the variable overhead cost over- or under-recovered due to efficiency. The formula for this variance is:

(standard hours allowed for production – actual hours taken) × standard variable overhead absorption rate per hour.

See also efficiency variances.

overhead expenditure variance *See* expenditure variance.

overhead productivity variance *See* overhead efficiency variance.

overhead total variance The variances in respect of fixed and variable overheads arising in *standard costing representing the differences between the overhead recovered and the overhead incurred for a period. Where the overhead recovered exceeds the overhead incurred an over-recovery or favourable variance results. Where the overhead incurred exceeds that recovered then an under-recovery or adverse variance results.

overhead volume variance (fixed overhead volume variance) That part of the *fixed overhead total variance in *standard costing that measures the over- or under-recovery of fixed overheads as a result of the level of activity actually achieved differing from the level of activity budgeted. The formula is:

(actual production – budgeted production) × fixed overhead recovery rate, or alternatively:

recovered fixed overheads – budgeted fixed overheads.

overseas-income taxation Income that has been subject to taxation outside the jurisdiction of the UK tax authorities. When the same income is subject to taxation in more than one country, relief for the double tax is given either under the provisions of the *double taxation agreement with the country concerned or unilaterally.

over-the-counter market (OTC market) A market in which shares are bought and sold outside the jurisdiction of a recognized stock exchange; it was originally so named in the 1870s, from the practice of buying shares over bank counters in the USA. OTC markets acquired a reputation for providing reduced investor protection but they have since become more formalized. The world's largest OTC market is the US *National Association of Securities Dealers Automated Quotation System (NASDAQ). The UK has considered the OTC market as less than respectable and it disappeared altogether with the formation of the third market, with its minimal entry requirements, by the London Stock Exchange in 1987. This market was subsequently abolished in 1990 with the introduction of less stringent requirements for the *unlisted securities market (USM).

owners' equity The funds of an organization that have been provided by its owners, i.e. its total assets less its total liabilities. The balance-sheet value of the owners' equity is unlikely to be equal to its market value.

own shares purchase The purchase or redemption of its own shares by a company; this is permitted subject to certain conditions set out in the Companies Act. For example, redeemable shares may only be redeemed if they are fully paid. If the redemption or purchase of a company's own shares would lead to a reduction of its capital, a *capital redemption reserve will need to be created. In certain cases private companies may reduce their capital in this way (*see* permissible capital payment).

package A set of computer programs designed to be sold to a number of users. They are used in computerized accounting systems for purchase and sales ledgers, stock control, payroll records, etc. Buying a software package from firms specializing in them saves users a considerable amount of time and money in developing their own.

paid-in capital In the USA, the section of stockholders' equity on a company's *balance sheet, which shows the amount of stock issued, the premiums or discounts from selling the stock, stock received from donations, and the resale of treasury stock.

paid-up share capital (fully paid capital) The total amount of money that the shareholders of a company have paid to the company for their fully paid shares.

P & L account Abbreviation for *profit and loss account.

paperless office *See* electronic office.

paper profit A profit shown by the books or accounts of an organization, which may not be a realized profit because the value of an asset has fallen below its book value, because the asset, although nominally showing a profit, has not actually been sold, or because some technicality of book-keeping might show an activity to be profitable when it is not. For example, a share that has risen in value since its purchase might show a paper profit but this would not be a real profit since the value of the share might fall again before it is sold.

parallel hedge A hedge (*see* hedging) in which exposure to fluctuation in one foreign currency is matched by a purchase or sale of another currency, which is expected to move in sympathy with the first currency.

parent undertaking (parent company) *See* holding company.

pari passu clause A *covenant in a loan agreement in which a borrower promises to ensure that the loan in question will rank pari passu (equally) with its other defined debts.

partial exemption A restriction in *value added tax legislation that can arise if a *taxable person makes a mixture of *taxable supplies and *exempt supplies. In these circumstances there is a restriction on the amount of *input tax that is available to set against *output tax. If the amount of input tax relating to the exempt supplies does not exceed the *de minimus* limit of £625 per month, or £7500 per annum, all the input tax is available to be set against the output tax of the business. From 1 Dec 1994 there has been a 50% limit on the amount of input tax relating to exempt supplies. If the *de minimus* limit is exceeded, none of the input tax relating to the exempt supplies is available to set against output tax.

partial intestacy The circumstances that arise if a will covers only part of the estate of the deceased. The part of the estate accounted for in the will is dealt with according to the wishes of the deceased as set out in the will, while the remainder is allocated in accordance with the rules of intestacy (*see* intestate).

participating interest An interest held by an undertaking in the shares of another undertaking, which it holds on a long-term basis for the purpose of securing a contribution to its activities by the exercise of control or influence arising from or related to that interest. This definition is based on that given in *Financial Reporting Standard 2, 'Accounting for Subsidiary Undertakings'. A holding of 20% or more of the shares of an undertaking is presumed to be a participating interest, unless the contrary is shown.

participating preference share A *preference share entitled to a fixed rate of *dividend and a further share in the profits of a company, for example after the *ordinary shares have received a certain percentage.

participative budgeting The setting of a budget in which various levels of management are involved in fixing the budgeted levels of performance against which their actual performance will ultimately be measured.

participator Any person having an interest in the capital or income of a company, e.g. a shareholder, loan creditor, or any person entitled to participate in the *distributions of the company.

partly paid shares Shares on which the full nominal or *par value has not been paid. Formerly, partly paid shares were issued by some banks and insurance companies to inspire confidence, i.e. because they could always call on their shareholders for further funds if necessary. Shareholders, however, did not like the liability of being called upon to pay out further sums for their shares and the practice largely died out. It has been revived for large new share issues, especially in *privatizations, in which shareholders pay an initial sum for their shares and subsequently pay one or more calls on specified dates (*see also* share capital).

partner A member of a *partnership.

partnership An association of two or more people formed for the purpose of carrying on a business. Partnerships are governed by the Partnership Act (1890). Unlike an incorporated *company, a partnership does not have a legal personality of its own and therefore partners are liable for the debts of the firm. **General partners** are fully liable for these debts, **limited partners** only to the extent of their investment. A **limited partnership** is one consisting of both general and limited partners and is governed by the Limited Partnership Act (1907). A **partnership-at-will** is one for which no fixed term has been agreed. Any partner may end the partnership at any time provided that notice of the intention to do so is given to all the other partners. **Nominal partners** allow their names to be used for the benefit of the partnership, usually for a reward but not for a share of the profits. They are not legal partners. Partnerships are usually governed by a *partnership agreement.

partnership accounts The accounts kept by a *partnership. They include an *appropriation account in which the *profit of a *partnership is shared between the partners in accordance with the *partnership agreement. This may be in the form of salaries, interest on capital, and a share of the profit in the appropriate *profit-sharing ratio. Each partner also has a *capital account and a *current account. The former is used to account for capital contributions, *goodwill, and revaluations; the latter for all other transactions, such as appropriations of profit and drawings.

partnership agreement An agreement made between the partners of a *partnership. In the absence of either an express or an implied agreement the provisions of the Partnership Act (1890) apply. These provisions are also applicable if an agreement is silent on a particular point. The provisions are:
• partners share equally in the *profits or losses of the partnership;
• partners are not entitled to receive salaries;
• partners are not entitled to interest on their capital;
• partners may receive interest at 5% per annum on any advances over and above their agreed capital;
• a new partner may not be introduced unless all the existing partners consent;
• a retiring partner is entitled to receive interest at 5% per annum on his or her share of the partnership assets retained in the partnership after his or her retirement;
• on dissolution of the partnership the assets of the firm must be used first to repay outside creditors, secondly to repay partners' advances, and thirdly to repay partners' capital. Any residue on dissolution should be distributed to the partners in the *profit-sharing ratio.

par value (face value; nominal value) The *nominal price of a share or other security. If the market value of a security exceeds the nominal price it is said to be **above par**; if it falls below the nominal price it is **below par**. Gilt-edged securities are always repayed **at par** (usually £100), i.e. at the par value.

patent The grant of an exclusive right to exploit an invention. In the UK patents are granted by the Crown through the Patent Office, which is part of the Department of Trade and Industry. An applicant for a patent (usually the inventor or the inventor's employer) must show that the invention is new, is not obvious, and is capable of industrial application. An expert known as a **patent agent** often prepares the application, which must describe the invention in considerable detail. The Patent Office publishes these details if it grants a patent. A patent remains valid for 20 years from the date of application (the **priority date**) provided that the person to whom it has been granted (the **patentee**) continues to pay the appropriate fees. During this time, the patentee may assign the patent or grant licences to use it. Such transactions are registered in a public register at the Patent Office. If anyone infringes the patentee's monopoly, the patentee may sue for an injunction and *damages or an account of profits. However, a patent from the Patent Office gives exclusive rights in the UK only: the inventor must obtain a patent from the European Patent Office in Munich and patents in other foreign countries to protect the invention elsewhere.

payable to bearer Describing a *bill of exchange in which neither the payee or endorsee are named. A holder, by adding his or her name, can make the bill *payable to order.

payable to order Describing a *bill of exchange in which the payee is named and on which there are no restrictions or endorsements; it can therefore be paid to the endorsee.

pay and file A procedure for companies introduced in the UK for
*accounting periods ended after 30 September 1993. *Corporation tax is due
nine months after the end of the accounting period. The company must file a
detailed return within twelve months of the end of the accounting period.
Under this system there is more responsibility placed on the company to
finalize the accounts and accompanying tax computations in order to pay the
correct amount of tax by the due date. Previously, estimated assessments were
issued by the Inland Revenue if the finalized computations were not available.
These enabled companies to defer payment, for a limited period, without
incurring interest charges. The new pay and file system means that it is
expensive for companies to be late in finalizing their corporate tax position.

pay as you earn (PAYE) The UK scheme by which both income tax and
*National Insurance contributions due from employees is collected by
employers and is paid over by the employers to the *Collector of Taxes.
Employers deduct tax and National Insurance from the weekly or monthly
*taxable income of their employees, using *income tax codes and tax tables
supplied to them by the *Board of Inland Revenue. The total amount deducted
for each *tax month, together with the employers' National Insurance
contribution, is paid over to the Collector of Taxes by the 19th of the month,
being 14 days after the end of the tax month. From 6 April 1993 interest is
payable on unpaid PAYE. If too much tax has been deducted throughout the tax
year, the refund due to the employee is paid by the employer, who then
reclaims this amount from the Collector of Taxes.

payback period method A method of *capital budgeting in which the time
required before the projected cash inflows for a project equal the investment
expenditure is calculated; this time is compared to a required payback period to
determine whether or not the project should be considered for approval. If the
projected cash inflows are constant annual sums, after an initial capital
investment the following formula may be used:
    payback (years) = initial capital investment/annual cash inflow.
Otherwise, the annual cash inflows are accumulated and the year determined
when the cumulative inflows equal the investment expenditure.

PAYE Abbreviation for *pay as you earn.

paying agent A bank or other organization that contracts under a **paying
agency agreement** to pay, upon presentation to one of its designated offices,
the interest and capital sums due on a *bearer bond.

payment in advance *See* prepayment.

payment on account *See* progress payment

PCP Abbreviation for *permissible capital payment.

PCTCT Abbreviation for profits chargeable to corporation tax. *See* total profits.

PDR (P/D ratio) Abbreviations for *price–dividend ratio.

penalties Amounts demanded by the Inland Revenue in excess of the tax due
when certain statutory requirements have not been satisfied. The penalty
regime for *income tax and *corporation tax differs from that for *value
added tax. For income tax and corporation tax the Inland Revenue has powers

to impose penalties when it has been established that there has been a loss of tax as a result of the taxpayer's fraudulent or negligent conduct. Failure to submit a tax return attracts a fixed sum together with a daily penalty. The penalty for negligence or fraud depends on the amount of tax lost and can equal the tax lost. However, there is a mitigation procedure to reduce the penalty under certain circumstances. Value added tax penalties are more automatic without the same level of mitigation procedures. From 1 December 1993 the main VAT penalties are the persistent *misdeclaration penalty and the *penalty for repeated errors.

penalty for repeated errors A penalty used in the collection of *value added tax. It applies when there has been a material inaccuracy in a VAT return, being the lower of £500,000 and 10% of the total true amount of VAT due for the quarter. The trader must also have received a *surcharge liability notice resulting from a previous error within the 15 months prior to the current VAT period. In these circumstances a penalty for repeated errors of 15% of the VAT lost will be charged.

penny shares Securities with a very low market price (although they may not be as low as one penny) traded on a stock exchange. They are popular with small investors, who can acquire a significant holding in a company for a very low cost. Moreover, a rise of a few pence in a low-priced share can represent a high percentage profit. However, they are usually shares in companies that have fallen on hard times and may, indeed, be close to bankruptcy. The investor in this type of share is hoping for a rapid recovery or a takeover.

pension scheme Any arrangement the main purpose of which is to provide a defined class of individuals (called members of the scheme) with pensions. A pension scheme may include benefits other than a pension and may provide a pension for dependants of deceased members. *See also* occupational pension scheme; personal pension schemes.

PEP Abbreviation for *personal equity plan.

P/E ratio Abbreviation for *price–earnings ratio.

percentage on direct labour cost A basis used in *absorption costing for absorbing the production overheads into the cost units produced. The formula used is:

(budgeted production overheads × 100)/budgeted direct labour cost.

percentage on direct material cost A basis used in *absorption costing for absorbing the *manufacturing overhead into the cost units produced. The formula used is:

(budgeted manufacturing overhead × 100)/budgeted direct material cost.

percentage on prime cost A basis used in *absorption costing for absorbing the *manufacturing overhead into the cost units produced. The formula used is:

(budgeted manufacturing overhead × 100)/budgeted prime cost.

performance measures Ways in which the performance of whole organizations or parts of organizations, such as *profit centres, *cost centres, divisions, departments, and sections, and the managers responsible for these parts of the business, can be measured. Performance measures, which may be in the form of quantitative, qualitative, or financial measures, include measures based on profitability or comparison with budgets and standard-cost-based measures as well as the figures for previous periods.

performance standard A standard, used in *standard costing, of the level of performance to be achieved during a period. For example, a standard performance for direct labour of two standard hours to complete a task would be combined with the *rate per standard hour for labour to create the *standard direct labour cost for the task.

period concept The accounting concept that the *financial statements of a company should be produced after regular periods. The *profit and loss account and *balance sheet are prepared at regular intervals, for example annually instead of after each transaction or event. This provides comparability, consistency, and regular communications.

period costs Items of expenditure that tend to be incurred on a time basis, such as rent, insurance, and business rates. Because they are not related to an activity, they are usually treated as *fixed costs.

periodic inventory *See* periodic stocktaking.

periodic stocktaking (periodic inventory) The counting or evaluating of the *stock held by an organization at the end of an *accounting period. Movement of stock is restricted during the period of *stocktaking.

period of account The period for which a business prepares its accounts, which is usually 12 months.

perks Benefits arising as a result of employment, in addition to regular remuneration. *See* benefits in kind.

permanent difference A difference between profits or losses computed for tax purposes and profits presented in the *financial statements. For example, UK entertaining expenditure will be shown as an expense in the financial statements but will not be allowed as a deduction in deriving the profit or loss for tax purposes. Such differences are dealt with under *Statement of Standard Accounting Practice 15, 'Accounting for Deferred Tax'. *Compare* originating timing difference.

permanent diminution in value A fall in the value of an *asset that is unlikely to be reversed. The *fixed asset must be shown in the *balance sheet at the reduced amount, which will be the estimated recoverable amount. A provision has to be made through the *profit and loss account; if this is subsequently found to be no longer required, it should be written back to the profit and loss account. *Compare* temporary diminution in value.

permanent interest bearing share (PIBS) A fixed-interest non-redeemable security that pays interest at a rate fixed at issue. This is often 10–13.5%, giving investors a high yield for perpetuity. However, these shares carry the risks associated with fixed-interest securities, being the last to be paid out should an issuing building society go into liquidation.

permissible capital payment (PCP) A payment made out of *capital when a company is redeeming or purchasing its own *shares and has used all available distributable profits as well as the proceeds of any new issue of shares. *See* own shares purchase.

perpetual annuity The receipt or payment of a constant annual amount in perpetuity. Although the word annuity refers to an annual sum, in practice the constant sum may be for periods of less than a year. The *present value of a perpetual annuity is obtained from the formula:

$$P = a \times 100/i,$$

where P = present value, a = annual sum, and i = interest rate (%).

perpetual audit *See* continuous stocktaking.

perpetual inventory The process of keeping records in a *stock ledger or on a *bin card in which the balance of the quantity in stock is entered after each receipt or issue of stock. In some systems the value of the stock balance is also entered after each transaction.

personal accounts Accounts used to record transactions with persons, for example *debtors and *creditors.

personal allowance The allowance to which every individual resident in the UK is entitled in calculating their *taxable income for *income tax. The allowance depends on the age of the taxpayer; for the *age allowance it depends on the level of income. For 1995–96 the personal allowance for those under 65 is £3525, for those between 65 and 74 the allowance is £4630, and for those aged 75 and over it is £4800. *See also* income tax allowances.

personal equity plan (PEP) A UK government scheme introduced in 1987 under the Finance Act (1986) to encourage individuals to invest directly in UK quoted companies, offering investors certain tax benefits. The investment is administered by an authorized plan manager. Plans are either discretionary (in which the plan manager makes the investment decisions, sometimes called a **managed PEP**) or non-discretionary (in which the investor makes the decisions, a **self-select PEP**). Investors may put in a lump sum or regular monthly amounts. Re-invested dividends are free of *income tax and *capital gains tax is not incurred, as long as the investment is retained in the plan for at least a complete calendar year. There is a limit of £6000 on the amount an individual can invest in an authorized plan in any one year and a limit of £3000 in a **single-company PEP**.

personal financial planning Financial planning for individuals, which involves analysing their current financial position, predicting their short-term and long-term needs, and recommending a financial strategy. This may involve advice on pensions, the provision of independent school fees, mortgages, life assurance, and investments.

Personal Investment Authority (PIA) A *Self-Regulating Organization that took over many of the responsibilities of FIMBRA and LAUTRO, and some of those of IMRO, in October 1994. It regulates investment business carried out mainly for private investors.

personal ledger A *ledger containing *personal accounts, for example the debtors' ledger and the creditors' ledger.

personal pension schemes Arrangements in which individuals contribute part of their salary to a pension provider, such as an insurance company or a bank. The pension provider invests the funds so that at retirement a lump sum is available to the pensioner. This is used to purchase an annuity to provide regular pension payments.

PERT Abbreviation for programme evaluation and review technique. *See* critical-path analysis.

PET Abbreviation for *potentially exempt transfer.

petroleum revenue tax (PRT) A tax on the profits from oil exploration and mining occurring under the authority of licences granted in accordance with the Petroleum (Production) Act (1934) or the Petroleum (Production) Act (Northern Ireland) (1964). This tax was the principal means enabling the UK government to obtain a share in the profits made from oil in the North Sea.

petty cash The amount of cash that an organization keeps in notes or coins on its premises to pay small items of expense. This is to be distinguished from cash, which normally refers to amounts held at banks. Petty-cash transactions are normally recorded in a petty-cash book, the balance of which should agree with the amounts of petty cash held at any given time.

petty cash book A book used to record *petty cash transactions. It is usually kept in an *imprest account.

physical capital maintenance *See* capital maintenance concept.

physical inventory (physical stock check) The process of counting the physical balance of stock items at a particular time with a view to carrying out a stocktaking under a system of either *inventory control or *continuous stocktaking.

physical stock check *See* physical inventory.

PI *See* profitability index.

PIA Abbreviation for *Personal Investment Authority.

PIBS Abbreviation for *permanent interest bearing share.

PINC Abbreviation of *property income certificate.

placed deal A transaction in which a bank, or group of banks, undertakes to market an entire new issue of bonds or similar securities. Unlike a *bought deal, the borrower is not guaranteed that the new issue will be successful. Such transactions are favoured by the smaller financial institutions, such as *merchant banks, who do not have large marketing departments.

placing The sale of shares by a company to a selected group of individuals or institutions. Placings can be used either as a means of *flotation or to raise additional capital for a quoted company (*see also* pre-emption rights; rights issue). Placings are usually the cheapest way of raising capital on a *stock exchange and they also allow the directors of a company to influence the selection of shareholders. The success of a placing usually depends on the placing power of the company's stockbroker. Placings of public *companies are sometimes called **public placings**. In the USA a placing is called a **placement**. *Compare* introduction; issue by tender; offer for sale; public issue.

placing power A measure of a bank's ability to sell bonds issued in the *primary market to its own customers, compared to syndicating their sales through other banks.

planning One of the functions of *management accounting in which plans for the future activities and operations of an organization are incorporated into its *budgets, etc.

planning, programming, budgeting system (PPBS) A budgeting system developed particularly for use in non-profitmaking organizations, such as national and local government. The system is based on the grouping together of activities with common objectives and a long-term plan relating to the objectives of the organization as a whole, which is subdivided into programmes. Conventional annual expenditure budgeting procedures are applied within this framework.

planning variance *See* revision variance.

plant and equipment A category of tangible fixed assets that includes plant, machinery, fixtures and fittings, and other equipment.

plant and machinery The equipment required to operate a business. No formal definition is given in the tax legislation. However, from the tax point of view the definition often used is that given in the taxation case Yarmouth *v.* France (1887). This defines plant and machinery as 'whatever apparatus is used by a businessman for carrying on his business – not his stock in trade which he buys or makes for resale: but all goods and chattels, fixed or moveable, live or dead, which he keeps for permanent employment in the business'. Subsequent cases have been concerned with the distinction between plant actively used in a business, and so qualifying as plant and machinery for *capital allowances purposes, and expenditure on items that relate to the setting up of the business, which do not qualify for capital allowances.

plant register *See* fixed-assets register.

plc Abbreviation for *public limited company.

ploughed-back profits *See* retained earnings.

point of sale (POS) The place at which a consumer makes a purchase, usually a retail shop. It may, however, also be a doorstep (in door-to-door selling), a market stall, or a mail-order house.

poison pill A tactic used by a company that fears an unwanted takeover by ensuring that a successful takeover bid will trigger some event that substantially reduces the value of the company. Examples of such tactics include the sale of some prized asset to a friendly company or bank or the issue of securities with a conversion option enabling the bidder's shares to be bought at a reduced price if the bid is successful. Poison pills are used all over the world but were developed in the USA. *See also* staggered directorships.

policy cost An item of expenditure incurred as a consequence of a policy determined by the management of an organization. For example, the insurance premium determined by a key-man insurance policy taken out by an organization will be directly related to the sum assured.

political and charitable contributions Donations for political or charitable purposes made by an organization. Under the Companies Act a disclosure of such a donation has to be made by companies that are not wholly owned *subsidiary undertakings of another British company and which have on their own or with their subsidiaries given in the financial year in aggregate more than £200. Charitable purposes is taken to mean purposes that are exclusively charitable. A donation for political purposes is taken to mean the giving of money either directly or indirectly to a political party of the UK or any part of it, or to a person who is carrying on activities likely to affect support for a political party. The total amounts given for both political and charitable purposes must be separately disclosed. If the payments are for political purposes, where applicable, the following information must be provided: (a) the name of each person to whom money exceeding £200 in amount has been given for those purposes and the amount given; and (b) if more than £200 has been given as a donation or subscription to a political party, the identity of the party and the amount given must be disclosed.

political credit risk The *credit risk that arises as a result of actions by a foreign government, which may affect the management of a foreign business, control of its assets, and its ability to make payments to its creditors. *Compare* transfer credit risk.

pooling-of-interests method In the USA, the method of accounting used in a business combination in which the acquiring company has issued voting common *stock in exchange for voting common stock of the acquired company. The features of the method are that the acquired company's net *assets are brought forward at book value, retained *earnings and *paid-in capital are brought forward, the net income is recognized for the full financial year regardless of the date of acquisition, and the expenses of pooling are immediately charged against earnings. In order to use the method there are a number of criteria to be met concerning the prior independence of the companies and the nature and timing of the acquisition.

portfolio 1. The list of holdings in securities owned by an investor or institution. In building up an investment portfolio an institution will have its own investment analysts, while an individual may make use of the services of a *merchant bank that offers **portfolio management**. The choice of portfolio will depend on the mix of income and capital growth its owner expects, some investments providing good income prospects while others provide good prospects for capital growth. **2.** A list of the loans made by an organization. Banks, for example, attempt to balance their portfolio of loans to limit the risks.

portfolio insurance (portfolio protection) The use of a *financial futures and *options market to protect the value of a portfolio of investments. For example, a fund manager may expect the general level of prices to fall on the stock exchange. The manager could protect the portfolio by selling the appropriate number of index futures, which could then be bought back at a profit if the market falls. Alternately, the manager could establish the value of the portfolio at current prices by buying put options, which would provide the opportunity to benefit if there was a rise in the general level of prices.

portfolio theory The theory that rational investors are averse to taking increased risk unless they are compensated by an adequate increase in expected return. The theory also assumes that for any given expected return, most rational investors will prefer a lower level of risk and for any given level of risk they will prefer a higher return than a lower return. A set of efficient *portfolios can be calculated from which the investor will choose the one most appropriate for their risk profile. *See also* portfolio insurance.

POS Abbreviation for *point of sale.

positive accounting theory A theory that attempts to explain the nature of accounting, the role and activities of accountants, and relationships of accountancy to the economy. Unlike *normative theories of accounting, it does not set out to state what accounting procedures and policies should be, but rather to explain why they are what they are.

post-balance-sheet events *See* adjusting events; non-adjusting events.

post-cessation receipts Amounts accruing from a trading activity that are received after the trade has ceased. For tax purposes the receipts are treated as income in the year of receipt, from which any relevant trade expenses incurred can be deducted. An election can be made to treat post-cessation receipts as income in the year the trade ceased rather than the year of receipt.

post-date To insert a date on a document that is later than the date on which it is signed, thus making it effective only from the later date. A **post-dated** (or **forward-dated**) **cheque** cannot be negotiated before the date written on it, irrespective of when it was signed. *Compare* ante-date.

post-retirement benefits Benefits provided by an employer to an employee who has retired. For example, some employers provide health care and other benefits in addition to pensions, particularly in the USA. In the USA, *Financial Accounting Standard 106 requires that such benefits are dealt with on an *accruals basis and not a *cash basis. In 1992, the *Urgent Issues Task Force in the UK stated that as a matter of principle such benefits, in accordance with the accruals and *prudence concepts, should be recognized in *financial statements. This applied to all financial periods ending after 23 December 1994.

potentially exempt transfer (PET) A lifetime gift made by an individual to another individual, or into an *interest-in-possession trust that does not attract a liability to *inheritance tax at the date of the gift. No charge occurs if the donor survives seven years after the date of the gift. If death occurs within seven years of the gift, the total lifetime gifts in the seven years preceding death are reviewed. The gifts are taken in chronological order with the first £154,000 worth of gifts being covered by the *nil-rate band. Gifts in excess of this sum are charged at death rates with abatement for gifts made between three and seven years before death. *See also* exempt transfers.

PPBS Abbreviation for *planning, programming, budgeting system.

Practice Notes Notes issued by the *Auditing Practices Board to assist *auditors when applying *Statements of Auditing Standards of general application to particular cirumstances and industries. These notes are intended to indicate good practice and to be persuasive rather than prescriptive. *See also* auditing standards.

pre-acquisition profits The *profits of an acquired company that were made prior to the takeover.

preceding-year basis (PYB) A basis for assessing the profits made by a business in which the profits assessed in any given *fiscal year are based on the accounts that ended during the previous tax year. For example, in an ongoing business with accounts drawn up to 30 April, the profits assessed in 1995–96 will be based on the profits as set out in the accounts for the year ended 30 April 1994 (the accounts ending in the previous tax year, 6 April 1994 to 5 April 1995).

precept A command by the Commissioners of Inland Revenue to a taxpayer to make certain relevant documents available, usually by a specified date.

predetermined overhead rate An overhead *absorption rate computed in advance of operations. In practice, most absorption rates are computed from budgeted figures and are therefore predetermined overhead rates, which usually cover one year.

pre-emption rights A principle, established in company law, according to which any new shares issued by a company must first be offered to the existing shareholders as the legitimate owners of the company. To satisfy this principle a company must write to every shareholder (*see* rights issue), involving an expensive and lengthy procedure. Newer methods of issuing shares, such as *vendor placings or *bought deals, are much cheaper and easier to effect, although they violate pre-emption rights. In the USA pre-emption rights have now been largely abandoned but controversy is still widespread in the UK.

preference dividend A *dividend payable to the holders of *preference shares. Preference dividends not paid in previous periods will only be due to the holders of *cumulative preference shares.

preference share A share in a company that is entitled to a fixed percentage *dividend rather than a variable dividend; for example, a 6% preference share pays a dividend of 6% per annum. If the company goes into *liquidation, the preference shares are paid out after *debt capital, but before *ordinary share capital. According to *Financial Reporting Standard 4, 'Capital Instruments', preference shares should be classified as *non-equity shares. *See also* preference share capital.

preference share capital *Share capital consisting of *preference shares. Under *Financial Reporting Standard 4, 'Capital Instruments', preference share capital should be classified as *non-equity share capital. The amount attributable to non-equity shares in the analysis of shareholders' funds and the allocation of finance costs should be disclosed separately in the *financial statements.

preferential creditor A creditor whose debt will be met in preference to those of other creditors and who thus has the best chance of being paid in full on the bankruptcy of an individual or the winding-up of a company. Preferential creditors, who are usually paid in full after *secured liabilities and before ordinary creditors, include: the Inland Revenue in respect of PAYE, Customs and Excise in respect of VAT and car tax, the DSS in respect of National Insurance Social Security contributions, the trustees of occupational pensions schemes, and employees in respect of any remuneration outstanding.

preferential debt A debt that will be repaid in preference to other debts. *See* preferential creditor.

preferred stock The US term for a *preference share.

preliminary announcement An early announcement of their profit or loss for the year that *listed companies are required to make under *London Stock Exchange Regulations. The minimum information is a summarized *profit and loss account, although there has been a trend for companies to provide other information, such as *balance sheets. Companies must lodge their preliminary announcement with the Stock Exchange, but there is no requirement to send the information to shareholders. A number of companies publish some of the information in national newspapers and provide *investment analysts and journalists with substantial information, which receives considerable comment in the press.

preliminary expenses Expenses incurred in the setting up of a *company, for example the cost of issuing *shares. These expenses may be written off to the *share premium account.

premium 1. The consideration payable for a contract of insurance or life assurance. *See also* renewal notice. 2. An amount in excess of the nominal value of a share or other security. 3. An amount in excess of the issue price of a share or other security. When dealings open for a new issue of shares it may be said that the market price will be at a premium over the issue price (*see* stag).

premium on capital stock In the USA, the excess amount received from *stockholders over the *par value of the stock issued. The premium account is shown in the *balance sheet under the *paid-in-capital section of stockholders' *equity and should not be regarded as income.

prepayment (payment in advance) A payment made for goods or services before they are received. It is treated as *deferred debits under the *accruals concept, and is shown as a *debit balance under *debtors in the *circulating assets of the balance sheet.

present value (discounted value) The result arrived at in a *discounted cash flow calculation by multiplying a projected annual cash flow figure by a *discount factor derived from a *hurdle rate of interest and a time period.

present-value factor *See* discount factor.

price–dividend ratio (PDR; P/D ratio) The current market price of a company share divided by the dividend per share for the previous year. It is a measure of the investment value of the share.

price–earnings ratio (P/E ratio) The current market price of a company share divided by the *earnings per share (eps) of the company. The P/E ratio usually refers to the annual eps and is expressed as a number (e.g. 5 or 10), often called the **multiple** of the company. Loosely, it can be thought of as the number of years it would take the company to earn an amount equal to its market value. High multiples, usually associated with low *yields, indicate that the company is growing rapidly, while a low multiple is associated with dull no-growth stocks. The P/E ratio is one of the main indicators used by fundamental analysts to decide whether the shares in a company are expensive or cheap, relative to the market.

price-level accounting A system of accounting that attempts to take into account changes in price levels, thus avoiding some of the criticisms of *historical cost accounting. There have been many proposed methods but they have not often been implemented, usually because of the practical difficulties in operating them.

price-sensitive information Information (usually unpublished) about a company that is likely to cause its share prices to move.

price variance *See* direct materials price variance.

pricing The setting of selling prices for the products and services supplied by an organization. In many cases selling prices will be based on market prices but in other circumstances pricing will be based on costs, using information provided by the *management accounting system.

primary auditor The *auditor of the primary company, i.e. the *holding company, when *group accounts are being prepared. The primary auditor is responsible for the *audit opinion on the group's financial statement.

primary earnings per share In the USA, a calculation for assessing the performance of companies with complex *capital instruments. The net income available to holders of *common stock is divided by the weighted average of the common stock outstanding plus common-stock equivalents; common-stock equivalents are securities that can be converted into common stock. The figure is shown on the face of the income statement.

primary market The market into which a new issue of bonds, or any other form of medium- or long-term money-market paper, is launched. *Compare* secondary market.

prime cost The total of *direct materials, *direct labour, and direct expenses.

prime documents The documents used to initiate and record the accounting entries in an accounting or management accounting system. Prime documents include *invoices, *materials requisitions, *materials returns notes, and *direct charge vouchers.

prime rate The rate of interest charged by US banks to their best borrowers. This is not the same as the UK *base rate, as even the best borrowers in the UK normally pay a margin over the base rate for an overdraft. The prime rate is therefore a lending rate, while the base rate is a yardstick.

principal 1. The sum on which interest is paid. **2.** A person who has given express or implied authority for another person to act on his or her behalf. *See* agency relationship.

principal budget factor *See* limiting factor; constraint.

principal private residence The main private dwelling house of an individual. Gains arising on the disposal of this dwelling are exempt for *capital gains tax.

prior-period adjustments Material adjustments applicable to prior *financial periods arising from changes in *accounting policies or from the correction of fundamental errors. They do not include normal recurring adjustments or corrections of accounting estimates made in prior periods. Under *Financial Reporting Standard 3, if prior-period adjustments fall within these definitions, the *financial statements for the current period should not be distorted, but the prior periods should be restated with an adjustment to the opening balance of the retained *profit.

private ledger A *ledger containing confidential accounts. A control account may be used to link it to the general ledger.

private limited company Any *limited company that is not a *public limited company. Such a company is not permitted to offer its shares for sale to the public and it is free from the rules that apply to public limited companies.

privatization The process of selling a publicly owned company to the private sector. Privatization may be pursued for political as well as economic reasons. The economic justification for privatization is that a company will be more efficient under private ownership, although most economists would argue that privatization will only achieve this if it is accompanied by increased competition. Recently, privatizations in the form of *share offers to the general public have been advocated as a means of increasing the participation of individuals in the capitalist system. The process can also be called **denationalization**.

probability The likelihood that a particular outcome will occur, on a scale of 0 (zero probability or certainty that it will not occur) to 1 (certainty that it will occur). Where probabilities are used in decision-making models they are usually subjective in nature. *See* expected value; expected monetary value.

probate value A valuation of all the assets included in the estate of a deceased person at the date of his or her death. The valuation must take account of any restrictions on the use of the assets.

process An operation in the production cycle of an organization that contributes to the completion of a product or *cost unit.

process costing A method of *cost accounting applied to production carried out by a series of chemical or operational stages or processes. Its characteristics are that costs are accumulated for the whole production process and that average unit costs of production are computed at each stage (*see* average costing). Special rules are applied in process costing to the valuation of *work in progress, *normal losses, and *abnormal losses. In process costing it is usual to distinguish between the *main product of the process, *by-products, and *joint products. *Compare* continuous-operation costing.

product An item, sub-assembly, part, or *cost unit manufactured or sold by an organization.

product costs The costs of production when charged to the *cost units and expressed as costs of individual products. Product costs may include both *direct costs and *indirect costs or *overhead; many approaches to *cost accounting, such as *absorption costing and *process costing, are concerned with computing product costs.

production The *cost units manufactured by an organization. Production may be measured in units, *direct labour hours, *machine hours, or *direct labour cost.

production budget (operating budget) A budget set for the production function of an organization under a system of *budgetary control, which includes, inter alia, the production volumes and the *production cost to be incurred in a budget period. It will usually provide an analysis of the budgets by product and by accounting period.

production cost (total cost of production) The total of all the costs incurred in producing a product or *cost unit. In a manufacturing account the production cost is represented by the total of the *prime costs and the *manufacturing overhead.

production cost centre An area of an organization, such as a function, department, section, individual, or any group of these, in which production is carried out. *See also* cost centre.

production cost of sales The production cost of the goods sold during an accounting period. It is made up of the *direct cost of sales and the *manufacturing overhead incurred during the period, adjusted by the opening and closing values of *work in progress and the opening and closing values of the stocks of finished goods.

production cost variance The variance arising in *standard costing when the standard cost of the actual production is compared with the actual cost incurred. If the standard cost is higher than the actual cost a favourable variance arises, while if the actual cost exceeds the standard cost an adverse variance occurs. The production cost variance is usually analysed into the *direct materials variances, the *direct labour variances, and the fixed and variable overhead variances.

production department A section of an organization in which production is carried out.

production herd A group of living animals or other livestock kept for their products, such as milk or wool, or for their young.

production order (manufacturing requisition) A form issued to the production department of an organization specifying the production to be carried out by the department. A production order gives, inter alia, a description of the operations to be carried out, the quantities to be produced, the time allowed, and the completion times.

production overhead *See* manufacturing overhead.

production planning The administrative operations ensuring that the material, labour, and other resources necessary to carry out production are available when and where they are required in the necessary quantities.

production profit *See* profit on manufacture.

production-unit method (units of production method of depreciation) A method of computing the depreciation charge for a period on a piece of machinery in which the depreciation charge is based on the number of production units manufactured by the machine. When the machinery to be depreciated is purchased an estimate is made of the total number of units of production that will be made by the machine over its lifetime. A rate per production unit is then computed and applied to the production over the life of the machinery. The formula per production unit is as follows:

original cost − estimated residual value/estimated number of production units. Unlike the *straight-line method of depreciation, which treats depreciation as a *fixed cost, the production-unit method treats depreciation as a variable cost.

production–volume ratio (PV ratio) *See* contribution margin ratio.

productivity variance *See* overhead efficiency variance.

profit The excess of the selling price over the cost of providing the goods or service sold. **Gross profit** is the excess of the selling price over the cost of the goods sold. **Net profit** is the gross profit less all further costs, such as administration and distribution costs.

profitability index (PI) A method used in *discounted cash flow for ranking a range of projects under consideration in which *standard cash flow patterns are projected. It is based on the ratio:

(total present values of net cash inflows)/initial investment,

the value of which is compared for each project.

The projects with a PI of less than 1 are not expected to earn the *required rate of return and are rejected. The projects with a PI in excess of 1 are ranked according to the magnitude of the PI.

profit and loss account (P & L account) **1.** An *account in the books of an organization showing the profits (or losses) made on its business activities with the deduction of the appropriate expenses. **2.** A statement of the profit (or loss) of an organization derived from the account in the books. It is one of the statutory accounts that, for most limited companies, has to be filed annually with the UK Registrar of Companies. The profit and loss account usually consists of three parts. The first is a trading account, showing the total sales income less the costs of production, etc., and any changes in the value of stock or work in progress from the last accounting period. This gives the gross profit (or loss). The second part gives any other income (apart from trading) and lists administrative and other costs to arrive at a net profit (or loss). From this net profit before taxation the appropriate corporation tax is deducted to give the net profit after taxation. In the third part, the net profit after tax is appropriated to dividends or to reserves. The Companies Act (1985) gives a choice of four formats, one of which must be used to file a profit and loss account for a registered company.

profit and loss account formats The four formats given for *profit and loss accounts by the Companies Act (1985):
• vertical format, analysing costs by type of operation and function;
• vertical format, analysing costs by items of expense;
• horizontal format, analysing costs by type of operation or function;
• horizontal format, analysing costs by items of expense.
The following three items must be disclosed on the face of the profit and loss account irrespective of which format is selected.
1. Profit or loss on ordinary activities before taxation.

2. Any amount set aside or proposed to be set aside to, or withdrawn or proposed to be withdrawn from, reserves.

3. The aggregate amount of *dividends paid and proposed.

*Financial Reporting Standard 3, 'Reporting Financial Performance', issued in October 1992, has developed the format given in the Companies Act, by adopting a layered format requiring the following components to be shown:
• the results of continuing operations, including the results of any acquisitions;
• the results of discontinued operations;
• profits and losses on the sale or termination of an operation, costs of fundamental reorganization or restructuring, and profits or losses on the disposal of *fixed assets;
• any extraordinary items.

profit and loss account reserve A reserve that contains the balance of *retained earnings to carry forward. It is fully distributable and shown as part of *shareholders' reserves on the *balance sheet.

profit and loss appropriation account A statement showing how the net profits or losses have been dealt with. In a company, the *retained earnings brought forward is added to the net profit for the year; from this total *taxation and *dividends paid and proposed are deducted; other transfers to and from reserves are deducted or added as appropriate. In *partnership accounts the profit or loss available for appropriation is given at the beginning of the statement. Each partner's contribution of interest on drawings and entitlement to salary and interest on capital, as appropriate, are deducted, leaving a balance to be shared between the partners in the *profit-sharing ratio.

profit centre A section or area of an organization to which revenue can be traced, together with the appropriate costs, so that profits can be ascribed to that area. Profit centres may be divisions, subsidiaries, or departments.

profit forecast A forecast by the directors of a public company of the profits to be expected in a stated period. If a new flotation is involved, the profit forecast must be reported on by the reporting accountants and the sponsor to the share issue. An existing company is not required to make a profit forecast with its *accounts, but if it does it must be reported on by the company's auditors.

profit margin *See* gross margin; net margin.

profit on manufacture (production profit) The margin obtained when manufactured items or finished goods are transferred from the factory at a price in excess of the cost of production. The technique is used in organizations wishing to submit the production departments to market prices and therefore credit production according to some formula; for example, at a price per unit. The system may also create a **loss on manufacture**. *See also* manufacturing account; manufacturing profit.

profit-related pay (PRP) A UK scheme enabling employees to be paid part of their salary tax-free. The profit-related pay scheme has to be registered with the *Board of Inland Revenue by the employer and the application must be accompanied by a certificate from an independent accountant confirming that the scheme complies with the regulations. Payments to employees under a registered scheme can be tax-free up to a maximum of £4000 or 20% of total pay, whichever is the lower. For profit-related pay purposes, total pay excludes *benefits in kind.

profits available for distribution *See* distributable profits.

profit-sharing ratio (PSR) The ratio in which the profits or losses of a business are shared. For a partnership, the profit-sharing ratios will be set out in the partnership agreement. This will show the amount, usually given as a percentage of the total profits, attributable to each partner. In some agreements there is a first charge on profits, which is an allocation of the first slice of the profits for the year. The remainder will then be split in the profit-sharing ratios as specified in the agreement. The profit-sharing ratios can also apply to the capital of the partnership, but this does not always follow. The partnership agreement can specify a different capital-sharing ratio. If no specific agreement has been made, profits and losses will be shared equally in accordance with the Partnership Act (1890).

profit-sharing scheme An approved share option scheme in the UK, introduced in the Finance Act (1978). The scheme involves setting up a trust to hold the shares, for at least two years, before the employee to whom the shares are allocated can sell them. Provided the employee does not sell the shares for five years there will be no *income tax charge on their disposal, although *capital gains tax will be due on any profit.

profit variance A variance in *standard costing made up of the difference between the *standard operating profit budgeted to be made on the items sold and the actual profits made. The analysis of the profit variance into its constituent sales, direct labour, direct material, and overhead variances provides the management of the organization with information regarding the source of the gains and losses compared to the predetermined standard.

profit–volume chart (PV chart) A graph showing the profits and losses to be made at each level of activity. The profit/loss line is usually plotted as a linear function, and the graph shows the total fixed cost level as the loss at zero activity, the *breakeven point activity level, and the profits or losses at each level of production or sales.

profit–volume ratio (PV ratio) *See* contribution margin ratio.

pro-forma financial statements *Financial statements for a period prepared before the end of the period, which therefore contain estimates.

proforma invoice An invoice sent in certain circumstances to a buyer, usually before some of the invoice details are known. For example, in commodity trading a proforma invoice may be sent to the buyer at the time of shipment, based on a notional weight, although the contract specifies that the buyer will only pay for the weight ascertained on landing the goods at the port of destination. When the missing facts are known, in this case the landed weight, a final invoice is sent.

programme evaluation and review technique (PERT) *See* critical-path analysis.

progress payment (payment on account) A stage payment made to a contractor based on the level of work completed at a specified date, as certified by an agreed authority. It is used in the costing of *long-term contracts, such as civil engineering, shipbuilding, or large items of plant and machinery.

project finance Money or loans put up for a particular project (e.g. a property development), which are usually secured on that project rather than forming part of the general borrowing of the company carrying out the development.

promissory note A document that is a negotiable instrument and contains a promise to pay a certain sum of money to a named person, to that person's order, or to the bearer at a specified time in the future. It must be unconditional, signed by the maker, and delivered to the payee or bearer. They are widely used in the USA but are not in common use in the UK. A promissory note cannot be reissued, unless the promise is made by a banker and is payable to the bearer, i.e. unless it is a banknote.

proper accounting records *Accounting records that are sufficient to show and explain an organization's transactions. For a company, the Companies Act requires that these records should be able to disclose with reasonable accuracy, at any time, the financial position of the company and enable the directors to ensure that the *balance sheet and *profit and loss account comply with the statutory regulations. In particular, the accounting records shall contain entries of all money received and spent and a record of the *assets and *liabilities of the company. If goods are being bought and sold, stock records must also be sufficient. In forming an *audit opinion an *auditor performing a statutory audit under the Companies Act will consider whether proper accounting records have been kept and proper returns adequate for audit have been received from branches not visited. Furthermore, the auditor will consider whether the accounts are in agreement with the accounting records and returns. *See* auditors' report; qualified audit report.

property income certificate (PINC) A certificate giving the bearer a share in the value of a particular property and a share of the income from it. PINCs can be bought and sold.

property tax A tax based on the value of property owned by a taxpayer. In the UK, council tax is charged on the value of a property, as defined by a series of value bands, which depend on the region of the UK in which the property is situated.

proportional consolidation A method of consolidation used in *group accounts in which subsidiaries are not fully owned; a proportionate share of each category of a joint venture's revenue, expenditure, *assets, and *liabilities is included line by line. *Compare* full consolidation.

proposed dividend A *dividend that has been recommended by the directors of a company but not yet paid. *See* final dividend.

proprietary company *See* Pty.

proprietary view The view of an accounting entity in which the enterprise is seen from the shareholders' perspective rather than stressing the importance of the enterprise itself. *Compare* entity view; residual equity theory.

proprietor An owner of property or of a business. The owners of a company are the *shareholders of the company.

provision An amount set aside out of profits in the accounts of an organization for a known liability (even though the specific amount might not be known) or for the diminution in value of an asset. Common provisions are for bad debts (*see* provision for bad debts) and for depreciation (*see* provision for depreciation) and also for accrued liabilities. According to the Companies Act (1981) notes must be given to explain every material provision in the accounts of a limited company.

provision for bad debts A provision calculated to cover the debts during an *accounting period that are not expected to be paid. A **general provision**, e.g. 2% of debtors, is not allowed as a deduction for tax purposes. A **specific provision**, in which specific debts are identified, is allowed if there is documentary evidence to indicate that these debts are unlikely to be paid. A **provision for doubtful debts** (or **allowance for doubtful accounts**) is treated in the same way for tax purposes.

provision for depreciation *See* depreciation.

proxy A person who acts in the place of a member of a company at a company meeting at which one or more votes are taken. The proxy need not be a member of the company but it is quite common for directors to offer themselves as proxies for shareholders who cannot attend a meeting. Notices calling meetings must state that a member may appoint a proxy and the appointment of a proxy is usually done on a form provided by the company with the notice of the meeting; it must be returned to the company not less than 48 hours before the meeting. A **two-way proxy form** is printed so that the member can state whether he wants the proxy to vote for or against a particular resolution. A **special proxy** is empowered to act at one specified meeting; a **general proxy** is authorized to vote at any meeting.

PRP Abbreviation for *profit-related pay.

PRT Abbreviation for *petroleum revenue tax.

prudence concept The accounting concept that insists on a realistic view of business activity and stresses that anticipated revenues and profits have no place in a *profit and loss account until they have been realized in the form of cash or other assets for which the ultimate cash value can be assessed with reasonable certainty. Moreover, provision should be made for all known expenses and losses whether the amount of these is known with certainty or is a best estimate in the context of the information available.

PSBR Abbreviation for *public sector borrowing requirement.

PSR Abbreviation for *profit-sharing ratio.

Pty Abbreviation for proprietary company, the name given to a *private limited company in Australia and the Republic of South Africa. The abbreviation Pty is used after the name of the company as Ltd is used in the UK. It is also used in the USA for an insurance company owned by outside shareholders.

public issue A method of making a new issue of shares, loan stock, etc., in which the public are invited, through advertisements in the national press, to apply for shares at a price fixed by the company. *Compare* introduction; issue by tender; offer for sale; placing.

publicity costs Items of expenditure incurred in carrying out the publicity function in an organization. Such items might include the publicity manager's salary, the advertising costs, promotions, and point-of-sale material.

public limited company (plc) A company registered under the Companies Act (1980) as a public company. Its name must end with the initials 'plc'. It must have an authorized share capital of at least £50,000, of which at least £12,500 must be paid up. The company's memorandum must comply with the format in Table F of the Companies Regulations 1985. It may offer shares and securities to the public. The regulation of such companies is stricter than that of private companies. Most public companies are converted from private companies, under the re-registration procedure in the Companies Act.

public sector borrowing requirement (PSBR) The borrowing required by the UK government if its expenditure exceeds its income.

published accounts Accounts of organizations published according to UK law. The most common, according to the Companies Act (1981), are the accounts of *limited companies, which must be provided for their shareholders and filed with the Registrar of Companies at Companies House, Cardiff. The accounts comprise the *balance sheet, the *profit and loss account, the statement of *source and application of funds, the *directors' report, and the *auditors' report. In the case of *groups of companies, consolidated accounts are also required. *Small companies and *medium-sized companies, as defined by the Act, need not file some of these documents.

purchase day book (purchases journal) The *book of prime entry in which invoice amounts for purchases are entered.

purchased goodwill *Goodwill acquired when a business is purchased as opposed to that which has been internally generated.

purchase method In the USA, a method of accounting for business combinations in which cash and other assets are distributed or liabilities incurred. The purchase method is used if the criteria are not met for the *pooling-of-interests method. With the purchase method, the acquirer records the net assets acquired at the *fair value on the market. Any excess of the purchase price over fair market value is recorded as *goodwill. The net income of the acquired company is recognized from the date of acquisition.

purchase requisition A form, completed by a user department of an organization and issued to the purchasing department, requiring the latter to effect the purchase of the items specified in the requisition. The requisition usually includes the quantity and specification of the items required, the possible supplier, the date required, and the delivery point.

purchases account An account in which records are kept of transactions involving the buying of goods, either on credit or for cash. The double entries involved will be: debit the purchases account with the amount purchased and credit the creditors' account for purchases on credit and the bank account for purchases for cash.

purchases budget A budget set for the purchasing function of an organization under a system of *budgetary control, which plans the volumes and cost of the purchases to be made in a budget period. It will usually provide an analysis of the budgets by material and by *accounting period.

purchases invoice An invoice sent by a supplier to a purchaser, detailing the goods sent, amounts payable, discount applicable, VAT, and any other relevant information. This is entered into the *purchase day book of the business buying the goods.

purchases journal *See* purchase day book.

purchases ledger *See* creditors' ledger.

purchases ledger control account *See* creditors' ledger control account.

purchases returns Goods purchased from a supplier but returned to the supplier because they are faulty, are not exactly what was ordered, etc.

purchasing power The ability to purchase goods and services. In times of inflation a loss of purchasing power occurs when *monetary assets are held because of the decline in the purchasing power of the currency. If a company has monetary liabilities, a purchasing power gain will arise because the absolute sum of the loans will be repaid with currency with less purchasing power.

purchasing power parity theory The theory that the exchange rate between one currency and another is in equilibrium when their domestic purchasing powers at that rate of exchange are equivalent.

put option *See* option.

PV chart *See* profit–volume chart.

PV ratio Abbreviation for profit–volume ratio or production–volume ratio. *See* contribution margin ratio.

PYB Abbreviation for *preceding-year basis.

Q

qualified audit report An *audit report in which some qualification of the *financial statements is required because the *auditor feels there is a limitation on the scope of the audit examination or because the auditor disagrees with the treatment or disclosure of a matter in the financial statements. The type of qualification used will depend upon the degree of *materiality of the limitation or disagreement. If the limitation of scope is very material, a *disclaimer of opinion will be issued; if it is less material the 'except for the limitation of scope' form of qualification will be issued in the report (*see* except for). If the auditor disagrees with the accounting treatment or disclosure in the financial statements and feels the effect is material and potentially misleading, an *adverse opinion will be expressed. If the disagreement is not so material, a qualified opinion will be given using the 'except for the effects of the disagreement' form of qualification.

qualified stock option In the USA, an agreement giving employees the right to purchase company *stock at a later date at a specified option price, which is normally lower than the market price.

qualifying distribution A distribution from a company resulting in *advance corporation tax being paid. Qualifying distributions include:
• dividends,
• distributions from any company assets to shareholders (except for capital repayments),
• issues of redeemable preference shares,
• bonus issues of shares followed by a repayment of share capital.

qualifying loss A trading loss arising in a current accounting period as a result of computing the profits and losses of an organization in accordance with accepted *corporation-tax principles.

qualitative characteristics of accounting information The characteristics information should have to be of maximum usefulness to readers of financial reports. The *Financial Accounting Standards Board, in its 'Statement of Financial Accounting Concepts No. 2', identifies the specific qualities useful to decision makers and to making the documents understandable. Information must be both reliable and relevant; it must have predictive value, feedback value, timeliness, comparability, consistency, verifiability, neutrality, and representational faithfulness. The *Accounting Standards Board, in its *Statement of Principles, identifies similar qualities, although there are some differences in the relationships and importance of these qualities.

quality of earnings The degree to which the net *profit of an organization reflects accurately its operating performance; it is particularly important to ensure that *creative accounting has not taken place and that no events have occurred to distort the profit figure.

quango Acronym for quasi-autonomous non-governmental organization.

Such bodies, some members of which are likely to be civil servants and some not, are appointed by a minister to perform some public function at the public expense. While not actually government agencies, they are not independent and are usually answerable to a government minister.

quantitative budgets Budgets that cover the non-financial aspects of *budgetary control, such as the number of units of product planned to be produced and sold and the number of direct labour hours or machine hours to be worked.

quarter days Four days traditionally taken as the beginning or end of the four quarters of the year, often for purposes of charging rent. In England, Wales, and Northern Ireland they are Lady Day (25 March), Midsummer Day (24 June), Michaelmas (29 September), and Christmas Day (25 December). In Scotland they are Candlemas (2 February), Whitsuntide (15 May), Lammas (1 August), and Martinmas (11 November).

quarterly report In the USA, a financial report issued by a company every three months. The usual contents are an income statement, *balance sheet, statement of changes in financial position, and a narrative overview of business operations.

quasi-contract A legally binding obligation that one party has to another, as determined by a court, although no formal contract exists between them.

quasi-loan An arrangement in which a creditor agrees to meet some of the financial obligations of a borrower, on condition that the borrower reimburses the creditor.

quasi-subsidiary A company, trust, partnership, or other arrangement that does not fulfil the definition of a *subsidiary undertaking but is directly or indirectly controlled by the reporting entity and gives rise to benefits for that entity that are in substance no different from those that would arise if it was a subsidiary. This definition is based on that given in *Financial Reporting Standard 5, 'Reporting on the Substance of Transactions'. If a reporting entity has a quasi-subsidiary, the substance of the transactions entered into by the quasi-subsidiary should be reported in *consolidated financial statements.

quick assets *See* liquid assets.

quick ratio *See* liquid ratio.

quick-succession relief Relief available when property is assessed for *inheritance-tax purposes in the estates of two separate individuals, if the death of the second individual occurs within 5 years of the first. For example, B inherits property from A, which was subject to inheritance tax on A's death of £X. If B dies within one year of the date of the gift, the inheritance tax, £X, that was paid on A's estate will be allowed in full against the inheritance-tax liability on B's estate. If B dies within 1–2 years after the date of A's death the relief is 80% of £X, within 2–3 years relief is 60% of £X, within 3–4 years relief is 40% of £X, and within 4–5 years relief is 20% of £X. The relief is deducted from the whole estate, not simply a particular part of it.

quoted company A company listed on a stock exchange.

R

RAFT Abbreviation for *revolving acceptance facility by tender.

random-walk theory The theory that share prices move, for whatever reason, without any memory of past movements and that the movements therefore follow no pattern. This theory is used to refute the predictions of *chartists, who do rely on past patterns of movements to predict future prices.

ratchet effect An irreversible change to an economic variable, such as prices, wages, exchange rates, etc. For example, once a price or wage has been forced up by some temporary economic pressure, it is unlikely to fall back when the pressure is reduced. This rise may be reflected in parallel sympathetic rises throughout the economy, thus fuelling *inflation.

rate of interest *See* interest; interest rate.

rate of return The gain earned from the investment of resources in a commercial or economic activity, usually expressed as a percentage. In a *discounted cash flow appraisal, for example, the rate of return may be expressed as an *internal rate of return, whereas investment in a division or subsidiary may be expressed as an *accounting rate of return or *return on capital employed.

rate of return pricing Setting the prices of a range of products so that they earn a predetermined *required rate of return or *return on capital employed.

rate of turnover The frequency, expressed in annual terms, with which some part of the assets of an organization is turned over. The total sales revenue is often referred to as *turnover and in order to see how frequently stock is turned over, the sales revenue (or if a more accurate estimate is needed the cost of goods sold) is divided by the average value of the stock to give the number of times the stock is turned over. This provides a reasonable measure in terms of stock. However, some accountants divide the sales figure by the value of the fixed assets to arrive at turnover of fixed assets. This is less realistic, although it does express the relationship of sales to the fixed assets of the organization, which in some organizations could be significant.

rate per direct labour hour A basis used in *absorption costing for absorbing the *manufacturing overhead into the *cost units produced. The formula is:

budgeted manufacturing overhead/budgeted direct labour hours.

rate per machine hour A basis used in *absorption costing for absorbing the *manufacturing overhead into the *cost units produced. The formula is:

budgeted manufacturing overhead/budgeted machine hours.

rate per standard hour A basis used in *absorption costing for absorbing the *manufacturing overhead into the *cost units produced. The formula is:

budgeted manufacturing overhead/budgeted standard hours.

rate per unit A basis used in *absorption costing for absorbing the *manufacturing overhead into the *cost units produced. The formula is:

  budgeted manufacturing overhead/budgeted units.

rating agency An organization that monitors the credit backing of bond issues and other forms of public borrowings. The two best known are Standard & Poor and Moody, both of which have been in existence for over 100 years.

ratio analysis The use of ratios to evaluate a company's *operating performance and financial stability. Ratios, such as *return on capital employed and *profit margin, can be used to assess *profitability. The *current ratio can be used to examine solvency and *gearing ratios to examine the financial structure of the company. In conducting an analysis comparisons will be made with other companies and with industry averages over a period of time.

ratio covenant A form of *covenant in a loan agreement that includes conditions relating to such ratios as the *gearing ratio and *interest cover. Breaching such a covenant could indicate significant deterioration in the company's business or a major change in its nature; this will usually empower the lender to request repayment of any of the loan then outstanding, and the loan then becomes null and void.

raw materials *Direct materials used in a production process, which are at a low level of completion compared to the final product or *cost unit. Examples include steel plate, wood, and chemicals.

raw materials stock The inventory of *raw materials held at a specified time. The raw materials appear in the balance sheet under the heading of current assets. *See* inventory valuation.

real account A *ledger account for some types of property (e.g. land and buildings, plant, investments, stock) to distinguish it from a *nominal account, which would be for revenue or expense items (e.g. sales, motor expenses, discount received, etc.). This distinction is now largely obsolete and both sets of accounts are maintained in the same ledger, usually referred to as the *nominal ledger.

real estate In the USA, land, land improvements, and buildings held for business use in the generation of income.

realizable account An account drawn up on the dissolution of a *partnership. The account is debited with the assets of the partnership and any expenses on realization; it is credited with the proceeds of any sales made. The difference between the total debits and credits is either a *profit or loss on realization and must be shared between the partners in the *profit-sharing ratio.

realizable assets *See* liquid assets.

realization convention The general basis used in *financial statements prepared under *historical cost accounting in which increases or decreases in the market values of assets and liabilities are not recognized as gains or losses until the assets are sold or the liabilities paid.

realized profit (or **loss)** A profit (or loss) that has arisen from a completed transaction (usually the sale of goods or services or other assets). In accounting terms, a profit is normally regarded as having been realized when an asset has been legally disposed of and not when the cash is received, since if an asset is sold on credit the asset being disposed of is exchanged for another asset, a debtor. The debt may or may not prove good but that is regarded as a separate transaction.

real rate of interest The rate of *interest charged for the use of financial resources adjusted for the effect of the inflation rate within an economy. For example, if the rate charged for borrowed funds is 12% and the inflation rate is 5% per annum, the real rate of interest is about 7%.

real terms A representation of the value of a good or service in terms of money, taking into account fluctuations in the price level. Economists are usually interested in the relationship between the prices of goods in real terms, i.e. by adjusting prices according to a price index or some other measure of inflation.

real terms accounting A system of *accounting in which the effects of changing prices are measured by their effect on a company's financial capital (i.e. *shareholders' funds) to see if its value is maintained in real terms. *Assets are measured at *current cost. Profit is defined as any surplus remaining after the shareholders' funds (determined by reference to the current cost of *net assets) have been maintained in real terms. The unit of measurement may be either the nominal pound or the unit of constant purchasing power.

real-time processing The processing of data by a computer as soon as it is input so that the results can be output almost immediately.

rebate 1. A discount offered on the price of a good or service, often one that is paid back to the payer, e.g. a tax rebate is a refund to the taxpayer. 2. A discount allowed on a *bill of exchange that is paid before it matures.

recapitalization In the USA, the process of changing the balance of *debt and *equity financing of a company without changing the total amount of *capital. Recapitalization is often required as part of reorganization of a company under bankruptcy legislation.

receipts and payments basis The basis of accounting in which accounts are prepared on a cash basis, i.e. when amounts are actually received or paid, as opposed to the *accruals concept.

receivables Claims held against customers and others for money, goods, or services. These will appear on the *balance sheet of a company.

receiver A person exercising any form of *receivership. In *bankruptcy, the *official receiver becomes receiver and manager of the bankrupt's estate. Where there is a *floating charge over the whole of a company's property and a crystallizing event has occurred, an **administrative receiver** may be appointed to manage the whole of the company's business. The administrative receiver will have wide powers under the Insolvency Act to carry on the business of the company, take possession of its property, commence *liquidation, etc. A receiver appointed in respect of a *fixed charge can deal with the property covered by the charge only, and has no power to manage the company's business.

receivership A situation in which a lender holds a mortgage or charge (especially a *floating charge) over a company's property and, in consequence of a default by the company, a receiver is appointed to realize the assets charged in order to repay the debt.

reciprocal costs Costs apportioned from a *service cost centre to a *production cost centre that carries out work for the original service cost centre. Consequently, a proportion of the production cost centre costs should also be re-apportioned to the service cost centre. Cost apportionment can be calculated either by the use of simultaneous equations or by a continuous apportionment method, until all the costs are charged to the production cost centre.

recognition The process of incorporating an accounting item into the *financial statements of an organization. Not only is the process essential for revenue and expenditure items, but it has became increasingly important in the proper treatment of *off balance sheet finance.

recognized professional body (RPB) A professional body recognized by the *Securities and Investment Board as being able to authorize its members to carry out investment business when it does not form part of their main activity.

recognized supervisory body A body recognized in the UK by the Secretary of State for Trade and Industry as supervising and maintaining the conduct and technical standards of *auditors performing statutory *audits. Currently the *Institute of Chartered Accountants in England and Wales, the *Institute of Chartered Accountants of Scotland, and the *Institute of Chartered Accountants in Ireland are recognized, together with the *Chartered Association of Certified Accountants; in principle, the *Association of Authorized Public Accountants is also recognized.

reconciliation of movements in shareholders' funds A *financial statement bringing together the performance of an organization in a financial period, as shown in the *statement of total recognized gains and losses, with all other changes in *shareholders' equity in the period, including *capital contributed by or repaid to shareholders. This statement is provided for in *Financial Reporting Standard 3, 'Reporting Financial Performance'.

recourse *See* without recourse.

recoverable advance corporation tax *Advance corporation tax that has been paid and can be set off in full against the current year's *gross corporation tax liability or set back against gross corporation tax for accounting periods beginning six years preceding the current accounting period.

recoverable amount The value of an *asset treated as the greater of its *net realizable value and its *net present value. The value of an asset to a business can be regarded as the lower of the recoverable amount and the current *replacement cost.

recovered overhead *See* absorbed overhead.

recovery rate *See* absorption rate.

rectification note A form issued to the production department of an organization requiring a piece of work to be reworked or rectified. The form includes a specification of the work to be done, the number of units, the processes involved, and the date required.

redeemable shares *Shares (either *ordinary shares or *preference shares) in a company that the issuing company has the right to redeem, under terms specified on issue. Redemption may be funded from *distributable profits or from a fresh issue of shares. If the shares were issued at a premium and are to be redeemed at a premium and subject to a maximum amount, the premium may be funded from the *share premium account. If redemption reduces the total capital of the company, i.e. no fresh issue is made or the proceeds of the fresh issue do not fully replace the nominal value of the shares redeemed, a *capital redemption reserve will need to be credited, to ensure that the *creditors' buffer is maintained.

redemption The repayment of *shares, *stocks, *debentures, or *bonds. The amount payable on redemption is usually specified on issue. The **redemption date**, or dates, may or may not be specified on issue. *See also* gilt-edged security; maturity date.

redemption date *See* maturity date; redemption.

redemption premium An addition to the *par value of a bond issued with a call *option, if the issuer exercises the option.

redemption yield *See* gross redemption yield; yield.

reducing-balance method *See* diminishing-balance method.

reduction of capital A reduction in the *issued share capital of a company. The Companies Act states that, subject to confirmation by the court, a company may, if authorized by its *articles of association, pass a *special resolution to reduce its issued share capital. It may (a) cancel any paid-up capital that is lost or no longer represented by available assets, (b) extinguish or reduce the *liability on any of its shares in respect of share capital not paid up, (c) pay off any paid-up share capital that is in excess of its *warrants.

reference bank A bank nominated under the terms of a loan agreement to provide the marker rates for the purposes of fixing interest charges on a variable-rate loan.

refer to drawer Words written on a cheque that is being dishonoured by a bank, usually because the account of the person who drew it has insufficient funds to cover it and the manager of the bank is unwilling to allow the account to be overdrawn or further overdrawn. Other reasons for referring to the drawer are that the drawer has been made bankrupt, that there is a garnishee order against the drawer, that the drawer has stopped it, or that something in the cheque itself is incorrect (e.g. it is wrongly dated, words and figures don't agree, etc.). The words 'please re-present' may often be added, indicating that the bank may honour the cheque at a second attempt.

registered auditor An *auditor approved by the authorities of the European Union to carry out *statutory audits, in accordance with the European Community 8th Directive. This was brought into UK legislation by the Companies Act (1989). Under this legislation, *recognized supervisory bodies were given the authority for approval. Registers of individuals and firms eligible to act as registered auditors have been set up.

registered book-keeper A member of the *International Association of Book-keepers.

registered capital *See* authorized share capital.

registered company A *company incorporated in England and Wales or Scotland by registration with the *Registrar of Companies. It may be a *limited company or an *unlimited company, a private *company or a public company.

registered office The official address of a UK company, to which all correspondence can be sent. Any change must be notified to the Registrar of Companies within 14 days and published in the *London Gazette*. Statutory registers are kept at the registered office, the address of which must be disclosed on stationery and in the company's annual return.

registered trader A *taxable person who has complied with the *registration for value added tax regulations.

register of charges **1.** The register maintained by the Registrar of Companies on which certain charges must be registered by companies. A charge is created when a company gives a creditor the right to recover a debt from specific assets. The types of charge that must be registered in this way, and the details that must be given, are set out in the Companies Act (1985). Failure to register the charge within 21 days of its creation renders it void, so that it cannot be enforced against a liquidator or creditor of the company. The underlying debt remains valid, however, but ranks only as an unsecured debt. **2.** A list of charges that a company must maintain at its registered address or principal place of business. Failure to do so may render the directors and company officers liable to a fine. This register must be available for inspection by other persons during normal business hours.

register of debenture-holders A list of the holders of *debentures in a UK company. There is no legal requirement for such a register to be kept but if one exists it must be kept at the company's registered office or at a place notified to the Registrar of Companies. It must be available for inspection, to debenture-holders and shareholders free of charge and to the public for a small fee.

register of directors and secretaries A statutory book in which a company must list the names, addresses, nationalities, dates of birth, other directorships, and business occupations of all its *directors and the secretary or secretaries of the company.

register of directors' interests A statutory book in which a company must detail the interests of its *directors in the *shares and *debentures of the company. The register must be available for inspection during the *annual general meeting of the company.

register of interests in shares A statutory book required to be maintained by *public companies. Interests in shares disclosed to the company by those persons knowingly interested in 3% or more of any class of the voting share capital must be disclosed in the register. Investments held by a spouse, children under 18 years, and corporate bodies over which the person has control are added to the person's own interests.

register of members (share register) A list of the *members of a company, which all UK companies must keep at their *registered office or where the register is made up, provided that this address is notified to the Registrar of Companies. It contains the names and addresses of the members, the dates on which they were registered as members, and the dates on which any ceased to be members. If the company has a share capital, the register must state the number and class of the shares held by each member and the amount paid for the shares. As legal, rather than beneficial, ownership is registered, it is not always possible to discover from the register who controls the shares. The register must be available for inspection by members free of charge for at least two normal office hours per working day. Others may inspect it on payment of a small fee. The register may be rectified by the court if it is incorrect.

Registrar of Companies An official charged with the duty of registering all the companies in the UK. There is one registrar for England and Wales and one for Scotland. The registrar is responsible for carrying out a wide variety of administrative duties connected with registered companies, including maintaining the **register of companies** and the *register of charges, issuing certificates of incorporation, and receiving annual returns.

registration for value added tax An obligation on a person making *taxable supplies to register for *value added tax if at the end of any month the amount of taxable supplies in the period of 12 months ending in that month exceeds the **registration threshold** of £46,000, according to the Finance Act (1995).

registration statement In the USA, a lengthy document that has to be lodged with the *Securities and Exchange Commission. It contains all the information relevant to a new *securities issue that will enable an investor to make an informed decision whether or not to purchase the security.

reinvestment rate The interest rate at which an investor is able to reinvest income earned on an existing investment.

related party An individual, partnership, or company that has the ability to control, or exercise significant influence over, another organization.

related-party transaction A transfer of resources or obligations between *related parties, regardless of whether a price is charged.

relationship banking The establishment of a long-term relationship between a bank and its corporate customers, often in the form of a bilateral bank agreement. The main advantage is that it enables the bank to develop in-depth knowledge of a company's business, which improves its ability to make informed decisions regarding loans to the company. The company expects to benefit by increased support during difficult times. *See also* bilateral bank facility; syndicated bank facility.

relevance The principle in decision making that the impact of a particular decision on the performance of an organization can only be determined by identifying those elements of cost or revenue that are affected by the decisions made. *See* relevant cost; relevant income.

relevant accounts The *accounts that should be used to determine the amount of *distributable profit of a company. These accounts are the most recent audited *annual accounts of the company, prepared in compliance with the Companies Act. If the accounts are qualified by the *auditors (*see* qualified audit report), the auditors must state in their report whether they consider that the proposed distribution would contravene the Companies Act.

relevant cost An item of expenditure that changes as the result of a proposed decision. A cost that remains unchanged as the result of a particular decision is irrelevant to that decision.

relevant income (relevant revenue) An item of revenue that changes as a result of a proposed decision. An item of revenue that remains unchanged as the result of a particular decision is irrelevant to that decision.

relevant information Information that is able to influence an economic decision likely to be made by the user of that information. To be relevant, information must have the *qualitative characteristics of timeliness and must either have predictive value or act as confirmation or correction of earlier expectations.

relevant range The range of levels of activity between which valid conclusions can be drawn from the *linear cost functions normally associated with a *breakeven analysis. Outside this range it is recognized that the linear relationships between fixed costs, variable costs, and revenue do not apply.

relevant revenue *See* relevant income.

reliability The verifiability, neutrality, and representational faithfulness of *accounting information as defined by the *Financial Accounting Standards Board's 'Statement of Financial Accounting Concepts No. 2'. The *Accounting Standards Board's *Statement of Principles considers that reliable information has the *qualitative characteristics of faithful representation, substance, neutrality, *prudence, and completeness.

remainderman The recipient of the remainder (residue) of an estate after the expenses, specific legacies, and *inheritance tax have been paid.

remitting bank *See* collecting bank.

remote job entry The entry of data into a computer system when the inputting device is physically remote from the actual computer.

remote terminal A computer terminal connected to a physically remote computer.

remuneration 1. A sum of money paid for a service given. *See also* audit fee. 2. A salary.

renewal notice An invitation from an insurer to continue an insurance policy that is about to expire by paying the **renewal premium**. The renewal premium is shown on the notice; it may differ from the previous premium, either because insurance rates have changed or because the insured value has changed. Many insurers increase the insured value of certain objects automatically, in line with inflation.

rent A payment made for the use of land or property usually, but not necessarily, based on a *lease.

rent-a-room A tax relief for individuals who receive payment for letting furnished accommodation in their only or main residence. Income of up to £3250 is exempt from tax, unless payment is made to two individuals, in which case the limit is £1625 each.

renting back *See* leaseback.

reorder level The number of units of a particular item of stock to which the balance can fall before an order for replenishment is placed. A **reorder-level system** is a stock-control system based on the principle that orders for the replenishment of items of stock are only placed when the balance of stock for a particular item falls to a predetermined level. The **reorder quantity** is the quantity ordered to replenish stock when the stock level falls to the reorder level.

reorganization costs The costs of restructuring a business. Financial Reporting Standard 3, 'Reporting Financial Performance', requires that reorganization costs, if they have a material effect on the nature and focus of a reporting entity's operations, should be shown separately as an *exceptional item on the face of the *profit and loss account after operating profit and before interest, under continuing operations or *discontinued operations as appropriate.

repairs and maintenance The revenue expenditure incurred in maintaining the assets of an organization in their original condition (as far as this is possible). Any expenditure incurred in improving the assets would normally be regarded as *capital expenditure and therefore not repairs and maintenance.

repayment claim A claim made by a taxpayer for repayment of tax overpaid in the *fiscal year. This can occur if *basic rate tax is deducted at source from all or most of the taxpayer's income without any relief for *personal allowances. Where trading losses occur, which are set against other income in the year of the loss or in the three previous years, as in the case of losses in the opening years of a business, any overpayment of tax on other sources of income can be reclaimed by making a repayment claim to the *Board of Inland Revenue.

replacement cost The cost of replacing an *asset, either in its present physical form or as the cost of obtaining equivalent services. If the latter is lower in amount than the former, the conclusion is that the assets currently used by the company are not those it would choose to acquire in the market place. Replacement cost may be used to value tangible fixed assets and in some circumstances such *circulating assets as stock.

replacement of business asset relief *See* roll-over relief.

report and accounts *See* annual accounts.

reporting accountants A firm of accountants who report on the financial information provided in a prospectus. They may or may not be the company's own auditors. It is usual for reporting accountants to have had previous experience of new issues and the preparation of prospectuses.

reporting currency The currency used by an organization in its *financial statements.

reporting partner The partner in a firm of *auditors who forms an *audit opinion on the *financial statements of a client company and signs and dates the *audit report after the financial statements have been formally approved by the directors of the company.

report of the auditor(s) *See* auditors' report.

representation and warranty A clause in a loan agreement in which the borrower gives a contractual undertaking confirming certain fundamental facts. These will include the borrower's power to borrow and to give guarantees, as well as confirmation that it is not involved in any major litigation.

representative member The company within a group of companies that must account for the *output tax and *input tax for *value added tax of all the companies in the group and be responsible for the quarterly VAT return for the group. All the companies within the group have *joint and several liability for any VAT due.

repurchase of own debt The buying back by a company of its own *debt at an amount different from the amount of the *liability shown in the *balance sheet. *Urgent Issues Task Force, Abstract 8, states that any difference on repurchase should be taken to the *profit and loss account, except in specified exceptional circumstances.

repurchase transaction A form of discounting in which a corporation raises funds from a bank by selling negotiable paper to it with an undertaking to buy the paper when it matures (*see* negotiable instrument).

required rate of return The *rate of return, usually expressed as a percentage, that an organization determines is necessary before an investment can be regarded as profitable and therefore justified. In a *discounted cash flow appraisal the required rate of return may be expressed as an *internal rate of return and in other circumstances the *return on capital employed or *accounting rate of return may be regarded as appropriate.

requisition A form that requires the recipient department or organization to carry out a specified procedure. Examples are *purchase requisition, *materials requisition, and manufacturing requisition (*see* production order).

research and development costs The costs to a company of its research and development. *Statement of Standard Accounting Practice 13, 'Accounting for Research and Development', distinguishes between pure research, applied research, and development. Pure research is original investigation undertaken to gain new scientific or technical knowledge and understanding, but without any specific applications. Applied research is original investigation undertaken to gain new scientific or technical knowledge with a specific practical aim or objective. Development is the use of scientific or technical knowledge to produce new or substantially improved materials, devices, products, processes, systems, or services prior to the commencement of commercial production. Under this Statement the costs of pure and applied research should be written off in the year in which they were incurred. Development expenditure, if it conforms with certain criteria, may be either written off immediately or capitalized and *amortized. The decision is left to the company and by capitalizing development costs a company will be creating an *intangible fixed asset to be shown on the *balance sheet.

reservation of title A sale of goods in which the seller retains title to the goods sold, or any products made from them, or the resulting sale proceeds, until the buyer pays for the goods. *See also* Romalpa clause.

reserve Part of the *capital of a company, other than the share capital, largely arising from retained profit or from the issue of share capital at more than its nominal value. Reserves are distinguished from *provisions in that for the latter there is a known diminution in value of an asset or a known liability, whereas reserves are surpluses not yet distributed and, in some cases (e.g. share premium account or capital redemption reserve), not distributable. The directors of a company may choose to earmark part of these funds for a special purpose (e.g. a **reserve for obsolescence** of plant). However, reserves should not be seen as specific sums of money put aside for special purposes as they are represented by the general net assets of the company. Reserves are subdivided into *retained earnings (revenue reserves), which are available to be distributed to the shareholders by way of dividends, and *capital reserves, which for various reasons are not distributable as dividends, although they may be converted into permanent share capital by way of a bonus issue.

reserve accounting The transfer of items directly to *reserves, rather than through the *profit and loss account. In certain instances this may be permitted, for example in adjusting for *prior-period items.

reserve asset cost *See* mandatory liquid assets.

resident A person living or based in the UK to whom one of the following applies for a given tax year:
• the person is present in the UK for 183 days or more during that year;
• the person pays substantial visits to the UK, averaging 90 days or more for four or more consecutive years;
• the person has accommodation available for use in the UK and one visit is made during the year. This does not apply if the taxpayer is working abroad full-time nor to individuals who visit the UK for a temporary purpose only.
From 15 March 1988 companies incorporated in the UK are regarded as resident in the UK for corporation-tax purposes, irrespective of where the management and control of the company is exercised. Prior to 15 March 1988 a company was regarded as resident in the UK if its management and control were in the UK.

residual equity theory The theory holding that emphasis should be given to ordinary shareholders as they are the real owners of a business. The theory is reflected in the *earnings per share figure, which assists ordinary shareholders in making investment decisions. Residual equity theory falls between the *proprietary view and the *entity view.

residual income (residual return) The net income that a *subsidiary undertaking or division of an organization generates after being charged a percentage return for the book value of the net assets or resources deemed to be under its control. The residual income approach by the headquarters or holding company of an organization is to require the subsidiary or division to maximize its profits after the charge for the use of those assets.

residual value *See* net residual value.

resolution A binding decision made by the members of a company. If a motion is put before the members of a company at a general meeting and the required majority vote in favour of it, the motion is passed and becomes a resolution. A resolution may also be passed by unanimous informal consent of the members. An **ordinary resolution** may be passed by a bare majority of the members. The Companies Act prescribes this type of resolution for certain actions, such as the removal of a director. Normally, no particular length of notice is required for an ordinary resolution to be proposed, beyond the notice needed to call the meeting. However, ordinary resolutions of the company require **special notice** if a director or an auditor is to be removed or if a director who is over the statutory retirement age is to be appointed or permitted to remain in office. In these circumstances 28 days' notice must be given to the company and the company must give 21 days' notice to the members. An **extraordinary resolution** is one for which 14 days' notice is required. The notice should state that it is an extraordinary resolution and for such a resolution 75% of those voting must approve it if it is to be passed. A **special resolution** requires 21 days' notice to the shareholders and a 75% majority to be effective. The type of resolution required to make a particular decision may be prescribed by the Companies Acts or by the company's articles. For example, an extraordinary resolution is required to wind up a company voluntarily, while a special resolution is required to change the company's articles of association.

responsibility accounting A *management accounting system designed to provide information to all levels of an organization, based on the responsibility of the individual managers for particular items of expenditure or income. Budgetary control and *standard costing are both examples of responsibility accounting.

responsibility centre A section or area of an organization the costs or income of which can be assigned to be the responsibility of a particular manager. A responsibility centre may be a department, *cost centre, division, *profit centre, or *investment centre.

restrictive covenant **1.** A clause in a contract that restricts the freedom of one of the parties in some way. Employment contracts, for example, sometimes include a clause in which an employee agrees not to compete with the employer for a specified period after leaving the employment. Such clauses may not be enforceable in law. **2.** A clause in a contract affecting the use of land. *See* covenant.

retailer schemes Twelve special schemes used by retailers to identify and allocate the total amount of *taxable supplies made into the *value added tax categories standard-rated, zero-rated, and exempt.

Retail Price Index (RPI) An index of the prices of goods and services in retail shops purchased by average households, expressed in percentage terms relative to a base year, which is taken as 100. For example, if 1987 is taken as the base year for the UK (i.e. average prices in 1987 = 100), then in 1946 the RPI stood at 7.4, and in 1990 at 126.1. The RPI is published by the Central Statistical Office on a monthly basis and includes the prices of some 130 000 different commodities. The RPI is one of the standard measures of the rate of *inflation. In the USA and some other countries the RPI is known as the *Consumer Price Index.

retained earnings (retained profits; ploughed-back profits; retentions) The *net profit available for *distribution, less any distributions made, i.e. the amount kept within the company. Retained earnings are recorded in the profit and loss reserve.

retentions *See* retained earnings.

retirement relief A *capital gains tax relief available against a gain arising on a qualifying disposal. There are two main categories of qualifying disposals:
• a material disposal of business assets,
• an associated disposal.
Business assets include the whole or part of a business, including a partnership share, shares or other securities in a personal company, and assets used for business purposes when the business ceased. An associated disposal refers to the disposal of assets used in the business, which were not included in the accounts as business assets. A property owned personally, which was disposed of at the same time as the business, would be an associated disposal. Retirement relief was increased, from 1 December 1993, to full relief on the first £250,000 of a gain on disposal and 50% relief on the next £750,000 slice of gain. The amount of the gain in excess of £1 million is charged to capital gains tax in full.

return on assets An *accounting ratio expressing the amount of *profit for a *financial period as a percentage of the *assets of a company.

return on capital employed (ROCE) An *accounting ratio expressing the *profit of an organization for a *financial period as a percentage of the capital employed. It is probably one of the most frequently used ratios for assessing the performance of organizations. In making the calculation, however, there are a number of differing definitions of the terms used. Profit is usually taken as profit before interest and tax, while capital employed refers to fixed assets plus *circulating assets minus *current liabilities.

Sometimes the expression **return on investment (ROI)** is used, in which case even greater care must be used in understanding the calculation of the separate items. Management may consider that profit before interest and tax, expressed as a percentage of total assets, is a useful measure of performance. Shareholders, however, may be more interested in taking profit after interest and comparing this to total assets less all liabilities. The ratio can be further analysed by calculating *profit margins and *capital turnover ratios.

return on equity (ROE) The net income of an organization expressed as a percentage of its equity capital.

return on investment (ROI) *See* return on capital employed.

return period The quarterly *accounting period for *advance corporation tax and income tax payable by companies, to 31 March, 30 June, 30 September, and 31 December. If the end of the accounting period does not coincide with one of these dates, there are five return periods in the year. The year end identifies the fifth return period; e.g. for an accounting period to 31 May, the return periods would be 31 March, 31 May, 30 June, 30 September, and 31 December.

returns inwards (sales returns) Goods returned to an organization by customers, usually because they are unsatisfactory.

returns inwards book (sales returns book) The *book of prime entry used to record any returns of goods sold. Returns are posted to the individual *debtor's account in the *debtors' ledger and the total returns are posted to the *debtors' ledger control account and returns inwards accounts in the *nominal ledger.

returns on investments and servicing of finance A heading required on *cash-flow statements by *Financial Reporting Standard 1, 'Cash Flow Statements', to show receipts resulting from the ownership of investments and payments to the providers of finance. Cash inflows include interest and dividends received, while cash outflows include interest and dividends paid and the interest element of *finance lease rental payments.

returns outwards Goods returned by an organization to its suppliers, usually because they are unsatisfactory.

returns outwards book The *book of prime entry used to record any returns to suppliers of goods purchased. Returns are posted to the individual *creditor's accounts in the *creditors' ledger and the total returns are posted to the *creditors' ledger control account and returns outwards accounts in the *nominal ledger.

revalorization of currency The replacement of one currency unit by another. A government often takes this step if a nation's currency has been devalued frequently or by a large amount. *Compare* revaluation of currency.

revaluation An increase in the value of an asset to reflect its current market value. The asset cost account is debited and the *revaluation reserve is credited. Under the *alternative accounting rules, certain assets may be revalued.

revaluation account In a *partnership to which a new partner is admitted or if an existing partner dies or retires, *assets and *liabilities must be revalued to their current market value. The differences between historical values and the revaluations are debited or credited to the revaluation account. The balance on the revaluation account will represent a profit or loss on revaluation, which must be shared between the partners in the *profit-sharing ratio.

revaluation method A method of determining the *depreciation charge on a *fixed asset against profits for an accounting period. The asset to be depreciated is revalued each year; the fall in the value is the amount of depreciation to be written off the asset and charged against the profit and loss account for the period. It is often used for such depreciating assets as loose tools or a mine from which materials are extracted.

revaluation of assets A revaluation of the assets of a company, either because they have increased in value since they were acquired or because *inflation has made the balance-sheet values unrealistic. The Companies Act (1985) makes it obligatory for the directors of a company to state in the directors' report if they believe the value of land differs materially from the value in the balance sheet. The Companies Act (1980) lays down the procedures to adopt when fixed assets are revalued. The difference between the net book value of a company's assets before and after revaluation is shown in a revaluation reserve account or, more commonly in the USA, an **appraisal-surplus account** (if the value of the assets has increased).

revaluation of currency An increase in the value of a currency in terms of gold or other currencies. It is usually made by a government that has a persistent balance of payments surplus. It has the effect of making imports cheaper but exports become dearer and therefore less competitive in other countries; revaluation is therefore unpopular with governments. *Compare* devaluation; revalorization of currency.

revaluation reserve account (asset revaluation reserve) The reserve account to which the *unrealized profit or loss on *revaluation must be taken when the *alternative accounting rules are used for the valuation of an *asset. Companies have the option of choosing another name for this reserve if they wish. The revaluation reserve should be reduced to the extent that the amounts transferred to it are no longer necessary for the purpose of the valuation method used. The treatment for *taxation purposes of any amounts credited or debited to the revaluation reserve must be disclosed in a note to the accounts.

revenue 1. Any form of income. 2. Cost and income items that are either charged or credited to the *profit and loss account for an accounting period.

revenue bonds Loans in which the *principal and *interest are payable from the earnings of the project financed by the loan. They are sometimes issued in the USA by municipalities, to finance such projects as toll bridges.

revenue centre The area of an organization for which income is collected. Revenue centres are determined by individual organizations and they may be a function, department, section, individual, or any group of these that generates income.

revenue expenditure Expenditure written off to the *profit and loss account in the *financial period in which it is made. Such expenditure is deemed to have been incurred by the *revenue generated within that financial period.

revenue function A formula or equation representing the way in which particular items of income behave when plotted on a graph. For example, the most common revenue function is that for total revenue in the equation $y = bx$, where y = total revenue, b = selling price per unit of sales, and x = number of units sold.

revenue recognition The process of recording *revenue in the accounts of an organization in the appropriate *financial period. Revenue could be recognized at various points; for example, when an order is placed, on delivery of the goods, or on receipt of payment. It is essential to recognize revenue correctly to be able to calculate the appropriate amount of *profit for a correctly to be able to calculate the appropriate amount of *profit for a financial period. Normally, revenue is recognized when the buyer assumes the significant risks and rewards of ownership and the amount of revenue must be capable of reliable measurement. However, the complexity of some business transactions may make it difficult to determine in which financial period revenue should be recognized.

revenue reserve A reserve that is not a *capital reserve, i.e. a reserve that is distributable.

revenue transaction A transaction that is generally of a short-term nature and is only expected to benefit the current period. Revenue transactions appear in the *profit and loss account of the period.

reverse premium A cash payment made to a lessee as an encouragement to enter into a *lease agreement. Under *Urgent Issues Task Force, Abstract 12, such payments received by a lessee should be spread on a *straight-line basis over the lease term or, if shorter than the full lease term, over the period to the review date on which the rent is first expected to be adjusted to the prevailing market rate.

reverse takeover 1. The buying of a larger company by a smaller company. 2. The purchasing of a public company by a private company. This may be the cheapest way that a private company can obtain a listing on a stock exchange, as it avoids the expenses of a *flotation and it may be that the assets of the public company can be purchased at a discount. However, on the *London Stock Exchange there are regulations stipulating that the nature of the target company's business must be compatible with that of the private company. Usually the name of the public company is changed to that of the private company, who takes over the listing.

reversionary bonus A sum added to the amount payable on death or maturity of a with-profits policy for life assurance. The bonus is added if the life-assurance company has a surplus or has a profit on the investment of its life funds. Once a reversionary bonus has been declared it cannot be withdrawn if the policy runs to maturity or to the death of the insured. However, if the policy is cashed, the bonus is usually reduced by an amount that depends on the length of time the policy has to run.

Review Panel *See* Financial Reporting Review Panel.

revision variance (planning variance) A variance in *standard costing that adjusts the *basic standard to take into account any changed circumstances since the original standard was set. Establishing revision variances avoids having to reset standards for marginal changes in the underlying circumstances, while at the same time retaining the ability to identify the *operational variances during an accounting period.

revolving acceptance facility by tender (RAFT) An underwritten facility from a bank to place sterling *acceptance credits through the medium of a tender panel of eligible banks.

revolving bank facility (standby revolving credit) A loan from a bank or group of banks to a company in which the company has flexibility with regard to the timing and the number of *drawdowns and repayments; any loan repaid can be reborrowed subject to fulfilment of the conditions of the *committed facility. The facility can be a *bilateral bank facility or a *syndicated bank facility.

rights issue A method by which quoted companies on a stock exchange raise new capital, in exchange for new shares. The name arises from the principle of *pre-emption rights, according to which existing shareholders must be offered the new shares in proportion to their holding of old shares (a **rights offer**). For example in a 1 for 4 rights issue, shareholders would be asked to buy one new share for every four they already hold. As rights are usually issued at a discount to the market price of existing shares, those not wishing to take up their rights can sell them in the market. *Compare* bought deal; vendor placing; scrip issue.

ring-fence 1. To allow one part of a company or group to go into receivership or bankruptcy without affecting the viability of the rest of the company or group. 2. To assign a sum of money to a particular purpose so that it does not become part of the general resources of an organization.

risk analysis The measurement and analysis of the risk associated with financial and investment decisions. Risk arises when future events cannot be predicted with certainty but a range of possible outcomes enable an estimate to be made of their probability. Risk analysis is particularly important with *capital-investment decisions because of the large amount of capital usually required and the long-term nature of the projects.

risk-based audit An auditing technique that responds to the risk factors in an *audit by assessing the levels of risk attached to different areas of an organization's system and using the results to devise audit tests. The purpose is to focus the audit on the areas of highest risk in order to improve the chances of detecting errors. *See also* systems-based audit; audit risk.

risk-free rate of return The rate of interest that an investment carrying no risk is capable of earning. In the UK, for example, gilt-edged government securities are risk-free because they are underwritten by the UK Treasury.

risk premium (market-risk premium) The difference between the expected *rate of return on an investment and the risk-free return (e.g. on a government stock) over the same period. If there is any risk element at all, the rate of return will be higher than that if no risk is involved.

ROCE Abbreviation for *return on capital employed.

ROE Abbreviation for *return on equity.

ROI Abbreviation for return on investment. *See* return on capital employed.

rolling budget A budget that is regularly updated by adding a further budget period, such as a month or a quarter, while at the same time dropping out the earliest month or quarter as appropriate.

roll-over relief (replacement of business asset relief) A relief from *capital gains tax on certain disposals. A gain arising on the disposal of a business asset may be rolled over in full, resulting in no payment of capital gains tax on its disposal. This can occur only if all the proceeds received from the disposal of the asset are re-invested in a new business asset. Both the old and new asset must both be business assets, which are defined as:

- land or buildings,
- fixed plant and machinery,
- ships, aircraft, and hovercraft,
- goodwill,
- satellites, space stations, and spacecraft,
- milk and potato quotas,
- premium quotas for ewes and suckler cows.

The old asset and the new asset do not have to belong to the same category. The proceeds on disposal of land (the old asset) could be rolled over into the acquisition of a milk quota (the new asset). Full roll-over relief would be available if all the proceeds from the land were used to acquire the milk quota.

Romalpa clause A clause included in a contract of sale in which the seller retains the title of the goods sold until they have been paid for. This is of importance to accountants as it may affect the ownership of *stocks; it is essential to determine whether the commercial substance of a transaction rests ownership of an *asset in the purchaser, irrespective of any legal agreement. This clause derives its name from the case of Aluminium Industrie Vasseen BV v. Romalpa Aluminium Ltd (1976), which was concerned with the practice of selling goods subject to *reservation of title.

rotation of directors Under the articles of association of most UK companies, the obligatory retirement of one third of the directors each year (normally at the annual general meeting), so that each director retires by rotation every three years. Retiring directors may be re-elected.

round tripping An opportunity to make a profit by making use of a bank overdraft facility to deposit funds in the money market at rates that exceed the cost of the overdraft. The practice is frowned upon by banks because they may be having to use the money market to fund their customers' overdrafts. This accounts for the name 'round tripping'.

royalty A payment made for the right to use the property of another person for gain. This may be an intellectual property, such as a book or an invention. It may also be paid to a landowner, who has granted mineral rights to someone else, on sales of minerals extracted from the land. A royalty is regarded as a wasting asset as copyrights, patents, and mines have limited lives.

RPB Abbreviation for *recognized professional body.

RPI Abbreviation for *Retail Price Index.

running costs The expenditure incurred in order to carry out the operations of a fixed asset. Examples are power, maintenance, and consumable materials for a machine or fuel, oil, tyres, and servicing for motor vehicles.

running yield See yield.

S

SAEF Abbreviation for *Stock Exchange Automatic Execution Facility.

safety stock A level of stock that provides a safety buffer in the event of increased demand or reduced receipt of stocks. The level for any item should not be allowed to fall below the safety stock.

sale and leaseback A transaction in which the owner of an *asset sells it and immediately purchases back from the buyer the right to use the asset under a *lease. The lease may be a *finance lease or an *operating lease.

sale and repurchase agreement An arrangement in which an *asset is sold by one party to another on terms that provide for the seller to repurchase the asset under certain circumstances. Sale and repurchase agreements, which are examples of *off balance sheet finance, are dealt with by *Financial Reporting Standard 5, 'Reporting the Substance of Transactions'. In a number of cases the agreement will in substance be that of a secured loan in which the seller retains the risks and rewards of ownership of the asset. In these cases the seller should show the original asset on the balance sheet, together with a *liability for the amounts received from the buyer.

sale or return Terms of trade in which the seller agrees to take back from the buyer any goods that he has failed to sell, usually in a specified period. Some retail shops buy certain of their goods on sale or return.

sales account An *account used to record cash and credit sales transactions resulting from the sale of goods or services.

sales budget A budget set for the sales function of an organization under a system of *budgetary control; it includes, inter alia, the *sales volumes and the *sales revenue to be achieved in a budget period. It will usually provide an analysis of the budgets by product, market segment, and by accounting period.

sales cost budget A budget that determines the expenditure the *sales function is allowed to incur in achieving the *sales volumes and *sales revenue budgets during a budget period. It includes such costs as sales personnel salaries, advertising expenditure, and promotional costs.

sales credit note A credit note sent by a seller to a customer to cancel, or partly cancel, an invoiced charge.

sales day book (sales journal; sold day book) The *book of prime entry in which an organization records the invoices issued to its customers for goods or services supplied in the course of its trade. Postings are made from this book to the personal accounts of the customers, while the totals of the invoices are posted to the sales account in the *nominal ledger.

sales discount A cash discount given by the seller of goods or services.

sales forecast An estimate of future sales volumes and revenue. It is usually based on past trends and takes into account current and future directions, such as government regulations, economic forecasts, and industry conditions.

sales function The section of an organization responsible for selling its products and services.

sales invoice A document sent by the seller of goods or services to the buyer, detailing the amounts due, discounts available, payment dates, and such administrative details as the account numbers and credit limits.

sales journal *See* sales day book.

sales ledger *See* debtors' ledger.

sales ledger control account *See* debtors' ledger control account.

sales margin mix variance (sales mix profit variance) The adverse or favourable variance arising in *standard costing as a result of a difference between the actual mix of sales achieved and the budgeted mix of sales. It is made up of the difference between the actual total sales volume based on the actual mix by product and the actual total sales volume based on the budgeted mix by product, multiplied by the standard margin per product.

sales margin price variance (selling price variance) The adverse or favourable variance arising in *standard costing as a result of the difference between the actual sales revenue achieved and the actual sales quantities at budgeted or *standard selling prices.

sales margin volume variance (sales volume variance) The adverse or favourable variance arising in *standard costing as a result of the difference between the actual number of units sold and those budgeted, valued at the standard profit margin.

sales mix The relative proportions of individual products that make up the total units sold.

sales mix profit variance *See* sales margin mix variance.

sales returns **1.** *See* returns inwards. **2.** A report on sales made in a period.

sales returns book *See* returns inwards book.

sales revenue The income arising from the sales of products or services.

sales tax A tax imposed at the point of sale. In the UK *value added tax is the main sales tax.

sales values **1.** The prices charged for items when they are sold. **2.** A method of apportioning the *joint costs between the *joint products in *process costing. From the *sales revenue of each independent product, the costs of the independent processes are deducted to give a sales value of each joint product at the *separation point. The joint costs are then apportioned between the joint products, in proportion to their relative sales values.

sales volume The number of units sold of each product.

sales volume variance *See* sales margin volume variance.

salvage value (scrap value) The realizable value of an asset at the end of its useful life, when it is no longer suitable for its original use. Fixed assets, stock, or waste arising from a production process can all have a salvage value.

sample **1.** A small quantity of a commodity, etc., selected to represent the bulk of a quantity of goods. **2.** A small quantity of a product, given to potential buyers to enable them to test its suitability for their purposes. **3.** A small group of items selected from a larger group to represent the characteristics of the larger group. Samples are often used in marketing research because it is not feasible to interview every member of a particular market; however, conclusions about a market drawn from a sample always contain a sampling error and must be used with caution. The larger the sample, in general, the more accurate will be the conclusions drawn from it. In **quota sampling** the composition of the sample reflects the known structure of the market. Thus, if it is known that 60% of purchasers of household DIY products are men, any sample would reflect this. An alternative sampling procedure is **random sampling**, which ensures that everyone in a particular market has an equal chance of selection. Although more accurate than quota sampling, it is also more expensive.

sampling frame A listing of the population from which a *sample is to be drawn.

samurai bond A bond issue, denominated in yen, made in the Japanese domestic market by a foreign (non-Japanese) issuer; it is thus the Japanese equivalent of a *Yankee bond.

Sandilands Committee A committee chaired by Sir Francis Sandilands, set up in 1975 by the UK government to consider the most appropriate way to account for the effects of inflation in the published accounts of companies. It recommended *current cost accounting in preference to the *current purchasing power accounting favoured by the accountancy bodies.

sans recours *See* without recourse.

SAS Abbreviation for *Statement of Auditing Standards.

save-as-you-earn (SAYE) A method of making regular savings (not necessarily linked to earnings), which carries certain tax privileges. This method has been used to encourage tax-free savings in building societies or National Savings and also to encourage employees to acquire shares in their own organizations.

savings ratio The ratio of savings by individuals and households to disposable income. Savings are estimated in the national income accounts by deducting consumers' expenditure from disposable income. Variations in the savings ratio reflect the changing preferences of individuals between present and future consumption. Countries, such as Japan, with very high savings ratios have tended to experience faster growth in GDP than countries, such as the USA, with low savings ratios.

savings related share option scheme An approved share option scheme established by an employer. An employee or director, who is granted rights to acquire shares by such a scheme, was not charged to income tax on the receipt of the right nor on the exercise of the right until 1995. *Capital gains tax will be payable on disposal of the shares for a consideration in excess of the allowable cost, taking into account the *indexation allowance. *See also* save-as-you-earn.

SAYE Abbreviation for *save-as-you-earn.

scalpers Traders in the *futures and *options markets who deal very frequently and may hold a position only for a few minutes.

SCARF Abbreviation for *systems control and review file.

scatter diagram A graph on which observations are plotted on the y-axis for events on the x-axis. For example, the wages incurred (y-axis) for each level of activity (x-axis) would produce a scatter graph from which a relationship can be established between the two variables, say by *linear regression, as an aid to predicting *cost behaviour.

schedule 1. The part of legislation that is placed at the end of a UK act of parliament and contains subsidiary matter to the main sections of the act. **2.** One of several schedules of income tax forming part of the original income tax legislation, now used to classify various sources of income for tax purposes. Some of the schedules are further subdivided into cases. The broad classification is: Schedule A, rents from property in the UK; Schedule B, income from commercial woodlands; Schedule C, interest paid by public bodies; Schedule D, Case I, profits from trade; Case II, profits from professions or vocations; Case III, interest not otherwise taxed; Case IV, income from securities outside the UK; Case V, income from possessions outside the UK; Case VI, other annual profits and gains; Schedule E, Cases I, II, and III, emoluments of offices or employments (the cases depending on the residential status of the taxpayer); Schedule F, dividends paid by UK companies. **3.** Working papers submitted with tax returns or tax computations. **4.** Any scale of rates. **5.** A plan for undertaking some enterprise, especially one that details the timing of events.

scheme of arrangement A compromise agreement made between a company and its shareholders or *creditors as an alternative to *bankruptcy. This is usually achieved by applying the assets and income of the debtor in proportionate payments to the creditors. This is sometimes known as a **composition**. Once a scheme of arrangement has been agreed, a *deed of arrangement is drawn up. *See also* voluntary arrangement.

scorekeeping One of the functions of *management accounting in which the performance of the managers and operators is monitored and reported in accounting statements to the appropriate levels of management.

scrap 1. What is left of an asset at the end of its useful life, which may have a *salvage value. **2.** The waste arising from a production process, which may have a *salvage value.

scrap value *See* salvage value.

scrip The certificates that demonstrate ownership of *stocks, *shares, and *bonds (capital raised by subscription), especially the certificates relating to a *scrip issue.

scrip issue (bonus issue; capitalization issue; free issue) The issue of new share certificates to existing shareholders to reflect the accumulation of profits in the reserves of a company's balance sheet. It is thus a process for converting money from the company's reserves into issued capital. The shareholders do not pay for the new shares and appear to be no better off. However, in a 1 for 3 scrip issue, say, the shareholders receive one new share for every three existing shares they own. This automatically reduces the price of the shares by approximately 25%, catering to the preference of shareholders to hold lower-priced shares rather than heavy shares; it also encourages them to hope that the price will gradually climb to its former value, which will, of course, make them 25% better off. In the USA this is known as a **stock split**.

SEAQ Abbreviation for *Stock Exchange Automated Quotations System.

SEC Abbreviation for *Securities and Exchange Commission.

secondary auditor The *auditor of a subsidiary company who is not also the auditor of the parent company. *See also* primary auditor.

secondary market A market in which existing securities are traded, as opposed to a **primary market**, in which securities are sold for the first time. In most cases a *stock exchange largely fulfils the role of a secondary market, with the flotation of new issues representing only a small proportion of its total business. However, it is the existence of a flourishing secondary market, providing *liquidity and the spreading of risks, that creates the conditions for a healthy primary market.

second-hand goods scheme An arrangement in which the *value added tax due on second-hand goods sold is calculated on the trader's margin, rather than the total selling price of the goods. This applies regularly with sales of second-hand cars. In order to qualify, the trader must retain detailed records of car purchases and sales, which must be available for inspection at a VAT control visit.

secret reserve Funds accumulated by a company but not disclosed on the *balance sheet. They can arise when an *asset has been deliberately undervalued or a method has been used to account for a transaction with the intention of not showing the effect on the balance sheet. *Financial Reporting Standard 5, 'Reporting the Substance of Transactions', is aimed at *off balance sheet finance.

section 212 The section of the UK Companies Act (1985) that gives a company powers to require shareholders hiding behind nominee names to declare their identity.

secured creditor A *creditor who holds either a *fixed charge or a *floating charge over the *assets of its debtor.

secured liability A debt against which the borrower has provided sufficient assets as security to safeguard the lender in case of non-repayment.

Securities and Exchange Commission (SEC) In the USA, the federal government agency monitoring and controlling corporate financial reporting, auditing practices, and trading activity. The SEC follows, to a very large extent, the accounting and auditing pronouncements of bodies organized by the public accounting profession, such as the *Financial Accounting Standards Board and the *Auditing Standards Board.

Securities and Futures Authority Ltd (SFA) The *Self-Regulating Organization formed from the merger of The Securities Association Ltd (TSA) and the Association of Futures Brokers and Dealers Ltd (AFBD) in April 1991. It is responsible for regulating the conduct of brokers and dealers in securities, *options, and futures, including most of those on the *London Stock Exchange and the *London International Financial Futures and Options Exchange.

Securities and Investment Board (SIB) A regulatory body set up by the Financial Services Act (1986) to oversee London's financial markets (e.g. the stock exchange, life assurance, unit trusts). Each market has its own *Self-Regulating Organization (SRO), which reports to the SIB. The prime function of the SIB is to protect investors from fraud and to ensure that the rules of conduct established by the government and the SROs are followed. However, as the structure of City institutions and their regulation is not fixed for all time, the role of the SIB has to be capable of adapting to changing practices. Moreover, some City activities are outside its control; for example, takeovers remain under the supervision of the Takeover Panel (*see* City Code on Takeovers and Mergers). Members of the SIB are appointed jointly by the Secretary of State for Trade and Industry and the Governor of the Bank of England from leading City institutions; while this understandably leads to suggestions of partisanship, it is doubtful whether outsiders would have sufficient understanding of City practices to be effective as regulators. The SIB is authorized to grant recognition to investment institutions and is financed by the fees paid to achieve this recognition.

securitization An arrangement involving one party (the originator) selling a portfolio of high-quality *assets, such as house mortgages, to a special-purpose vehicle (the issuer), who issues loan notes to finance the purchase. The arrangement may be a form of *off balance sheet finance and now falls under the regulations of *Financial Reporting Standard 5, 'Reporting the Substance of Transactions'.

security **1.** An asset or assets to which a lender can have recourse if the borrower defaults on his loan repayments. In the case of loans by banks and other moneylenders the security is sometimes referred to as *collateral. **2.** A financial asset, including shares, government stocks, debentures, bonds, unit trusts, and rights to money lent or deposited. It does not, however, include insurance policies. *See also* bearer security; gilt-edged security; listed security.

segmental reporting **1.** The disclosure in the *annual accounts and report of certain results of major business and geographical segments of a diversified group of companies. Segmental reporting is required by *company law, the *stock exchange, and *Statement of Standard Accounting Practice 25. The argument for segmental reporting is that the disclosure of profitability, risk, and growth prospects for individual segments of a business will be of use to investors. Under SSAP 25 companies should disclose, for both business and geographical segments, turnover, profit or loss before tax, minority interests, extraordinary items, and net assets. **2.** The approach in *management accounting in which the financial and quantitative performance of each definitive part of an organization is reported to both the management of the *business segment and of the organization as a whole.

self-assessment A system that enables a taxpayer to assess his or her own *income tax and *capital gains tax liabilities for the year. Major changes to the current system in the UK will occur in the year 1996–97, when a self-assessment section will be contained in the tax return, in addition to the part requiring details of *taxable income, *chargeable gains, and claims for *personal allowances. At present the self-assessment is voluntary. The introduction of self-assessment will be accompanied by the *Board of Inland Revenue having extensive audit powers to enquire into any tax return.

Self-Regulating Organization (SRO) One of several organizations set up in the UK under the Financial Services Act (1986) to regulate the activities of investment businesses and to draw up and enforce specific codes of conduct. Five SROs were originally recognized by the *Securities and Investment Board, to whom they report, which was reduced to four in 1991 on the merger of The Securities Association Ltd (TSA) and the Association of Futures Brokers and Dealers Ltd (AFBD) to form the *Securities and Futures Authority Ltd (SFA). In 1994 the *Financial Intermediaries, Managers and Brokers Regulatory Association Ltd (FIMBRA) amalgamated with the *Personal Investment Authority. The other two SROs are the **Life Assurance and Unit Trust Regulatory Organization (LAUTRO)**, which regulates institutions offering life assurance and unit trusts as principals; and the **Investment Managers Regulatory Organization (IMRO)**, which regulates any institution that offers investment management.

self supply The *value added tax charge on a commercial building, which is used for an exempt purpose, on the grant of an interest in the building. *Output tax is charged on the land and the building costs. *Input tax is allowed on the building costs. The self supply is due to be assessed and paid within three months of the initial occupation.

selling overhead (selling costs) The expenses incurred by an organization in carrying out its selling activities. These would include salaries of sales personnel, advertising costs, sales commissions, etc.

selling price variance *See* sales margin price variance.

semi-fixed cost (stepped cost) An item of expenditure that increases in total as activity rises but in a stepped, rather than a *linear, function. For example, the costs of one supervisor may be required for a particular range of activity, although above this level the cost of an additional supervisor would be incurred.

semi-variable cost An item of expenditure that contains both a *fixed-cost element and a *variable-cost element. Consequently, when activity is zero, the fixed cost will still continue to be incurred. For example, in the UK the cost of gas is made up of a standing charge plus a cost per unit consumed; therefore while the consumption of gas varies with production the fixed standing charge will still be incurred when production is zero.

sensitivity analysis A form of analysis used in approaches to business problems, in which possible changes to the variables are subjected to the decision-making technique to examine the range of possible outcomes and to determine the sensitivity of the projected results to these changes. For example, in a *discounted cash flow calculation possible changes to interest rates, cash flows, and timing may be built into the calculation to determine the sensitivity of the project to each change.

separate-entity concept The concept that the *financial statements of an

set-off

organization should describe the business as if it were entirely separate from its owners.

separate taxation of wife's earnings An election available before April 1990, in which both parties to a marriage agreed to treat the wife's earnings separately from the husband's. For high-earning couples this could mean a saving of tax. This ceased to apply on the introduction of *independent taxation for husbands and wives.

separation point (split-off point) In *process costing, the point at which the *by-products or the *joint products separate and are subsequently processed independently of each other.

Serious Fraud Office (SFO) A body established in 1987 to be responsible for investigating and prosecuting serious or complex frauds in England, Wales, and Northern Ireland. The Attorney General appoints and superintends its director. Serious and complex fraud cases can go straight to the Crown Court without committal for trial. That court can hold preparatory hearings to clarify issues for the jury and settle points of law.

SERPS Abbreviation for *State Earnings-Related Pension Scheme.

service An economic good consisting of human worth in the form of labour, advice, managerial skill, etc., rather than a *commodity. **Services to trade** include banking, insurance, transport, etc. **Professional services** encompass the advice and skill of accountants, lawyers, architects, business consultants, doctors, etc. **Consumer services** include those given by caterers, cleaners, mechanics, plumbers, etc. Industry may be divided into extractive, manufacturing, and service sectors. The **service industries** make up an increasing proportion of the national income.

service contract (contract of employment; contract of service; service agreement) An employment contract between an employer and employee, usually a senior employee, such as a director, executive manager, etc. Service contracts must be kept at the registered office of a company and be open to inspection by members of the company. The Companies Acts (1980 and 1985) prohibit service contracts that give an employee guaranteed employment for more than five years, without the company having an opportunity to break the employment as and when it needs to. This measure prevents directors with long service agreements from suing companies for loss of office in the event of a takeover or reorganization. *See also* compensation for loss of office; golden parachute.

service cost centre (indirect cost centre; service department; support cost centre) A *cost centre to which costs are allocated or apportioned in *absorption costing; though the service cost centre is necessary to carry out the production process, it is incidental to it and does not handle the *cost unit. Examples of service cost centres are stores, canteens, and boiler houses.

service department *See* service cost centre.

set-off An agreement between the parties involved to set off one debt against another or one loss against a gain. A banker is empowered to set off a credit balance on one account against a debit balance on another if the accounts are in the same name and in the same currency. It is usual, in these circumstances, for the bank to issue a **letter of set-off**, which the customer countersigns to indicate agreement. A letter of set-off is also needed if the accounts are not in the same name, e.g. differently named companies in the same group.

settled property Property that is included in an *interest-in-possession trust. A person entitled to benefit from the settled property is known as the life tenant. When the estate of the life tenant is assessed for *inheritance tax, the value of the settled property is included, provided the property does not comprise excluded property. The inheritance tax attributable to the settled property is payable by the trustees of the interest-in-possession trust and this is shown separately in the inheritance-tax computation of the life tenant.

settlement day The day on which trades are cleared by the delivery of the securities or foreign exchange.

set-up time The time taken to prepare a machine, process, or operation to carry out production. It may involve such operations as tool setting, calibration, and the initialization of the production process.

Seventh Directive A directive approved by the European Community in 1983 and implemented in the UK by the Companies Act (1989) concerning *consolidated financial statements prepared by *groups.

several liability *See* joint and several liability.

severe long-term restrictions Restrictions that hinder the exercise of the rights of a *holding company over the *assets or management of a *subsidiary undertaking. Severe long-term restrictions may be used as grounds for excluding a subsidiary from *consolidation; if it is so excluded, a subsidiary should be treated as a fixed-asset investment. *See also* exclusion of subsidiaries from consolidation.

SFA Abbreviation for *Securities and Futures Authority Ltd.

SFAC Abbreviation for *Statement of Financial Accounting Concepts.

SFAS Abbreviation for *Statement of Financial Accounting Standards.

SFO Abbreviation for *Serious Fraud Office.

shadow director A person in accordance with whose instructions the directors of a company are accustomed to act although that person has not been appointed as a director. A shadow director influences the running of the company and some provisions of the Companies Acts, including wrongful trading and the regulation of loans to directors, relating to directors also extend to shadow directors.

shadow price The *opportunity costs that arise in the solution to a *linear programming model.

shallow discount bond A bond issued in a *primary market at a price exceeding 90% of its face value, i.e. a bond in which the discount does not exceed 10%.

share One of a number of titles of ownership in a company. Most companies are limited by shares, thus if a company fails an investor has a liability that is limited to the amount paid for (or owing on) the shares. A share confers on its owner a legal right to the part of the company's profits (usually by payment of a *dividend) and to any voting rights attaching to that share (*see* voting shares; A shares). Companies are obliged to keep a public record of the rights attaching to each class of share. The common classes of shares are: *ordinary shares, which have no guaranteed amount of dividend but carry voting rights; and *preference shares, which receive dividends (and/or repayment of capital on winding-up) before ordinary shares, but which have no voting rights. Shares in public companies may be bought and sold in an open market, such as a stock exchange. Shares in a private company are generally subject to restrictions on sale, such as that they must be offered to existing shareholders first or that the directors' approval must be sought before they are sold elsewhere. *See also* cumulative preference share; deferred ordinary share; founders' shares; partly paid shares; redeemable shares.

share capital That part of the finance of a company received from its owners (i.e. its members or *shareholders) in exchange for *shares. *See also* authorized share capital; called-up share capital; issued share capital; paid-up share capital.

share certificate A document that provides evidence of ownership of shares in a company. It states the number and class of shares owned by the shareholder and the serial number of the shares. It is stamped by the common seal of the company and usually signed by at least one director and the company secretary. It is not a negotiable instrument. *See* bearer security.

shareholder An owner of shares in a limited company or limited partnership. A shareholder is a member of the company.

shareholders' equity (shareholders' funds) The *share capital and *reserves of a company. *Financial Reporting Standard 4, 'Capital Instruments', requires that share capital be split into ^equity shares and ^non-equity shares.

share issued at a discount A share issued at a price (the *issue price) below its *par value. The discount is the difference between the par value and the issue price. It is illegal to issue shares at a discount in the UK.

share issued at a premium A share issued at a price (the *issue price) above its *par value. The premium is the difference between the issue price and the par value. Except in special circumstances, the premium must be credited to a *share premium account. *See also* share premium.

share option The right to buy a fixed quantity of *shares at a particular date, at a particular price. An option is a right, not an obligation, so the holder does not have to buy the shares. Share options are sometimes given to employees and company executives on favourable terms.

share premium The amount payable for shares in a company and issued by the company itself in excess of their nominal value (*see* nominal price). Share premiums received by a company must be credited to a *share premium account, which cannot be used for paying dividends to the shareholders, although it may be used to make *scrip issues.

share premium account The account to which the premium must be credited for *shares issued at a premium. The balance on the share premium account may be used for specified purposes:
• the issue of *bonus shares;

• the writing-off of preliminary expenses;
• the writing-off of underwriting commissions;
• the provision of a premium to be paid on the *redemption of *debentures;
• the provision of a premium to be paid on the redemption or purchase of *share capital, subject to certain limits.

The share premium account may not be used to write off *goodwill on consolidation. Relief from the creation of a share premium account is given in section 131 of the Companies Act; this is known as *merger relief and is available in specified circumstances.

share register *See* register of members.

share splitting The division of the share capital of a company into smaller units. The effect of a share split is the same as a *scrip issue although the technicalities differ. Share splits are usually carried out when the existing shares reach such a high price that trading in them becomes difficult.

share transfer (stock transfer) A change in the ownership of a *share or *stock. On the *London Stock Exchange a **stock transfer form** (or **transfer deed**) has to be signed by the seller of registered securities to legalize the transaction.

share warrant A certificate giving the holder the right to purchase a security at a particular price at a particular date or dates in the future.

shell company **1.** A non-trading company, with or without a stock-exchange listing, used as a vehicle for various company manoeuvres or kept dormant for future use in some other capacity. **2.** A company that has ceased to trade and is sold to new owners for a small fee to minimize the cost and trouble of setting up a new company. Some business brokers register such companies with the sole object of selling them to people setting up new businesses. The name and objects of such a company can be changed for a small charge. **3.** A company, normally with a stock exchange quotation, that has become relatively inactive and has little by way of earnings or assets. An entrepreneur with a profitable private company can sometimes gain control of a shell company and inject his private business into it to avoid the requirements and costs of a *listing, thus acquiring a ready-made stock-market presence.

short-form audit report In the USA, a standard *audit report that conforms to the short-form reporting requirements of the *Securities and Exchange Commission and the *American Institute of Certified Public Accountants. The first paragraph of the report indicates what the *auditor has done and the second paragraph gives the findings.

short lease A lease that has less than 50 years to run, as defined by the Companies Act (1985). *Compare* long lease.

short position A position held by a dealer in securities (*see* market maker), commodities, currencies, etc., in which sales exceed holdings because the dealer expects prices to fall, enabling the shorts to be covered at a profit. *Compare* long position.

short-term interest rates The rates of interest on **short-term loans**, i.e. loans that are made for a short period. Banks will usually pay higher rates for short-term loans, in which no withdrawal is permitted until the money is withdrawn on an agreed date, usually within three months. However, when banks are asked to make loans for a short term (usually less than one year), their interest rate charged may be lower than for a long-term loan, which will involve a higher risk.

short-termism Any policy that aims to maximize current profits rather than long-term development and wealth. For example, cutting back on *research and development reduces immediate costs but may lead to products becoming obsolescent in the future.

SIAS Abbreviation for *Statement on Internal Auditing Standards.

SIB Abbreviation for *Securities and Investment Board.

sight draft *See* documentary draft.

significant influence An influence by one company on the financial and operating policy decisions of another company (including *dividend policy) in which it has an interest. This definition is given in *Statement of Standard Accounting Practice 1, 'Accounting for the Results of Associated Companies'. The influence does not need to amount to control. *See also* associated company; equity accounting.

simple interest *See* interest.

simplex method (simplex algorithm) A method of obtaining a *linear programming solution by producing a series of tableaux. The technique, a step by step iterative process, tests a number of feasible solutions in turn until the final optimal solution is obtained. It lends itself to computer applications.

simplified financial statements Simplified versions of the *annual accounts and report intended for readers who do not possess sophisticated financial knowledge. The financial information may be made easier to understand by using simple financial terminology, showing the information in the forms of graphs and diagrams, providing fuller explanations, and reducing the amount of information. One form of simplified financial statement is the *employee report, which is intended for employees and not covered by legislation; another form is the *summary financial statement intended for shareholders and subject to legislation.

SIN Abbreviation for stores issue note. *See* materials requisition.

single capacity system *See* dual-capacity system.

single-entry book-keeping A *book-keeping system that only records one aspect of each transaction, i.e. either a debit or a credit. *Compare* double-entry book-keeping.

single property ownership trust (SPOT) A single property trust; shares in the trust entitle their holder to a direct share of the property's income and capital. A form of *securitization, a share in a SPOT is similar to a *property income certificate (PINC).

sinking fund A holding by a borrower or the borrower's agent of the borrower's own bonds, purchased in the market or otherwise acquired to meet future redemption commitments. The reason may be a requirement of the loan agreement or it may be due to *defeasance.

sleeping partner A person who has capital in a *partnership but takes no part in its commercial activities. He has all the legal benefits and obligations of ownership and shares in the profits of the partnership in accordance with the provisions laid down in the partnership agreement.

small companies relief *See* marginal relief.

small company A *company that meets the following criteria for the current and preceding financial year:
• its *balance-sheet total does not exceed £1.4 million (i.e. assets before deducting *current liabilities and *long-term liabilities);
• its *turnover does not exceed £2.8 million. This must be proportionally adjusted when the *financial year is longer or shorter than 12 months;
• the average number of employees should not exceed 50.
A company that is in its first financial year may still qualify as a small company if it falls within these limits. Alternatively, if the company has qualified in the two preceding financial years, it may qualify. If a company is a member of a *group containing a public *company, a banking or insurance company, or an authorized person under the Financial Services Act (1986), it is not eligible for the exemptions for small or *medium-sized companies.

A small company with a turnover of not more than £90,000 (and balance-sheet total of not more than £1.4 million) is exempt from a *statutory audit of its *annual accounts. A company with a turnover of between £90,001 and £350,000 (and balance-sheet total of not more than £1.4 million) may also take advantage of the small company audit exemption, but will need an *audit exemption report.

A small company is entitled to reduce the amount of information in its annual report to members. The exemptions allow a number of combinations of format-heading items in the balance sheet and notes.

A small company may also file *abbreviated accounts with the *Registrar of Companies.

small group A *group that meets two out of three of the following criteria for the current and preceding year, or the two preceding financial years:
• its *balance-sheet total should not exceed £1.4 million (i.e. assets before deducting *current liabilities and *long-term liabilities);
• its *turnover should not exceed £2.8 million. This must be proportionally adjusted when the financial year is longer or shorter than 12 months;
• the average number of employees should not exceed 50.
If a group is in its first financial year, it may still qualify if it falls within these limits.

An *intermediate holding company or an ultimate *holding company cannot qualify as a small company or a *medium-sized company unless the group headed by it qualifies as a small group or a medium-sized group. A group containing a public *company, a banking or insurance company, or an authorized person under the Financial Services Act (1986) is ineligible for the exemptions for small groups or medium-sized groups.

Under the Companies Act, a parent company is not required to prepare *group accounts for a financial year in which the group headed by that parent qualifies as a small group. *See also* exemption from preparing consolidated financial statements.

A small group may file *abbreviated accounts instead of full accounts with the *Registrar of Companies.

SNIF Abbreviation for short-term *note issuance facility.

social accounting issues Issues that concern the impact of an entity on society, both within the organization and externally. Social accounting issues may include charitable donations of equipment and time, education initiatives (such as sponsorships and research funding), product safety, community involvement, employment of disadvantaged groups, and the provision of sports equipment or sponsorship. Environmental issues that are often also included under this heading include energy conservation and control of pollution.

social audit An *audit of the impact of an organization on society. For example, an *environment audit is one kind of social audit. *See also* social responsibility reporting.

socially responsible investment *See* ethical investment.

social responsibility reporting The reporting of the costs and benefits of *social accounting issues by a business. This may be included in a separate report or as part of the *annual accounts. The costs are the costs to the business, for example of equipment donated, of sponsorship given, or of charitable donations. The benefits should be expressed as a monetary quantification of social benefits, which are often very hard to measure and necessarily subjective.

soft currency A currency that is not freely convertible and for which there is only a *thin market.

software package A set of computer programs that work together to achieve a specific purpose; for example, a spreadsheet package, a word-processing package, or an accounting package. Many accounting packages for large organizations are broken down into specific aspects of book-keeping and control.

sold day book *See* sales day book.

sold ledger *See* debtors' ledger.

sole practitioner A *sole proprietor who has a professional practice as an accountant, solicitor, etc.

sole proprietor An individual who runs an unincorporated business. Generally, a sole proprietor of a business is known as a **sole trader** and a sole proprietor of a professional practice is known as a *sole practitioner.

sole trader *See* sole proprietor.

solicitors' accounts Accounts prepared under the Solicitors' Account Rules, a key feature of which is that money held on behalf of clients is accounted for separately from the money owned by the practice.

Solomons Reports **1.** *Prospectus for a Profession* (1974), written by Professor David Solomons, which deals with the education and training of accountants. **2.** *Guidelines for Financial Reporting Standards* (1989), by the same author, which sets out a *conceptual framework for financial accounting.

solvency 1. The financial state of a person or company that is able to pay all debts as they fall due. **2.** The amount by which the assets of a bank exceed its liabilities.

SORP Abbreviation for *Statement of Recommended Practice.

source and application of funds (source and disposition of funds) A statement describing how a business has raised and used its funds for a specified period. Originally, a statement of source and application of funds was required by *Statement of Standard Accounting Practice 10, 'Statements of Source and Application of Funds', to be produced by a company if its turnover or gross income was at least £25,000. However, this is now obsolete since SSAP 10 has been withdrawn and replaced by *Financial Reporting Standard 1, 'Cash Flow Statements'. *See* cash-flow statement.

source document The first document to record a transaction.

sovereign risk The risk inherent in an overseas project that the assets on which the cash flow for repaying loans or generating profits is dependent could be expropriated by the local government.

Special Commissioners A body of civil servants who are specialized tax lawyers appointed by the Lord Chancellor after consultation with the Lord Advocate to hear appeals against assessments to income tax, corporation tax, and capital gains tax. A taxpayer may generally choose to appeal to the Special Commissioners, rather than the *General Commissioners, particularly in cases in which legal matters rather than questions of fact are at issue.

special resolution A resolution of the members of a *company that must be approved by at least 75% of the members to be valid. Members must have been given at least 21 days' notice of the meeting at which the resolution is proposed and the notice of meeting must give details of the special resolution. *See also* ordinary resolution; extraordinary resolution.

specific bank guarantee An unconditional guarantee from the *Export Credits Guarantee Department to a UK bank enabling that bank to finance an exporter's medium-term credit to an export customer without recourse; the arrangement is known as **supplier credit** in contrast to the buyer credit under which the bank finances the overseas buyer to pay the exporter on cash terms.

specific order costing *See* job costing.

split-off point *See* separation point.

spoilage *See* waste.

sponsor The issuing house that handles a new issue for a company. It will supervise the preparation of the prospectus and make sure that the company is aware of the benefits and obligations of being a public company.

SPOT Abbreviation for *single property ownership trust.

spot market A market that deals in commodities or foreign exchange for immediate delivery. Immediate delivery in foreign currencies usually means within two business days. For commodities it usually means within seven days.

spread 1. The difference between the buying and selling price made by a *market maker on the stock exchange. **2.** The diversity of the investments in a

*portfolio. The greater the spread of a portfolio the less volatile it will be.
3. The simultaneous purchase and sale of commodity futures (*see* futures
contract) in the hope that movement in their relative prices will enable a profit
to be made. This may include a purchase and sale of the same commodity for
the same delivery, but on different commodity exchanges, or a purchase and
sale of the same commodity for different deliveries.

spreadsheet A computer program used for numerical tabular operations,
such as financial forecasting and planning. It displays on the computer screen a
large table of columns and rows. Numbers are entered by the user to show, for
example, financial results or items of income and expenditure. If instructed,
the spreadsheet can automatically calculate those numbers that are derived
from figures already entered. The program can also update the figures shown
in all columns when a single figure is changed by the user.

square position An *open position that has been covered or hedged.

SRN Abbreviation for stores returns note. *See* materials returns note.

SRO Abbreviation for *Self-Regulating Organization.

SSAP Abbreviation for *Statement of Standard Accounting Practice.

SSP Abbreviation for *statutory sick pay.

stabilization The activities of the *lead manager of a bond issue in the *grey
market that are intended to reduce fluctuations in the price of the bond before
and just after issue.

stag A person who applies for shares in new issues in the hope that the price
when trading begins will be higher than the issue price. Often measures will be
taken by the issuers to prevent excessive stagging; it is usually illegal for
would-be investors to attempt to obtain large numbers of shares by making
multiple applications. Issuers will often scale down share applications to
prevent such quick-profit taking, e.g. by ballot.

staggered directorships A measure used in the defence against unwanted
takeover bids. If the company concerned resolves that the terms of office
served by its directors are to be staggered and that no director can be removed
from office without due cause, a bidder cannot gain control of the board for
some years, even with a controlling interest in the share capital. *See* poison pill.

stakeholders Those with interests in an organization; for example, as
*shareholders, employees, suppliers, or customers. Stakeholders may be users of
the *annual accounts and report of the organization and dependent to some
degree on its financial position and performance.

stale cheque A cheque that, in the UK, has not been presented for payment
within six months of being written. The bank will not honour it, returning it
marked 'out of date'.

stand-alone computer A self-contained computer that can be operated
without having to be connected to a central computing facility or to a network.

standard cash flow pattern The circumstances applying in a *discounted
cash flow calculation in which the projected cash flows are made up of an initial

cash outflow followed by subsequent cash inflows over the life of the project, there being no net cash outflows in subsequent years.

standard cost allowance The level of expenditure allowed to be incurred under a *standard costing system for variable costs, taking into account the actual levels of activity achieved. For example, the standard cost allowance for *direct materials is obtained from the actual number of units produced multiplied by the *standard direct materials cost per unit.

standard cost card The cards on which the standard costs of products (*see* standard costing) are built up and recorded. The standard cost card records the standard quantities of material and the standard prices, the standard labour times, and the standard rates of pay, as well as the fixed and variable overhead rates per unit of product. Traditionally, this information was kept on a series of cards, but it is now usually held in computer databases.

standard costing A system of *cost ascertainment and control in which predetermined **standard costs** and income for products and operations are set and periodically compared with actual costs incurred and income generated in order to establish any variances.

standard direct labour cost In *standard costing, a standard cost derived from the standard time allowed for the performance of an operation and the *standard direct labour rate for the operators specified for that operation.

standard direct labour rate A predetermined rate of pay for *direct labour operators used for establishing *standard direct labour costs in a *standard costing system; it provides a basis for comparison with the actual direct labour rates paid.

standard direct materials cost In *standard costing, a standard cost derived from the standard quantity of materials allowed for the production of a product and the *standard direct materials price for the materials specified for that product.

standard direct materials price A predetermined price for *direct materials used for establishing *standard direct materials costs in a *standard costing system in order to provide a basis for comparison with the actual direct material prices paid.

standard fixed overhead cost In *standard costing, a standard cost derived from the standard time allowed for the performance of an operation or the production of a product and the standard fixed overhead absorption rate per unit of time for that operation or product.

standard hour A measure of production (not time) that represents the amount of work, number of units produced, etc., that can be achieved within an hour under normal conditions. It is used to calculate the *efficiency ratio and *efficiency variances.

standard marginal costing A system of *cost ascertainment and control in a *marginal costing system in which predetermined standards for marginal costs and income generated for products and operations are set and periodically compared with actual marginal costs incurred and income generated in order to establish any variances.

standard materials usage A predetermined quantity of materials to be used in the production of a product, which is ultimately compared with the actual quantity of material used to provide a basis for *material control. The difference between standard and actual usage is used in *standard costing to calculate the *direct materials usage variance.

standard minute One sixtieth of a *standard hour.

standard mix 1. The predetermined proportions in which a mixture of different materials are intended to be used in a manufacturing process. It is set as a standard for the purposes of calculating the *direct materials mix variance. 2. The budgeted total volume of sales of an organization expressed in predetermined proportions of its range of related products. It is set as a standard for the purposes of calculating *sales margin mix variances.

standard operating cost The total of all the *standard cost allowances for the actual level of activity achieved by an organization.

standard operating profit The *budgeted revenue from an operation less the *standard operating cost.

standard operator performance *See* standard performance.

standard overhead cost A standard cost for the fixed and/or variable overhead of an operation derived from the standard time allowed for the performance of the operation or the production of a product and the standard overhead *absorption rate per unit of time for that operation or product.

standard performance (standard operator performance)
A predetermined level of performance for an operator or a process used as a basis for determining *standard overhead costs. For example, standard performance may be expressed as the number of units of production per *standard hour, *standard minute, or per working day.

standard price *See* standard purchase price; standard selling price.

standard production cost The *production costs of products and operations calculated from predetermined levels of performance and cost in order to provide a yardstick against which actual production costs can be compared for the purposes of *cost ascertainment and control.

standard purchase price A predetermined price set for each commodity of *direct material for a specified period. These prices are compared with the actual prices paid during the period in order to establish *direct materials price variances in a system of *standard costing.

standard rate The rate of *value added tax applied to all items sold by *taxable persons that are not specified as either *exempt supplies or *zero-rated goods and services. The rate for 1995–96 is 17.5%, which has been the rate since 1 April 1991. From 18 June 1979 to 1 April 1991 the standard rate was 15%.

standard rate of pay A predetermined rate of pay set for each classification of labour for a period. These rates are compared with the actual rates paid during the period in order to establish *direct labour rate of pay variances in a system of *standard costing.

standard selling price A predetermined selling price set for each product sold for a specified period. These prices are compared with the actual prices obtained during the period in order to establish *sales margin price variances in a system of *standard costing.

standard time The time allowed to carry out a production task in a *standard costing system. It may be expressed as the standard time allowed or alternatively, when expressed in *standard hours, as the output achieved.

standard variable overhead cost A standard cost derived from the standard time allowed for the performance of an operation or the production of a product and the standard variable overhead *absorption rate per unit of time for that operation or product.

standby revolving credit *See* revolving bank facility.

standing data Information held on file in a computer for long-term use because it does not often change. An example is the names and addresses of clients.

start-up costs The initial expenditure incurred in the setting up of an operation or project. The start-up costs may include the capital investment costs plus the initial revenue expenditure prior to the start of operations.

State Earnings-Related Pension Scheme (SERPS) A scheme, started in 1978, run by the UK government to provide a pension for every employed person in addition to the basic state flat-rate pension. The contributions are paid from part of the National Insurance payments made by employees and employers. Payment of the pension starts at the state retirement age (65 for men, 60 for women) and the amount of pension received is calculated using a formula based on a percentage of the person's earnings. Persons who wish to contract out of SERPS may subscribe to an *occupational pension scheme or a *personal pension scheme.

statement of affairs A statement showing the assets and liabilities of a person who is bankrupt or of a company in liquidation.

Statement of Auditing Standards (SAS) Any of the statements issued by the *Auditing Practices Board on basic principles and essential procedures in auditing. Auditors are required to comply with an SAS, except where otherwise stated in the SAS concerned, in the conduct of any *audit of *financial statements. Some SASs are also published containing auditing standards that apply to other audits and to related services provided by auditors. *See also* auditing standards.

Statement of Financial Accounting Concepts (SFAC) In the USA, any of the reports issued by the *Financial Accounting Standards Board to identify the fundamental concepts of *financial accounting and reporting. They reflect the *objectives of financial statements.

Statement of Financial Accounting Standards (SFAS) In the USA, any of the statements detailing the *financial accounting and reporting requirements of the *Financial Accounting Standards Board. These *accounting standards are *generally accepted accounting principles and should be followed by accountants responsible for the preparation of *financial statements.

statement of movements in shareholders' funds A statement that reconciles changes in the financial position of an organization that are not shown on the *statement of total recognized gains and losses covered by *Financial Reporting Standard 3, 'Reporting Financial Performance'.

Statement of Principles A discussion paper issued by the *Accounting Standards Board; it is intended to form a *conceptual framework. There are seven chapters:
1. The Objectives of Financial Statements
2. Qualitative Characteristics of Financial Information
3. The Elements of Financial Statements
4. The Recognition of Items in Financial Statements
5. Measurement in Financial Statements
6. Presentation of Financial Information
7. The Reporting Entity

Statement of Recommended Practice (SORP) Non-mandatory statements dealing with accounting topics issued by the *Accounting Standards Committee (ASC). Some **franked SORPs** were prepared by other bodies, mainly on an industry basis, and were approved by the ASC, a process known as franking. The ASC's successor, the *Accounting Standards Board, does not issue or frank SORPs.

Statement of Standard Accounting Practice (SSAP) Any of the *accounting standards prepared by the *Accounting Standards Committee and issued by the six members of the *Consultative Committee of Accountancy Bodies. The first SSAP was issued in 1971 and in total 25 SSAPs were issued. Before a SSAP was issued a discussion document known as an *exposure draft was circulated for comment. The SSAPs issued are given below, although some of these were withdrawn by the ASC, amended, or superseded by the later *Financial Reporting Standards:
1. Accounting for the Results of Associated Companies
2. Disclosure of Accounting Policies
3. Earnings per Share
4. The Accounting Treatment of Government Grants
5. Accounting for Value Added Tax
6. Extraordinary Items and Prior Year Adjustments
7. Accounting for the Changes in the Purchasing Power of Money (provisional)
8. The Treatment of Taxation under the Imputation System
9. Stocks and Work in Progress
10. Statement of Sources and Application of Funds
11. Accounting for Deferred Taxation
12. Accounting for Depreciation
13. Accounting for Research and Development
14. Group Accounts
15. Accounting for Deferred Taxation
16. Current Cost Accounting
17. Accounting for Post Balance Sheet Events
18. Accounting for Contingencies
19. Accounting for Investment Properties
20. Foreign Currency Translation
21. Accounting for Leases and Hire Purchase Contracts

22. Accounting for Goodwill
23. Accounting for Acquisitions and Mergers
24. Accounting for Pension Costs
25. Segmental Reporting

statement of total recognized gains and losses A primary statement showing the extent to which *shareholders' equity has increased or decreased from all the various gains and losses recognized in the period. It includes profits and losses for the period, together with all other movements on *reserves reflecting recognized gains and losses attributable to shareholders. The statement is dealt with under *Financial Reporting Standard 3, 'Reporting Financial Performance'.

Statement on Internal Auditing Standards (SIAS) Any of the statements issued by the Internal Responsibilities Committee of the *Institute of Internal Auditors, based in the USA.

Statements on Auditing Documents issued by the *Institute of Chartered Accountants in England and Wales, covering the current practice of the larger auditing firms. The statements are withdrawn when an *auditing standard is issued on the same topic.

static budget *See* fixed budget.

statistical sampling The use of random selection and probability theory to determine the size of a sample and to evaluate the results using this sample. Statistical sampling provides a measure of the sampling risk to assist an *auditor to draw conclusions on the total population. *See also* judgmental sampling.

statutory accounts Accounts required by law, for example by the Companies Act. *See also* statutory books.

statutory audit An *audit of a company as required by the Companies Act (1985), subject to *small company exemptions. The *auditors are required to report to the company's members on all accounts of the company, copies of which are laid before the company in general meeting (*see also* qualified audit report). Companies with a *turnover of not more than £350,000 (£250,000 for charitable companies) and gross *assets of not more than £1.4 million may be exempt from the statutory audit. Companies with a turnover of £90,000 or less do not need to have any form of accountant's or auditor's report. Companies with a turnover of between £90,001 and £350,000 need a reporting accountant's *audit exemption report.

statutory books The books of account that the Companies Act (1985) requires a company to keep. They must show and explain the company's transactions, disclose with reasonable accuracy the company's financial position at any time, and enable the directors to ensure that any accounts prepared therefrom comply with the provisions of the act. They must also include entries from day to day of all money received and paid out together with a record of all assets and liabilities and statements of stockholding (where appropriate).

statutory sick pay (SSP) A compulsory scheme operated by an employer. Payments are made to an employee for up to 28 weeks of absence as a result of sickness. There are two rates of statutory sick pay, the applicable level being determined by the employee's earnings. The two qualifying conditions for SSP are:

• there must be a period of incapacity for work,
• there must be one or more qualifying days.

The first three days do not count and so it is only on the fourth consecutive day that an entitlement to SSP begins.

statutory total income *See* total income.

step-function cost An item of expenditure that when plotted on a graph against activity levels gives a stepped function; i.e. increments of cost are incurred as activity rises. *See also* semi-fixed cost; linear cost function.

stepped cost *See* semi-fixed cost.

stewardship A traditional approach of accounting that places an obligation on stewards or agents, such as directors, to provide relevant and reliable financial information relating to resources over which they have control but which are owned by others, such as shareholders. Not only are stewards responsible for providing information, but they must also submit to an *audit.

stock **1.** In the UK, a fixed-interest security (*see* gilt-edged security) issued by the government, local authority, or a company in fixed units, often of £100 each. They usually have a *redemption date on which the *par value of the unit price is repaid in full. They are dealt in on stock exchanges at prices that fluctuate, but depend on such factors as their *yield in relation to current interest rates and the time they have to run before redemption. *See also* tap stock. **2.** The US name for an *ordinary share. **3.** The stock-in-trade of an organization. **4.** Any collection of assets, e.g. the stock of plant and machinery owned by a company.

stockbroker An agent who buys and sells securities on a stock exchange on behalf of clients and receives remuneration for this service in the form of a commission.

stock budgets *Budgets set under a system of *budgetary control, which plan the levels of stocks of *materials, *work in progress, and *finished goods both in volumes and values at various times throughout a *budget period.

stock control *See* inventory control.

stock exchange (stock market) A market for the sale and purchase of securities, in which the prices are controlled by the laws of supply and demand. The first stock exchange was in Amsterdam, where in 1602 shares in the United East India Company could be traded. UK exchanges date from 1673, with the first daily official price lists being issued in London in 1698. Stock markets have developed hand-in-hand with capitalism, gradually growing in complexity and importance. Their basic function is to allow public companies, governments, local authorities, and other incorporated bodies to raise capital by selling securities to investors. They perform valuable secondary functions in allowing those investors to buy and sell these securities, providing liquidity, and reducing the risks attached to investment. Stock markets were abolished after World War II in communist-dominated states but with the collapse of communism many restarted. The major international stock exchanges are based in London, New York, and Tokyo. Outside the UK and English-speaking countries, a stock exchange is usually known as a **bourse**.

Stock Exchange Automated Quotations System (SEAQ)
A computerized system used on the *London Stock Exchange to record the prices at which transactions in securities have been struck, thus establishing the market prices for these securities; these prices are made available to brokers through *TOPIC. When a bargain is concluded, the details must be notified to the central system within certain set periods during the day. **SEAQ International** is the system used on the London Stock Exchange for non-UK equities; it operates on similar lines to SEAQ.

Stock Exchange Automatic Execution Facility (SAEF) A computerized system used on the *London Stock Exchange to enable a broker to execute a transaction in a security through an SAEF terminal, which automatically completes the bargain at the best price with a *market maker, whose position is automatically adjusted. The price of the transaction is then automatically recorded on a trading report and also passes into the settlement system. The system has greatly reduced the administrative burden on brokers and market makers but has been criticized for eliminating the personal element between brokers and market makers on the floor of the exchange.

Stock Exchange Daily Official List A record of all the bargains made on the *London Stock Exchange. It also provides details of dividend dates, rights issues, prices, etc., of all *listed companies. It is also known as the *Official List.

stockholders In the USA, individuals, businesses, and groups owning stocks in a corporation.

stockholders' equity In the USA, the ownership interest of stockholders in a corporation. It is the difference between the total *assets and the total *liabilities.

stock-in-trade *See* inventories.

stock ledger The accounting book in which the movements of *inventories are recorded. The stock ledger records the receipts and issues of material as well as the balance in hand, in terms of both material quantities and values.

stock market *See* stock exchange.

stock out The circumstance that pertains when the balance of the physical stock of a particular commodity has been used and none remains in store.

stock reconciliation *See* stocktaking.

stock record The record in an *inventory control system of movements in items of stock. The stock record may be made up of entries in the *stock ledger, which records stock movements in both quantities and values, or on the *bin cards, which record quantities only.

stocks *See* inventories.

stock split *See* scrip issue.

stocktaking The process of counting and evaluating stock-in-trade, usually at an organization's year end in order to value the total stock for preparation of the accounts. In more sophisticated organizations, in which permanent stock records are maintained, stock is counted on a random basis throughout the year to compare quantities counted with the quantities that appear in the, usually, computerized records.

stock transfer *See* share transfer.

stock turnover *See* inventory turnover.

stock valuation *See* inventory valuation.

stock watering The creation of more new shares in a company than is justified by its tangible assets, even though the company may be making considerable profits. The consequences of this could be that the dividend may not be maintained at the old rate on the new capital and that if the company were to be liquidated its shareholders might not be paid out in full.

stop loss order An order given by an investor to a broker to sell a financial instrument, commodity, etc., when its price falls to a specified level in order to limit loss.

store card *See* bin card.

stores The part of an organization in which *inventories are stored. Depending on the arrangements within particular organizations, there may be separate stores for stationery stocks, maintenance components, production tools, *raw materials, *work in progress, and *finished goods.

stores issue note (SIN) *See* materials requisition.

stores oncost *See* oncost.

stores requisition *See* materials requisition.

stores returns note (SRN) *See* materials returns note.

straight bond A *bond issued in the *primary market that carries no equity or other incentive to attract the investor; its only reward is an annual or biannual interest coupon together with a promise to repay the capital at par on the redemption date.

straight-line method A method of calculating the amount by which a *fixed asset is to be depreciated in an accounting period, in which the *depreciation to be charged against income is based on the original cost or valuation, less the asset's estimated *net residual value, divided by its estimated life in years. This has the effect of a constant annual depreciation charge against profits year by year. In some circumstances the net residual value is ignored.

strategic investment appraisal An appraisal of an investment decision based on wider grounds than that provided by a purely financial appraisal. It is also necessary to evaluate possible long-term strategic benefits and any intangible factors that may be relevant to the decision, particularly if advanced manufacturing technology is concerned. *See also* capital budgeting.

strategic management accounting A management accounting system organized so that it is capable of providing the information needed by management to help in making long-term strategic decisions rather than being limited to the more traditional approach of providing short-term costs.

Strategic management accounting, for example, provides information that will assist in the pricing strategy for new products and decisions relating to the expansion of capacity.

stratified sampling The division of a total population into strata or bands. The sample is then drawn from each stratum individually.

strike price *See* exercise price.

subjective goodwill The *goodwill of an enterprise calculated by deducting its net tangible assets from the *net present value of its estimated future *cash flows.

subjective probabilities *See* probability.

subject to opinion A qualification by an *auditor stating that there was a material but not fundamental matter of uncertainty in the accounts being audited. The *audit report in these circumstances would have been given 'subject to' any adjustments that may have been necessary had the scope of the work not been limited or had the outcome of an inherent uncertainty been known. This procedure was contained in the auditing standard 'The Audit Report', issued by the *Auditing Practices Committee. This auditing standard has been replaced by the *Auditing Practices Board's Statement of Auditing Standards titled 'Auditors' Reports on Financial Statements', which does not include the 'subject to' qualification. *See also* qualified audit report.

sublease A *lease granted from a *head lease.

subordinated debt A debt that can only be claimed by an unsecured creditor, in the event of a liquidation, after the claims of secured creditors have been met. In **subordinated unsecured loan stocks** loans are issued by such institutions as banks, in which the rights of the holders of the stock are subordinate to the interests of the depositors. Debts involving *junk bonds are always subordinated to debts to banks, irrespective of whether or not they are secured.

subrogation The principle that, having paid a claim, an insurer has the right to take over any other methods the policyholder may have for obtaining compensation for the same event. For example, if a neighbour is responsible for breaking a person's window and an insurance claim is paid for the repair, the insurers may, if they wish, take over the policyholder's legal right to claim the cost of repair from the neighbour.

subscribed share capital *See* issued share capital.

subsidiary undertaking (group undertaking) An undertaking that is controlled by another undertaking (the parent or holding undertaking). The extent of the control needed to define a subsidiary is given in the Companies Act (1985). The *financial statements of a subsidiary undertaking are normally included in the *consolidated financial statements of the group.

substance over form An important concept in accounting, according to which transactions and other events are accounted for by their commercial reality rather than their legal form. *Off balance sheet finance and *creative accounting depended on accounting according to the legal form, often established in complex agreements. The purpose of *Financial Reporting

Standard 5, 'Reporting the Substance of Transactions', has been to give more strength to the substance aspect as well as guidance in specific transactions.

substantive tests *Audit tests designed to check the completeness, ownership, existence, valuation, and disclosure of the information contained in the accounting records and financial statements of an organization being audited. These tests may include *vouching, inspection, and *analytical review.

subsubsidiary A *subsidiary undertaking of a company that is itself a subsidiary company.

summary financial statement An abbreviated form of the *annual accounts and report that, providing certain conditions are met, may be sent by *listed companies to their *shareholders instead of the full report. Summary financial statements were introduced by section 251 of the *Companies Act (1985), which took effect from 1 April 1990.

sum-of-the-digits method A method of calculating the amount by which a *fixed asset is depreciated in an accounting period. The estimated life is expressed in years, and the digits for each year of its life are totalled. The proportion of the asset's cost or valuation less residual value to be written off as depreciation in a particular year is determined by the number of years remaining before the asset's removal from commission, expressed as a proportion of the sum of the years; the greatest amount is therefore written off in the early years of the asset's life. For example, for an asset with an estimated life of 5 years, the sum of the digits is $5 + 4 + 3 + 2 + 1 = 15$. Thus 5/15 is written off in the first year, 4/15 in year 2, 3/15 in year 3, and so on. In some circumstances the *net residual value is ignored.

sundry expenses Costs incurred as small items of expenditure, which do not lend themselves to easy classification under any other heading. Sometimes they refer to a specific area, such as sundry office expenses or sundry production costs.

sunk costs Expenditure, usually on capital items, that once having been incurred can be included in the books of account as an asset, although this value cannot be recovered. An example of this form of expenditure would be creating a railway embankment or dredging to create a berth in a harbour.

superannuation An occupational pension scheme. Contributions are deducted from an employee's salary by the employer and passed to an insurance company or the trustees of a pension fund. After retirement, the employee receives a pension payment from the scheme.

supplier credit *See* specific bank guarantee.

supply risk The inherent risk in *limited recourse financing of a construction project that the raw materials necessary for the operation of the plant to be constructed may become unavailable. *Compare* completion risk; technological risk.

support cost centre *See* service cost centre.

surcharge liability notice A notice issued when a trader is late with a *value added tax return or with the payment of the tax. The surcharge period is specified on the notice and it will run to the anniversary of the end of the period in which the default occurred. Any default in the liability notice period will result in a further notice extending the notice period to the anniversary of the end of the VAT period in which the second default occurred. *See also* penalty for repeated errors.

surplus advance corporation tax The *advance corporation tax paid in an accounting period in excess of the maximum available for set-off against the current accounting period's *gross corporation tax. In a group of companies the advance corporation tax can be surrendered by the parent company to a subsidiary, if 51% of the subsidiary company is owned by the parent company.

surplus franked investment income The amount by which the *franked investment income exceeds the *franked payments in an accounting period.

surrender value The sum of money given by an insurance company to the insured on a life policy that is cancelled before it has run its full term. The amount is calculated approximately by deducting from the total value of the premiums paid any costs, administration expenses, and a charge for the life-assurance cover up to the cancellation date. There is little or no surrender value to a life policy in its early years. Not all life policies acquire a surrender value; for example, term assurance policies have no surrender value.

sushi bond A bond issued in the *euromarket by a Japanese-registered company in a currency other than yen but targeted primarily at the Japanese institutional investor market.

suspense account A temporary account in the books of an organization to record balances to correct mistakes or balances that have not yet been finalized (e.g. because a particular deal has not been concluded).

swap The means by which a borrower can exchange the type of funds most easily raised for the type of funds required, usually through the intermediary of a bank. For example, a UK company may find it easy to raise a sterling loan when they really want to borrow Deutschmarks; a German company may have exactly the opposite problem. A swap will enable them to exchange the currency they possess for the currency they need. The other common type of swap is an *interest-rate swap, in which borrowers exchange fixed- for floating-interest rates. Swaps are most common in the *eurocurrency markets.

swaption An *option to enter into a *swap contract.

swingline bank facility (swingline loan) A facility that enables a borrower to avail itself of funds at very short notice, usually on a same-day basis, often to cover shortfalls in other credit arrangements. It may form part of a multi-option facility.

SWOT analysis An analysis of the Strengths, Weaknesses, Opportunities, and Threats of an organization as a form of appraisal of its current position at a particular time and future potential.

syndicated bank facility (syndicated loan) A very large loan made to one borrower by a group of banks headed by one lead bank, which usually takes only a small percentage of the loan itself, parcelling out the rest to other banks and financial institutions. The loans are usually made on a small margin. The borrower can reserve the right to know the names of all the members of the syndicate. If the borrower states which banks are to be included, it is known as a **club deal**. A syndicated bank facility is usually a *revolving bank facility. There is only one loan agreement.

synergy An effect in which the value of the sum of the parts is greater than the value of the whole. It is usually associated with mergers and acquisitions, because overheads can often be cut in the newly formed group by combining a number of functions previously carried out separately. *See also* coupon stripping.

systems-based audit An approach to auditing based on the concept that by studying and assessing the internal control system of an organization an *auditor can form an opinion of the quality of the accounting system, which will determine the level of *substantive tests needed to be carried out on the items in the financial statements. This approach is now less popular than formerly because it does not focus on *audit risk. The *risk-based audit is now generally considered to be more flexible, efficient, and effective.

systems control and review file (SCARF) An *embedded audit facility in a computer that consists of a program code or additional data provided by an *auditor and incorporated into a computerized accounting system. The auditor designates files as SCARF or not and also specifies a monetary value threshold. All transactions posted to a SCARF file that are above the threshold are also written to a SCARF file, the contents of which can only be altered or deleted by the external auditors of the company. *See also* integrated test facility.

systems development controls The internal controls ensuring that the development of a computerized system is properly controlled. For example, segregation of duties should ensure that an employee involved in the development of a system should not usually be involved in testing the system.

Table A A model set of *articles of association that a *company may adopt in full or in part, as set out in the Companies Act (1985).

T-account An account laid out so that the left-hand side records debits and the right-hand side records credits, with a vertical rule between them. A single horizontal rule above the entries forms the shape of the letter 'T'.

takeover bid (offer to purchase) An offer made to the shareholders of a company by an individual or organization to buy their shares at a specified price in order to gain control of that company. In a welcome takeover bid the directors of the company will advise shareholders to accept the terms of the bid. This is usually known as a *merger. If the bid is unwelcome, or the terms are unacceptable, the board will advise against acceptance. In the ensuing **takeover battle**, the bidder may improve the terms offered and will then usually write to shareholders outlining the advantages that will follow from the successful takeover. In the meantime bids from other sources may be made (*see* grey knight; white knight) or the original bidder may withdraw as a result of measures taken by the board of the *target company (*see* poison pill). In an **unconditional bid**, the bidder will pay the offered price irrespective of the number of shares acquired, while the bidder of a **conditional bid** will only pay the price offered if sufficient shares are acquired to provide a controlling interest. Takeovers in the UK are subject to the rules and disciplines of the *City Code on Takeovers and Mergers.

Takeover Panel *See* City Code on Takeovers and Mergers.

TALISMAN Abbreviation for Transfer Accounting Lodgement for Investors and Stock Management. This is the *London Stock Exchange computerized transfer system, which covers most UK securities; it also covers claims for dividends on shares being transferred. It is operated by a special company set up for the purpose, the Stock Exchange Pool Nominees Ltd, known as SEPON Ltd.

tangible assets *Assets that can be touched, such as land, buildings, and machinery, as compared to *intangible fixed assets, such as *goodwill. *See* fixed assets.

tap stock A gilt-edged security from an issue that has not been fully subscribed and is released onto the market slowly when its market price reaches predetermined levels. **Short taps** are short-dated stocks and **long taps** are long-dated taps.

TAR Abbreviation for throughput accounting ratio. *See* throughput accounting.

target company A company that is subject to a *takeover bid.

target costing A form of costing in which the manufacture of a product or the provision of a service is aimed to be restricted within a predetermined total cost ceiling so that a competitive price is achieved.

taxable income Income liable to taxation. It is calculated by deducting *income tax allowances and any other tax-deductible expenses from the taxpayer's gross income.

taxable person An individual, partnership, limited company, club, association, or charity as defined by the *value added tax legislaton. Value added tax is charged on *taxable supplies made by taxable persons in the course or furtherance of a business.

taxable supply A supply of goods or services made in the UK, other than an *exempt supply. The term is used in *value added tax legislation.

tax accountant A person who assists a taxpayer in preparing a *tax return. The term is used in the *Taxes Management Act (1970).

tax advantage A benefit enjoyed as a result of a reduction in a charge to taxation.

tax allocation The allocation of a charge to tax between different sources of income.

tax allowance A deduction, e.g. the *personal allowance, from the income of an individual, made in calculating the *taxable income.

tax assessment A schedule issued by the *Board of Inland Revenue showing a calculation of a taxpayer's liability to income tax. The income sources are identified separately on the tax assessment and an individual could receive several tax assessments for each *fiscal year, depending on the number of different sources of income for the year. These assessments can be based on estimated figures, in which case the schedule is known as an *estimated assessment.

taxation A levy on individual or corporate bodies by central or local government in order to finance the expenditure of that government and also as a means of implementing its fiscal policy. Payments for specific services rendered to or for the payer are not regarded as taxation. In the UK, an individual's income is taxed by means of an *income tax (*see* pay as you earn), while corporations pay a *corporation tax. Capital profits are taxed by means of a *capital gains tax while gifts, made during an individual's lifetime or on death, are taxed by means of an *inheritance tax. *See also* council tax; value added tax.

tax base The specified domain on which a tax is levied, e.g. an individual's income for *income tax, the estate of a deceased person for *inheritance tax, the profits of a company for *corporation tax.

tax bracket Figures between which income is subjected to a specific rate of tax. For 1995–96 taxable income between £3201 and £24,300 is taxed at *basic rate of income tax of 25%. Above £24,300 is the *higher-rate tax bracket.

tax code 1. *See* income tax code. 2. The body of tax law applicable in a country, in which the tax law is codified rather than laid down by statute.

tax commissioners *See* General Commissioners; Special Commissioners.

tax credit The tax allowance associated with the *dividend paid by a company. *Advance corporation tax is paid at a rate of 20/80 of a dividend payment when the dividend is paid. The shareholder is given allowance for the tax paid at source by the tax credit, at the same rate, 20/80, for 1995–96; i.e. a dividend of £80 received by the shareholder has an associated tax credit of £20. For *basic-rate taxpayers there is no further tax to pay. For *higher-rate taxpayers the difference between the tax credit rate, 20%, and the higher rate, 40%, is due on the higher-rate tax assessment.

tax-deductible Denoting an amount that can be deducted from income or profits, in accordance with the tax legislation, before establishing the amount of income or profits that is subject to tax.

tax-effective Denoting a procedure that is in accordance with the tax legislation and results in a reduction in the tax charge.

Taxes Management Act (1970) The UK legislation consolidating the law relating to the administration and collection of *income tax, *corporation tax, and *capital gains tax.

tax exempt special savings scheme (TESSA) A savings scheme in which interest payments are not subject to tax. Payments are made to a bank or building society by an individual within the specified limits, £3000 maximum in year 1 and £1800 in subsequent 12-month periods, with an overall maximum of £9000, and are held on deposit. Provided no withdrawals are made during a five-year period the resulting interest is tax-free. No individual can have more than one TESSA and TESSAs cannot be shared.

tax-free Denoting any payment, allowance, benefit, or other amount of income that is not subject to taxation.

tax harmonization The process of increasing the compatibility of various taxation systems by limiting the variations between them. The main areas of difference in taxation are the *tax base and the rates of tax applicable. There is often strong resistance to tax harmonization between independent states as, by setting limits within which the tax rates can be set, the authority of individual governments is eroded. The level of taxation is often a cornerstone of government policy and if harmonization is to succeed there would have to be an agreement to follow the limits set centrally; this would impinge on the sovereignty of individual governments.

tax haven A country or independent area that has a low rate of tax and therefore offers advantages to retired wealthy individuals or to companies that can arrange their affairs so that their tax liability falls at least partly in the low-tax haven. In the case of individuals, the cost of the tax saving is usually residence in the tax haven for a major part of the year. For multinational companies, an office in the tax haven, with some real or contrived business passing through it, is required. Monaco, Liechtenstein, the Bahamas, and the Cayman Islands are examples of tax havens.

tax invoice A detailed *value added tax invoice that must be provided by a *taxable person to another taxable person when the *taxable supply is made for £100 or more. The tax invoice must show:
• the supplier's name, address, and VAT registration number,
• the tax point and invoice number,
• the name and address of the customer,

• a description of the transaction and the goods supplied,
• the amount of VAT and the amount excluding VAT.
A less detailed invoice is required for a supply of less than £100.

taxman An informal name for an *Inspector of Taxes.

tax period The period covered by a *value added tax return, usually three calendar months. The VAT return should be completed and sent to the *Board of Customs and Excise within one month of the end of the tax period.

tax planning The arrangement of a taxpayer's affairs, in accordance with the requirements of the tax legislation, in order to reduce the overall charge to tax.

tax point The date on which goods are removed or made available to a customer or the date on which services to a customer are completed. The tax point determines the *tax period for which the *output tax must be accounted for to the *Board of Customs and Excise.

tax rebate A repayment of tax paid. A *repayment claim must be made and approved by an *Inspector of Taxes and the refund due to the taxpayer will be made by the *Collector of Taxes following the Inspector's instructions.

tax return A form upon which a taxpayer makes an annual statement of income and personal circumstances enabling claims to be made for personal allowances. In the UK an income tax return also requires details of *capital gains in the year. The onus is on the taxpayer to give the Inland Revenue the appropriate information even if the taxpayer receives no tax return. The completed return is used by the *Inspector of Taxes to assess the appropriate tax liability.

Separate returns are required for *inheritance tax purposes and by the *Board of Customs and Excise in repect of VAT and excise duties. *See also* self-assessment.

tax shield The amount of earnings required to cover a tax-deductible payment, taking account of the tax relief that can be obtained by making the payment.

tax system The means by which taxes are raised and collected in accordance with the tax legislation.

tax tables Tables issued by the *Board of Inland Revenue to employers to assist them in calculating the tax due from their employees under the *pay as you earn system. The tables are provided either for weekly or monthly payments. They enable the taxable pay to be calculated for an *income tax code number supplied by the Inspector of Taxes for each employee; they also give the tax due in each week or month of the year for the taxable pay so calculated. In practice, most employers now calculate salaries, wages, and tax deductions by computer, using a program into which the tax tables are incorporated.

tax treaty An agreement between two countries, identifying the treatment of income, profits, or gains that are subject to tax in both countries. The amount of *double taxation relief will be specified in the treaty.

tax voucher *See* dividend.

tax week Any of the series of weeks starting 6 April, the beginning of the tax year (*see* fiscal year). The first tax week ends on 13 April, the second ends on 20 April, etc.

tax year *See* fiscal year.

technological risk The inherent risk in *limited recourse financing of a construction project that a newly designed plant will not operate to specification. *Compare* completion risk; supply risk.

teeming and lading *See* lapping.

telegraphic transfer (TT) A same-day method of transferring funds from one party to another. In the UK, instructions are given to the bank by telephone or by smart card.

temporal method A method of converting a foreign currency involved in a transaction in which the local currency is translated at the exchange rate in operation on the date on which the transaction occurred. If rates do not fluctuate significantly, an average for the period may be used as an approximation. Any exchange gain or loss on translation is taken to the *profit and loss account. This contrasts with the closing rate or *net-investment method of translation, which uses the exchange rate ruling at the *balance-sheet date for translation and takes exchange differences to *reserves. *Statement of Standard Accounting Practice 20, 'Foreign Currency Translation', allows either method to be adopted.

temporary diminution in value A fall in the value of an *asset that is only expected to be for the short term. Under *historical cost accounting, no adjustments are made for temporary diminutions (unless they become permanent). *See also* permanent diminution in value.

tender panel A group of banks forming a panel to tender competitively to lend money to a company.

tenor The time that must elapse before a *bill of exchange or *promissory note becomes due for payment, as stated on the bill or note.

ten-year charge An *inheritance tax charge made every ten years on certain *discretionary trusts. As a discretionary trust does not attach to the life of an individual there is no inheritance-tax charge on passing through the generations. To compensate for this a ten-year charge, calculated at 30% of the lifetime rate, is assessed, so that a full charge is made every 33.33 years. Assets are valued at *open-market value at the tenth anniversary of the trust after 31 March 1984, and every ten years thereafter. The current rate is 6%, being 30% of the current lifetime rate of 20%.

terminal bonus An additional amount of money added to payments made on the maturity of an insurance policy or on the death of an insured person, because the investments of the insurer have produced a profit or surplus. Bonuses of this kind are paid at the discretion of the life office and usually take the form of a percentage of the sum assured.

terminal-loss relief Relief for a loss made by a business or profession during the last 12 months of trading. The business or profession must be permanently discontinued. The loss of the last 12 months can be set against the profits of the three years prior to the final tax year, taking the most recent year first.

Terminal-loss relief is also available for companies. The trading loss arising in the accounting period in which the trade ceases may be carried back and offset against the profits of the three years ending immediately before the commencement of the final period of trading.

terminal value (TV) The value of an investment at the end of an investment period taking into account a specified rate of interest over the period. The formula is the same as that for compound *interest, i.e.

$$TV = P(1+r)^t,$$

where TV = the final amount at the end of period, P = the principal amount invested, r = the interest rate, and t = the time in years for which the investment takes place.

term loan A loan from a bank to a company. The term of the loan is fixed and it is drawn down (*see* drawdown) immediately or within a short period of signing the loan agreement as set out in the *amortization schedule.

terotechnology The technology that encompasses management, financial, and engineering skills in installing, operating, and maintaining plant and machinery. *See* life-cycle costing.

TESSA Abbreviation for *tax exempt special savings scheme.

test data Data used by an *auditor in computer processing to check the operation of an organization's computer programs. The main use of test data is in conducting *compliance tests on *application controls; for example, to check that batch totals are being correctly produced. *See also* computer-assisted audit techniques; embedded audit facility; integrated test facility; systems development controls.

thin capitalization A form of company capitalization in which the capital of a company consists of too few shares and too much loan stock in the view of the tax authority. Some countries reserve the right in such cases to treat some of the interest on the loan stock as if it were a dividend, thus denying the right to a tax deduction on the interest payment.

thin market A market in which the price of the underlying commodity, currency, or financial instrument may change if sizable transactions are carried out. *Compare* deep market.

three-column cash book A *cash book in which details of *discounts allowed and discounts received are included in addition to receipts and payments made. Periodically these totals will be posted to the discounts allowed and received accounts, respectively. *Compare* two-column cash book.

throughput accounting The approach to short-term decision making in manufacturing in which all *conversion costs are treated as though they were fixed and products are ranked if a particular *constraint or scarce resource exists. Decisions are made using the throughput accounting ratio (TAR) as follows:

return per factory hour/cost per factory hour,

where return per factory hour =

(sales price − material cost)/hours on scarce resource;

cost per factory hour =

total factory cost/total available hours of constraint.

time card (clock card) A card on which is recorded the time spent by an employee at the place of work or the time spent on a particular job. The card is usually marked by mechanical or electronic means by recording the starting and ending times, enabling the elapsed time to be calculated.

time draft *See* documentary draft.

time of supply The date on which goods are removed or made available to a customer or when services for a customer are completed, i.e. the *tax point. Goods on sale or return are treated as supplied on the date of adoption by the customer or 12 months after despatch, whichever is the earlier. Continuous services paid for periodically are charged to tax on receipt of payment or issue of each tax invoice, whichever is the earlier.

time sheet A form on which is recorded the employee time or machine time spent on each activity during a period. It is used for costing jobs, operations, or activities.

time value of money The concept, used as the basis for *discounted cash flow calculations, that cash received earlier is worth more than a similar sum received later, because the sum received earlier can be invested to earn interest in the intervening period. For the same reasons, cash paid out later is worth less than a similar sum paid at an earlier date.

TLF Abbreviation for *transferable loan facility.

tombstone An advertisement in the financial press giving brief deals of the amount and maturity of a recently completed bank facility. The names of the *lead managers are prominently displayed, as well as the *co-managers and the managers. It is customary for the borrower to pay although he or she receives little benefit from the advertisement.

tom next A deal starting from tomorrow and maturing the following day.

TOPIC Abbreviation for Teletext Output Price Information Computer. This computerized communication system provides brokers and market makers on the *London Stock Exchange with information about share price movements and bargains as they are transacted. Input is from the *Stock Exchange Automated Quotations System (SEAQ).

total cost of production *See* production cost.

total costs The sum of all the expenditure incurred during an accounting period, either within an organization, on a product, or on a process. It is often convenient to analyse the total costs into *fixed costs and *variable costs.

total income The income of a taxpayer from all sources. This is often referred to as **statutory total income**, which consists of income from sources based on the income of the current year and income from other sources based on income of the preceding year. This artificial concept is used to calculate a person's income tax for a given year.

total production cost of finished goods *See* manufacturing cost of finished goods.

total profits Profits chargeable to corporation tax (PCTCT), including profits from trading, property, investment income, overseas income, and chargeable gains, less charges.

total standard cost The *total standard production cost plus the *standard cost allowance for the non-production overhead.

total standard production cost The total of *standard direct materials cost, *standard direct labour cost, the *standard fixed overhead cost, and the *standard variable overhead cost.

total standard profit The difference between the sales at *standard selling prices and the *standard overhead cost of these sales.

town clearing A special same-day clearing service for high value cheques drawn on accounts within the City of London and paid into another City account. All other cheques (known as **country cheques**) go into the general clearing system and take two or more days to clear. From 1995 the town clearing service ceased to be available. To guarantee a same-day transfer of funds, bank customers have to use the *telegraphic transfer service.

trade creditors *See* accounts payable.

trade debtors *See* accounts receivable.

trade discount A reduction in the list price of goods; for example, a discount given to a customer who makes bulk purchases.

trademark A distinctive symbol that identifies particular products of a trader to the general public. The symbol may consist of a device, words, or a combination of these. A trader may register a trademark at the Register of Trade Marks, which is held at the Patent Office. The trader then enjoys the exclusive right to use the trademark in connection with the goods for which it was registered. Any manufacturer, dealer, importer, or retailer may register a trademark. Registration is initially for seven years and is then renewable. The right to remain on the register may be lost if the trademark is not used or is misused. The owner of a trademark may assign it or, subject to the Registrar's approval, allow others to use it. If anyone uses a registered trademark without the owner's permission, or uses a mark that is likely to be confused with a registered trademark, the owner can sue for an injunction and *damages or an account of profits.

trade reference A reference concerning the creditworthiness of a trader given by another member of the same trade, usually to a supplier. If a firm wishes to purchase goods on credit from a supplier, the supplier will usually ask for a trade reference from another member of the same trade, in addition to a *banker's reference.

trading account The part of a *profit and loss account in which the cost of goods sold is compared with the money raised by their sale in order to arrive at the gross profit.

trading profit The profit of an organization before deductions for such items as interest, directors' fees, auditors' remuneration, etc.

tranche (French: slice) A part or instalment of a large sum of money. In the International Monetary Fund the first 25% of a loan is known as the **reserve** (formerly **gold**) **tranche**. In **tranche funding**, successive sums of money become available on a prearranged basis to a new company, often linked to the progress of the company and its ability to reach the targets set in its *business plan.

transaction An external event (e.g. purchase or sale) or internal event (e.g. depreciation of an asset) that gives rise to a change affecting the operations or finances of an organization.

transaction costs Costs arising from such transactions as buying and selling.

transaction date The date on which a transaction in the money market took place.

transaction exposure The risk that the cost of a transaction will change because of exchange-rate movements between the date of the transaction and the date of settlement.

transaction file A computer file used to record an external or internal *transaction. *Compare* standing data.

transferable loan facility (TLF) A bank loan facility that can be traded between lenders, in order to reduce the credit risk of the bank that provided the loan. It is a form of *securitization but can have an adverse effect on *relationship banking.

Transfer Accounting Lodgement for Investors and Stock Management *See* TALISMAN.

transfer credit risk The *credit risk that arises, especially on long-term contracts, as a result of a foreign debtor's inability to obtain foreign currency from the central bank at the appropriate time. This may occur even when the debtor is able and willing to pay. *Compare* political credit risk.

transfer deed *See* share transfer.

transfer of a going concern The disposal of a business by a *registered trader under *value added tax regulations to another VAT-registered trader on which VAT is not charged. This results in no *output tax for the vendor and no *input tax for the purchaser.

transfer prices The prices at which goods and services are bought and sold between divisions or subsidiaries within a group of companies.

translation exposure (accounting exposure) A risk that arises from the translation of the assets and liabilities in a *balance sheet into a foreign currency.

treasurer A person who is responsible for looking after the money and other assets of an organization. This may include overseeing the provision of the organization's finances as well as some stewardship over the way in which the money is spent.

trial balance A listing of the balances on all the *accounts of an organization with debit balances in one column and credit balances in the other. If the processes of double-entry book-keeping have been accurate, the totals of each column should be the same. If they are not the same, checks must be carried out to find the discrepancy. The figures in the trial balance after some adjustments, e.g. for closing stocks, prepayments and accruals, depreciation, etc., are used to prepare the final accounts (profit and loss account and balance sheet). *See also* extended trial balance.

true and fair view Auditors of the published accounts of companies are required to form an opinion as to whether the accounts they audit show a 'true and fair view' of the organization's affairs. This is an important concept in the UK and may be used as an override to depart from legal requirements. Despite its importance there is no legal definition of the expression.

Trueblood Report A report, *Objectives of Financial Statements*, prepared by a committee chaired by Robert M. Trueblood and published by the *American Institute of Certified Public Accountants in 1971. The report identified the basic *objective of financial statements as the provision of information useful for making economic decisions. The report was influential in the preparation by the *Financial Accounting Standards Board of Statement of Financial Accounting Concepts No. 1.

truncation Simplification of banking procedures. For example, to avoid the movement of such documents as cheques, banks are expanding the space available on bank statements to improve the description of the transaction.

trust An arrangement enabling property to be held by a person or persons (the *trustees) for the benefit of some other person or persons (the beneficiaries). The trustee is the legal owner of the property but the beneficiary has an equitable interest in it. A trust may be intentionally created or it may be imposed by law (e.g. if a trustee gives away trust property, the recipient will hold that property as constructive trustee for the beneficiary). Trusts are commonly used to provide for families and in commercial situations (e.g. pensions trusts).

trust deed The document creating and setting out the terms of a *trust. It will usually contain the names of the trustees, the identity of the beneficiaries, and the nature of the trust property, as well as the powers and duties of the trustees. Trusts of land must be declared in writing; trusts of other property need not be although there is often a trust deed to avoid uncertainty.

trustee A person who holds the legal title to property but who is not its beneficial owner. Usually there are two or more trustees of a *trust and for some trusts of land this is necessary. The trustee may not profit from the position but must act for the benefit of the beneficiary, who may be regarded as the real owner of the property. Either an individual or a company may act as trustee. It is usual to provide for the remuneration of trustees in the trust deed, otherwise there is no right to payment. Trustees may be personally liable to beneficiaries for loss of trust property.

trustee in bankruptcy A person who administers a bankrupt's estate and realizes it for the benefit of the creditors (*see* bankruptcy).

trustee investments Investments in which trustees are authorized to invest trust property. In the UK the Trustees Investment Act (1961) regulates the investments of trust property that may be made by trustees. The act applies unless excluded by a trust deed executed after the act was passed. Half of the trust fund must be invested in **narrow-range securities**, largely specified in fixed-interest investments. The other half may be invested in **wider-range**

securities, most importantly ordinary shares in companies quoted on the London Stock Exchange. In some cases, trustees must take advice before investing. The act considerably enlarged the range of trustee investments.

TT Abbreviation for *telegraphic transfer.

turnover **1.** The total sales figure of an organization for a stated period. Turnover is defined in the UK Companies Act (1985) as the total revenue of an organization derived from the provision of goods and services, less trade discounts, VAT, and any other taxes based on this revenue. **2.** More generally, the rate at which at some asset is turned over, e.g. stock turnover is obtained by dividing the total sales figure by the value of the particular asset. **3.** The total value of the transactions on a market or stock exchange in a specified period.

turnover ratio An *accounting ratio showing the number of times an item of *circulating assets has been replaced by others of the same class within a *financial period.

TV Abbreviation for *terminal value.

two-column cash book A *cash book that records receipts and payments made but does not record discounts allowed and discounts received. *Compare* three-column cash book.

two-tier board A method of running a large organization in which, in addition to a board of management, there is a supervisory board. It is claimed that this provides an effective method of *corporate governance and is used in some European countries. In the UK, the normal practice is for a single board to consist of both executive and non-executive directors.

UITF Abbreviation for *Urgent Issues Task Force.

ultimate holding company (ultimate parent company) A *company that is the *holding company of a group in which some of the subsidiary companies are themselves *immediate holding companies of their own groups. *See also* subsubsidiary.

ultra vires (Latin: beyond the powers) Denoting an act of an official or corporation for which there is no authority. The powers of officials exercising administrative duties and of companies are limited by the instrument from which their powers are derived. If they act outside these powers, their action may be challenged in the courts. A company's powers are limited by the objects clause in its memorandum of association. It it enters into an agreement outside these objects, the agreement may be unenforceable, although a third party may have a remedy under the Companies Act (1985) if it was dealing with the company in good faith (or there may be other equitable remedies).

uncommitted facility An agreement between a bank and a company in which the bank agrees in principle to make funding available to the company but is under no obligation to provide a specified amount of funding; if a loan is made it will be for only a short period. Examples of an uncommitted facility include a *money market line or an *overdraft. *Compare* committed facility.

unconsolidated subsidiary An *undertaking that, although it is a *subsidiary undertaking of a group, is not included in the *consolidated financial statements of the group. *See* exclusion of subsidiaries from consolidation.

uncontrollable costs (non-controllable costs) Items of expenditure appearing on a manager's management accounting statement that are not able to be controlled or influenced by that level of management. Costs regarded as uncontrollable by one level of management may, however, be controllable at a higher level of management. *See also* responsibility accounting.

undated security A fixed-interest security that has no *redemption date.

underabsorbed overhead (underapplied overhead) The circumstance in *absorption costing in which the *absorbed overhead is less than the overhead costs incurred for a period. The difference, also known as an adverse variance, represents a reduction of the budgeted profits of the organization. *Compare* overabsorbed overhead.

undercapitalization The state of a company that does not have sufficient *capital or *reserves for the size of its operations. For example, this may be due to the company growing too quickly. Although such a company may be making profits it may be unable to convert these profits sufficiently quickly into cash to pay its debts.

undertaking A body corporate, *partnership, or an unincorporated association carrying on a trade or business with a view to making a *profit.

underwriter **1.** A person who examines a risk, decides whether or not it can be insured, and, if it can, works out the premium to be charged, usually on the basis of the frequency of past claims for similar risks. Underwriters are either employed by insurance companies or are members of Lloyd's. The name arises from the early days of marine insurance, when a merchant would, as a sideline, *write* his name *under* the amount and details of the risk he had agreed to cover on a slip of paper. **2.** A financial institution, usually an issuing house or *merchant bank, that guarantees to buy a proportion of any unsold shares when a new issue is offered to the public. Underwriters usually work for a commission (usually 2%), and a number may combine together to buy all the unsold shares, provided that the minimum subscription stated in the prospectus has been sold to the public.

underwriting group A group of financial institutions that receive a fee for underwriting a new securities issue.

undischarged bankrupt A person whose *bankruptcy has not been discharged. Such persons must not obtain credit (above £250) without first informing their creditors that they are undischarged bankrupts, become directors of companies, or trade under another name. Undischarged bankrupts may not hold office as a JP, MP, mayor, or councillor. A peer who is an undischarged bankrupt may not sit in the House of Lords.

undistributable reserves *Reserves that may not be distributed according to the Companies Act (1985). They include *share capital, *share premium account, *capital redemption reserve, certain *unrealized profits, or any other reserve that the company may not distribute according to some other act or its own articles of association.

undistributed profit Profit earned by an organization but not distributed to its shareholders by way of dividends. Such sums are available for later distribution but are frequently used by companies to finance their trade.

unearned income Income not derived from trades, professions, or vocations, or from the emoluments of office. In the UK, until 1984, it was thought that as investment income was more permanent than earned income and did not depend on the labours of the taxpayer, it should be taxed more heavily than earned income. This was achieved by an investment-income surcharge, which was an extra 15% over the normal rate of income tax. In the UK both earned and unearned income are now taxed at the same rates.

unexpired cost The balance of an item of expenditure, recorded in the books of account of an organization, that has not been written off to the profit and loss account. For example, the *net book value of an asset represents the unexpired cost of that asset.

unfavourable variance *See* adverse variance.

unfranked investment income Income received by a company that has suffered *income tax at source, e.g. debenture interest received. Unfranked investment income is the net amount received plus the income tax suffered.

uniform commercial code In the USA, a legal code that standardizes business law. It consists of regulations on *commercial paper, *warranties, uncertified cheques, security agreements, written agency agreements, and *bankruptcy.

uniform costing The use of the same basic costing system by a number of different organizations by adopting common costing principles and practices.

unincorporated association An association of people that is not a *corporation and whose members have not formed themselves into a partnership.

unissued share capital The excess of the *authorized share capital over the *issued share capital, i.e. that part of the authorized share capital that has not yet been issued.

unit cost Expenditure incurred by an organization expressed as a rate per unit of production or sales.

unit price The price paid per unit of item purchased or charged per unit of product sold.

units of production method of depreciation *See* production-unit method.

unit standard operating profit The *standard operating profit, expressed as a rate per unit of production or sales.

unit standard production cost The *standard production cost, expressed as a rate per unit of production or sales.

unit standard selling price The *standard selling price, expressed as a rate per unit sold.

unit trust **1.** A trust formed in the UK to manage a portfolio of stock-exchange securities, in which small investors can buy units. This gives the small investor access to a diversified portfolio of securities, chosen and managed by professional fund managers, who seek either high capital gains or high yields, within the parameters of reasonable security. The trustees, usually a commercial bank, are the legal owners of the securities and responsible for ensuring that the managers keep to the terms laid down in the trust deed. Prices of unit trusts are quoted daily, the difference between the bid and offer prices providing a margin for the management costs and the costs of buying and selling on the *London Stock Exchange. Basic-rate tax is deducted from the dividends paid by unit trusts and capital gains on the sale of a holding are subject to capital gains tax, although transactions involved in creating the portfolio are free of capital gains tax. UK unit trusts are authorized and controlled by the Department of Trade and Industry and most belong to the Unit Trust Association. In the USA unit trusts are called **mutual funds**. Many trusts are now available, specializing in various sectors of the market, both at home and abroad; there is also a wide spectrum of trusts catering for both those seeking growth and those seeking income. **2.** A trust scheme (also called a **unit investment trust**) in the USA in which investors purchase **redeemable trust certificates**. The money so raised is used by the trustees to buy such securities as bonds, which are usually held until they mature. Usually both the number of certificates issued and the investments held remain unchanged during the life of the scheme, but the certificates can be sold back to the trustees at any time.

unlimited company A *company whose *shareholders do not benefit from limited liability (*compare* limited company). Such companies are exempt from filing accounts with the *Registrar of Companies.

unlimited liability A liability to pay all the debts incurred by a business. For a *sole proprietor or *partnership, the liability of the owners is not limited to the amount the owner has agreed to invest. All debts of the business must not only be paid out of the *assets of the business but also, if necessary, out of personal assets.

unlisted securities Securities (usually *equities) in companies that are not on an official stock-exchange list. They are therefore not required to satisfy the standards set for listing (*see* listed security). Unlisted securities are usually issued in relatively small companies and their shares usually carry a high degree of risk. In London, unlisted securities are traded on the **unlisted-securities market** (USM) and other exchanges have their own USMs. The existence of a USM enables owners of small companies to realize their investments and raise capital, without having to satisfy the more stringent requirements of the main market. For full listing a company has to have a capital of at least £700,000, a three-year trading record, and 25% of the equity has to be available to the public. For unlisted securities the capital figure is the same but only 10% of the equity need be available for purchase on the USM, and there is a minimum two-year trading period.

unpaid cheque A cheque that has been sent to the payee's bank and then through the clearing process only to be returned to the payee because value cannot be transferred. If the reason is lack of funds the bank will mark the cheque 'refer to drawer'.

unrealized profit (or loss) A profit or loss that results from holding *assets rather than using them; it is therefore a profit or loss that has not been realized in cash.

Urgent Issues Task Force (UITF) A body established in 1991 as part of the *Accounting Standards Board. It is responsible for tackling urgent matters not covered by existing standards in which the timescale of the normal standard-setting process would not be practicable.

usage rate The speed at which a commodity, raw material, or other resource is used up.

usage variance *See* direct materials usage variance.

usance **1.** The time allowed for the payment of short-term foreign *bills of exchange. It varies from country to country but is often 60 days. **2.** Formerly, the rate of interest on a loan.

useful economic life The period for which the present owner of an *asset will derive economic benefits from its use. Under *Statement of Standard Accounting Practice 12, 'Accounting for Depreciation', an asset should be depreciated over its useful economic life.

user-friendly Denoting a computer system that is intended to be easy to use by people who are not computer specialists. The term was coined to distinguish such systems from older systems, in which the priority was efficient utilization of machine resources with few concessions to the convenience of the user. Commonly, a user-friendly system can be started up with a minimum of trouble and provides on-screen guidance to the user, usually in the form of menus. If the user becomes completely confused, a help menu lists the action to be taken to correct all common mistakes. Some input devices, such as the mouse, are considered easier to use than the traditional keyboard, and user-friendly machines therefore make use of them.

user terminal An input and output unit that enables a user of a computer system to communicate with the system.

USM Abbreviation for unlisted securities market. *See* unlisted securities.

value-added statement (added-value statement) A *financial
statement showing how much wealth (value added) has been created by the
collective effort of capital, employees, and others and how it has been allocated
for a *financial period. Value added is normally calculated by deducting
materials and bought-in services from *turnover. The value added is then
allocated to employees in the form of wages, to shareholders and lenders in the
form of dividends and interest, and to the government in the form of taxes,
with a proportion being retained in the company for reinvestment. Although
popular as a *simplified financial statement in *employee reports in the 1970s,
it has never become a major feature of the *annual accounts and report given
to *shareholders.

value added tax (VAT) A charge on *taxable supplies of goods and services
made in the UK by a *taxable person in the course or furtherance of a business.
Where appropriate, each trader adds VAT to sales and must account to the
*Board of Customs and Excise for the *output tax. The *input tax paid on
purchases can be deducted from the output tax due. VAT, *indirect taxation
that falls on the final customer, was introduced in 1973 when the UK joined the
European Economic Community. In the UK, since April 1991, all goods and
services bear VAT at a rate of 17.5%, unless they are *zero-rated goods and
services or *exempt supplies.

value date The time at which a remittance sent through the bank *clearing
cycle becomes available to the payee for use.

value for money audit An audit of a government department, charity, or
other non-profitmaking organization to assess whether or not it is functioning
efficiently and giving value for the money it spends.

value to the business The value of an *asset taken as the lower of the
*replacement cost and the *recoverable amount. The latter is the greater of the
*net realizable value and *net present value. It is claimed that generally an
asset should never be worth more to a business than its replacement cost,
because if the business were deprived of the asset it would replace it. If an asset
is not worth replacing it would be sold (net realizable value), unless the net
present value were higher. The concept is also known as the **deprival value** and
was a feature of *current cost accounting as required by *Statement of
Standard Accounting Practice 16.

variable cost An item of expenditure that, in total, varies directly with the
level of activity achieved. For example, *direct materials cost will tend to
double if output doubles, a characteristic being that it is incurred as a constant
rate per unit. *Compare* fixed cost; semi-variable cost.

variable costing *See* marginal costing.

variable cost ratio The ratio of variable cost to *sales revenue, expressed as
a percentage.

variable overhead cost The elements of an organization's indirect costs for a product that vary in total in proportion to changes in the levels of production or sales. Examples can include power, commission earned by sales personnel, and consumable materials.

variable production overhead The elements of an organization's indirect manufacturing costs that vary in total in proportion to changes in the level of production or sales. Examples can include factory power and depreciation of machinery using the *production-unit method.

variable-rate note (VRN) A *bond, usually with a fixed maturity, in which the interest coupon is adjusted at regular intervals to reflect the prevailing market rate (usually a margin over the *London Inter Bank Offered Rate). A VRN differs from a *floating-rate note in that the margin is not fixed and will be adjusted to take into account market conditions at each coupon setting date.

variance In *standard costing and *budgetary control, the difference between the standard or budgeted levels of cost or income for an activity and the actual costs incurred or income achieved. If the actual performance is better than standard then a *favourable variance results, while if actual performance is worse than standard there is an *unfavourable variance.

variance analysis The analysis of variances in *standard costing and *budgetary control, in order to seek their causes. Expenditure, usage, and efficiency variances are typical parameters to be examined in variance analysis.

VAT Abbreviation for *value added tax.

VATman An informal name for an employee of the *Board of Customs and Excise dealing with *value added tax. It is often used to refer to a VAT Inspector responsible for routine VAT inspections.

vendor placing A type of *placing used as a means of acquiring another company or business. For example, if company X wishes to buy a business from company Y, it issues company X shares to company Y as payment with the prearranged agreement that these shares are then placed with investors in exchange for cash. Vendor placings have been popular with some companies as a cheaper alternative to a *rights issue. *See also* bought deal.

verification A *substantive test in an *audit that checks on the existence, ownership, and valuation of *assets and *liabilities. It is used to gather *audit evidence.

vertical form The presentation of a *financial statement in which the debits and credits are shown one above the other. *Compare* horizontal form.

vertical integration The combination of two or more companies at different stages in the same industry. For example, a manufacturer of raw materials could purchase a manufacturer of components and an organization that assembles the components. *Compare* horizontal integration.

vested interest **1.** In law, an interest in property that is certain to come about rather than one dependent upon some event that may not happen. For example, a gift to 'A for life and then to B' means that A's interest is **vested in possession**, because A has the property now. B's gift is also vested (but not in possession) because A will certainly die sometime and then B (or B's estate if B is dead) will inherit the property. A gift to C 'if C reaches the age of 30' is not vested, because C may die before reaching that age. An interest that is not vested is known as a **contingent interest**. **2.** An involvement in the outcome of some business, scheme, transaction, etc., usually in anticipation of a personal gain.

view to resale The grounds on which a *subsidiary undertaking is excluded from the *consolidated financial statements of a group, because the group's interest in the subsidiary is held exclusively with a view to subsequent resale. *Financial Reporting Standard 2, 'Accounting for Subsidiary Undertakings', defines the circumstances appropriate for this exclusion as if a purchaser has been identified or is being sought for a subsidiary and it is reasonably expected that the interest will be disposed of within approximately one year of its date of acquisition. The subsidiary undertaking should not previously have been consolidated in group accounts prepared by the *holding company. Where a subsidiary undertaking is excluded on these grounds, it should be recorded in the consolidated financial statements as a *circulating asset at the lower of cost and *net realizable value. *See also* exclusion of subsidiaries from consolidation.

virement The practice allowed in some systems of *budgetary control in which overspending under one budget expenditure head may be offset by underspending under another budget expenditure head. If virement is not allowed, each head of expenditure must be treated individually.

volume variances *Standard costing variances that arise as a result of differences between the fixed overhead absorbed and the fixed overhead budgeted.

voluntary arrangement A procedure provided for by the Insolvency Act (1986), in which a company may come to an arrangement with its creditors to pay off its debts and to manage its affairs so that it resolves its financial difficulties. This arrangement may be proposed by the directors, an administrator acting under an *administration order, or a *liquidator. A qualified insolvency practitioner must be appointed to supervise the arrangement. This practitioner may be the administrator or liquidator, in which case a meeting of the company and its creditors must be called to consider the arrangement. The proposals may be modified or approved at this meeting but, once approved, they bind all those who had notice of the meeting. The court may make the necessary orders to bring the arrangement into effect. The arrangement may be challenged in court in the case of any irregularity. The aim of this legislation is to assist the company to solve its financial problems without the need for a winding-up (*see* liquidation).

voluntary liquidation (voluntary winding-up) *See* creditors' voluntary liquidation; members' voluntary liquidation.

voluntary registration Registration for *value added tax by a *taxable person whose taxable turnover does not exceed the registration threshold.

voting shares Shares in a company that entitle their owner to vote at the annual general meeting and any extraordinary meetings of the company. Shares that carry **voting rights** are usually *ordinary shares, rather than *A shares or *debentures. The company's articles of association will state which shares carry voting rights.

voucher A receipt for money or any document that supports an entry in a book of account.

vouching A *substantive test in an *audit to check that the underlying records correctly show the nature of transactions entered into by the business being audited.

VRN Abbreviation for *variable-rate note.

WACC Abbreviation for *weighted-average cost of capital.

wages The remuneration paid to hourly paid employees for the work done, usually based on the number of hours spent at the place of work.

wages costs *See* labour costs.

wages oncost *See* oncost.

waiting time The period during which the operators of a machine or the machinery itself are idle or waiting for work, material, or repairs. *See also* idle time.

walk-through test A test that takes a few transactions from the records of a business and follows them through every stage of the accounting system. For example, a walk-through test of a purchases system would follow through from the material requisition to settlement of the supplier's invoice.

war loan A government stock issued during wartime; it has no redemption date and pays only 3% interest.

warrant **1.** A security that offers the owner the right to subscribe for the *ordinary shares of a company at a fixed date, usually at a fixed price. Warrants are themselves bought and sold on *stock exchanges and are equivalent to stock options. Subscription prices usually exceed the market price, as the purchase of a warrant is a gamble that a company will prosper. They have proved increasingly popular in recent years as a company can issue them without including them in the balance sheet. **2.** A document that serves as proof that goods have been deposited in a public warehouse. The document identifies specific goods and can be transferred by endorsement. Warrants are frequently used as security against a bank loan. Warehouse warrants for warehouses attached to a wharf are known as **dock warrants** or **wharfinger's warrants.**

waste (spoilage) The amount of material lost as part of a production process. Acceptable levels of waste, known as a *normal loss, are part of the cost of production and as such are allowed for in the product costs. *See also* abnormal loss; process costing.

wasting asset An asset that has a finite life; for example, a lease may lose value throughout its life and become valueless when it terminates. It is also applied to such assets as plant and machinery, which wear out during their life and therefore lose value.

watered stock *See* stock watering.

WDA Abbreviation for *writing-down allowance.

WDV Abbreviation for *written-down value.

wealth tax A tax used in some European countries, not including the UK, consisting of an annual levy on wealth. In practice, the implementation of a wealth tax requires a clear identification of the assets to be charged and an unassailable valuation of these assets. In 1975, the issue of a wealth tax was considered by the UK government, but as no agreement on the identification and valuation of chargeable assets could be reached, it failed to reach the statute book.

wear and tear A diminution in the value to an organization of a fixed asset due to the use and damage that it inevitably sustains throughout its working life.

weighted average (weighted mean) An arithmetic average that takes into account the importance of the items making up the average. For example, if a person buys a commodity on three occasions, 100 tonnes at £70 per tonne, 300 tonnes at £80 per tonne, and 50 tonnes at £95 per tonne, the purchases total 450 tonnes; the simple average price would be $(70 + 80 + 95)/3 = £81.7$. The weighted average, taking into account the amount purchased on each occasion, would be:

$$[(100 \times 70) + (300 \times 80) + (50 \times 95)]/450 = £79.4 \text{ per tonne.}$$

weighted-average cost *See* average cost.

weighted-average cost of capital (WACC) A method of establishing an organization's *cost of capital by taking each source of funds from its balance sheet and assigning a *required rate of return to each individual source. The amounts of each of the sources of funds are used as weights applied to the required returns, and the total return is divided by the total weights to give the WACC expressed as a percentage.

white knight A person or firm that makes a welcome *takeover bid for a company on improved terms to replace an unacceptable and unwelcome bid from a *black knight. If a company is the target for a takeover bid from a source of which it does not approve or on terms that it does not find attractive, it will often seek a white knight, whom it sees as a more suitable owner for the company, in the hope that a more attractive bid will be made. *Compare* grey knight.

wholly owned subsidiary A *subsidiary undertaking that is owned 100% by a holding company (i.e. there is no *minority interest).

will A document giving directions as to the disposal of a person's property after death. It has no effect until death and may be altered as many times as the person (the testator) wishes. To be binding, it must be executed in accordance with statutory formalities. It must be in writing, signed by the testator or at the testator's direction and in the testator's presence. It must appear that the signature was intended to give effect to the will (usually it is signed at the end, close to the last words dealing with the property). The will must be witnessed by two persons, who must also sign the will. The witnesses must not be beneficiaries.

windfall gains and losses Gains and losses arising from actual or prospective receipts that differ from those originally predicted or from changes in the *net present value of the receipts as a result of unexpected changes in discount rates.

winding-up *See* liquidation.

winding-up petition A document presented to a UK court seeking an order for a company to be put into *compulsory liquidation.

window dressing Any practice that attempts to make a situation look better than it really is. It has been used extensively by accountants to improve the look of balance sheets. For example, banks used to call in their short-term loans and delay making payments at the end of their financial years, in order to show spuriously high cash balances. It can also take the form of writing down goodwill (since goodwill is not tax-deductible and does not count as risk-based bank capital as recognized and regulated by the Bank for International Settlements) and accounting for trademarks and exceptional items. These practices now fall within the remit of the *Accounting Standards Board.

WIP Abbreviation for *work in progress (or process).

withholding tax Tax deducted at source from *dividends or other income paid to non-residents of a country. If there is a *double taxation agreement between the country in which the income is paid and the country in which the recipient is resident, the tax can be reclaimed.

without prejudice Words used as a heading to a document or letter to indicate that what follows cannot be used in any way to harm an existing right or claim, cannot be taken as the signatory's last word, cannot bind the signatory in any way, and cannot be used as evidence in a court of law. For example, a solicitor may use these words when making an offer in a letter to settle a claim, implying that the client may decide to withdraw the offer. It may also be used to indicate that, although agreement may be reached on the terms set out in the document on this occasion, the signatory is not bound to settle similar disputes on the same terms.

without recourse (sans recours) Words that appear on a *bill of exchange to indicate that the holder has no recourse to the person from whom it was bought, if it is not paid. It may be written on the face of the bill or as an endorsement. If these words do not appear on the bill, the holder does have recourse to the drawer or endorser if the bill is dishonoured at maturity.

with the exception of See except for.

working capital The capital of a business that can be used in its day-to-day trading. It consists of its *circulating assets (e.g. *stocks, *debtors, *prepayments, cash-in-hand, and cash at bank) less *current liabilities (e.g. *accruals and trade creditors; see accounts payable).

working-capital adjustment (monetary working-capital adjustment) A *current cost accounting adjustment made to the *working capital of a business. Bank balances and overdrafts may fluctuate with the volume of stock held, the *debtors, and the *creditors. If the bank balances and overdrafts arise from such fluctuations, they too should be included in the monetary working capital, together with any cash required to support the daily operations of the business.

working-capital ratio See current ratio.

work in progress (work in process; WIP) The balance of partly finished work remaining in a manufacturing operation or a long-term contract at a particular time. It is normally valued at the lower of cost or *net realizable value, using either the *first-in-first-out cost, the *last-in-first-out cost, or the *average cost method of valuation. In the USA, 'work in process' is the more common term.

work measurement An estimate of the time required to carry out a series of manufacturing procedures, by studying the operations involved by means of time, methods, and work studies.

World Bank The name by which the *International Bank for Reconstruction and Development combined with its affiliates, the International Development Association and the International Finance Corporation, is known.

writ An order issued by a court. A **writ of summons** is an order by which an action in the High Court is started. It commands the defendant to appear before the court to answer the claim made in the writ by the plaintiff. It is used in actions in tort, claims alleging fraud, and claims for *damages in respect of personal injuries, death, or infringement of *patent. A **writ of execution** is used to enforce a judgment; it is addressed to a court officer instructing that officer to carry out an act, such as collecting money or seizing property. A **writ of delivery** is a writ of execution directing a sheriff to seize goods and deliver them to the plaintiff or to obtain their value in money, according to an agreed assessment. If the defendant has no option to pay the assessed value, the writ is a **writ of specific delivery**.

write off 1. To reduce the value of an asset to zero in a balance sheet. An expired lease, obsolete machinery, or an unfortunate investment would be written off. 2. To reduce to zero a debt that cannot be collected (*see* bad debt). Such a loss will be shown in the *profit and loss account of an organization.

writing-down allowance (WDA) A *capital allowance available to a UK trader; from 1 November 1993 it is the only allowance available for *plant and machinery used in trade. Any additions to plant and machinery are added to the *written-down value of assets acquired in previous years and the writing-down allowance is calculated as 25% of the total. For cars the allowance is restricted to £3000, for vehicles whose initial cost is in excess of £12,000. For *industrial buildings the allowance is calculated at 4% of the initial cost, on the *straight-line method.

		£
Year 1	Cost	1000
	WDA 25%	(250)
	WDV	750
Year 2	WDA 25%	(187)
	WDV	563

written-down value (WDV) The value of an asset for tax purposes after taking account of its reduction in value below the initial cost, as a result of its use in the trade. An asset acquired for a trade is eligible for *capital allowances. A *writing-down allowance (WDA) of 25% is available in the year of purchase, which is deducted from the initial cost to establish the written-down value. In the following year the written-down value is subject to the 25% writing-down allowance, which is deducted to arrive at the written-down value at the end of the second year. The table above shows the WDA and WDV for an asset acquired for £1000. The written-down value of the asset, for tax purposes, at the end of year 2 is £563.

wrongful trading Trading during a period in which a company had no reasonable prospect of avoiding insolvent *liquidation. The liquidator of a company may petition the court for an order instructing a director of a company that has gone into insolvent liquidation to make a contribution to the company's assets. The court may order any contribution to be made that it thinks proper if the director knew, or ought to have known, of the company's situation. A director would be judged liable if a reasonably diligent person carrying out the same function in the company would have realized the situation: no intention to defraud need be shown.

Yankee bond A bond issued in the US domestic market by a borrower that is not a US-resident company.

Yellow Book The colloquial name for *Admission of Securities to Listing*, a book issued by the Council of the *London Stock Exchange that sets out the regulations for admission to the *Official List and the obligations of companies with *listed securities.

yield **1.** The income from an investment expressed in various ways. The **nominal yield** of a fixed-interest security is the interest it pays, expressed as a percentage of its *par value. For example, a £100 stock quoted as paying 8% interest will yield £8 per annum for every £100 of stock held. However, the **current yield** (also called the **interest yield**, **running yield**, **earnings yield**, or **flat yield**) will depend on the market price of the stock. If the 8% £100 stock mentioned above was standing at a market price of £90, the current yield would be 100/90 × 8 = 8.9%. As interest rates rise, so the market value of fixed-interest stocks (not close to redemption) fall in order that they should give a competitive current yield. The capital gain (or loss) on redemption of a stock, which is normally redeemable at £100, can also be taken into account. This is called the **yield to redemption** (**gross redemption yield** or **maturity yield**). The redemption yield consists approximately of the current yield plus the capital gain (or loss) divided by the number of years to redemption. Thus, if the above stock had nine years to run to redemption, its redemption yield would be about 8.9 + 10/9 = 10%. The yields of the various stocks on offer are usually listed in commercial papers as both current yields and redemption yields, based on the current market price. However, for an investor who actually owns stock, the yield will be calculated not on the market price but the price the investor paid for it. The annual yield on a fixed-interest stock can be stated exactly once it has been purchased. This is not the case with *equities, however, where neither the dividend yield (*see* dividend) nor the capital gain (or loss) can be forecast, reflecting the greater degree of risk attaching to investments in equities. Yields on fixed-interest securities and equities are normally quoted gross, i.e. before deduction of tax. **2.** The income obtained from a tax.

yield curve A curve on a graph in which the *yield of fixed-interest securities is plotted against the length of time they have to run to maturity. The yield curve usually slopes upwards, indicating that investors expect to receive a premium for holding securities that have a long time to run. However, when there are expectations of changes in interest rate, the slope of the yield curve may change. *See also* negative yield curve.

yield to maturity *See* gross redemption yield.

ZBB Abbreviation for *zero-base budget.

zero-base budget (ZBB) A *cash-flow budget in which the manager responsible for its preparation is required to prepare and justify the budgeted expenditure from a zero base, i.e. assuming that initially there is no commitment to spend on any activity. *Compare* incremental budget.

zero coupon bond A *bond issued at a discount to mature at its face value; the discount is set so that no interest is paid during the life of the bond. It is the ultimate *deep discount bond. *See also* coupon stripping.

zero-rated goods and services Goods and services that are taxable for *value added tax purposes but are currently subject to a tax rate of zero. These include:
• certain food items,
• sewerage and water services for non-industrial users,
• periodicals and books,
• charities for certain supplies, such as 'talking books',
• new domestic buildings,
• transport fares for public services (carrying more than 12 passengers),
• banknotes,
• drugs and medicines,
• clothing and footwear for children.

Z-score A single statistic that attempts to measure the susceptibility of a business to failure. It is computed by applying beta coefficients to a number of selected ratios taken from an organization's final accounts using the technique of multiple discriminant analysis.